FOUNDATIONS
OF MENU PLANNING

FOUNDATIONS OF MENU PLANNING

Second Edition

Daniel Traster, CCP

330 Hudson Street, NY, NY 10013

Vice President, Portfolio Management: Andrew Gilfillan
Portfolio Manager: Pamela Chirls
Editorial Assistant: Lara Dimmick
Development Editor: Melissa Mashburn
Senior Vice President, Marketing: David Gesell
Field Marketing Manager: Thomas Hayward
Marketing Coordinator: Elizabeth MacKenzie-Lamb
Director, Digital Studio and Content Production:
   Brian Hyland
Managing Producer: Cynthia Zonneveld
Managing Producer: Jennifer Sargunar
Content Producer: Rinki Kaur

Content Producer: Purnima Narayanan
Manager, Rights Management: Johanna Burke
Manufacturing Buyer: Deidra Smith
Full-Service Management and Composition:
   iEnergizer Aptara®, Ltd.
Full-Service Project Manager: Megha Bhardwaj
Cover Design: Studio Montage
Cover Photo: Marcel Kriegl/Shutterstock
Printer/Binder: LSC Communications
Cover Printer: LSC Communications
Text Font: Sabon LT Pro-Roman 10/12 pt

Library of Congress Cataloging-in-Publication Data

Names: Traster, Daniel, author.
Title: Foundations of menu planning / Daniel Traster, CCC, CCE, CCCP.
Description: Boston : Pearson, [2018] | Includes bibliographical references
   and index.
Identifiers: LCCN 2016051965 | ISBN 9780134484471 (alk. paper) | ISBN
   0134484479 (alk. paper)
Subjects: LCSH: Menus. | Food service—Planning.
Classification: LCC TX911.3.M45 T73 2018 | DDC 642—dc23 LC record available at
https://lccn.loc.gov/2016051965

ISBN 10:   0-13-448447-9
ISBN 13: 978-0-13-448447-1

To Rebecca, Elizabeth,
and Benjamin, for continuing to share, celebrate,
and support through all that life has to dish out.

BRIEF CONTENTS

CONTENTS

PREFACE

When I was a student in culinary school many years ago, I learned a great deal about a range of culinary subjects, but menu planning was not among them. After some time in the industry and years of creating numerous menus, I found myself working at two different culinary schools. In both cases, the schools subsumed menu planning under the subject of nutrition, as if the only challenge to writing a menu were to accommodate a special diet. This is not to say that nutrition is not a critical subject for a chef to study; however, the act of writing even the most basic menu is not as easy as it might seem.

Thousands of restaurants open across the country every year only to shut down after their first few years of operation. Plenty of chefs with spectacular culinary talent fail to tailor their menus to the local market. Others simply do not know how to price their menus effectively. Still others start off well only to see their profits erode over time under the yoke of a static menu. In all of these cases, the restaurants might have survived had they managed the menu-planning process better from the start.

These challenges afflict not only restaurants but all forms of culinary operations. Caterers, hotels, bars, and noncommercial operations all live or die by the effectiveness of their menus. Menus are marketing mechanisms, cost control tools, and critical communication devices. Without them, revenue and profits wither away. Sadly, anyone looking to study the subject would be hard-pressed to find a comprehensive, easy-to-grasp textbook. I believe culinary and hospitality students deserve better.

New to the Second Edition

This second edition includes updated and expanded content to reflect changes to the industry in the years since the first edition was published. Major changes and updates are described subsequently.

In order to showcase a wider range of modern approaches to food, nearly all of the menus in the text are new. These menus represent a variety of foodservice operations across the United States and reflect both regional and national industry trends. The book's pedagogical value has been enhanced through the addition of two new end-of-chapter elements: Case Studies provide more complex challenges to drive classroom discussion and the Capstone Project leads students through the process of creating their own menus rather than just reading about the theory behind menu planning. The Technology Assistance sections in Chapters 6 and 11 lead students through the process of creating their own templates in Excel to conduct recipe costing and menu analysis. Additional key updates are as follows:

- Changes in nutritional advice for menu planners as reflected in the *Dietary Guidelines for Americans 2015–2020* (Chapter 2)
- Shifts in modern menu pricing approaches from the traditional table d'hôte to the more modern prix fixe with supplemental charges approach (Chapter 3)
- The small plates trend in modern menus (Chapter 4)
- The trend toward signature cocktails made from house-crafted mixers (Chapter 5)
- The incorporation of industry terminology for menu content, including "menu copy," "descriptive copy," and "institutional copy" (Chapter 8)

- Software and other options for laying out the menu during the design phase as well as a discussion on the various ways to organize an online menu (Chapter 10)
- More detailed explanations on how to engineer menus for greater profitability after conducting a menu analysis (Chapter 11)

Finally, I have updated the PowerPoint slides, test bank, and teacher's manual to help teachers facilitate a lively and informative class.

The Book's Structure

Foundations of Menu Planning guides students through the menu-planning process in the same order in which a menu planner typically conducts the process in the real world. The book begins with the resources commonly used to understand and define a target market. The text then progresses to a survey of general nutrition concerns that most menu planners must address in their work. Two chapters on menu styles follow, highlighting how they differ and how different menus organize items under various headings to reinforce their company's brand and theme. The focus then shifts specifically to the unique elements of beverage menus. The book moves next to recipe costing and menu pricing to ensure future menu planners can learn how to make their menu items profitable, and then to a chapter on the art of writing appealing and accurate menu item descriptions, known as descriptive copy. A chapter on unwritten menus is included to address how to replicate the functions of a menu when the customer is not given a written menu. The chapter on menu layout and design guides readers through the process of selecting a menu design that supports the business's brand. The study of menu analysis and evaluation trains readers on how to engineer a menu to make it even more profitable with each iteration. The book closes with a discussion of the pros and cons of a menu-first approach to menu planning.

In addition to addressing the "how" of menu planning from a logical, sequential approach, *Foundations of Menu Planning* delves into the "why," so students understand the purpose behind each step. That the book deals with broad menu-planning concepts but also expounds upon variations specific to certain types of foodservice operations makes the material applicable to undergraduate culinary and hospitality students no matter where in the industry they work.

In addition to the primary content of the book, I have included several pedagogical tools to enhance the educational experience of the reader. Because words are no substitute for pictures of real menus, the book contains a great many images of menus from foodservice operations across the country. These menus (and other images) reinforce the book's narrative and illustrate how menu-planning principles are applied in the real world. In the math-based chapters, examples permeate the text to illustrate how each equation is executed in practice.

Each chapter concludes with a summary of the chapter's main points, comprehension questions to ensure that students have grasped key concepts from the chapter, and discussion questions to push students to think beyond the chapter and to apply the learning to their own personal experiences. The discussion questions do not necessarily have a single correct answer, but they can spark class discussions to help students probe challenging menu-planning concepts. For more extended analysis of each chapter's content, most chapters now include a case study at the end of the chapter. Chapters 6 and 11 also include a section to guide students through the process of setting up their own worksheets, complete with formulas, in Excel or similar software. There are many products available for purchase that claim to perform recipe costing and menu analysis, but there is no reason a menu planner should remain dependent on purchasing additional software when the process of setting up one's own template is easy enough to learn.

A Note on Gender and Pronouns

Readers will notice that the text alternates by chapter between male and female pronouns. While men and women both have much to contribute to and learn from the culinary industry, the English language makes gender-neutral communication difficult and clumsy. Rather than using "he/she" or similar constructs, I have opted to use male pronouns in the odd chapters and female ones in the even chapters. The use of one set of pronouns in a given subject area is not meant to insinuate anything about the relationship of one sex to that particular material. Rather, the alternation is an attempt to convey the relevance of the book's entirety to both sexes equally.

How to Use This Book

Students: This book includes a great deal of information. Trying to understand and retain it all becomes much easier when you realize that the world is your classroom. As you read through each chapter's content, see how the lessons apply not only to the menus included in that chapter but to the menus located in other chapters as well. Do not quickly gloss over the menus just to finish the chapter; instead, read and analyze them carefully to understand them better. The menus included in this text have been selected as excellent examples of various approaches to menu planning, but you can learn from foodservice operations' menus in your neighborhood and online as well. Just as you develop your palate by tasting food critically and thinking about what you would do differently, start to look at menus critically to consider how you might improve them. By applying this book's lessons to your own restaurant experiences, you'll secure your learning for the future and more easily employ it when you need to create a menu.

Teachers: As a former culinary educator, I have written the book to accommodate the realities of teaching in a classroom. The opening chapter is shorter than average to allow sufficient time for coverage on the first class day when introductions and syllabus distribution are necessary elements of that first session. Similarly, the final chapter, also brief, gives you time to conduct a course review prior to the final exam or to have your students present their capstone projects. With twelve total chapters, the book is flexible enough to be used effectively in a quarter or a semester system school.

The book includes not only comprehension questions that may be assigned as homework, but also discussion questions, case studies, and a capstone project for those of you who would like your students to go through the step-by-step process of designing their own menu. My intention in including these additional end-of-chapter tools is to help your students effectively apply chapter material to the actual process of menu creation.

Finally, no textbook is complete without a range of supporting material for students and instructors. This text's teacher's manual includes not only key chapter points but also recommended in-class educational activities and assessments. PowerPoint slides of the chapters and a test bank are available as well. To access supplementary materials online, instructors need to request an instructor access code. Go to www.pearsonhighered.com/irc, where you can register for an instructor access code. Within forty-eight hours after registering, you will receive a confirming email, including your instructor access code. Once you have received your code, go to the site and log on for full instructions on downloading the materials you wish to use.

What's at Stake

Most culinary professionals know the statistics showing the vast percentage of restaurants that fail in their first few years. Surely, other types of foodservice operations face similarly grim odds. Many students come to culinary school with dreams of opening their own businesses, and of course, a strong desire to learn how to cook really well. Yet of the many reasons that so many foodservice businesses shut down prematurely, the chef's inability to cook doesn't even make the top ten. A poorly written menu, on the other hand, sets a restaurant on the road to certain failure. A great menu may not guarantee a company's success, but it provides a strong foundation on which the business can build.

No book is perfect, but I sincerely hope that students will find *Foundations of Menu Planning* an informative, inspirational, and comprehensive study of the subject matter. Writing an effective menu is no easy task, but with the right book and the right teacher menu-writing skills can be learned. Through this book, I believe readers will gain an understanding of the menu-planning process and the ability to create an effective and profitable menu as they head off to become successful industry leaders.

Daniel Traster

ACKNOWLEDGMENTS

This textbook would surely have fallen victim to exhaustion and frustration were it not for the incredibly passionate and inspiring team of people who have helped me to create this wonderful book. Thank you to Pearson's Andrew Gilfillan, Daryl Fox, Susan Watkins, Melissa Mashburn, Pamela Chirls, Lara Dimmick, Megha Bhardwaj Azad, Jennifer Sargunar, and Subhanjan Dasgupta; it is their continued support and hard work that is most responsible for this book coming out on time and at such a high level of quality. I owe a great many thanks to all of the chefs, restaurateurs, hotel managers, catering directors, and other industry professionals who provided the images that greatly enhance the educational value of this book. Their generosity is a testament to their commitment to the industry, their support of education, and their dedication to hospitality and its mission of helping others. I hope all of my readers have a chance to patronize their establishments, credited next to or within each image. Thanks also go to the professors who helped review the manuscript.

Earl Arrowood, Bucks County Community College

Barry Karrh, East Central Community College

Charles King, Wayland Baptist University

Charlie Martin, Spokane Community College

A special thank-you goes to graphic designer Linsey Silver, who provided support and guidance on issues of menu design and typography. To all of my past employers who gave me a chance to learn, practice, and teach menu writing of all sorts—thank you. I am truly blessed for my parents, who inspired my career in the culinary arts despite their best efforts to the contrary. To my wife and daughter, I owe the deepest gratitude; without their love, support, and patience, I would never have become an author.

Finally, thank you to all of those schools and teachers who adopted the first edition of *Foundations of Menu Planning*. Without you, this book would never have made it to a second edition.

ABOUT THE AUTHOR

Keith Erickson

Daniel Traster, CCP, has over eight years of formal culinary arts education experience, mostly at the program management level. He worked as the Dean of Culinary Arts and Hospitality Management at Stratford University in Falls Church, VA, and as the Academic Director for Culinary Arts at the Art Institute of Washington. Additionally, Traster served two years as the Chair of the Cooking Schools and Teachers section of the International Association of Culinary Professionals after two years as the section's Vice-Chair. Currently working as a culinary and education consultant for multiple organizations and as a writer, Traster has relished the opportunity to experience firsthand the wide range of career options available in the culinary field. Prior to teaching, Chef Traster cooked in various types of foodservice operations including "Bagels and . . ." in New Jersey; the Four Seasons Hotel in Philadelphia; Provence Restaurant in Washington, DC; Occasions Caterers in Washington, DC; and as a private chef. Over his career, he has served on the boards of the Restaurant Association of Metropolitan Washington and its Education Foundation; the Nation's Capital Chefs Association (a chapter of the American Culinary Federation); the Epicurean Club of Washington; and the National Capital chapter of The American Institute of Wine & Food. Chef Traster has also served on the advisory boards for DC Central Kitchen, the Center of Applied Technology North, Stratford University, and Lincoln College of Technology. A strong believer in lifelong education, he holds a B.A. in English and Theater from Yale University, an A.O.S. in Culinary Arts from The Culinary Institute of America, and an M.S. in Adult Learning and Human Resource Development from Virginia Tech. In addition to this text, Traster has authored *Welcome to Culinary School: A Culinary Student Survival Guide* and *Foundations of Cost Control*, both published by Pearson. Daniel Traster lives with his wife, Katie, and his daughter, Abigail, in Washington, DC.

As any textbook can be improved through the collective input of culinary school students, teachers, and industry professionals around the country, Daniel Traster welcomes feedback, comments, and suggestions for future editions. He can be reached via email at WelcometoCulinarySchool@gmail.com.

CHAPTER 1

Factors That Define a Menu

INTRODUCTION

What is a menu? In the most basic sense, a menu is a list of products that may be purchased at a foodservice establishment, but a menu can and should be much more than that. A menu is a communication vehicle that describes for the clientele each dish's components. It markets food and drink to encourage sales. Used as a control mechanism, it helps to keep a business efficient, functional, and profitable. The menu can add to the dining experience by providing history, entertainment, and support of the restaurant's theme. An effective menu meets the needs of both the business and the guests.

Menu planning is the process of creating a menu that achieves all of the aforementioned goals and more. Proper menu planning does not operate in a vacuum but rather begins after a significant amount of research. After all, a menu planner cannot meet the needs of a foodservice establishment and a customer base if he does not first know what those needs are. A menu planner begins by analyzing each of the variables that impact a menu, so, too, this text opens with a study of the multiple factors that define a menu.

CHAPTER 1 LEARNING OBJECTIVES

As a result of successfully completing this chapter, readers will be able to:

1. List several factors that impact and define a menu.

2. Describe how a menu supports a brand.

3. Define a market using demographic and psychographic studies.

4. Describe how staff skill levels, equipment and space constraints, and product availability define a menu.

5. List all of the stakeholders commonly involved in the menu-planning process.

CHAPTER 1 OUTLINE

Which Comes First, the Menu or the Market?

Learning Objective 1
List several factors that impact and define a menu.

A menu planner does not create a menu solely out of instinct and personal preferences. There are many factors that impact and define a menu, and the menu planner must take all of them into account throughout the menu-planning process. The menu planner must consider the logistical constraints of the operation, such as employee skill levels, available kitchen equipment, work flow, and product availability. Stakeholder needs help define the menu as does the business's brand. Finally and equally important, the composition and desires of the market and the presence of competing businesses all impact the final menu.

Learning Objective 2
Describe how a menu supports a brand.

Because a menu often determines which individuals from the broader market will choose to patronize an establishment, a business should begin by first analyzing the potential market and then tailoring a menu to meet the needs of one or more segments of that market. Creating the menu first can lead to a business that appeals to a market segment that does not exist in that community. For example, a chef may envision a restaurant that serves the most upscale cuisine in the world, but if his restaurant is located in a blue-collar town with an average household income of $30,000 per year, the locals will likely not dine there.

With a new business, an owner typically identifies a target market and then attempts to envision a brand that will appeal to that customer base. A brand is a business's identity, its soul. It is the set of qualities and characteristics that people associate with the business and often the reason that they spend their money there. A foodservice operation's mission and vision, its décor and location, its style of service, and, yes, its menu all define the business's brand. While the items on a menu may change, the "feel" of the menu (price point, cuisine, types of ingredients, caliber of cooking, etc.) usually does not. For example, a restaurant that serves local, organic, from-scratch dishes at a high price point on one menu will not likely change to a low-cost, mass-produced burger and fries menu during the next round of menu revisions. The brand draws customers, and a properly constructed menu supports the brand. For existing businesses, a menu overhaul continues to support the operation's brand and the needs of the business and the market. A business may choose to modify its brand, but the menu should follow and support a carefully considered brand change, not the other way around.

Learning Objective 3
Define a market using demographic and psychographic studies.

A business that attempts to be all things to all people ultimately ends up appealing to no one; its undefined brand fails to fully meet the needs of any target market. Identifying a target market and determining the type of business that might meet the market's needs is no easy task. Fortunately, there are several tools available to assist a menu planner or business owner in defining the local market segments: demographic studies, psychographic studies, competitive analyses, and feasibility studies.

Demographic Studies

A demographic study compiles certain data about the population in a given area. If a potential business owner knows exactly where he wishes to open his business, the demographic study should reflect the population of the small area around that location—a zip code, for example, rather than a large city or a state. The smaller the area studied, the more accurate the depiction of the local market will be. Menu planners can acquire demographic studies through the local chamber of commerce, local government, or Census Bureau. (Explore the website of the United States Census at www.census.gov to find demographic data for any U.S. state, county, or city.) A demographic study typically includes the following information:

Age. Listed as both raw numbers and percentages for a series of age ranges, age tells the menu planner whether the local customer is more likely to be older or younger. The foodservice needs of teenagers, middle-aged adults, and seniors will vary greatly from each other.

Marital Status. Singles and married couples may visit restaurants during different hours or prefer different types of establishments.

Housing Type and Household Size. Larger households (families) have different dining needs that impact business decisions from table sizes to menu options. Depending on the area, the ratio of apartments to houses may suggest the level of disposable income locals have to spend in restaurants.

Gender. Owners may choose to adjust their business concept to meet the needs of one sex if the population is significantly tilted toward men or women.

Ethnicity. People from different ethnic backgrounds may prefer different kinds of cuisines, particularly ones that reflect their family's country of origin or historical roots. For example, a significant population of Salvadoran immigrants may prefer classic dishes from El Salvador.

Religion. Individuals from some cultures may have religious dietary restrictions or food taboos as well. Offering fish during Lent for a Catholic community or kosher foods for an Orthodox Jewish community will appeal to that segment of the local market.

Education. Often, people with higher levels of education seek out healthier foods, display a greater willingness to try unfamiliar foods, and have more disposable income to spend on dining out.

Occupation and Income. The average income and popular occupations alert a business owner to the price point that is most likely to appeal to the local community.

Vehicles. When fewer locals own cars, a business should be located where people can access it easily on foot or via public transportation; otherwise, the restaurant may need to appeal to a larger audience beyond the local area.

Psychographic Studies

Psychographic studies provide insight into the values, interests, and habits of the population studied. Such studies provide information on how people get involved in the community, what their hobbies are, where they shop, what sports they support, where they spend their free time, and what their opinions are on a range of subjects from politics to business to education.

While all of the psychographic data contributes to a more complete depiction of the average customer, the most important data for a foodservice business owner reveals where and how people spend their money on food. If most of the population eats at home except on special occasions, a restaurateur may choose to create a destination restaurant. However, all of the psychographic data must be taken in context. If the town has a huge interest in sports but has only recently grown large enough to support any restaurants at all, perhaps the time is right to open a little sports bar.

Embedded within psychographic data may be a market's receptiveness to current and emerging trends; however, menu planners may need to research the specific trends themselves. For example, in 2016, culinary trends included farm-to-table menus, environmental sustainability and local sourcing of ingredients, healthier and less meat-focused dishes, small plates (tapas, mezze, etc.), artisanal products, in-house canning and curing, and the use of social media applications in restaurants. Menu planners may discover emerging trends by reading periodicals and blogs, or they may travel to see the dining patterns in trendsetting cities. Most importantly, before deciding to factor for a trend in a menu, the smart planner confirms that the target market values the trend. A large city's restaurants may boast several of the trends mentioned earlier, but if the citizens in a nearby small community only want large, meat-heavy portions of fried food when they go out, a trendy vegetarian tapas restaurant will not draw their business. Similarly, customers may prefer to follow trends for special occasion meals but revert to comfort foods during the week. Just as a menu planner should know the current culinary trends, he should also know whether the psychographic studies of the target market depict people who are trend followers or customers more set in their ways. If the market changes its tastes in the future, the business should adjust with the next menu revision.

Competitive Analyses

Demographic and psychographic data can be hard to interpret if the business owner or menu planner has no familiarity with the local food scene. A competitive analysis describes the foodservice competition in the area and informs a menu planner of the likely competitors to a given business concept. Such information helps a restaurateur or menu planner theorize whether a restaurant would fulfill a customer need that is currently unmet in the community or if the business concept has been so overdone in the market as to make a similar business unsustainable. Culinary entrepreneurs should investigate other businesses to see whether similar concepts might attract more customers by providing better service or cheaper prices. A little historical research may also suggest which business concepts have consistently failed in the area.

WHO IS DOWNTOWN?

Downtowners are a diverse group of workers, residents and visitors. It is a relatively young population, with high levels of income, education, and professional accomplishment.

The LIVE segment is characterized by young (average age 38), upwardly mobile professionals, the largest proportion of whom are employed in arts and entertainment, and business, professional, educational and medical services. A majority of respondents live in South Park, The Historic Core or Bunker Hill.

The WORK segment tends to be older (average age 45), and are more likely to be employed in the fields of business, professional, finance, insurance, real estate, and government, in positions such as professional/senior staff or top level executive/managers. They are more often homeowners and work primarily in the Financial District (and to a lesser extent, Bunker Hill and South Park).

The LIVE-WORK segment is even younger (average age 37), with higher income and education, and is more likely to be self-employed or an entrepreneur/business owner.

GENDER	Live	Live/Work	Work	Visit
Male	43%	47%	31%	36%
Female	57	53	69	64

AGE	Live	Live/Work	Work	Visit
18 - 22	1%	2%	1%	3%
23 - 29	18	19	12	11
30 - 34	22	25	13	12
35 - 44	25	24	24	24
45 - 54	16	19	26	24
55 - 64	10	10	21	20
65+	6	3	3	11

KIDS	Live	Live/Work	Work	Visit
Yes	11%	17%	26%	18%
No	89	83	74	82

RELATIONSHIP	Live	Live/Work	Work	Visit
Married	32%	37%	46%	38%
Living together	20	16	12	12
Single, never married	36	35	27	33
Other	12	12	15	17

ETHNICITY	Live	Live/Work	Work	Visit
Caucasian (non-Hispanic)	47%	48%	41%	43%
Hispanic/Latino	17	19	22	24
Asian/Asian American	17	18	15	13
African/African American	8	3	8	8
Pacific Islander	2	1	1	1
Native American	1	1	--	1
Other group	3	5	3	3
Prefer not to answer	6	5	9	7

EMPLOYMENT STATUS	Live	Live/Work	Work	Visit
Employed full time	61%	76%	93%	53%
Employed part time	4	4	2	6
Self-employed	7	18	3	13
Not employed	28	2	2	28

FIGURE 1.1

This segment of a larger demographic and psychographic study includes information on the places people visit in the area and the types of retail shops they patronize.

Reprinted with permission of The Downtown Center Business Improvement District.

MEDIAN HOUSEHOLD INCOME	Live	Live/Work	Work	Visit
Under $40,000	15%	8%	5%	19%
$40,000 to $74,999	18	21	24	26
$75,000 to $99,999	14	17	15	12
$100,000 to $149,999	21	20	21	15
$150,000 to $249,999	16	19	17	10
$250,000 and over	5	7	7	3
Prefer not to answer	11	8	11	15

EDUCATION	Live	Live/Work	Work	Visit
Less than high school completed	--	--	--	1%
High school or equivalent	11	6	8	10
Trade school/community college	13	14	20	21
Undergraduate/four-year college	42	45	46	40
Graduate or professional degree	34	35	27	29

INDUSTRY OF EMPLOYMENT	Live	Live/Work	Work	Visit
Arts & entertainment (artist, actor, writer, production, etc.)	21%	9%	2%	13%
Architecture, design	3	10	10	4
Business/professional/technical services	13	19	24	13
Educational services, health care & social assistance	13	5	5	11
Financial services and insurance	6	10	15	4
Government (including military)	5	7	14	6
Information media, telecom., Internet & data processing	4	5	4	5
Manufacturing (apparel, hard goods, etc.)	3	2	1	2
Medical/health services	10	2	2	8
Non-profit/civic/religious organizations	4	3	5	5
Real estate (e.g., development, brokerage)	4	9	8	7
Other	11	15	11	19

JOB TITLE	Live	Live/Work	Work	Visit
Professional or senior staff (including educators)	41%	41%	46%	33%
Clerical or general staff	9	11	25	15
Top level executive/manager	15	13	12	9
Technical/development staff	7	5	7	5
Small business owner/entrepreneur	5	10	2	9
Independent consultant, contractor or agent	6	8	2	11
Writer, artist, entertainer	6	7	1	7
Other	12	6	6	11

FIGURE 1.1 *(Continued)*

ACTIVITIES

Downtowners engage in a broad range of social, cultural, and entertainment activities, and are more likely to do them Downtown than in other parts of LA. This is especially true for sporting events, concerts, trade shows and tours. Generally, the residential and live-work populations have the highest rate of participation.

The most popular activities range from museum exhibitions and concerts to nightlife and sporting events, while the most frequented venues include "mainstream" locations such as Staples Center, high culture establishments like The Music Center, and more "niche" attractions such as ArtWalk.

Downtowners also actively frequent retail-oriented locations such as FIGat7th, Grand Central Market and LA LIVE, and public places such as Pershing Square, Grand Park, and the Los Angeles Public Library.

Downtowners utilize a range of transportation modes, including car, Metro, bus, and increasingly, walking. They are also particularly receptive to the BikeShare concept. *(See page 11)*

For information about DTLA, Downtowners show their community-orientation with the highest proportion relying on word-of-mouth. L.A. Downtown News and Los Angeles Times run 2nd and 3rd. Not surprisingly, this Internet-savvy population also frequently turns to web sites such as DowntownLA.com. *(See page 11)*

MOST FREQUENTLY VISITED LANDMARK VENUES

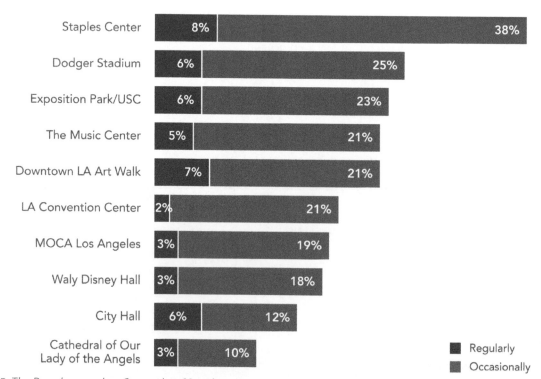

NOTE: The Broad opened on September 30 and so was not included in the survey

FIGURE 1.1   *(Continued)*

SUPERMARKETS: AVERAGE SHARE OF TOTAL SHOPPING

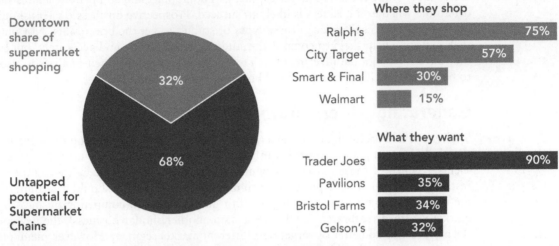

Downtown share of supermarket shopping

32%

68%

Untapped potential for Supermarket Chains

Where they shop

Ralph's	75%
City Target	57%
Smart & Final	30%
Walmart	15%

What they want

Trader Joes	90%
Pavilions	35%
Bristol Farms	34%
Gelson's	32%

NOTE: Whole Foods opened on November 4 and so was not included in the survey

HEALTH & BEAUTY: AVERAGE SHARE OF TOTAL SHOPPING

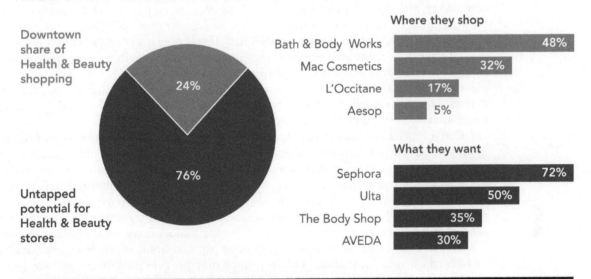

Downtown share of Health & Beauty shopping

24%

76%

Untapped potential for Health & Beauty stores

Where they shop

Bath & Body Works	48%
Mac Cosmetics	32%
L'Occitane	17%
Aesop	5%

What they want

Sephora	72%
Ulta	50%
The Body Shop	35%
AVEDA	30%

CLOTHING/APPAREL: AVERAGE SHARE OF TOTAL SHOPPING

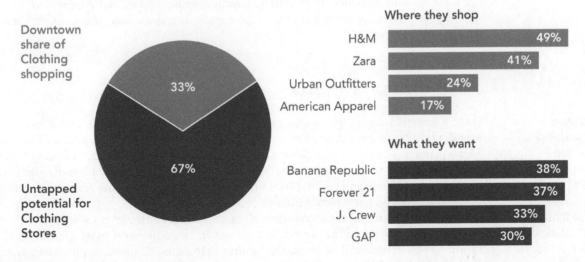

Downtown share of Clothing shopping

33%

67%

Untapped potential for Clothing Stores

Where they shop

H&M	49%
Zara	41%
Urban Outfitters	24%
American Apparel	17%

What they want

Banana Republic	38%
Forever 21	37%
J. Crew	33%
GAP	30%

FIGURE 1.1   *(Continued)*

Feasibility Studies

A feasibility study combines demographic, psychographic, and competitive analysis data to determine whether a business is likely to succeed. Prospective business owners should hire professionals who specialize in these types of studies to get the best results. Not only does their expertise help them to compile the study more efficiently and accurately, but because they have no emotional investment in a given business concept, their analysis is also likely to be more objective than a potential business owner's would be.

Generating a Menu from the Data

Studies provide useful data, but generating a menu from that data requires some interpretive skill. A menu planner must hypothesize the needs of the various market segments and then see which of those market segments' needs are not being met by the competition. A restaurateur should not be put off by a similar competitor, but he should determine whether the market is large enough to support both his concept and competing businesses. If the market is already saturated (unable to sustain another similar business), the newcomer to the market may do better by targeting a different market segment. However, menu planners and entrepreneurs should always confirm that there is a large enough market to sustain a given business concept even if there is no competition. For example, a hip, loud, experimental restaurant targeted at 20-somethings will fail to find customers in a retirement community with no one under the age of 55. Sometimes, competition for a particular market segment does not exist for a reason.

Analysis of the various market studies may reveal obvious constraints to a menu. The market's average income, for example, may limit the menu's flexibility with price points. If a target market does not usually spend more than $30 per person for dinner, then the menu's prices should permit a guest to order one or two courses with drinks for that price. A restaurant that exceeds a market's typical price point may need to focus on special occasion business, as it is unlikely to attract regular customers.

Certain menu constraints only become obvious with personal knowledge of the community. Consider a restaurant targeted toward seniors. While most older patrons prefer quieter dining rooms with sufficient lighting for menu reading, all seniors do not prefer the same limited menu selections. Some mature diners prefer the comfort foods of 1950s America, while others opt for ethnic foods reminiscent of their foreign travels. Softer foods may be a physical necessity for certain seniors, but others may prefer the variety of textures that lend interest to a typical dish. Whether seniors favor cosmopolitan or homey fare may not be obvious from a demographic or psychographic study, but some familiarity or interaction with local senior citizen groups may provide a definitive answer. Making assumptions based on stereotypes alone can lead to an underperforming and ineffective menu, but proven behaviors for a market segment allow a menu planner to design a product for a built-in audience. Fortunately, psychographic studies and competitive analyses describe the proven spending patterns of the community as a whole, if not for each individual market segment.

Logistical Constraints on Menus

Learning Objective 4
Describe how staff skill levels, equipment and space constraints, and product availability define a menu.

Once a business owner and menu planner have selected a business's target market and brand, they should next determine any other factors that would limit a menu's feasibility. Menu planners should avoid writing a menu that the staff cannot execute. Listing barbecue on a menu makes no sense if the restaurant cannot fit a grill or smoker into its kitchen. For a menu to be feasible and profitable, it must make efficient use of the employees' skills, the physical space, and purveyors' available products.

In a new restaurant, the menu determines the caliber of employees sought and the minimal equipment required for the kitchen. However, menu planners must keep in mind that future menu changes will be impacted by that first menu. Equipment purchases and staff skill levels should be versatile enough to support the business's brand in future menu iterations. For established operations, the menu planner must account for the existing equipment and staff limitations in the menu-planning process.

Employee Skill Level

Complex menus with lots of handmade components per dish typically require highly skilled labor. The same is true for menus that call for servers to perform some form of cooking or carving tableside. Since a higher-caliber workforce often necessitates higher wages, the employee skill level required to execute a menu impacts the menu's price point.

If an existing business has a kitchen team that is only capable of reheating and plating prefabricated dishes, then the menu planner must create a menu that does not exceed this skill level. While the employees could be replaced with a more highly trained staff, to do so would increase labor cost and call for significantly higher menu prices. If the business has been successful and a change in prices would undermine the brand, replacing the workers with a higher-caliber team could drive away business and erode profits. Similarly, there is no value to writing a menu that exceeds the current staff's abilities. The employees would likely put out substandard food that does not meet the menu planner's or manager's goals. If managers choose to train the employees to increase their skill level, they should confirm the training's effectiveness before the new menu is put in place.

Whereas a new restaurant does not have the skill-level constraints of an existing operation, it does have some staffing limitations that impact the menu. As mentioned above, a higher-caliber staff requires higher wages. Additionally, some communities may not possess the trained workforce envisioned by the menu planner. If none of the restaurants in a given community prepare their food from scratch, most foodservice workers in the area will have had no opportunity to practice or learn a higher level of culinary skill.

Equipment

Equipment availability places significant constraints on menu planners and what their menus can offer. The most obvious limitation stems from cooking equipment. A kitchen that consists of nothing more than ovens and a deep fryer cannot effectively serve a la carte sautéed or grilled foods. Chefs can create a workaround for certain pieces of equipment—steaming in a pot with a basket rather than in a commercial steamer, for example—but such equipment alternatives should be kept to a minimum. In the steamer example, a pot with a basket could probably handle a single component for one dish, but it would significantly slow production if four entrées required steamed ingredients.

Refrigeration also impacts menu choices. If a kitchen only has a single-door, reach-in freezer, the number of frozen menu components offered on the menu should be limited. Because more extensive menus require larger storage capacity for ingredients, a small kitchen with little refrigeration and dry storage space will perform better with a small menu rather than with a larger set of offerings.

Work flow also comes into play when deciding upon a menu. If a kitchen is laid out with a set number of workstations, the menu should attempt to balance the amount of production coming from each station. For example, if a restaurant kitchen has only a grill station and a sauté station, it would not make sense to write a menu with six grilled items and only one sautéed dish; otherwise, the sauté cook would be fairly idle while the grill cook becomes overwhelmed. It would be better to divide the menu such that half of the dishes come from one station and the other half from the other station.

While a brand-new establishment may design its kitchen around the opening menu, the menu planner should consider whether or not the initial menu inordinately constrains future menus. If the vision for a restaurant is to serve a variety of modern American dishes cooked in a range of ways, it would not make sense to open with an all-barbecue menu that requires a large bank of smokers on the hot line. To do so would effectively force future menus to replicate the barbecue theme. That said, if a restaurant is going for a specific theme (like barbecue or fried seafood), it may make sense to design a menu that begs for a hot line of all one piece of equipment (all smokers or all fryers, for example).

Product Availability

A menu planner must ensure that the ingredients required to execute a given menu are available during the time that the menu will be in place. Some products are available year-round while others are only in season during a short period of time. Ingredients found in one part of the country may be difficult to source elsewhere. For example, walleye, a fish native to the Great Lakes, may be easy to find in Ohio but nearly impossible to source in Louisiana. Similarly, while blood oranges may be a spectacular addition to a winter menu, they are out of season in the United States during the summer and thus would be an inappropriate component to a year-round menu. Including items on a menu that cannot be purchased during the lifetime of the menu only leads to menu shortages, unexpected substitutions, and, ultimately, dissatisfied customers.

The Stakeholders

Learning Objective 5
List all of the stakeholders commonly involved in the menu-planning process.

Nearly everyone involved in a foodservice business has a stake in producing an effective, quality menu. The owners and investors want a menu that will attract business and assist in the operation's profitability. Managers and employees need a menu that can be executed effectively and efficiently given the equipment, product, and employee constraints of the business. Customers want a menu that appeals to their tastes and works within their personal budgets. In short, the menu serves a lot of people, so the menu planner should involve all of these stakeholders in the menu development process.

For a new business, owners, managers, and the executive chef usually work together to generate a menu that will meet the needs of the target market. To some degree, this is a guessing game, as the customer preferences are inferred from psychographic data for the area rather than obtained by polling the customers directly. Some restaurants gather customer input by hosting a series of pre-opening meals from which managers observe which dishes are popular and which do not sell well. The more input the management collects prior to opening its doors officially, the better.

For an existing restaurant, menu changes should incorporate known data on prior sales. Slow-moving dishes should be adjusted or removed entirely. Popular and profitable ones should be retained. Menu planners should interview employees to see where problems with work flow or product sourcing exist. They should also consult customers to see whether certain changes would encourage them to return more or less frequently to the establishment.

Before a foodservice business opens its doors, a poorly researched menu will still define the market, the caliber of the staff, and the design of the kitchen, though not necessarily in the way that the menu planner had hoped. It is often better for all of the stakeholders to determine these variables first and then allow those factors to suggest a menu that supports the brand. For a foodservice operation that already exists, these factors are already in place and often are quite difficult to change simply to accommodate a new menu.

Summary

The identity of any foodservice operation is its brand. Each brand innately appeals to a specific market. Business owners should research the potential markets in the area to see whether they are large enough to support a business and if their needs are currently being met by competing businesses. Data that defines a market comes from demographic and psychographic studies. Demographic studies describe the population's age, marital status, housing type, household size, gender, race, ethnicity, religion, education, occupations, income, and vehicles, among other information.

Psychographic studies describe the values, interests, and habits of the population. A competitive analysis provides a depiction of competing businesses in the area while a feasibility study suggests whether a potential business is likely to make a profit. A foodservice business's brand and its menu must appeal to the target market described in the studies, and they must do so in a way that does not put the business at risk of losing out to the competition. Other variables limit and define a menu as well. Employee skill level, equipment and space constraints, and product availability all impact what a menu planner can include in a menu. As the process of creating a menu is a complex one, it is best to involve as many stakeholders as possible. For new businesses, the stakeholders may be only the owners and managers. For existing operations, guests and frontline employees should be consulted as well.

Comprehension Questions

1. List four variables that help to define a menu.

2. What role does a menu play in relation to a business's brand?

3. List the two primary tools that help to define a market. What type of information does each one provide?

4. If a chef wants to create a menu that exceeds his staff's ability, why can't he just hire new staff?

5. How does a kitchen's space and work flow impact a menu?

6. Who are the typical stakeholders who contribute to the menu-planning process in a new business? Who is normally added to the process in an existing business?

Discussion Questions

1. A demographic study shows that the largest percentage of the local population is age 30–50 with a middle-class income and an average household size of 3.7. Many of them own their own homes and at least one car. Describe a restaurant concept that would appeal to this target market. (Describe the brand and the menu, but do not write out a menu.)

2. A nearby community has the demographic makeup described in question 1. A psychographic study shows that the community spends the majority of their disposable income on recreational activities for their children (sports, dance, music, movies, travel, etc.), not on food. What kind of foodservice business might you set up in this community to appeal to the local market? Describe the business's brand.

3. Describe the demographic and psychographic qualities that define the target market into which you personally fall. What kinds of foodservice establishments are those in that market segment likely to patronize?

4. Envision a restaurant concept and describe it. Describe the kind of employees, the kitchen layout, and the kitchen equipment you would need to support that concept across several consecutive menus.

5. Imagine that you are the general manager for an existing restaurant. What kind of information would you want to know from the various stakeholders before creating a new menu?

Capstone Project

Overview: Working alone or in a team, you will create a menu for a given business concept. As menu planning is not a quick, off-the-cuff process, this project will span all of the chapters of the book to allow you to work in small, manageable steps.

Step 1: Imagine a business concept. Describe in one to two pages the business's concept and target market, the average price point, approximate business location, and required staff skill level. You should also include, using online census or other tools, demographic data for your desired business location. The target market should be well represented in this data. You should include in your written descriptions where in the demographic data your target market is represented and how your business concept meets the needs of that market. (Large companies often spend months on this step and might invest significant money into researching the local market, but this brief exercise will give you a taste of what the process is like while providing sufficient grounding to begin the capstone project.)

CHAPTER 2
Nutrition and Menu Planning

INTRODUCTION

Accounting for nutrition in the menu-planning process should be a major consideration. While some special occasion restaurants may expect to see the same customers return only once each year, most foodservice establishments aim to attract repeat business far more frequently. As customers return more regularly, culinary businesses have an increasing ethical obligation to serve the nutritional needs of their clientele appropriately. One unhealthy meal may not harm a diner, but a regular diet of unhealthful meals impacts the consumer's quality of life and life expectancy. While most restaurants need not serve only healthy dishes, they should offer at least some healthy choices to allow guests to patronize the establishment when they crave something more nutritious.

When a customer has no alternative dining choice (think schools, hospitals, prisons, etc.), meeting the consumer's nutritional needs becomes imperative. However, attending to nutrition in menu planning serves two other purposes beyond maintaining a guest's health. First, as Americans continue to focus on nutrition, diet, and weight loss while increasing the number of meals they consume outside the home, they increasingly clamor for healthier meal options. Many national restaurant chains have already adjusted their menus to accommodate dietary needs and retain the nutrition-minded

market segment. Some of these chains have merely put a nutritional spin on their current menus without actually making their menus healthier, but those that have genuinely adopted a healthier approach to menus will fare better as the population becomes more informed. Second, America continues to battle an obesity epidemic. If the epidemic worsens, the government will increase pressure on all foodservice establishments to provide healthier menus. It is far more cost-effective for the industry to preempt government by proactively addressing nutrition than it is to have government regulations thrust upon it. The rule that a foodservice operation should appeal to the needs of its target market is still paramount; what is changing is the American market's increasing awareness of and desire for nutrition on foodservice menus.

This chapter is not intended to be an in-depth study of nutrition, but it will provide some nutrition basics on the more common dietary concerns among Americans. While most foodservice operations do not need to prepare for every conceivable dietary restriction, they should be able to accommodate the most common ones to better serve their clientele. Whether factoring for general health, special diets, or even allergies, the menu planner should always consider nutrition and dietary restrictions when creating a menu.

CHAPTER 2 LEARNING OBJECTIVES

As a result of successfully completing this chapter, readers will be able to:

1. Describe why nutrition is a critical component of menu planning.

2. State how market captivity relates to the healthfulness of menus.

3. List the major categories of nutrients and broadly describe their functions.

4. List the principles of a healthy diet.

5. List the most common food allergens for the population.

6. Create a healthy menu that addresses the nutritional needs of the majority of the population.

7. List several common dietary restrictions and create a menu item that accommodates individuals with those restrictions.

CHAPTER 2 OUTLINE

Why Is Nutrition Important to Menu Planning?

Learning Objective 1
Describe why nutrition is a critical component of menu planning.

While some foodservice businesses rely on constant marketing to attract new clients each day, the best scenario for a culinary operation is to maintain a core of regular customers who frequent the establishment. Regular customers require less investment in marketing dollars, and they ensure a steady flow of revenue for the business, even during slow periods. However, customers who acquire health problems from a steady diet of unhealthy food from a given restaurant are likely to reduce or eliminate their patronage of that restaurant. To attract a regular customer, a restaurant must offer food that that customer can eat frequently without negatively impacting her health. Providing a healthy menu (or at least some healthy options) to customers who have a choice in where to dine is a business decision that usually helps to build a steady customer base.

Learning Objective 2
State how market captivity relates to the healthfulness of menus.

Some diners have no choice in which establishment they patronize. Hospital patients have no alternative but to eat the food provided by the hospital. Schoolchildren who do not bring a lunch with them (and this includes the vast numbers of students who survive on federally subsidized school lunches) must eat the meal provided to them by the school or go hungry. While businesspeople can leave work to eat at a nearby restaurant, those in a rush may have no choice but to dine in the company's corporate cafeteria. When a foodservice operation has a clientele who must use its services, those customers are called a *captive market*.

Culinary businesses that serve a captive market have an ethical obligation to provide healthy food to their customers. To do otherwise is to force a person to choose between going hungry or eating food that will make her sick. Additionally, in a noncommercial operation—in which supporting a parent organization in its mission takes precedence over generating significant profits—creating a pool of sluggish, unhealthy workers or students may undermine the efforts of the parent company (school, business, or hospital). Businesses with captive markets may not need to attract customers with nutritional offerings, but they still must provide healthy, appealing options to their guests.

Addressing nutrition in menu planning also helps the industry as a whole in terms of public perception and government regulation. Several states have enacted or are considering legislation that regulates nutrition in restaurants. The most prominent efforts have centered on nutrition labeling for chain restaurant menus. As the obesity epidemic persists in the country, it is likely that more local and state governments will enact laws regulating nutrition in restaurants.

The *Dietary Guidelines for Americans 2015–2020* is one of the foundational documents that inform American nutrition education programs. Educators turn to this document to learn what they should tell their students about healthy lifestyle habits. The *Dietary Guidelines* lists the food and beverage industry among the many sectors (including government, health care, public health organizations, marketing, media, and agriculture, to name a few) that impact an individual's eating patterns.[1] When restaurants do not offer healthy options, patrons of those restaurants end up making poor choices in regard to their health. So how does the *Dietary Guidelines* recommend that foodservice providers deal with this situation? The document advises:

> The food and beverage and food service sectors and settings have a unique opportunity to continue to evolve and better align with the Dietary Guidelines. Reformulation and menu and retail modification opportunities that align with the Dietary Guidelines include offering more vegetables, fruits, whole grains, low-fat and fat-free dairy, and a greater variety of protein foods that are nutrient dense, while also reducing sodium and added sugars, reducing saturated fats and replacing them with unsaturated fats, and reducing added refined starches. Portion sizes also can be adapted to help individuals make choices that align with the Dietary Guidelines. Food manufacturers are encouraged to consider the entire composition of the food, and not just individual nutrients or ingredients when developing or reformulating products. Similarly, when developing or modifying menus or retail settings, establishments can consider the range of offerings both within and across food groups and other dietary components to determine whether the healthy options offered reflect the proportions in healthy eating patterns. In taking these actions, care should be taken to assess any potential unintended consequences so that as changes are made to better align with the Dietary Guidelines, undesirable changes are not introduced.[2]

While the *Dietary Guidelines* does not require the culinary industry to comply with these recommendations, foodservice operations ignore them at their own peril. Educators, government, nonprofits, and the media promote the *Dietary Guidelines* regularly to the public. As a business's market adopts the mantra of healthier eating, the business must cater to that changed market or lose some of its customer base. The operation need not restrict its menu solely to healthy choices, but if none are available, health-conscious customers will take their sales dollars elsewhere. Additionally, if the foodservice industry shifts to healthier menus, government may view the industry as a valued partner rather than as a contributor to the obesity problem.

As menu planners account for nutritional concerns in the menu-planning process, foodservice businesses are more likely to attract and retain nutrition-minded customers,

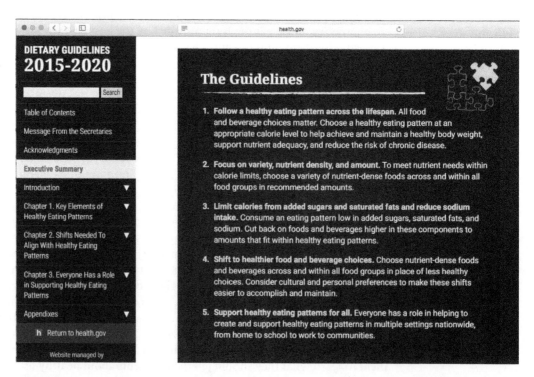

FIGURE 2.1

The executive summary section of the USDA's *Dietary Guidelines for Americans 2015–2020* shows the key recommendations that menu planners can use when designing healthy dishes for the general public.

Source: From Dietary Guidelines Executive Summary, U.S. Department of Health & Human Services.

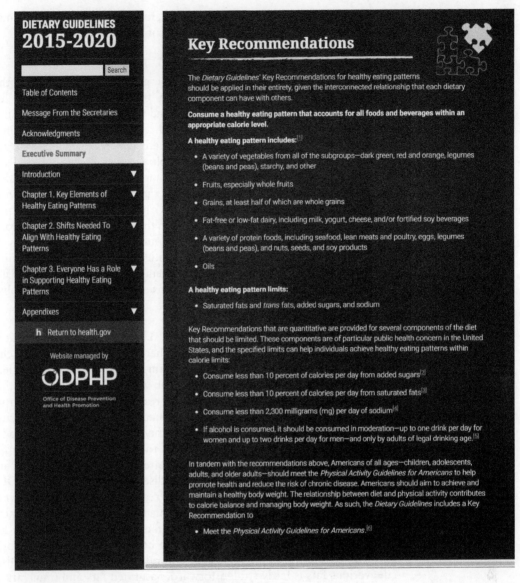

FIGURE 2.1 *(Continued)*

to meet the needs of the parent organizations they support, and to forestall government regulation designed to combat the obesity crisis in America. An entire restaurant menu need not be devoted to health and nutrition, but a menu should include some healthy choices to address those customers for whom nutrition is supreme in their dining selections.

Nutrition Basics

Learning Objective 3
List the major categories of nutrients and broadly describe their functions.

Prior to creating a healthy menu, a menu planner must understand some nutrition basics. Food and drink can be broken down into certain components that the body needs to survive. Carbohydrates, lipids, protein, and water are considered macronutrients as they are required in relatively large quantities—multiple ounces per day. Vitamins and minerals are called micronutrients as they are needed in much smaller quantities, measured in milligrams or micrograms per day. Carbohydrates, lipids, and proteins provide calories while water, vitamins, and minerals do not. A *calorie* (short for kilocalorie) is a measure of energy that food delivers to the body. When a person consumes more calories than she burns, the excess energy is stored as body fat. Foods that are termed *nutrient-dense* provide a large quantity of nutrients (specifically, vitamins and minerals) per calorie while *calorie-dense* food and drink supply little more than calories to the body. While this text is not a replacement for a thorough understanding of nutrition, following are some of the most important points to know about nutrition for the purposes of general menu planning:

Carbohydrates

Carbohydrates provide 4 calories of energy per gram. Although they are an essential component of any diet, they can be found in healthy and less healthy forms. While carbohydrates are present in fruits and vegetables, most Americans consume the majority of their carbohydrates from grains and refined sugars. Whole grains—those that deliver fiber along with calories—generate more gradual increases in blood sugar while refined grains and sugars tend to create sharp spikes in blood sugar. Spikes in blood sugar yield short-term energy "highs" followed by periods of lethargy and hunger. As a result, consumers of large quantities of refined grains and sugars find themselves hungry and craving calories soon after eating. The ongoing cycle of hunger pangs often leads to overeating throughout the day and ultimately to weight gain. Whole grains, on the other hand, provide a longer feeling of satiety or fullness that allows the eater to go without snacking between meals. Additionally, refined grains, unless they are enriched or fortified, lose many of their nutrients and become calorie-dense; whole grains, fruits, and vegetables are nutrient-dense. The *Dietary Guidelines* recommends that 45%–65% of calorie consumption come from carbohydrates.[3]

Lipids

Lipids are the category comprised of fats, oils, and cholesterol. As the body makes cholesterol in sufficient quantities for survival, there is no need to consume cholesterol in the diet. Fats and oils provide 9 calories per gram—the most of any nutrient. Thus, lipids are calorie-dense and contribute to weight gain when eaten in large quantities. Fats and oils are composed of fatty acids, but not all fatty acids are the same when it comes to physical health. The consumption of fatty acids impacts the levels of high-density lipoprotein (HDL) and low-density lipoprotein (LDL) that the liver produces in the body. (The media often refer to HDL as "good cholesterol" and to LDL as "bad cholesterol.") Higher levels of LDL and total cholesterol typically correlate to heavier deposits of cholesterol and plaque on arterial walls—a risk factor for heart disease. Higher levels of HDL and lower levels of LDL and total cholesterol in the bloodstream translate to a lower risk of heart disease. Monounsaturated and polyunsaturated fats maintain a healthy balance between HDL and LDL in the bloodstream while saturated fats and trans fats increase levels of LDL. (Most trans fats are unsaturated fats that have been made saturated through a process called hydrogenation; trace amounts occur naturally in meat and dairy.) Distinguishing between the various fats is fairly straightforward. Saturated fats and trans fats are typically solid at room temperature while monounsaturated and polyunsaturated fats are liquid oils at room temperature. Seafood is the rare exception that provides high levels of unsaturated fats that are solid at room temperature. Fats are an essential component of any diet, but most Americans consume far more than they need. The *Dietary Guidelines* recommends that 20%–35% of calories come from fat with no more than 10% coming from saturated fats.[4]

Proteins

Proteins provide 4 calories of energy per gram and are a component of most parts of the body. Proteins are made up of amino acids, and while the body can produce some of the amino acids that it needs, nine of the amino acids are not created by the body in sufficient quantity for survival. These nine are called *essential amino acids*. Foods that provide all nine essential amino acids are termed *complete proteins*; those that are missing at least one of the nine are called *incomplete proteins*. While the body needs all nine essential amino acids, they can be acquired by consuming either complete proteins or several incomplete proteins that supplement each other's missing amino acids. Proteins are found in both plant and animal sources, but animal sources often come with the addition of saturated fat. Lean proteins—those that deliver little fat with the protein—are generally considered the healthiest sources of protein. The *Dietary Guidelines* recommends that 10%–30% of calories come from protein.[5]

Water

Water delivers no calories to the body, but it is an essential nutrient for proper bodily function. While a human being can survive for weeks without food, she will die after just a week or two without water. The average person should consume at least eight 8-ounce glasses of water each day.

Vitamins and Minerals

Vitamins and minerals are critical for a wide range of bodily functions. Some work in tandem with each other while others work independently from the other micronutrients. For basic menu-planning purposes, it is more important to understand some general facts about the micronutrients than it is to understand each one's sources and functions. Some vitamins are water-soluble while others are fat-soluble. Thus, cooking liquids can dissolve some of a food's micronutrients and remove them from the meal if the cooking liquid is not served with the rest of the food. Many vitamins are destroyed with heat and time, too, so using fresh ingredients and avoiding overcooking help to preserve these delicate nutrients. While vitamins and minerals are a required part of a healthy diet, they can cause physical harm when consumed in excess. Thus, dietary supplements can aid a person with insufficient nutrient intake, but megadoses of vitamins and minerals may do more harm than good. Emphasizing variety in a diet is the best way to acquire the complete range of necessary vitamins and minerals.

Of the dietary vitamin and mineral spectrum, only a few are common sources for dietary concern. Calcium provides strength to bones and teeth; an insufficient quantity of calcium leads to osteoporosis—a weakening of the bones. Vitamin D works with calcium to strengthen bones. Both calcium and vitamin D are prevalent in dairy. Calcium can also be obtained through fish bones (commonly eaten in smaller fishes), certain leafy greens, and calcium-fortified foods. Vitamin D is produced by the body through exposure to sunlight, but some individuals require additional vitamin D through their diet. Sodium is often cited for its contribution to high blood pressure. As sodium is plentiful in processed foods, most Americans need to reduce or limit their dietary sodium rather than increase it. Iron deficiency leads to anemia, one of the few nutrient deficiency diseases common in America today. Good sources of iron include lean meats, poultry, seafood, legumes, spinach, and iron-fortified foods. Folate and vitamin B_{12}, which work in tandem with each other, are required for cell generation, so they are critical dietary components for pregnant women and for seniors (who have reduced ability to absorb B_{12}). Folate is found in "foliage"—lettuces and leafy greens. B_{12} is present only in animal products, so vegans must take B_{12} supplements.

Fiber

Though not absorbed by the body as a nutrient, fiber plays a critical role in digestion that impacts health in a positive way. Fiber is indigestible, so it helps to push foods along through the digestive tract and aids in solid waste elimination. Fiber provides a feeling of satiety, which leads to fewer calories consumed each meal. It also helps to regulate blood sugar by slowing the absorption of sugars during digestion and may reduce the risk of certain diseases, including colon cancer and type II diabetes. Fiber is prevalent in fruits, vegetables, whole grains, and legumes.

Alcohol

While alcohol is not a required component of any diet, it is mentioned here because it is consumed by many Americans and does impact health in several ways. Alcohol provides 7 calories of energy per gram, so it is not a calorie-free drink. Some studies have shown positive heart-health benefits stemming from the moderate consumption of wine, especially red wine; however, those benefits disappear with excessive consumption. Moderate consumption is defined as one drink per day for women and two per day for men, but because of the risk of alcoholism, alcohol consumption is not recommended for all individuals.

Principles of a Healthy Diet

Learning Objective 4
List the principles of a healthy diet.

With the range of dietary restrictions and allergies across the population, there is no single diet that works for everyone; however, there are some universal truths to healthy eating that apply to all Americans. First, any healthy diet should be balanced and varied. As there is no magical food that supplies all of the required nutrients in the right proportions, people must consume a wide range of foods to ensure that they acquire all of the nutrients they need. Balance implies that the foods should come from the several macronutrient categories

Monday:

Choice of:
- Orange Chicken Brown Rice Bowl
- "Breakfast for Lunch": whole grain pancakes and cheese omelet with syrup and ketchup
- Turkey and Cheddar Sandwich on a whole grain bun with green leaf lettuce and mayonnaise
- BBQ Chicken Wrap in whole grain lavash with yogurt BBQ ranch dipping sauce

All served with side vegetables of pinto beans and baby carrots as well as fresh fruit and choice of lowfat or fatfree milk.

Tuesday:

Choice of:
- Cheesy Chicken Quesadilla in a whole grain tortilla
- Veggie Chili with Mini Melted Cheese Sandwich on a whole grain roll
- Chillin' Chinese Chicken Noodles made with whole grain noodles with sesame soy dressing
- Ham and Cheddar Sandwich on a whole grain bun with green leaf lettuce and mayonnaise

All served with side vegetable of steamed corn as well as fresh fruit and choice of lowfat or fatfree milk.

Wednesday:
- Chicken Bites with whole grain breading and ketchup
- Whole Grain Penne with Zesty Beef Sauce
- Pinto Bean Taco Dip with whole grain lavash
- Sesame Chicken Wrap in whole grain lavash with sesame soy dressing

All served with side vegetable of celery sticks with ranch dressing as well as fresh fruit and choice of lowfat or fatfree milk.

Thursday:
- Beef/Turkey Cheeseburger on a whole grain bun with ketchup
- Buffalo Chicken Sandwich on a whole grain bun
- Chicken "Pizza Party" Salad with pizza vinaigrette and whole grain dinner roll
- Egg Salad Sandwich with green leaf lettuce on a whole grain bun

All served with side vegetable of green leaf lettuce and sliced tomatoes as well as fresh fruit and choice of lowfat or fatfree milk.

Friday:
- Whole Grain Spaghetti and Beef/Turkey Meatballs in marinara sauce
- Chicken Marinara Bake (whole grain penne with chicken breast in marinara sauce, topped with low fat mozzarella cheese)
- Turkey Chef Salad with whole grain dinner roll
- Build Your Own Sunbutter and Jelly Sandwich with low fat yogurt on the side

All served with side vegetable of glazed carrots as well as fresh fruit and choice of lowfat or fatfree milk.

FIGURE 2.2

Addressing nutrition is absolutely essential for a captive audience. This school lunch menu, with a vegetarian option each day, illustrates that nutritious can be delicious and appeal to children.

Reprinted with permission of Revolution Foods.

in appropriate proportions. Variety suggests that the foods within each category should rotate regularly so that all of the micronutrients are ultimately received.

A healthy diet should also be adequate but moderate. A certain percentage of the population does not receive sufficient calories and nutrients due to financial strain or other hardship. Some may have access to food but not necessarily to healthy options. These diets are inadequate to meet the nutritional needs of the individual. However, in America today, the more common dietary challenge is excess consumption. Overeating calories leads to weight gain. Overindulgence in sugars, fats, and sodium can lead to cardiovascular disease or diabetes. Imbibing too heavily on alcohol can lead to the various health concerns associated with alcoholism. Thus, maintaining a moderate diet is as important as consuming an adequate one. Selecting foods that are nutrient-dense tends to supply adequacy in micronutrients without sacrificing moderation in macronutrients and calories overall.

While no diet is perfect for everyone, a typical healthy diet is based mainly on fruits, vegetables, legumes, and whole grains with less emphasis on meat, salt, fat, sugar, refined grains, and alcohol. A menu that approaches food from this philosophy would generally be considered healthier than one that focuses on large portions of fatty meat, rich, sugary desserts, and lots of alcohol. (To further examine your own diet or someone else's, visit www. choosemyplate.gov. To learn more about dietary recommendations for the U.S. population as a whole, read the complete *Dietary Guidelines for Americans 2015–2020* at http:// health.gov/dietaryguidelines/2015/guidelines/.)

Allergies and Food Safety Warnings

Learning Objective 5 List the most common food allergens for the population.

Allergies are a physical reaction to certain stimuli, and for some people, specific foods can trigger an allergic reaction. Reactions differ from minor swelling or rash to death, so menu planners are wise to account for possible allergic reactions. Chefs must take customer notifications of allergies seriously and make every effort to accommodate the request or to notify the customer of a potential hazard.

While no menu can account for every possible allergy, there are several common food allergens that a menu planner should consider when creating a menu. The most common categories of food allergens are fish, shellfish, dairy, peanuts, tree nuts, eggs, wheat, and soy. It is not necessary to avoid all of these ingredients on a menu, but most menu planners should attempt to have at least one dish on the menu that could accommodate a customer with each of these allergies. Thus, at least one dish should contain no seafood, another should contain no dairy, and so on. There are exceptions, of course—a seafood restaurant can safely assume that someone with a seafood allergy would not likely dine there—but for most general audience menus, all of the allergy categories should be addressed.

Restaurants that do not plan for these allergy categories on their menu should anticipate periodic guest requests for a recipe modification. In most mid-level and high-end establishments, these requests should be accommodated. Consequently, if a steak is served with a lobster sauce, the chef ought to be able to serve it without the sauce to someone who requests it. A dish normally fried in peanut oil should be fried in a different oil upon request. When a chef cannot accommodate a request—for example, for a dish that is made in advance and for which the allergen cannot be removed—the chef and server should be honest with the customer and not attempt to pass off the dish as allergen-free. If a processed component is used and the chef does not know whether it contains the allergen in question, she should simply say so to the customer. A guest who must choose from a limited selection of dishes is much happier than a guest who suffers an allergic reaction in a restaurant.

To avoid surprising a guest with an allergic reaction, some establishments state hidden ingredients on the menu when they pose a common allergy risk. For example, a menu should state if it fries its food in peanut oil. It should note whether the stir-fry includes shrimp paste. To do otherwise puts at risk a diner who might assume that the dish does not contain a certain allergen.

Another type of safety warning, sometimes mandated by the local municipality, deals with the consumption of undercooked, potentially hazardous food. Most chefs and culinary students are familiar with the minimum internal temperatures required to kill pathogenic bacteria. But how can a restaurant serve a poached egg if the temperature will not reach 165 degrees? Can a chef ever put scallop ceviche or rare hamburgers on a menu? Of course the chef can, but the menu must alert the restaurant patrons to the potential safety risk. A common way of phrasing this alert is "Consuming raw or undercooked meats, poultry, seafood, shellfish, or eggs may increase your risk of foodborne illness." Such a warning is typically placed at the bottom of a menu beside an asterisk, and the relevant dishes are starred on the menu as well.

By properly notifying guests of potential allergens and food safety hazards, the menu planner helps to reduce the number of customers who leave the establishment with an unanticipated illness or allergic reaction and helps to mitigate legal liability should an affected customer sue the establishment.

Creating a Healthy Menu

The first step to creating a healthy menu is to develop nutritious dishes targeted to the general population, not necessarily for any specific diet. Per the *Dietary Guidelines* and mainstream nutrition advice, such dishes should be based primarily on fruits, vegetables, whole grains, and legumes, with smaller quantities of lean meats, poultry, or seafood. For the average adult, 50–70 grams of pure protein is sufficient for the day's intake. As most Americans get at least half of this protein requirement from grains, nuts, legumes, dairy, and/or eggs, 4 ounces of meat, fish, or poultry is enough for the entire day. Thus, a 4-ounce portion of meat, poultry, or fish more than suffices as a portion for one meal. A single serving of cooked grain or vegetable is ½ cup, and one serving of each is typically plenty for a meal that also includes a center-of-the-plate protein. (For raw, leafy greens, 1 cup is a single serving.) If the restaurant expects guests to also order appetizers and desserts, those should continue the fruit/vegetable/grain focus without overdosing guests on added fats and sugars.

As Americans tend to consume more sodium than necessary in their diets, a healthy menu should reduce the amount of salt it delivers and focus on alternative flavor enhancers instead. Herbs, spices, and highly acidic ingredients (citrus, wine, or vinegar) provide a flavor boost without the addition of salt and allow the chef to use less sodium in her cooking. When salt is used, it should be added only when each guest's order is placed. That way, if a guest asks for a salt-free or low-sodium version, the chef is able to adjust the recipe accordingly. By presalting a batch recipe, the chef has no such flexibility.

Proper portion sizes are critical on menus in a country that suffers from diseases of overconsumption rather than from insufficient caloric intake. Not only are guests able to eat from such a menu without undermining their health, but a restaurant can sell more courses to customers who don't fill up completely on a single dish. So how should a steakhouse deal with the argument that the proper portion size for protein is 4 ounces? Is it realistic to expect all restaurants to serve a 4-ounce prime rib or porterhouse steak? Of course not, but hefty portions of meat should not be the only options on the menu either. The best advice for how closely a restaurant should adhere to nutrition guidelines is to factor more for nutrition as customer frequency increases. In other words, a restaurant that sees the same customers return weekly should include a wider range of healthy menu options than a once-a-year special occasion restaurant does. When the customer base is a captive market, nutrition should be one of the main concerns of the menu planner, as the consumers have no alternatives. Even in special occasion restaurants, diners should be able to find at least some healthy options should they choose to follow a healthy diet. If no restaurants in a community offer healthy choices, then the local market must choose between an unhealthy diet or fewer meals eaten outside the home. When a restaurant delivers a wide range of healthy choices and proper portion sizes, patrons are able to eat there more frequently without detriment to their health.

So how is a menu planner to create dishes that fit the proper portion size mold? The center-of-the-plate concept in which a large piece of meat, fish, or poultry is accompanied by smaller (or nowadays, equally enormous) portions of starch and vegetable is perhaps the most common style of plate presentation and yet one of the most difficult challenges nutritionally. Stir-fries, risottos, curries, salads, pizzas, and pastas are just a few examples of dishes that can include animal proteins in small quantities without fomenting customer dissatisfaction. Slicing and fanning a poultry breast or steak is another approach to providing normal portion sizes that appeal to a customer's desire for visible "bounty." Except for truly captive audiences, such dishes need not be the only options available on the menu, but providing just a few of these healthy selections allows health-conscious customers to enjoy their experience at a restaurant.

One pitfall that can trip up menu planners is to differentiate between nutritious and delicious. The two can and must be synonymous, for food does not provide any nutrition until the guest swallows it. Focusing only on a dish's nutritional value to the exclusion of its taste and appearance results in excessive food waste. Even as a captive audience, consumers will throw out nutritious food and go hungry if they find the meal unpalatable. Menu planners must maintain a high standard for flavor and guest appeal for every dish on the menu, especially when focusing on a dish's nutritional role on that menu.

With a menu in place that addresses the nutritional needs of the general population, the menu planner should next take into consideration several dietary restrictions common

GOOD MORNINGS

NOURISH YOUR LYFE

BREAKFAST
Monday–Friday
until 11am

BRUNCH
Saturday & Sunday
until 2pm

SPINACH & AVOCADO FRITTATA $7.5
scallions, Cheddar, served with
chipotle potato hash, salsa fresca
405 Calories | 840 mg Sodium

CLASSIC BREAKFAST $7
LYFE eggs, turkey sausage,
chipotle potato hash
456 Calories | 800 mg Sodium

BREAKFAST BURRITO $6.5
whole wheat tortilla, LYFE eggs,
arugula, avocado, cherry tomatoes,
chipotle aioli, Cheddar, salsa fresca
576 Calories | 654 mg Sodium

MORNING VEGGIE WRAP $6.5
whole wheat tortilla stuffed with
tofu scramble, roasted mushrooms,
Daiya™ Cheddar, arugula, avocado,
cherry tomatoes, salsa fresca
590 Calories | 605 mg Sodium

EGG SANDWICH $5
LYFE eggs, tomatoes, arugula,
Cheddar on multi-grain griddle toast,
gluten-free upon request
447 Calories | 734 mg Sodium

add turkey sausage $1.5
90 Calories | 290 mg Sodium

NEW! **BLUEBERRY BUTTERMILK PANCAKES** $6
made from scratch with quinoa,
topped with Greek yogurt, lemon zest,
with pure maple syrup
541 Calories | 605 mg Sodium

GREEK YOGURT BOWL $4
blueberries, pomegranate, chia seeds,
toasted almonds
215 Calories | 47 mg Sodium

CARROT-ZUCCHINI WALNUT MUFFIN $3
190 Calories | 138 mg Sodium

TURKEY SAUSAGE PATTIES $3
180 Calories | 580 mg Sodium

MULTI-GRAIN GRIDDLE TOAST $1.5
219 Calories | 341 mg Sodium

CHIPOTLE POTATO HASH $3
213 Calories | 189 mg Sodium

lyfekitchen.com

167 HAMILTON AVE, PALO ALTO, CA 94301 • (650) 325-5933
All items available to go. Ask about our catering options.

Gluten-Free   Vegan   Contains Nuts

CHEF-INSPIRED MENU

EAT DRINK LYFE

FEED. YOUR. SELF.

FIGURE 2.3

This menu lists calorie and sodium content for each dish and uses symbols to highlight those dishes that accommodate various dietary and allergy concerns.

Reprinted with the permission of LYFE Kitchen of California, LLC.

among Americans. While each of these diets represents a small percentage of the population, combined they can become a significant portion of any foodservice business. By planning for them, a menu planner expands the potential market for the company. Not every dish need accommodate every diet—to do so would inevitably turn off that percentage of the population without dietary restrictions—but a guest following one of these diets ought to be able to find at least one menu item in each category that meets her needs. Often, a single dish can accommodate the needs of several different diets. Following are seven of the most common specialized diets among Americans.

Vegetarian and Vegan Diets

Vegetarians come in several different forms. Pesco-vegetarians shun meat and poultry but eat seafood. Lacto-ovo vegetarians eat dairy and eggs, but no animal flesh. Vegans do not eat (or use) anything that comes from an animal—no milk, eggs, or even honey. The rationale behind such diets varies greatly from person to person. People may choose

Learning Objective 7
List several common dietary restrictions and create a menu item that accommodates individuals with those restrictions.

BEVERAGES
SERVED ALL DAY

LYFE WATERS

⊱ CUCUMBER MINT $2.5
fresh cucumber juice, mint, lime, agave
62 Calories | 19 mg Sodium

HIBISCUS BEET $3
hibiscus tea infused with beet, apple, lemon, ginger
121 Calories | 49 mg Sodium

ORANGE GINGER CHIA $3
fresh-squeezed orange juice, filtered water, lime, ginger, mint, chia seeds
124 Calories | 20 mg Sodium

GINGER MINT CHIA $1.5
filtered water infused with ginger, lime, mint, chia seeds
56 Calories | 22 mg Sodium

SMOOTHIES

⊱ KALE BANANA $5
raw kale, fresh ginger, banana, cucumber, apple juice, lemon juice
209 Calories | 28 mg Sodium

BANANA DATE $5
sweetened naturally with dates
264 Calories | 118 mg Sodium

LOCAL CRAFT BEER & WINE ON TAP

FRESH-SQUEEZED

GINGER POMEGRANATE LEMONADE $3
149 Calories | 26 mg Sodium

CLASSIC LEMONADE $3
125 Calories | 21 mg Sodium

ORANGE JUICE $4
126 Calories | 3 mg Sodium

COFFEE & TEA

almond or soy milk upon request

ORGANIC COFFEE $2
our blend of artisan, shade-grown coffee, regular or decaffeinated
0 Calories | 10 mg Sodium

CAFÉ AMERICANO $3
0 Calories | 7 mg Sodium

CAFÉ LATTE $3
158 Calories | 158 mg Sodium

CAPPUCCINO $3
158 Calories | 158 mg Sodium

CAFÉ MOCHA $3
201 Calories | 147 mg Sodium

HOT TEA $2
ask about our selection
0 Calories | 10 mg Sodium

UNSWEETENED ICED TEA $2.5
black or hibiscus
0 Calories | 10 mg Sodium

LITTLE LYFERS

Isn't it about time for a grown-up approach to children's food?

Great food for growing bodies starts with great ingredients — local fruits and vegetables, fresh herbs and spices, vitamin-rich whole grains, and responsibly-raised meats.

LITTLE LYFERS JUICES

FRESH-SQUEEZED ORANGE JUICE $2.5
126 Calories | 3 mg Sodium

APPLE JUICE $2
128 Calories | 11 mg Sodium

BREAKFAST & BRUNCH

LITTLE LYFERS PANCAKES $4
served Monday-Friday until 11am, Saturday & Sunday until 2pm
399 Calories | 416 mg Sodium

CARROT-ZUCCHINI WALNUT MUFFIN $3
190 Calories | 138 mg Sodium

LUNCH & DINNER

CHEESY FLATBREAD $5
max 381 Calories | max 739 mg Sodium

LITTLE LYFERS UNFRIED CHICKEN STRIPS $5
max 391 Calories | max 786 mg Sodium

LITTLE LYFERS FISH TACO $6
max 358 Calories | max 710 mg Sodium

CRISPY GARDEIN™ TENDERS $5
max 360 Calories | max 790 mg Sodium

PASTA WITH TOMATO SAUCE $4.5
max 358 Calories | max 563 mg Sodium

Lunch and dinner entrées are served with a choice of baked sweet potato fries or fresh fruit, *some items may be prepared gluten-free or vegan upon request*

LYFE KITCHEN
FEED. YOUR. SELF.

lyfekitchen.com

12.15.2015 NP T2

FIGURE 2.3 *(Continued)*

vegetarianism for religious, ethical, financial, health, or environmental reasons. Some individuals may not be vegetarian all the time but may look for vegetarian options for a significant portion of their weekly meals. (Consider the Meatless Monday movement that has gained popularity in some parts of the country among people who are not otherwise vegetarian.)

Most foodservice establishments—with the possible exception of restaurants with a theme that focuses on animal products, such as a steakhouse, fried chicken joint, or seafood restaurant—should include one or more vegetarian options for each menu category. A vegetarian dish should be more than the operation's standard meat-centered dish with

PLATES & BOWLS

✳ ART'S UNFRIED CHICKEN $14
roasted brussels sprouts, butternut squash, dried cranberries, cashew cream sauce, Dijon vinaigrette, *gluten-free upon request*
Ⓝ 566 Calories | 758 mg Sodium

ROASTED SALMON, TOMATO & FENNEL $15
sustainably raised salmon served with pan-steamed fennel, red onion, broccoli, and our zesty tomato sauce
Ⓖ ⚠ 549 Calories | 795 mg Sodium

CHICKEN, MUSHROOM & SPINACH PENNE $12.5
whole grain pasta, scallions, lemon zest, Parmesan, cashew cream sauce
Ⓝ 570 Calories | 776 mg Sodium

✳ THAI RED CURRY BOWL
broccoli, eggplant, peppers, peas, wheatberries, thai basil in a coconut curry sauce
with garlic-lime tofu $12
Ⓥ Ⓝ 502 Calories | 662 mg Sodium
with grilled chicken $13
Ⓝ 465 Calories | 735 mg Sodium

ANCIENT GRAIN STIR-FRY $12
stir-fried vegetables and Gardein™ beefless tips served over quinoa, black rice and cilantro with sweet chile-ginger sauce
Ⓥ 581 Calories | 790 mg Sodium

DESSERTS & SWEETS

✳ CHOCOLATE BUDINO $4
pomegranate, chia seeds, toasted almonds
Ⓖ Ⓥ Ⓝ 206 Calories | 24 mg Sodium

BANANA COCONUT BUDINO $4
chia seeds, nut crunch, date caramel
Ⓖ Ⓥ Ⓝ 254 Calories | 26 mg Sodium

CHOCOLATE CHIP COOKIE $2
still warm, fresh out of the oven
156 Calories | 100 mg Sodium
three cookies $5

⚠ Thoroughly cooking foods of animal origin such as beef, eggs, fish, lamb, milk, poultry or shellfish reduces the risk of foodborne illness. Individuals with certain health conditions may be at higher risk if these foods are consumed raw or undercooked.

Gardein™ (Garden + Protein) is made from delicious plant-based foods slow cooked to have the authentic taste and texture of premium lean meat.

Prices subject to change. While LYFE Kitchen is proud to offer menu items with gluten-free ingredients, LYFE Kitchen is not a gluten-free environment. LYFE Kitchen is also not an allergen-free environment. Due to the handcrafted nature of our menu items, variations in vendor-supplied ingredients, and our use of shared cooking and preparation areas, we cannot assure you that our restaurant environment or any menu item will be completely free of gluten, nuts or any other allergens.

Ⓖ Gluten-Free   Ⓥ Vegan   Ⓝ Contains Nuts

the food policy that matters most is yours.
—mark bittman

SHAREABLES & FLATBREADS

NEW! GRILLED PEPPER QUESADILLA $7
with caramelized onions and mozzarella, served with fresh guacamole and salsa
507 Calories | 616 mg Sodium
add chicken $1
56 Calories | 73 mg Sodium

UNFRIED BUFFALO CHICKEN STRIPS $7
tossed in spicy buffalo sauce, served with buttermilk ranch, *vegan upon request*
412 Calories, 903 mg Sodium

SPICY VIETNAMESE LETTUCE WRAPS $7
stir-fried Gardein™ beefless tips, wheatberries, scallions, thai basil, chile-ginger sauce
Ⓥ 401 Calories | 636 mg Sodium

MARGHERITA FLATBREAD $8.5
fresh mozzarella, cherry tomatoes, basil, pomodoro sauce
Ⓥ 511 Calories | 606 mg Sodium

BBQ CHICKEN FLATBREAD $9
grilled chicken, sweet corn, caramelized onion, cilantro, smoky BBQ sauce, mozzarella cheese
Ⓥ 474 Calories | 601 mg Sodium

ROASTED MUSHROOM & GOAT CHEESE FLATBREAD $9
roasted criminis, caramelized onions, goat and mozzarella cheeses, balsamic, chives
Ⓥ 596 Calories | 564 mg Sodium

EDAMAME HUMMUS PLATE $7
fresh crunchy vegetables and grilled multi-grain bread
Ⓥ 535 Calories | 669 mg Sodium

Ⓖ Gluten-Free   Ⓥ Vegan   Ⓝ Contains Nuts

FIGURE 2.3   *(Continued)*

the meat removed. Vegetarians are not usually looking for a side of rice and steamed green beans to make a meal. Instead, a proper vegetarian meal should take into consideration the specific nutritional challenges faced by people who do not eat animal products.

The biggest nutritional challenge for vegetarians is protein. Lacto-ovo vegetarian meals should include dairy and/or eggs to provide some protein as well as vitamin B_{12}. However, vegans must obtain their protein in other ways. Most plant protein sources are incomplete proteins, meaning they do not contain all of the nine essential amino acids humans must consume in their diets. To provide a complete protein in one meal, the menu planner should

food is an important part
of a balanced diet.

—fran lebowitz

QUINOA CRUNCH BOWL $10

quinoa tabbouleh, fresh crunchy vegetables, avocado, arugula, edamame hummus, chipotle vinaigrette, fireman's hot sauce
541 Calories | 498 mg Sodium

SALADS

all salads can be made gluten-free or vegan upon request

KALE CAESAR **$8**
crunchy Romaine, baby kale, cherry tomatoes, cucumbers, broccoli, Parmesan, breadcrumbs, Caesar dressing
362 Calories | 363 mg Sodium

FARMER'S MARKET **$9**
arugula, blackberries, house-pickled red onions, spiced pecans, goat cheese, balsamic vinaigrette
453 Calories | 281 mg Sodium

GRILLED VEGGIE **$9**
Romaine, baby spinach, roasted peppers, eggplant, onions, tomatoes, snap peas, fresh mozzarella, croutons, garlic-herb vinaigrette
490 Calories | 417 mg Sodium

PROTEIN ADD-ONS

GRILLED CHICKEN BREAST **$2**
167 Calories | 219 mg Sodium

GARLIC-LIME TOFU **$2**
163 Calories | 95 mg Sodium

GRILLED MAHI **$5**
131 Calories | 402 mg Sodium

GRILLED SALMON **$6**
368 Calories | 358 mg Sodium

SOUPS

SWEET CORN CHOWDER **$5**
made with cashew cream
164 Calories | 953 mg Sodium

THE - PERFECT - PAIR

ADD ANY SOUP WITH YOUR SALAD FOR $3

SANDWICHES

GRILLED CHICKEN & AVOCADO **$9**
roasted tomatoes, Romaine, red onion, tarragon aioli on ciabatta, *gluten-free upon request*
598 Calories | 627 mg Sodium

NEW! BLACKENED MAHI **$9.5**
crunchy Romaine, tomato, onion, avocado, lemon-caper mayo on ciabatta, *gluten-free upon request*
520 Calories | 683 mg Sodium

ITALIAN FLATBREAD **$7.5**
grilled vegetables, goat cheese, mozzarella, basil in a stuffed pizza sandwich, served with pomodoro dipping sauce
561 calories | 792 mg sodium
add chicken **$1**
56 calories | 73 mg sodium

BURGERS

FARMHOUSE **$9**
100% grass-fed beef, crunchy Romaine, tomato, red onion, farmhouse pickle, Dijonnaise on ciabatta, *gluten-free upon request*
590 Calories | 814 mg Sodium
add Cheddar 25¢
45 Calories | 68 mg Sodium
add burger patty **$2**
216 Calories | 487 mg Sodium

LYFE VEGGIE **$8**
crunchy Romaine, tomato, red onion, avocado, smoky pepper aioli on ciabatta, *gluten-free upon request*
570 Calories | 578 Sodium
add Daiya™ Cheddar 25¢
45 Calories | 125 mg Sodium

ADD ANY SIDE FOR $2
burgers, wraps, sandwiches or tacos

MAHI FISH TACOS $11

chayote slaw, avocado, cilantro, chipotle aioli, corn tortillas, salsa fresca, *gluten-free and vegan upon request*
437 Calories | 695 mg Sodium

add a third taco $3
215 Calories | 334 mg Sodium

WRAPS

QUINOA CRUNCH **$9**
quinoa tabbouleh, crunchy vegetables, avocado, edamame hummus, fireman's hot sauce on the side
591 Calories | 486 mg Sodium

BUFFALO CHICKEN **$9.5**
avocado, black beans, corn, chayote, Romaine, and Greek yogurt ranch
568 calories | 692 mg sodium

SIDES

SWEET POTATO FRIES **$3**
baked, served with house ketchup
327 Calories | 733 mg Sodium

GARLIC PARMESAN SWEET POTATO FRIES **$3.5**
with chipotle aioli, *vegan upon request*
528 Calories | 883 mg Sodium

NEW! ITALIAN QUINOA SALAD **$3.5**
roasted tomatoes, cucumber, garlic-herb vinaigrette
156 Calories | 246 mg Sodium

NEW! KALE & CRANBERRY SALAD **$3.5**
house-pickled red onion, balsamic vinaigrette
216 Calories | 129 mg Sodium

BROCCOLI & SNAP PEAS **$3.5**
tossed with a hint of garlic
75 Calories | 56 mg Sodium

ROASTED BRUSSELS & SQUASH **$4**
with dried cranberries, Dijon vinaigrette
280 Calories | 243 mg Sodium

Gluten-Free   Vegan   Contains Nuts

FIGURE 2.3   *(Continued)*

combine plant proteins from different sources. The main sources of protein from the plant kingdom are grains, nuts, and legumes. Fortunately, each of these categories is lacking in a different essential amino acid, so combining two of the three categories results in a complete protein. Examples of classic complete protein combinations include pita and hummus, beans and rice, almond croissants, and falafel sandwiches. Quinoa and soybeans are particularly high in protein, so soy products are commonly found in vegetarian dishes. A properly composed vegetarian dish factors these protein needs heavily into the plate's design. Unlike a meat-heavy dish, which often separates the meat, starch, and vegetables on the plate, a vegetarian dish is perfectly acceptable as a single integrated set of ingredients on the plate

---

Example 2.1: Appropriate versus Inappropriate Vegan Menu Items

Appropriate Vegan Menu—The menu provides complete proteins without using animal products.	**Inappropriate Vegan Menu**—The first two courses do not constitute a complete protein and the dessert contains animal products.
Mixed Green Salad with Toasted Almonds, Soy Nuts, Dried Cranberries, and Citrus Vinaigrette	Mixed Greens with Cucumbers, Tomato, Bell Pepper, Red Onion, and Balsamic Vinaigrette
Quinoa and Black Bean Chili with Tomatoes, Squash, and Vegetable Broth, served with an Eggless Cornbread	Sautéed Green Beans and Mashed Potatoes
Chocolate Sorbet with Peanut Brittle Crunch	Honey-Corn Bavarian made with Honey, Citrus Juice, Gelatin, and Corn Foam

---

en masse, such as a bowl of pasta, a stir-fry, or a pizza. When the menu planner includes dairy or eggs in the dish, options for a preparation without those ingredients should be noted on the menu for vegans. If the removal of eggs or dairy from a vegetarian dish would result in an incomplete protein, the menu planner should consider a substitution with a nut, grain, or legume as an alternative. Providing bean or nut spreads with bread at the table may eliminate the need to provide complete proteins with each dish. Finally, as the purpose of creating vegetarian and vegan dishes is to accommodate and attract guests with those dietary needs, any dishes that are not obviously vegan should be noted as such on the menu.

Low-Fat Diets

Whether for the purpose of losing weight, recovering from heart disease, or just general health, some Americans seek low-fat options whenever and wherever they eat. Foodservice establishments that can accommodate this dietary request are likely to attract that business. As lower-fat dishes do not fill up the consumer on a single entrée, they also help to drive sales of multicourse meals.

Low-fat should not translate to no flavor. Low-fat dishes generally rely on certain cooking techniques—poaching, steaming, sautéing, grilling, broiling, and roasting. Fried components do not belong on a low-fat dish. If a chef uses processed foods in her recipes, she should confirm that they, too, are low in fat. When meats are used, lean cuts should be employed to avoid adding hidden fat to a dish. Spices, herbs, and strongly flavored ingredients (garlic, chiles, etc.) help to deliver flavor without fat. For dishes in which fat delivers unctuousness, starch thickeners may replicate the thicker viscosity.

Menu planners may wish to highlight their low-fat dishes on a menu. Common symbols include hearts or checkmarks to denote a low-fat selection. The symbols are typically defined at the bottom of the menu. To meet the legal definition of low-fat, a dish must include no more than 3 grams of fat per 100 grams of food, and no more than 30% of the calories may come from fat.[6] Some restaurants prefer to leave nutrient claims off the menu. In such establishments, menu descriptions should make a low-fat dish obvious by stressing low-fat cooking techniques and by highlighting flavors that do not stem from fatty ingredients.

Example 2.2: *Sake-Poached Flounder with Ponzu Sauce, Steamed Bok Choy, and Sesame Sticky Rice* is a menu description that immediately alerts the customer that this dish is low-fat. "Poached" and "steamed" highlight low-fat cooking techniques while ingredients such as sake and ponzu sauce illustrate a deliberate effort to add flavor without fat. If written as *Flounder with Ponzu Sauce, Bok Choy, and Rice*, the menu description would be ineffective at communicating the dish's low-fat qualities.

Low-Sodium Diets

Consumers battling hypertension may look for low-sodium menu choices. While salt is the most prevalent source of sodium in a restaurant, sodium is also hidden in most processed foods, cured meats and fish, and certain other ingredients, such as soy sauce. Since a person's sensitivity to salt changes as she gets used to a certain consumption level, chefs who normally use salt heavily in their cooking may consider low-sodium dishes bland.

Conversely, diners who shun salt would find a "properly seasoned" dish salty. Chefs should keep in mind that it is the diner's taste preference, not the chef's, that matters most.

Chefs can create flavorful, low-sodium dishes by relying on fresh ingredients and by incorporating copious quantities of spices, herbs, and other highly flavorful ingredients. Cooks should not add salt to recipes until an order is placed, so a cook could easily prepare a dish without added salt. Chiles, garlic, ginger, and onions provide a salt-free flavor boost. Other ingredients, such as aged cheese, anchovies, and sundried tomatoes, contain some salt, but they also come with high levels of glutamates, which are strong flavor enhancers. Using glutamate-rich ingredients may reduce the need to add straight salt to enhance a dish's flavor. Flavor extracts also help to boost flavor without salt.

Menu planners with a market concerned about sodium should denote the low-sodium options on their menus with a symbol. Unlike low-fat dishes, low-sodium dishes are not usually easy to identify simply by reading a menu description. By law, low-sodium dishes must contain 140 milligrams or less of sodium per 100 grams of food.[7] One approach to addressing guests seeking low-sodium dishes may be to note on the menu that any dish can be made without added salt upon customer request. Chefs may prefer, instead, to create certain dishes with enough alternate flavor sources that added salt is not necessary; servers can recommend those dishes to customers requesting low-sodium options. Either way, having a plan to accommodate low-salt dieters is imperative for operations with captive audiences and for restaurants and hotels seeking to attract this segment of the market.

Example 2.3: *Sliced Flat-Iron Steak with Chimichurri, Chile-Garlic Roasted Corn, and Grilled Asparagus with Lemon Zest* is a dish that can easily be made low-sodium. The herb-garlic-vinegar chimichurri provides strong flavors that come through well even without salt. The chile and lemon zest do the same for the side dishes. By slicing the steak, the chef ensures that the sauce covers a greater surface area of the meat for a more effective flavor hit with each bite.

Low-Carbohydrate Diets

While not recommended by most mainstream nutritionists, the low-carbohydrate diet is popular among some Americans. The diet severely restricts the quantity of carbohydrates consumed per day, which leaves the body to subsist on protein and fat—the reason that most nutritionists do not recommend the diet. A few restaurants have attempted to capitalize on this trend by promoting their already unhealthy foods as appropriate for a low-carbohydrate diet. The merits of the diet may be debatable, but if a restaurant intends to capture this market segment, it ought to at least promote low-carbohydrate dishes honestly and accurately.

Low-carbohydrate dishes are based primarily in meat, poultry, and seafood, but they also consist of a good number of low-starch vegetables as a source of fiber. While mashed potato or bread might not be appropriate for a low-carbohydrate meal, mashed cauliflower or braised greens would be. Sugar is pure carbohydrate, so it has no place in a low-carbohydrate meal. Thus, a rack of ribs with a sugarless spice rub is low-carbohydrate; ribs with a sugary sauce are not. Calorie counts for this diet should not be any greater than they are with other diets, but fats and proteins make up the majority of the macronutrients consumed. With animal protein typically representing the majority of the plate, low-carbohydrate dishes can be expensive to deliver.

The main reason to create low-carbohydrate dishes in a restaurant is to attract a certain segment of the market. Low-carbohydrate dishes should be promoted as such. Some restaurants denote these dishes explicitly in the menu descriptions or with symbols; however, most diners can identify a low-carbohydrate dish if the description references various vegetables but no starches. Similarly, traditional dishes that have had the starch replaced, such as a burger wrapped in lettuce instead of a bun, are understood as low-carbohydrate items by most restaurant patrons.

Example 2.4: *12-ounce Rib-Eye Steak with Herb Butter, Sautéed Spinach, and Celeriac Puree* communicates "low-carb" to the customer by pairing an oversized portion of meat with a butter sauce and two vegetables rather than with a sweet sauce or starch. The large portion of meat makes up for the calories lost by eliminating the starch.

Diabetes Diets

People with diabetes either do not produce sufficient insulin to properly process blood sugar or they have developed a resistance to insulin. Either way, diabetics end up with high levels of glucose (a sugar) in their blood, which can cause a range of health problems. While no one knows what spurs the body's immune system to attack insulin-producing cells in the pancreas, thus causing type I diabetes, type II diabetes develops over time from lifestyle choices. Type II diabetes can be triggered by overweight, insufficient exercise, and/ or poor diet. While type II diabetes may require insulin injections, it is possible for most people to manage it through their diet. Thus, accommodating diabetics in a foodservice operation is critical to those guests' management of their illness.

The diet for diabetics is similar to the diet for good overall health—lots of vegetables and whole grains, lean meats, moderate portions. As type II diabetes often stems from overweight or obesity, diabetics typically need portions with calorie counts that allow them to control their weight. Additionally, spikes in blood sugar are worse for diabetics than are meals that provide a slow, steady supply of glucose across several hours. Unless the foodservice business plans on providing small snacks throughout the day, the best way to prevent blood sugar spikes is through fiber intake and carbohydrate counting. Fiber, present in fruits, vegetables, and whole grains but not in refined sugars, slows the rate at which blood sugar increases. A menu item planned for a diabetic should include these sources of fiber while limiting refined sugars or low-fiber carbohydrates. Diabetes-friendly meals should provide only moderate quantities of carbohydrates and calories to prevent spikes in blood sugar; some diabetics may manage that blood sugar spike by requesting an extra portion of low-starch vegetables to replace a starch on the dish. Appropriate meals are also low in fats, refined sugars, and calories to prevent weight gain, which contributes to diabetes.

Because the diet for people with diabetes is similar to that for overall good health, menus do not typically identify diabetes-friendly meals except in captive market environments. That said, a menu planner may consider partnering with a local diabetes association to identify or develop a menu item or two that are highly recommended for diabetics. Such a menu choice might be highlighted or identified as having the recommendation of the local association, assuming the association is willing to give its approval.

Example 2.5: *Grilled Chicken Breast with Sautéed Mushroom and Onion Sauce, Barley-Brown Rice Pilaf, and Wilted Spinach* is potentially a diabetes-friendly dish. With the skin removed, the chicken becomes low-fat. The mushroom and onion sauce must be made without added sugar (think reduced chicken stock rather than Madeira, which contains sugar). The pilaf and spinach can be made low-fat as well, and both contain significant amounts of fiber to slow sugar increases in the bloodstream. Assuming the portion sizes are moderate, this dish would be appropriate for a person with diabetes.

Gluten-Free Diets

A small but significant portion of the population suffers from celiac disease or gluten intolerance. For celiac sufferers, the gluten component proteins found in wheat, rye, barley, and to some degree oats impact the intestines and damage the intestinal lining. In short, individuals with gluten intolerance cannot consume any of these ingredients or products made from these ingredients.

While creating a celiac-friendly menu item may seem as simple as avoiding wheat, rye, barley, and oats, there are many processed foods that contain these ingredients. Soy sauce, for example, often contains wheat. Certain alcohols may be made from rye, wheat, or barley. It is critical that chefs using prefabricated products read their labels to ensure that none of the ingredients are wheat, rye, or barley derivatives. Cooks must also take care not to cross-contaminate a celiac-friendly preparation by using dirty utensils or equipment that contains traces of the problematic grains. Even in small amounts they can be harmful to celiac sufferers. Fortunately, other than avoiding the forbidden wheat, rye, barley, and oats, gluten-free dishes may contain anything else. In order to provide proper nutrition, they should include an appropriate balance of protein, fat, and carbohydrate, but the carbohydrates should come from potatoes, rice, corn, or other grains beyond the forbidden four. As many desserts are made from wheat flour, this final course in a meal is often the most challenging, but a gluten-free dessert is likely to be popular among the non–gluten intolerant as well.

Restaurants that take the time to create a gluten-free menu item ought to promote that effort to attract customers. A small notation or icon on the menu to identify gluten-free dishes is all that is required. In upscale restaurants, chefs may be asked to modify a dish to make it gluten-free. While customer service is paramount in the hospitality and foodservice industry, a chef should not agree to modify a dish unless she can guarantee that it will be gluten-free. In other words, celiac disease is a serious condition, and attempting to pass off as gluten-free a dish containing wheat, rye, barley, or oats is both dangerous and unethical.

Example 2.6: Appropriate versus Inappropriate Menus for People with Gluten Intolerance

Appropriate—Avoids wheat, rye, barley, and oats	**Inappropriate**—Croutons, Soy Sauce, and Pie Crust all contain wheat
Mixed Greens Salad with Cucumbers, Tomatoes, Scallions, and a Red Wine Vinaigrette	Classic Caesar Salad
Grilled Tuna with a Ketchup-Cider Vinegar BBQ Sauce, Steamed Rice, and Roasted Carrots	Soy-Glazed Tuna Steak with Steamed Rice and Carrots
Flourless Chocolate Torte with Raspberries	Chocolate Pie with Raspberry Sauce

---

Lactose-Free Diets

Lactose is a sugar found naturally in milk. The body normally digests it with the enzyme lactase, but for people with a lactase deficiency, the lactose is not digested properly and causes gastrointestinal distress. The best way to manage this condition is either through lactase pills or drops or through dietary changes. From the menu planner's perspective, the restaurant cannot rely on a diner to bring her lactase pills, so accommodating menu options are required to attract lactose-intolerant guests. This translates to some menu options that do not include dairy.

The range of sensitivity to lactose varies from person to person. While some lactose-intolerant people can eat low-lactose dairy products like yogurt or hard cheese, others cannot. Thus, it is best to have at least a few menu items that do not contain dairy at all. At a minimum, the chef should be able to modify a dish on the fly to remove any dairy components. For the average menu, this means that not every salad should come with cheese on it, and not every entrée should have a cream or butter sauce. Desserts may be more challenging, as they often contain dairy, but guests will be grateful to have just one nondairy choice for dessert. The biggest obstacle to accommodating lactose-intolerant guests is hidden dairy in processed foods. Ingredient lists may not include a familiar dairy term; lactose, whey, and curds are all dairy byproducts, as are dried milk and milk solids. The chef should know which of her processed ingredients contain dairy and notify any guest with a declared lactose-intolerance issue.

Example 2.7: Dairy-Based Desserts and Lactose-Free Versions

Includes Lactose	**Adjusted to Lactose-Free**
Apple Pie with a Butter Crust	Use a shortening crust and do not add butter to the apple filling
Milk Chocolate Soufflé	Use dark chocolate and margarine or oil as the base before adding the whipped egg white
Ice Cream Sundae	Substitute a fruit sorbet garnished with nuts and fresh fruit rather than whipped cream

Because dairy sources are typically obvious in menu descriptions, most restaurants do not identify a dish specifically as lactose-free. However, menu planners should take care to state any dairy products used in a dish, so a customer can easily navigate around any lactose-containing ingredients.

In a hospital, prison, or other environment in which the consumers are captive, it is an ethical necessity for a menu planner or chef to accommodate every dietary restriction and allergy that threatens the health of the diner. However, for most foodservice operations, the decision to accommodate the most popular dietary restrictions is simply smart business. The more diners that an establishment can service, the greater the potential revenue for the company. In restaurants, this translates to return business. For corporate cafeterias, it could mean the difference between renewing versus losing the contract for the cafeteria. Guests with special dietary needs are far more likely to become regular patrons when they have their needs accommodated. And the general population can dine out more often when they can find food that does not impact their health negatively.

Summary

Factoring nutrition into the menu-planning process maintains the health of the consumers in a captive market and attracts nutrition-minded individuals with a choice of dining options. All food and drink contain one or more of the major categories of nutrients: carbohydrates, lipids, proteins, water, vitamins, and minerals. Each category promotes good health in a different way. Calories provide energy, but their intake should be managed so that excess energy is not consumed and stored as body fat. Fiber is not digested, but it does play a role in maintaining health. A proper diet should be balanced, varied, adequate, and moderate. In the United States, overconsumption is as big a problem as inadequate nutrition intake. Allergies impact a person's diet, as someone with an allergy cannot consume certain foods. Menu planners should ensure that someone with one of the more common allergies can find something to eat in their foodservice establishments. When creating or modifying a menu, the menu planner should include some items that adhere to the recommendations of the *Dietary Guidelines for Americans 2015–2020*. These recommendations include focusing on fruits, vegetables, and whole grains, choosing lean meats and dairy, and minimizing refined sugars, fats, and sodium. Keeping in mind that all menu items must be delicious and appealing to customers, menu planners should also consider some menu options for those market segments that follow certain popular diets, such as vegetarian, vegan, low-fat, low-sodium, low-carbohydrate, diabetic, gluten-free and lactose-free diets. By accommodating a wide range of diets as well as a diet for general good health, a foodservice business can attract a wider audience and, for a captive market, better serve its clientele.

Comprehension Questions

1. List one reason why nutrition should be considered in the menu-planning process.

2. What is a captive market, and why is nutrition an important consideration for a captive market?

3. How many calories per gram are provided by carbohydrates, lipids, proteins, and alcohol?

4. What is the difference between HDL and LDL? How does consumption of each type of fat impact the levels of HDL and LDL?

5. What is a complete protein, and how does one eat complete protein from only plant products?

6. Name three vitamins and minerals that are concerns for modern American diets.

7. What does fiber do, and what foods are significant sources of fiber?

8. List the common categories of food allergies.

9. Write a common menu phrasing for a warning about eating undercooked, potentially hazardous food.

10. List three guidelines for creating a healthy menu option for the general public.

11. Create a three-course menu (one option for each course) that qualifies as healthy and nutritious for the general public.

12. Select one of the specialized diets common among Americans. Describe the principles of that diet and create a three-course menu that meets the needs of those dieters.

Discussion Questions

1. Think of a restaurant you have visited that markets its healthy menu options. How were the menu items identified? What type of diet was addressed in those options?

2. When you go out to eat, how big a factor is a dish's nutritional value in your decision making? Can you think of anyone you know for whom nutrition or diet plays a bigger role in their menu selection?

3. Some restaurateurs have argued that the obesity crisis in America is not due to restaurant food but rather to Americans' lack of physical activity. Why do you think restaurateurs might make this argument? Is there any problem that stems from the fact that restaurateurs are making this case?

4. What nutrition or diet issues have you heard in the news in the past three months? How could a menu planner address this issue? Should a menu planner or restaurant bother addressing this issue? Why?

5. Of the several specialized diets described in the chapter, which is the most common among your friends and family? How easily are those people able to find food that meets their dietary needs?

Case Study

This chapter provides two examples of menus that emphasize nutrition. One is a cycle menu for an elementary school, and the other is a restaurant menu. Analyze each from the perspective of a potential customer. What dietary needs does each menu address? How does the communication of dietary information change for the market (children versus adults)? Do the menu items appear both appealing and nutritious for the intended market? Consider visiting these companies' websites (www.lyfekitchen.com and www.revolutionfoods.com) to learn more about their approach to food and nutrition. Select another menu included in a different chapter in this text and consider its approach to nutrition and dietary concerns.

Capstone Project

Step 2: Building on your business concept, write one to two paragraphs on how you will address nutrition and dietary concerns in your establishment. The written description must specify which common dietary restrictions, if any, will be accommodated.

References

1. http://health.gov/dietaryguidelines/2015/guidelines/chapter-3/social-ecological-model/#callout-align, accessed 23 March 2016.
2. Ibid.
3. http://health.gov/dietaryguidelines/2015/guidelines/appendix-7/, accessed 23 March 2016.
4. Ibid.
5. Ibid.
6. http://www.fda.gov/iceci/inspections/inspectionguides/ucm114045.htm, accessed 23 March 2016.
7. Ibid.

CHAPTER 3

Menu Styles and Headings I— Traditional Basics

INTRODUCTION

As a menu reflects the theme of its corresponding food-service establishment and target market, it is difficult to provide a universal set of guidelines for menu categories, called "headings." A casual Italian restaurant might have a menu heading just for pizzas, but other types of restaurants may not offer pizza at all on their menus. To address this challenge, the menu planner must balance the restaurant's marketing goals with customer familiarity with menu conventions. While Chapter 4 deals with a wide variety of modern menus and niche dining environments, this chapter focuses on the most traditional formats and headings for restaurant breakfast, lunch, and dinner menus.

In addition to determining menu headings, the menu planner creates specific menu items. However, a listing of random dishes, no matter how delicious, is not automatically appropriate for a menu. The menu planner must take into account how the menu items will impact kitchen work flow, food cost, customer dining speed, and guest satisfaction with the variety of choices. When done properly, a one-page menu allows every guest to find something he wants to eat; done poorly, a ten-page menu still leaves some customers feeling that there's nothing listed they would like to order. Understanding the basics of menu item selection and categorization helps a menu planner to create a menu that meets the needs of the consumers and the employees.

CHAPTER 3 LEARNING OBJECTIVES

As a result of successfully completing this chapter, readers will be able to:

1. Describe the menu pricing approaches of à la carte, semi à la carte, table d'hôte, and prix fixe menus.

2. Create a menu of food options that incorporates balance and variety while satisfying management concerns for work flow and product utilization.

3. List the most common menu headings found on traditional breakfast, lunch, and dinner menus, and describe the types of menu items typically listed under each menu heading.

CHAPTER 3 OUTLINE

Menu Pricing Styles

Principles of Menu Item Selection
    Ingredient and Flavor
    Cooking Technique
    Temperature and Texture
    Color, Shape, and Size
    Composition and Plate Presentation

Traditional Menu Headings
    Breakfast Menus

    Beverages
    Entrées
    Eggs and Omelets
    Griddle Items
    Cereals
    Other Breakfast Entrées
    À La Carte or Sides
    Lunch and Dinner Menus
    Appetizers
    Soups

Menu Pricing Styles

Learning Objective 1
Describe the menu pricing approaches of à la carte, semi à la carte, table d'hôte, and prix fixe menus.

While a single menu item's price does not normally impact the selection of menu headings, how the entire menu is priced does influence the category headings appropriate for that menu. Menus typically fall into one of four pricing types: à la carte, semi à la carte, table d'hôte, and prix fixe.

On an à la carte menu, each menu item is priced separately and nothing is bundled together. For example, at an à la carte steakhouse, a guest who orders a grilled porterhouse steak receives only the steak and nothing else. Any vegetable or starch accompaniments must be ordered separately for an additional cost. A modern sushi menu often works the same way but with accompaniments ordered and eaten as separate courses rather than as sides. Some foodservice operations provide à la carte pricing for some or all of their menu items in addition to another pricing approach; this is particularly common on breakfast menus and in fast food establishments. À la carte menus allow for the most extensive set of menu headings and should include at least one heading for any side dishes/accompaniments available (vegetables, starches, etc.).

A semi à la carte menu packages all of the components of the entrée into a single price but charges separately for other courses. For example, a semi à la carte menu might offer a main protein, vegetable, starch, and sauce for one price. If a guest wishes to purchase an appetizer or dessert, those items must be ordered separately and will cost extra. This is the type of menu most common in American restaurants. As with an à la carte menu, this style of menu pricing allows for a large number of menu headings, but "side dishes" may or may not be among them.

Both à la carte and semi à la carte operations may offer multiple price points for products that differ only in portion size. Fast food and fast casual restaurants with small, medium, and large size offerings commonly use this approach, but upscale restaurants employ this pricing structure on occasion, too. For example, a fancy restaurant might offer a full-size dessert for one price and the same dessert in miniature for a lower price to help promote dessert purchases among more customers. While pricing for portion size does not impact menu category headings, menu planners should know upfront if portion size pricing is part of the operation's brand.

Table d'hôte and prix fixe menus offer a complete set of courses for one set price. The appetizers, soups, salads, and desserts are included with the price of the entrée. The difference between the two styles is that a table d'hôte menu lists different prices next to each entrée, so the price that the customer pays depends on his choice of entrée. For a prix fixe menu, a single set price includes all of the courses no matter which entrée the guest selects. Currently in the United States, the term "table d'hôte" is less common than it is in other countries, but the pricing concept persists even if the terminology does not. Casual table d'hôte restaurants in the United States usually list under the entrée heading the extra courses (salad, soup, etc.) that come with the purchase of an entrée; dessert may not be included. (See Figure 8.2, The Blue Lion restaurant menu, in Chapter 8 for an example of a table d'hôte menu where the purchase of an entrée includes a salad course.) Some American upscale operations today use the term "prix fixe" but then list a "supplement" or additional charge next to certain entrée selections, essentially creating a price structure that straddles prix fixe and table d'hôte.

Employing table d'hôte and prix fixe menus greatly impacts the names and number of the menu headings. Customers who pay one price for a set of courses usually want to experience something from each heading; otherwise, they feel cheated. If the price includes four

RAW BAR

Fresh Oysters ..... 1/2 Dozen 21.00 ..... Dozen 37.00		Little Neck Clams on the half shell .... Dozen 20.00	
Lincoln's Oysters ...... (30) 85.00 ...... (50!) 120.00		Lump Crab Cocktail............................25.00	
Iced Shrimp Cocktail...........................24.00		Lobster Salad 22.00	
		Half Lobster with Avocado and Grapefruit	

Chilled Seafood Tray 54.00
Oysters, Clams, Lobster, Shrimp

APPETIZERS

Oysters Rockefeller 20.00	Butter Lettuce House Salad 11.50
House-Cured Salmon 16.00	with Balsamic or Dijon Vinaigrette
Maryland Lump Crab Cakes 20.00	Iceberg Lettuce Wedges, Blue Cheese Dressing......13.00
Thick-Cut Smoked Bacon 15.00	with Chopped Tomatoes and Bacon 4.00
Charred Shishito Peppers 11.00	Caesar Salad 13.50
	Twice Baked Vermont Blue Cheese Puff 15.00

DINNER SPECIALS

➤ **WATCHING YOUR SALT INTAKE?** ◀
PLEASE LET US KNOW AND WE'LL LEAVE THE MEAT SEASONING UP TO YOU (WITH EXCEPTIONS)

KEENS'S CLASSIC DRY-AGED STEAKS AND MEATS
ALL OUR STEAKS ARE USDA PRIME GRADE, HAND-PICKED, AND THEN DRY-AGED ON PREMISE

Our Legendary Mutton Chop 52.00	Prime T-Bone Steak 56.00
Prime Rib of Beef, King's Cut.................59.00	Prime Porterhouse for two.................101.00
Steamed Maine Lobster and Filet Mignon 64.00	Prime Porterhouse for three................144.00
Roasted Buttermilk Chicken 28.00	Chateaubriand Steak for two, with three sauces 120.00
Two Double Lamb Chops 50.00	Prime Filet Mignon ...... (8 oz.) 44.00 (12 oz.) 57.00
Prime New York Sirloin 51.00	Au Poivre, Bearnaise, Mushroom or Red Wine Sauce 2.00

FISH AND SHELL FISH

Authentic Dover Sole 54.00	Pan-Seared Arctic Char 35.00

Sauteed Jumbo Shrimp with Spinach 34.00

STEAMED WHOLE MAINE LOBSTERS
YOU MAY CHOOSE FROM OUR TANK

Two, three, four or five pounders, and occasionally six ....MARKET

SIDE DISHES

Roasted Market Vegetables 13.00	Sauteed Field Mushrooms.....................13.50
Carrots with Brown Butter 11.50	Keens's Creamed or Sauteed Spinach 12.00
Fine String Beans.............................12.00	Pan-Roasted Broccoli and Cauliflower 12.00

Steamed Asparagus 13.50

POTATOES

Hand-Cut French Fries.........................10.50	Boiled Baby Potatoes with Parsley and Butter 10.00
Mashed Yukon Gold............................10.50	Hash Browns....................................10.00

Baked Idaho 9.50

18% VOLUNTARY GRATUITY WILL BE ADDED FOR PARTIES OF 6 OR MORE.
THE AMOUNT OF GRATUITY MAY BE CHANGED AND IS AT YOUR DISCRETION.

OUR MAIN BAR SERVES UNTIL 11:30 PM MON—SAT, AND UNTIL 10:30 PM ON SUNDAY.
EXECUTIVE CHEF: BILL RODGERS

FIGURE 3.1

In an à la carte menu, the entrée accompaniments are purchased separately from the main item.

Courtesy of Keens Steakhouse.

 KEENS STEAKHOUSE OWNS THE LARGEST COLLECTION OF CHURCHWARDEN PIPES IN THE WORLD. THE TRADITION OF CHECKING ONE'S PIPE AT THE INN HAD ITS ORIGINS IN 17TH CENTURY MERRIE OLD ENGLAND WHERE TRAVELERS KEPT THEIR CLAY AT THEIR FAVORITE INN – THE THIN STEMMED PIPE BEING TOO FRAGILE TO BE CARRIED IN PURSE OR SADDLEBAG. PIPE SMOKING WAS KNOWN SINCE ELIZABETHAN TIMES TO BE BENEFICIAL FOR DISSIPATING "EVIL HOMOURSE OF THE BRAIN." KEENS'S PIPE TRADITION BEGAN SHORTLY AFTER THE TURN OF THE CENTURY. THE HARD CLAY CHURCHWARDEN PIPES WERE BROUGHT FROM THE NETHERLANDS AND AS MANY AS 50,000 WERE ORDERED EVERY THREE YEARS. A PIPE WARDEN REGISTERED AND STORED THE PIPES, WHILE PIPE BOYS RETURNED THE PIPES FROM STORAGE TO THE PATRONS. THE MEMBERSHIP ROSTER OF THE PIPE CLUB CONTAINED OVER NINETY THOUSAND NAMES, INCLUDING THOSE OF TEDDY ROOSEVELT, BABE RUTH, WILL ROGERS, BILLY ROSE, GRACE MOORE, ALBERT EINSTEIN, GEORGE M. COHAN, J.P. MORGAN, STANFORD WHITE, JOHN BARRYMORE, DAVID BELASCO, ADLAI STEVENSON, GENERAL DOUGLAS MACARTHUR AND "BUFFALO BILL" CODY.

PRIOR TO 1885, KEENS WAS A PART OF THE LAMBS CLUB, A FAMOUS THEATRE AND LITERARY GROUP FOUNDED IN LONDON. ITS MANAGER WAS ALBERT KEEN.

IN 1885 KEENS CHOPHOUSE OPENED INDEPENDENTLY UNDER THE OWNERSHIP OF MR. KEEN, BY THEN A NOTED FIGURE IN THE HERALD SQUARE THEATRE DISTRICT. KEENS SOON BECAME THE LIVELY AND ACCEPTED RENDEZVOUS OF THE FAMOUS. ACTORS IN FULL STAGE MAKE-UP HURRIED THROUGH THE REAR DOOR TO "FORTIFY" THEMSELVES BETWEEN ACTS AT THE NEIGHBORING GARRICK THEATRE. YOU COULD GLANCE INTO THE PIPE ROOM TO SEE THE JOVIAL CONGREGATIONS OF PRODUCERS, PLAYWRIGHTS, PUBLISHERS AND NEWSPAPER-MEN WHO FREQUENTED KEENS. TODAY, KEENS IS THE ONLY SURVIVOR OF THE HERALD SQUARE THEATRE DISTRICT. IN AN AGE WHICH TEARS DOWN SO MUCH OF THE PAST IT IS COMFORTING TO FIND ONE LANDMARK WHICH SURVIVES...

IN 1905 LILLIE LANGTRY, ACTRESS AND PARAMOUR OF KING EDWARD OF ENGLAND, TOOK KEENS TO COURT FOR HAVING DENIED HER ACCESS TO ITS GENTLEMEN-ONLY PREMISES. SHE WON HER CASE, SWEPT INTO KEENS IN HER FEATHERED BOA AND PROCEEDED TO ORDER ONE OF OUR FAMOUS MUTTON CHOPS.

THE ELEGANCE AND SOPHISTICATION OF MUCH OF OLD NEW YORK MAY BE GONE. AT KEENS, HOWEVER, YOU MAY STILL DINE IN ITS FORMER SPLENDOR.

FIGURE 3.1   *(Continued)*

courses, then the menu typically lists only four menu headings. If the guest gets to select a soup, a salad, an entrée, and a dessert, then the menu headings may be simply "Soups," "Salads," "Entrées," and "Desserts." Alternatively, the menu might list "First Course," "Second Course," etc. If the diner must choose between a salad, soup, or appetizer for the first course, then all of those menu items should be listed under a single heading, usually

Caviars and Oysters

American Paddlefish	ounce 100; half ounce 50
Siberian Sturgeon	ounce 160; half ounce 80
White Sturgeon	ounce 185
Galilee Osetra	ounce 225
Chilled LiV potato vodka	(add 11)

Spearpoint oyster,* Edgartown, MA
Pleasant Bay oyster,* Orleans, MA
FOUR DOLLARS EACH, WITH MIGNONETTE PERLAGE

Winter Prix Fixe

NINETY-EIGHT DOLLARS

First Course

Salad of Winter greens and beets with cranberry sorbet, green apple, Vermont Creamery Fresh Crottin goat cheese and dill

Warm Spearpoint oyster stew with spinach pillows, smoked bone marrow emulsion and lardons

Roasted Hudson Valley foie gras with ginger beignets, King Oyster mushrooms, rum apple and mulled cider (*add 10*)

Seared Georges Bank scallops with honey nut squash, chestnut, Brussels sprouts and orange-raspberry confit

Braised rabbit cannelloni with Périgord Winter truffles, coddled egg, black pepper jus and warm truffle whipped cream (*add 35*)

Roasted Squab breast with pork belly, carrots: raw and roasted, golden raisin mostarda and smoked hazelnut sable*

Main Course

Pineland Farms beef tenderloin "Cacio e Pepe" with West Coast mushrooms, braised beef tongue and Arborio-parmesan crisp*

Butter poached Maine lobster with braised Belgium endive, walnut "polenta", grapefruit reduction and tarragon (*add 20*)*

East Coast black bass with dashi "noodles", black miso paste, petite shiitake and celeriac tofu

Roasted Amish chicken with Périgord truffle, herb spaetzle, little winter vegetables, foraged mushrooms and shallot nage

Venison loin with braised oxtail ragout, wild rice and smoked pine nut risotto, glazed Medjool dates and quince jam

Honey glazed Long Island duck for two with a caramelized onion and fig tart with chestnuts and roasted parsnips, toasted seeds (*add 20*)*

Jamison Farm's rack of lamb with bulgur salad, cumin spiced carrot purée, labne, sumac glazed carrot and garlic-herb sausage

Winter Degustation   (OFFERED FOR THE ENTIRE TABLE ONLY)

ONE HUNDRED EIGHTEEN DOLLARS

VINTNER'S TASTING
Four wine pairings 77
Six wine pairings 99
Four seasonal juice pairings 51

2014 PLANETA, "COMETA", FIANO, SICILY
Butter poached Maine lobster and crab with bergamot orange juice, ricotta gnudi and fresh apple roll

2014 CECILE LEBRUN, "EN MIREBEAU", CABERNET D'ANJOU
New York State foie gras royale with feuille de brick crisps, poached kumquat, pears and yuzu

2014 DROIN, "VAILLONS", PREMIER CRU, CHABLIS
East Coast black bass with dashi "noodles", black miso paste, petite shiitake and parsnip tofu

2009 CHATEAU SIAURAC, LALANDE-DE-POMEROL
Jamison Farm's rack of lamb with bulgur salad, cumin spiced carrot purée, labne, sumac glazed carrot and garlic-herb sausage

2013 RENACER, "ENAMORE", MENDOZA
Grand Fromage

BODEGAS CESAR FLORIDO, MOSCATEL ESPECIAL, JEREZ
Meyer lemon tart with sable breton and frozen parsley parfait

Degustation of Vegetables

A seasonal tasting of vegetarian dishes with optional wine or juice pairings

Chef McClelland's Tasting Journey   (OFFERED FOR THE ENTIRE TABLE ONLY)

TWO HUNDRED EIGHT DOLLARS

ADD VINTNER'S PAIRINGS
ONE HUNDRED FIFTY-TWO DOLLARS

A progressive tasting highlighting of the best seasonal ingredients including organic meats, lobster, foie gras and caviar

Private rooms are available for your special celebrations.

Gift Cards are available

Before placing your order, please inform your server if a person in your party has a food allergy

*Menu items are cooked to order or may contain undercooked meat or fish, which may increase your risk of food-borne illness
2.7 scd

FIGURE 3.2

This menu includes both a prix fixe option, where guests choose among several selections for each course for a set price, and a tasting menu, where the choices for each course are preset. The prix fixe option contains supplements for a few of the menu items.

Reprinted with permission of Frank McClelland L'Espalier.

WE ARE PROUD TO WORK WITH THE FOLLOWING
FARMS AND PURVEYORS:

Browne Trading Company, Portland, ME

Consider Bardwell Farm, Pawlet, VT

George Howell Coffee, Acton, MA

High Lawn Farm, Lee, MA

Hudson Valley Foie Gras, Ferndale, NY

Island Creek Oysters, Duxbury, MA

Jasper Hill Farm, Greensboro, VT

London Buzz Apiary, Hampstead, NH

Lovejoy Brook Farm, Andover, VT

River Rise Farm, Marshfield, MA

Shy Brothers' Farm, Westport, MA

Sparrow Arc Farm, Unity, ME

Vermont Creamery, Websterville, VT

Veta La Palma Estate, Guadalquivir River, Spain

Westport Rivers Winery, Westport, MA

Woodcock Farms, Weston, VT

FIGURE 3.2   *(Continued)*

"First Course" or "Appetizers." Some menu planners may skip the naming convention entirely for a prix fixe or table d'hôte menu and simply place lines, asterisks, or some other visual separator between the courses. Because of the nature of the table d'hôte and prix fixe menus, it is also acceptable to list a course that includes only one option—"Intermezzo" with a grapefruit sorbet being the only selection, for example. À la carte and semi à la carte menus would not normally list a menu heading with only one option beneath it.

Which pricing approach to take depends on the business's theme and its target market. If a restaurant wants to appeal to special occasion diners who spend several hours at dinner, it may adopt a prix fixe or table d'hôte style. That way, once guests have decided to patronize the establishment and pay the hefty per person cost to eat there, they can focus solely on their food choices rather than on how much each additional course will add to the bill. À la carte and semi à la carte menus attract guests who prefer flexibility in how many courses they order. These types of menus appeal to customers who are more price sensitive, have less time available to linger over a meal, or who do not want a multicourse dining

November 1st, 2016

First

Wood Fired *Virginia Salts* Oysters, Chili Miso Butter, Pepper Mash, Lemon   *$16*

Bibb Lettuces, Shaved Radish, Juliette Tomato, Crispy Butter Peas, *Split Creek* Feta, Cucumber-Dill Dressing   *$12*

Southern Fried Chicken Skins, Pimento Cheese *"Ranch,"* Scallions, Espelette   *$11*

Anson Mills Farro Verde, *Charleston* Brie "Fondue," Fall Greens, Asian Pear, Brown Butter   *$13*

Fire Roasted Brussels Sprouts, Caraway Hollandaise, Pastrami Spiced Bread Crisp   *$11*

General Tso's Glazed Pig's Ear Lettuce Wraps, Sweet Vinegar Marinated Cucumber, Red Onion, Benne   *$12*

Broadbent Country Ham, Buttermilk Biscuits, Dijonnaise, Bread-N-Butter Pickles   *$15*

Slow Smoked *TN* Pork Ribs, Sweet Potato BBQ, Toasted Pecan, Fall Spiced Pork Rinds   *$15*

Supper

NC Chicken, Wood Fired Brussels Sprouts, Herbed Spätzle, *NC Mountain* Apple, Roasted Chicken Jus   *$29*

Cornmeal Dusted *NC* Catfish, Carolina Gold Rice Purloo, Charred Juliette Tomato, Crispy Lacinato Kale   *$29*

Confit Duck Leg, Black Garlic, Embered Cabbage, *Heirloom* Snap Beans, Country Ham XO, *VA* Peanuts   *$32 Atlantic*

Grouper, *Owl's Nest Plantation* Carrots and Sugar Snaps, Hakurei Turnips, Bok Choy, Mushroom Tea   *$32 Coffee*

Rubbed *TN* Strip Steak*, *Anson Mills* Farro, Beef Fat Roasted Sweet Potato, Embered Brassicas, Cocoa   *$34*

Carolina Heritage Pork*, Field Peas and Butterbeans, *Heirloom* Kale, Kielbasa, Smoked Tomato, Boiled Peanut   *$32*

Sides for the Table

($8/each)

A Skillet of Real Cornbread, *Benton's* Bacon Crumble

New Potatoes, Grilled Snap Beans, *Mepkin Abbey* Mushrooms, Smoky Tomatoes, Sweet Onion

SC Delcata Squash, *Anson Mills* Farro, *Heirloom* Kale, Apple Cider, Spiced Pecan

843.577.2500

*Temperatures upon request. May be served raw or undercooked.
Consuming raw or undercooked meats, poultry, seafood, shellfish, or eggs may increase your risk of foodborne illness

FIGURE 3.3

This menu illustrates the semi à la carte pricing approach where each dish includes all accompaniments, but the courses are priced separately.

Reprinted with permission of Neighborhood Dining Group.

experience for that meal. Semi à la carte menus provide a sense of value over à la carte menus because the components of the entrée are packaged and priced together. À la carte menus work well when the portions are substantial enough that customers are satisfied with the purchase of a single item and one (or fewer) accompaniment; the sharing of side dishes at a table is common in a fully à la carte restaurant. Businesses typically choose a table d'hôte approach over a prix fixe pricing strategy when the food cost for each entrée varies significantly, but both types of menus appeal primarily to guests looking for a leisurely, indulgent dining experience.

Principles of Menu Item Selection

Learning Objective 2
Create a menu of food options that incorporates balance and variety while satisfying management concerns for work flow and product utilization.

The material from the earlier chapters is the foundation upon which menu items and headings are built. The menu must make sense with the business concept, appeal to the target market, and take into account any nutritional or dietary concerns as well as the menu's anticipated pricing style. Keeping those variables in mind, the menu planner considers the names and number of menu headings to include on the menu. Greater numbers of headings can increase the number of courses that people order. For example, a menu that lumps all first courses (soups, salads, and appetizers) into a single heading suggests that only one course should be selected prior to the entrée while a menu that separates those courses may encourage some customers to order multiple courses before the entrée. The names of the headings help to attract customers as well who are looking for a certain experience. For example, a menu that lists a pizza category separately from an entrée category suggests to customers that whether they prefer a fancy meal or simply an evening of pizza, this establishment can accommodate them.

Larger numbers of menu headings are not always a good thing, however. Although some operations include only a couple of options per heading, most à la carte and semi à la carte businesses offer five or more menu items per heading. Some restaurants have over a dozen menu items per heading. With more to read, diners in a restaurant with an extensive menu require more time to peruse the menu before placing their orders. The extra reading time leads to a longer dining experience overall, thus lowering the rate at which tables are turned over to new customers. Extensive menus cost more than limited menus not only in fewer table turns but also in the number of dollars tied up in inventory, the amount of space needed for inventory, and the cost of printing menus with multiple pages. However, if the restaurant's dining room is large and the broader menu attracts a significantly larger market, these extra costs may be justified.

Two of the most important considerations for selecting menu items are balance and variety. The menu should offer a wide range of options (variety) without focusing too heavily on any one product, cooking technique, or other variable (balance). As with any rule, there are always exceptions. A business with a narrowly focused concept—a BBQ shack, a pizza place, a fried-chicken joint, a seafood restaurant, a sandwich shop, etc.—must be true to its brand. In these examples, variety and balance are incorporated within the limits of the business. For example, a burger establishment can approach variety and balance by offering a range of burger patties and toppings; that the menu is skewed heavily or exclusively to burgers illustrates fidelity to the business concept rather than lack of attention to balance and variety.

The variables for which variety and balance are most relevant are as follows:

Ingredient and Flavor

Generally speaking, a menu should not rely too heavily on any single ingredient unless such uniformity is key to the business's concept. Thus, an entrée category might offer a lamb option, but not all of the entrée choices should include lamb. In fact, repetition of any main ingredient (protein, starch, vegetable, or sauce) is generally not a sound approach to menu planning. Imagine that a customer is repulsed by parsnips. If every entrée included parsnips, then that customer would have difficulty finding a dish to enjoy. The concept of flavor operates similarly. If every dish on a menu is somewhat sweet, then a person who dislikes sweetness will not enjoy the dining experience. The same is true for spicy, sour, or salty dishes that dominate a menu category. Similarly, menu planners may classify dishes as heavy or light, simple or complex, fresh or caramelized. If a menu relies too heavily on one flavor profile, it will appeal to a smaller audience than a menu with greater balance and variety will. There is one more exception to the rule of variety in ingredients. A menu planner should consider product utilization when creating menu items. Product utilization, incorporating the byproducts of a single ingredient into more than one dish, helps to keep a business's operating costs and menu prices low. To support the principles of variety and balance, the same ingredient may be used in a dish under a separate heading, during different meal periods, or in a very different form. Examples of appropriate product utilization abound. A chef might serve prime rib at dinner and utilize the leftovers in a sandwich at lunch. The potato "scraps" generated from making spherical Parisian potatoes may be turned into mashed potatoes for another dish. While the nice cuts of cod may be seared for an entrée, the irregular end pieces may be added to a seafood stew. When a chef can convert ingredient byproducts into something edible rather than throwing those items into the trash, he saves both the business and the customer money.

Cooking Technique

A quality menu typically varies the cooking techniques used within a single menu heading. Moist-heat cooking techniques (steaming, simmering, and poaching) yield delicate flavors and lower-fat dishes. The dry-heat cooking techniques of grilling, broiling, roasting, and sautéing generate low-fat dishes with more assertive, caramelized flavors, while frying creates heavier, richer dishes. The combination methods of braising and stewing create extremely rich and tender meals. As some guests prefer certain cooking techniques, a wider range of cooking techniques helps the menu to appeal to a broader audience. Variety and balance apply to the components within a dish as well. A dish that includes steamed, grilled, fried, and braised components is far more interesting than a dish in which all of the ingredients are fried.

Cooking technique impacts not only customer satisfaction but also kitchen work flow. A menu planner is limited to the equipment present (or purchasable) in the kitchen. For instance, grilling is not an option if the kitchen does not contain a grill, and the menu planner must take this into account. There is no point in including a menu item for which the kitchen lacks the proper cooking equipment. Creating balance among cooking techniques on a menu keeps a single line cook from becoming overloaded with orders. For example, if a heading with six menu items has four dishes coming from the sauté station, then the sauté cook will be extremely busy while the other stations remain relatively idle. A menu planner that divides the dishes evenly across the various kitchen workstations creates better balance and work flow within the kitchen. If separate components of a single dish come from different stations, the menu planner must consider whether the cooks can efficiently execute the dish given the kitchen layout and work flow. Otherwise, the dish may cause production problems for the entire kitchen.

Temperature and Texture

The mouth feel of a dish is as important to the dining experience as its flavor is. Menu items with a single texture are less interesting to eat than ones with multiple textures. Soft, chewy, crunchy, and crisp components make for an exciting salad or dessert, while a one-dimensional plate of salmon terrine, mashed potato, and butternut squash custard turns diversely textured ingredients into a uniform mouth feel of mush.

Variety in texture and temperature apply equally across menu items and headings. Offering an ice cream sandwich, a room temperature cake, and a warm peach cobbler aids the guest who is sensitive to certain temperature zones. Similarly, a selection of appetizers that are all crisp and crunchy will frustrate a diner who has trouble chewing, while an entrée category saturated with soft, stewed dishes will come across as boring. Incorporating variation in cooking technique and ingredients helps to provide variety in texture.

Color, Shape, and Size

Repetition of colors, shapes, or sizes across several dishes is less of an issue than it is within a single plate. A dish of all off-white components, such as poached chicken with cauliflower and rice, is unattractive and less appetizing than a dish with a variety of colors. Ingredient shapes and sizes operate similarly. It is far more interesting to eat a creation with different knife cuts than it is to eat a dish where everything is the same shape and size. Not only do different shapes and sizes provide different sensations within the mouth, but the visual impact is far more impressive. Since guests eat with their eyes before they consume with their mouths, providing variety and balance in color, shape, and size creates a more enjoyable dining experience for the customer.

Composition and Plate Presentation

Composition and plate presentation represent the final variables for which variety and balance enhance the guest's dining experience. A dish that is impossibly tall may seem spectacular to the guest, but it is less impressive if every dish is plated that way. Having some dishes presented in cast iron skillets, some on colored, rectangular china, and some on traditional round white plates lends interest to the dining experience as guests peer across the table at what others have ordered. Tableside preparations are exciting, but when every dish is assembled tableside, the service becomes tiresome. The best approach to plating is to offer variety in presentation and plate composition. Some plates may be tall and static; others may have a low, circular flow. Some may be intricately composed with each element in its place while others may be simply ladled into a large bowl or crock. The greater the variety, the more interesting the menu is for the guest.

Traditional Menu Headings

Learning Objective 3
List the most common menu headings found on traditional breakfast, lunch, and dinner menus, and describe the types of menu items typically listed under each menu heading.

While there are no hard and fast rules for naming menu headings, there are some traditional conventions that are commonly used throughout the industry. It is important to note that these naming conventions do not apply for all foodservice business concepts; the most important drivers for creating headings are the business's theme and the market's needs. A Chinese restaurant may prefer to categorize its entrées under the headings of "Beef," "Chicken," "Pork," and "Seafood." A tapas restaurant, on the other hand, may simply use "Hot Tapas" and "Cold Tapas." What follows are not the only or even the best options, just the most common ones.

Breakfast Menus

Because breakfast is typically a quick meal (except for destination restaurants), breakfast menus rarely divide their foods into sequenced courses. Most breakfast businesses assume that their customers will only order one course. Consequently, breakfast menus are usually categorized by the type of food rather than the order in which it is eaten.

Most breakfast menus include an à la carte section for guests who wish to have a lighter breakfast or snack. Not all breakfast customers are hungry in the morning, so they may prefer a simple piece of toast or a cup of yogurt. An à la carte section does not preclude the menu planner from offering a semi à la carte section as well. Semi à la carte options increase sales by packaging multiple items together for one price. The price is lower than it would be if the customer ordered all of the items à la carte, but the package deal usually encourages people to buy more than they would if they only had the à la carte option. Ordering semi à la carte also expedites the order-taking process, thus speeding service and improving the seat turnover rate.

Because many customers eat breakfast before heading off to work, most or all breakfast menu choices should be quick to prepare. Foodservice businesses may wish to consider portable menu options that can be eaten on the go. Everything from pastries to hot breakfast sandwiches are easy to sell without tying up table space, and guests can enjoy a meal out without significantly delaying their commute to work. Because of the popularity of certain breakfast foods and their relatively low cost, some operations offer breakfast all day. In such instances, the breakfast items are listed on their own menu page, separate from

BREAKFAST

SERVED UNTIL 2PM

PANCAKES, FRENCH TOAST AND WAFFLES

Side Car…1 egg with bacon, ham, or sausage   3

Bury It…covered in bananas, blueberries, or strawberries 4

Sub ice-cream for butter because you can   1.5

Two Pancakes   5

Two Blueberry or Chocolate Chip Pancakes   6

Special Breakfast (Tally's original)   4.25
one pancake, egg, bacon or sausage

Crepes   7.5
choose original ham and scrambled egg or with fresh fruit and whipped cream

French Toast   7

Really French Toast   13
foie gras, berries, granola, and maple cream

Cinnamon Swirl French Toast   7

Whole Wheat Oatmeal Waffles   9.5
 fresh fruit, vanilla yogurt sauce, basil

BREAKFAST DISHES

Meat Lovers   10
two eggs, hash browns, toast, two strips of bacon, one sausage

One Egg Breakfast   8
bacon, ham or sausage, hash browns, toast

Two Egg Breakfast   9
bacon, ham or sausage, hash browns, toast

Buffalo Hanger Steak and Eggs   15
two eggs, hash browns, toast (suggested MR-M)

Chicken Fried Steak   11.5
two eggs, hash browns, toast, country gravy

Eggs Benedict   11.5
two poached eggs, English muffin, ham, hollandaise, hash browns

Smoked Salmon Benedict   15
two poached eggs, smoked salmon, English muffin, hollandaise, Ikura roe, tarragon, red pepper coulis, hash browns

Breakfast Burrito   10.5
Onions, peppers, tomato, chorizo sausage, hash browns, scrambled eggs, cheddar, Monterey jack, green chili

Duck, Duck, Goose   14.5
duck confit, onion, arugula, sweet potatoes, foie gras, sunny egg, gooseberries, toast

Lox Plate   14.5
smoked salmon, cream cheese on a Black Hills Bagel, tomato, caper, red onion, arugula, four minute egg

Migas   12
chorizo sausage, onions, peppers, potatoes, tortilla strips, scrambled eggs, green chili, white cheddar

Vegetable Breakfast   12.5
garden greens, seasonal vegetables, herbs, hollandaise, sweet potatoes, sunny egg, toast

Gluten free options available for an additional $1

FIGURE 3.4

An example of an extensive and creative breakfast menu.

Source: From Tally's Silver Spoon Breakfast Menu, Chef Benjamin Klinkel, Tally's Silver Spoon.

BREAKFAST

SERVED UNTIL 2PM

FRENCH OMELETTES

Served with hash browns and toast, we use three eggs, fresh ingredients and imagination, ask your server about the omelette of the day.   10.5

BREAKFAST SANDWICHES

Bagel Sandwich   8.5
ham, sausage or bacon, egg, cheddar

Breakfast BLT   10
sourdough, bacon, arugula, tomato, egg, smoked gouda

OTHER FAVORITES

Fruit Risotto (oatmeal)   5.5
slow cooked with our house preserves

House made Pecan Vanilla Granola   6.5
fresh fruit and choice of yogurt, milk or half & half

Featured House Made Granola   6.5
fresh fruit and choice of yogurt milk or half & half

Caramel Roll   4.5

Biscuits and Gravy   5
house recipe

BREAKFAST SIDES

Toast   3.5
white, wheat, sourdough, rye, English muffin

Bagel   4.5
with cream cheese

Meat   4.5
bacon, ham or sausage

Potatoes   3.5
hash browns, American fries, sweet potatoes

Sauces   2.5
hollandaise, sausage gravy, vanilla yogurt sauce, maple cream, green chili

DRINKS

Juice   reg. 3   lg. 4
orange, apple, cranberry, tomato, grapefruit, and grape

Coffee   2.25

Hot tea, hot chocolate   2.5

Nestles Nesquick Chocolate Milk   3.5

Milk   reg. 2.5   lg. 3

Soda   2.5

Iced tea   2.5

Raspberry Lemonade   3

Gluten free options available for an additional $1

TALLY'S
SS
SILVER SPOON

FIGURE 3.4 *(Continued)*

the lunch and dinner menu options. Guests receive the same comprehensive menu all day long, but time frames printed on the menu state when each part of the menu is available.

Some of the most common headings for a breakfast menu are as follows:

Beverages

Beverages are an important part of the breakfast experience for most customers. Unlike lunch, brunch, and dinner, which may use a separate beverage menu for alcoholic options, breakfast beverages are almost always listed on the same menu as the food. Caffeinated drinks, such as coffee and tea, are a must. Casual operations may offer very few hot drinks, while fancier establishments may include espresso drinks and hot chocolate, too. Juice is an essential breakfast offering. Orange juice is the most popular juice option, but grapefruit, pineapple, apple, tomato, and others may be offered as well. Milk should also be listed; the number of milk options (whole, skim, 2%, soy, etc.) to include depends on the local market's taste preferences. The number and type of menu items listed under the beverage heading immediately conveys the style and theme of the establishment. Restaurants serving only coffee, decaf coffee, and tea suggest a small-town, homey feel, while those offering a range of espresso drinks and tea options imply a more cosmopolitan (and pricy) dining experience.

Entrées

Because of the nature of breakfast, some operations opt to list all of their multicomponent menu items under the single heading "Entrées." For a shorter menu with less than a dozen choices, this makes a lot of sense. It makes the number of choices appear bountiful and allows the menu planner to organize the options in any order. (The value of menu item placement will be discussed in Chapter 10.) Other breakfast places choose to categorize their menu items by main ingredient type.

Eggs and Omelets

Eggs are an extremely common offering at breakfast, and many establishments prefer to list them as their own category. An option of eggs cooked to order (customer choice) is popular in most operations, often served with meat, toast, and/or potatoes. However, offering a variety of egg dishes lends interest to the menu and may help increase sales revenue. Poached-egg dishes (e.g., Benedict or Florentine), frittatas, and omelets are high-value items for which a restaurant can charge more. Omelets, in particular, allow a menu planner to show off a wide range of classic and local flavor combinations that may include meat, vegetables, cheese, and/or seafood. Egg sandwiches also allow a restaurant to offer hot to-go options to its patrons. When the number of omelet and egg offerings is substantial, the menu planner may choose to separate "Eggs" and "Omelets" under two different headings.

Griddle Items

Another popular hot breakfast category is "Griddle Cakes" or items "From the Griddle." These include pancakes, French toast, waffles, and, in some cases, crepes and blintzes. Because of the high carbohydrate content of these items, they may be served with meat, eggs, or fruit, but not usually with toast or potatoes. Possibilities for flavor variation within this category abound. Pancakes may include a range of ingredients or toppings beyond the classic maple syrup. French toast and waffles may be stuffed or garnished with various sweet or savory toppings as well. Crepes and blintzes provide a similar canvas for culinary creativity. If the menu focuses exclusively on one type of griddle quick bread, the category heading may simply list that item by name, such as "Pancakes," or "Hot Cakes."

Cereals

While cereals are not as popular as some other breakfast options, they are an important component of any breakfast menu. Hot cereals and porridges provide high-fiber, low-fat nutrition for guests with dietary concerns. In some operations, they are incorporated creatively rather than relegated to "old standby" status. For example, grits might be served plain or with fish, cheese, and/or chiles. Oatmeal might be served simply with brown sugar and milk or more innovatively with other grains, dried fruit, and nut milk. Cold cereals, too, are important for guests, especially children, who prefer not to waiver from their morning routine. Cold cereals may be purchased ready-to-eat in individual boxes/bowls, or in bulk. If the operation serves a captive audience, the options should not all be sugary cereals but rather should include a range of flavor profiles. An upscale restaurant may choose to prepare certain cold cereals, such as granola or Birchermüesli, from scratch. When offering cold cereals, it is important to provide milk options—whole and reduced fat at a minimum.

Other Breakfast Entrées

Some foodservice establishments choose to offer specialty items that do not fit easily under any of the other category headings. Examples include steak and eggs, bagels and lox, corned beef hash, or Greek yogurt with fruit and honey. If these items are not simply placed under a general "Entrées" heading, they may be grouped under "House Specialties" or something similar. Such specialty items may be an attraction for customers as they are not readily available at all breakfast operations.

À La Carte or Sides

As stated earlier, most breakfast menus include an à la carte section, often entitled "À la Carte" or "Sides," depending on what options are included under the heading. Side dishes for a breakfast menu usually include breakfast meats, individual eggs, potatoes, bread/toast, and one or more fruit options. A more complete à la carte section will also include pastries, muffins, bagels, doughnuts, English muffins, and yogurt. À la carte sections, from which some entrée accompaniments are pulled, are an opportunity to show off regional products and to lend interest to a menu. In addition to bacon and sausage, meat options might include country ham or scrapple. Grits and biscuits reflect the flavors of the South. Muffins and pastries may be made from scratch in a variety of flavors. Potatoes can be prepared in a wide range of styles beyond basic hash browns. In short, while some menu planners treat the à la carte section as an afterthought, it should serve the customers' needs, lend interest to the menu, and work symbiotically with the entrée listings. Some of the à la carte choices will naturally be components intended as add-ons to entrées, but the section should also satisfy the needs of those guests who wish to patronize the establishment without indulging in a large meal.

Lunch and Dinner Menus

Lunch and dinner menus are generally more comparable to each other than they are to breakfast menus. In fact, some foodservice businesses use the same menu for lunch and dinner. While there are similarities in the ways that lunch and dinner menus are organized, there are a few differences between the two meals that are important to address. First, Americans typically eat less food over a shorter period of time at lunch than they do at dinner (special occasion lunches excepted). Consequently, lunch options should be quick to prepare, and they should be served in smaller portions at lower prices than their dinner counterparts. It is possible to offer the same menu at lunch and dinner but with smaller prices and portion sizes at the earlier meal. Second, sandwiches, soups, and salads are more popular as entrées at lunch than they are at dinner, where soups and salads are often treated as preludes or accompaniments to a more substantial entrée. Thus, lunch menus tend to rely more heavily on these menu items than dinner menus do. Otherwise, the headings for lunch and dinner menus tend to be the same. If the local market includes large numbers of individuals with lots of leisure time (stay-at-home parents or retirees, for example), lunch business may include guests willing to linger over several courses of food, just as they do at dinner. Other operations may only service guests with time for a single quick-service course. Tailoring the menu headings and offerings to the target market's eating habits is always the best approach.

The most commonly used menu headings for lunch and dinner are as follows:

Appetizers

The purpose of an appetizer is both to awaken the taste buds and to lengthen the dining experience. Appetizers should be flavorful but small in portion. Acidic or spicy ingredients work well as they foment salivation. Too often, restaurants serve rich, heavy appetizers that cause the consumer to fill up just as the meal is beginning. Portions that are too large or appetizers that are too filling can undermine the business's goal of increasing revenue. With some exceptions,

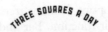

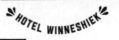

11:00 AM - 1:30 PM   RESTAURATION   LUNCH MENU

───────── **TO START** ─────────

red curry hummus   6
with crudité & grilled pita

french onion soup   cup 3 | bowl 5

soup of the day   cup 3 | bowl 5

───────── **SANDWICHES** ─────────

french fries, yam fries, cole slaw, sweet potato 'slaw,
or white bean salad served with pickle.

portabella mushroom   9
grilled over rosemary with smoked gouda
& red pepper ketchup

pulled pork sandwich   9
slow-cooked & topped with coleslaw

carson's ritzy pork tenderloin   9
cracker crust, honey mustard, pickled onion

turkey burger   9
smoked gouda, bacon, & avocado crema

winneshiek club   10
grilled chicken breast, bacon, swiss, & house-made aioli
with lettuce, red onion, & tomato

the winn burger*
1/3 lb: plain 9 | cheese 10 | go nuts 11
1/2 lb: plain 10 | cheese 11 | go nuts 12
go nuts: add cheese, mushrooms, bacon, & grilled onions

[⊗ indicates gluten-free options
gluten-free pasta, add $2
gluten-free bun on any sandwich, add $2]

───────── **SALADS** ─────────

mixed green salad   6

classic caesar salad   side 6 | full 9

chicken caesar salad   12

⊗ smoked turkey salad   13
field greens, milton cheddar, sliced apple, & rosemary
walnuts

cup of soup & salad   8

───────── **ENTREES** ─────────

add soup or salad, 1⁵⁰

telefonos   14
saffron risotto cakes, smoked gouda, greens, fennel slaw,
hazelnuts

fettuccine with smoked turkey   14
polashek's smoked turkey, lemon, roasted garlic, &
house made mascarpone

skewered beef lettuce wraps   10
tenderloin, sriracha-sorghum glaze, local bibb lettuce
& local yogurt

┌─────────────────────────────┐
│   res·tau·ra·tion   │
│ *archaic french variant, restoration* │
│ *"a returning to an improved condition"* │
└─────────────────────────────┘

Automatic gratuity of 18% for parties of six or more.

*Thoroughly cooking foods of animal origin such as beef, eggs, fish, lamb, pork, poultry, or shellfish reduces the risk of food-borne illness. Individuals with certain
health conditions may be at higher risk if these foods are consumed raw or under-cooked. Please consult your health care professional.

**We will make every attempt to meet your individual dietary request. Please inform your server of any allergies and dietary restrictions. Since our facility is not allergen-free,
we are not responsible for individual reaction to any foods. Although best practices are used in production, items may inadvertently come in contact with gluten,
shellfish, nuts, and/or non-vegan food items.

FIGURE 3.5
This lunch menu includes multiple sandwich and salad options.

Reprinted with permission of Hotel Winneshiek.

large numbers of guests opting for appetizers instead of entrées suggests that the appetizers are not properly serving their function. Bar and lounge environments in which many customers opt for drinks and appetizers rather than for full meals are the obvious exception to this rule.

As with other menu headings, appetizers should provide variety and balance within the category. Appetizers should include cold and hot options as well as meat, seafood, poultry, and vegetarian options. The cooking technique should vary as well. Appetizers are also excellent opportunities to utilize byproducts from ingredients used in the entrée section. No matter what ingredients and cooking techniques are used, foodservice businesses should be able to prepare appetizers quickly. As these are the first courses guests will consume, an extended cooking time for a single appetizer will leave guests without food for an uncomfortably long period of time after being seated.

In operations with shorter menus, the appetizer heading may include soups and salads; in other establishments, soups and salads may have their own headings. In upscale restaurants, separate headings for appetizers versus soups and salads may encourage sales of multiple pre-entrée courses in ways that a single heading will not.

Soups

Soup on a menu plays an important role both for the guest and for the establishment. Customers enjoy the homey, familiar feel of this nutrient-dense concoction. Hearty soups, sometimes paired with a salad, may be a complete meal for those on a tight budget or low-calorie diet. Soups serve as a welcoming introduction or liquid respite when part of a multicourse meal. From the chef's perspective, soups are the ultimate opportunity for product utilization. Scraps of vegetables, bits of meat or fish, leftover rice can all become part of an elegant soup even if they are inappropriately shaped for use in another dish.

When planning soup options for a menu, variety of type is critical. Soups come in many forms, including cream, broth, puree, and specialty. (Specialty encompasses many classic national and international soups that do not fall into the other categories.) Menu planners are wise to select soups of different types for their menus. For example, cream of broccoli, chicken noodle, lentil puree, and gazpacho soup will each appeal to different audiences, but a series of "cream of" soups will only attract guests who prefer that particular style. In warmer months, offering a cold soup helps to increase menu variety and soup sales.

Some operations offer soup in two sizes—a cup or a bowl. The bowl is always the bigger portion. Having two sizes allows for guests to enjoy a small cup of soup as an appetizer or a bowl as a main course. Restaurants that wish to encourage multicourse sales often offer only a single small size.

Salads

Salad, like soup, can be an accompaniment to a larger meal or a standalone entrée. The most basic of salads consists of simple mixed greens, but the garnish possibilities are endless. Vegetables, fruits (fresh or dried), nuts, seeds, cheeses, croutons, olives, legumes, eggs, seafood, meat, and poultry are all appropriate additions to a salad. Side salads usually rely on simplicity so as not to overshadow an entrée. Entrée salads typically include a hearty portion of protein, such as chicken, shrimp, steak, cheese, or beans. Sometimes, a restaurant allows the guest to choose whether to add animal protein to a salad for an additional cost, as is common with chicken Caesar salad. In some operations, entrée salads are listed under "Entrées," particularly on a lunch menu, or under their own "Entrée Salads" heading.

No matter its size or function, there are certain qualities that guests expect from a salad. Variety of texture, color, and flavor is critical in almost every salad. While the texture and color differences are obvious in a mixed green salad with dried cranberries, orange sections, chevre, red onion, and sunflower seeds, the variation is less conspicuous in a traditional Caesar salad. However, the crunch of the croutons, the crisp bite of the lettuce, and the creaminess of the dressing all lend a textural interest to the classic Caesar that is not present in a salad composed only of romaine lettuce, oil, and vinegar. A salad that includes only lettuce and dressing should use several lettuces to provide a variety of flavors and shapes. While some chefs prefer to pair a specific dressing with each salad, other operations offer guests their choice of dressing. When guests choose their own salad dressing, four to five dressing options are typically considered a minimum for the menu.

High-quality, fresh ingredients are essential for raw salads. Wilted, browned, or sandy lettuce is unappealing to eat, and it is impossible to hide in a salad. If certain fresh ingredients cannot be reliably sourced, then they should not be included in a raw salad. Cooked or processed ingredients make perfectly acceptable salads and are often easier to obtain during certain times of the year. Cabbage slaws, pickled vegetables, or cooked beans provide a nice contrast to the more common lettuce salad. And while many salads are served cold, they need not all be so; for example, a warm bacon dressing over spinach gives some temperature variation to this popular category of food. Finally, although salads are typically served prior to the entrée in the United States, there is no reason that a salad could not be offered after the entrée as is done in parts of Europe.

Sandwiches

Sandwiches come in almost limitless varieties. The outer wrappers may be tortillas, bread slices, biscuits, buns, or lettuce, just to name a few. They may be served hot or cold, closed or open faced. Typically, a sandwich includes one or more main items, a spread, and some garnish within the wrapper. The main items may be fresh or cured meat or fish, bound salads, cheeses, or vegan selections such as mushrooms or falafel. The spreads may be common condiments, like mustard or mayonnaise, or they may be house-made concoctions like herb oil or cranberry butter. Garnishes, too, span a range from the traditional lettuce, tomato, and onion found on hamburgers to anything that adds flavor and textural interest to the complete dish.

Sandwiches are often served with a side of fries, chips, or salad to add another element to the dish. Because they do not always require utensils, sandwiches make excellent options for meals made to go. Unlike the aforementioned menu categories, sandwiches may be a standalone heading for any meal of the day, including breakfast, but if they are few in number, they may be subsumed under the "Entrées" heading.

Entrées

The "Entrées" heading on a lunch or dinner menu is usually the longest and most important part of the menu for most foodservice concepts. This section contains the items that most guests order if they are only going to order one thing, and its contents are often the most expensive on the menu. Depending on the business's brand, the entrées may be portioned quite large to satisfy guests who do not order anything else, or they may be somewhat smaller in size with the expectation that customers always order multiple courses.

The term "Entrées" may not actually appear on the menu. Some operations use the term "Main Courses" while others divide the entrée options among several headings based on the main ingredients or on the cooking technique used. For example, a restaurant that focuses on just a few cooking techniques might use headings like "From the Hearth" or "From the Grill." Others may use the labels "Chicken," "Pork," "Beef," etc., as they do in many Chinese restaurants, or "Pasta," "Meat," "Seafood," as is done in some Italian restaurants. As always, the terminology used should mesh seamlessly with the business's concept and theme.

Unless the menu is strictly à la carte, the entrées include all sides and accompaniments that are part of the main course. Depending on the concept, these sides may be listed as part of the entrée description or under a separate heading that allows guests to choose their own sides. When the sides are predetermined by the menu planner, the entirety of the plate should be considered for variety and balance in shape, color, flavor, texture, and cooking technique. Variety and balance are important for the heading as a whole, too. Assuming the business concept permits it, the entrée section should include meat, poultry, seafood, and vegetarian options. In some operations, pizza, pasta, and casseroles represent a significant portion of the entrée offerings and may even merit their own headings.

Sides or Accompaniments

Some menus include a section entitled "Sides" or "Accompaniments" from which guests choose the starches and vegetables to pair with their entrée. Even businesses that predetermine the entrée accompaniments may include a list of sides for guests who wish to order additional portions or for eaters who prefer to make a meal out of side dishes. As with the other headings, this section should provide variety and balance. The vegetable choices should include lighter options, such as steamed with herbs, and heavier choices, such as fried or buttered. The vegetables should come from a range of colors (not all green, for example) and families (as in not all from the cabbage family). Several sides should be vegetarian for those who do not eat meat. In some operations, fruits like applesauce or peaches may be included among the choices, too. Starches follow a similar set of guidelines, though it is not uncommon to see potatoes listed several times with different preparations, as in fried, baked, or mashed. Still, potatoes should not be the only choice for a starch. Rice, beans, corn, quinoa, couscous, and pasta are only some of the possible options for starchy sides. Because nutrition-minded guests often select one starch and one vegetable (or two vegetables), it is important not to overload the "Sides" category with starches. For example, if only five sides are listed, potatoes, rice, beans, and couscous should not represent four of them. Vegetables provide a greater range of colors and flavors than starches do anyway.

Desserts

Some restaurants place desserts on a separate menu while others include them on the main menu. Generally speaking, the more upscale the dining experience, the more appropriate it is to give desserts their own menu. Desserts, like the other headings, offer a huge opportunity for variety and balance. Selections may include cakes, custards, fruit, nuts, chocolate, frozen treats, and other types of desserts. A dessert menu that offers six different pies is not as interesting as one that lists six vastly different desserts. Besides, a guest who does not care for pie would never order dessert if pie were the only option. Menu planners should plan for variety within a dessert, too. A single dessert may combine hot and cold temperatures, soft and crunchy textures, and sweet and tart flavors. As a dessert exhibits greater variety, not only does it become more interesting, but it also commands a higher sales price.

There are pros and cons to listing desserts on the main menu. As guests make their entrée selections, they may see a dessert and begin craving it early. Even if they are stuffed at the end of the main course, they may still order dessert just to satisfy the craving. Table tents, which market desserts throughout the meal, have a similar effect. On the other hand, a customer who sees interesting dessert options too early may avoid ordering appetizers in order to save room for dessert. The process of bringing an entire menu to a table just for a guest to read the tiny dessert section at the bottom of the page is also less elegant. It leaves less space for the marketing of dessert, and it reminds customers of everything they have already eaten. Simple, straightforward desserts in a casual restaurant do just fine under a single heading on the main menu; more complex desserts in need of description do not.

Cheese and Charcuterie

While a separate cheese heading on a menu is not particularly common, it is slowly seeing a resurgence in upscale restaurants in certain parts of the country. Cheese may serve as an appetizer, as the course between the entrée and dessert, or as a dessert alternative. Because it goes well with wine, guests may order cheese as they finish off their wine from the main course. Some menu planners list the cheese course on both the main menu and on a separate dessert menu to appeal to customers who prefer cheese at different points in the meal. Restaurants in cheese-making regions of the country often do well selling a local cheese course to tourists.

Variety in a cheese course comes from the milk source (cow, goat, sheep), the texture (soft, firm, hard), the origin (local or international), and the kind of processing (blue, smoked, aged). The menu planner may choose to offer a single plate that includes a predetermined set of cheeses or to list a range of cheeses from which the customer may choose. Either way, variety is key. With the cheese course, the menu planner may choose to offer fruit or other sweet condiments, such as jams, honey, or fig paste, to balance the saltiness of the cheese. An accompaniment of crackers, toast, or some other neutral base on which to spread the softer cheeses is essential.

One recent trend is to pair charcuterie and cheese as an appetizer or to list them under a menu heading of their own. As some operations focus on artisanal products, a few chefs have taken to creating and curing their own hams, fish, sausages, and deli meats. Some even make and/or age their own cheeses. These charcuterie boards, which sometimes allow

APPETIZERS

SIMPLY THE BEST CALAMARI
Buttermilk battered calamari, jalapeño lime aïoli, jalapeño chips. 12.95

ALE FONDUE WITH PRETZELS
White cheddar, BrewHouse IPA fondue sauce, fresh brick oven baked pretzels, crisp sweet gherkin. 10.95

BERING SEA KING CRAB CAKES
Roasted corn relish, Thai aïoli & cilantro oil. 14.95

TWICE FRIED CHICKEN WINGS
Asian style with seven spice chili pepper and salty caramel hot pepper sauce. 13.95

AMBER ALE BATTERED ALASKAN COD
Yogurt slaw, dill pickle tartar. 12.95

ALASKAN SMOKED SALMON DIP
Alder smoked ALASKAN sockeye salmon, lightly dressed with Greek yogurt, lemon zest, capers and dill. Served with alder-grilled artesian bread and crisp sweet gherkins. 12.95

BERING SEA KING CRAB LEGS
½ lb., drawn lemon butter. 27.95

STARTER SALADS & SOUPS

CLASSIC CAESAR
Crisp hearts of romaine, housemade croutons, Parmesan shavings. 7.50

BREWHOUSE BLUE*
Seasonal mixed greens, red flame grapes, caramelized pecans, blue cheese crumbles. 7.50

BLT CHOP CHOP
Crisp hearts of romaine, baby spinach, fresh herbed dressing, tomato, English cucumber, garbanzo beans, fresh avocado, crisp bacon, sweet corn and toasted artesian croutons. 9.95

DAILY SOUP
Our soup is always housemade. Ask your server about today's selection. cup, 5.95 bowl, 7.95

HEARTY ALASKA SEAFOOD CHOWDER
ALASKAN seafood, roasted corn, shaved fennel, sweet red peppers, crisp bacon, creamy crab broth, splash of dry sherry. cup, 6.95 bowl, 8.95

SIDES

BRUSSELS SPROUTS
Brussels sprouts, flash fried, lightly seasoned with kosher salt and black pepper. 6.95

GRILLED BROCCOLINI
Alder grilled with shaved parmesan. 6.95

SKILLET JALAPEÑO CORNBREAD
With maple butter. 6.95

SUCCOTASH
Tender asparagus, sweet corn, green beans, basil. 6.95

** Contains nuts or nut products*

WOOD GRILL & ROTISSERIE

We use KACHEMAK BAY Alder wood for rotisserie roasting & grilling. This imparts a unique subtle smoky flavor to ALASKA seafood & meats. The BREWHOUSE has the only wood fired rotisserie in ALASKA.

ALDER WOOD-GRILLED RIBEYE*
SIMPLY GRILLED 16 oz. 28 day-aged corn fed beef, garlic herb butter, alder grilled fingerling potatoes and Brussels sprouts. 35.95

ALDER WOOD-GRILLED FLAT IRON STEAK*
Root Beer birch syrup demi-glace, crispy buttermilk onions, broccolini, blue cheese, garlic mashed potatoes. 22.95

BARBECUED BABY BACK RIBS
Jamaican jerk rub, spicy BREWHOUSE signature whiskey BBQ sauce, yogurt slaw, jalapeño cornbread with maple butter. 24.95

STRIPLOIN & PRAWNS
28 day-aged custom cut striploin, PACIFIC white prawns, herb butter, alder grilled fingerling potatoes, radish salad, cilantro and avocado lime verde. 34.95

ROTISSERIE CHICKEN WITH SUCCOTASH
Pancetta, Rosemary, garlic served with succotash. 19.95

DINNER SPECIAL *
Our Chefs have utilized unique seasonal flavors to created a hearty special for your enjoyment. Ask your server about tonight's selection.

PASTA, BIG SALADS & SANDWICHES

SEAFOOD FETTUCCINE
ALASKAN sockeye salmon, shrimp, Manila clams and ALASKAN cod with mushrooms, spinach, red peppers and garlic cream. 24.95

FETTUCCINE JAMBALAYA
Pan seared chicken, Andouille sausage, shrimp, spicy Mamou sauce. 19.95

MAPLE CHICKEN SALAD*
Spring greens, shaved Brussels sprouts, quinoa, red onion, fresh mozzarella, WASHINGTON apples and sweet grapes dressed with maple vinnaigrette & topped with candied pecan and blue cheese. 15.95

CHILI LIME SHRIMP*
Alder wood grilled PACIFIC white prawns and sweet pineapple with chili glaze, sesame dressed romaine, spinach and arugula, crisp apple, candied pecan, cilantro and Mandarin orange. 15.95

ALASKAN SALMON BLT WEDGE
House smoked ALASKAN salmon, crisp iceberg, grape tomato, crisp bacon, toasted artesian croutons, fresh herbed dressing. 16.95

DOUBLE DIPPED CHICKEN
Fresh chicken breast with spicy aioli, crisp pepper bacon, aged Tillamook cheddar and jalapeno-pickle slaw. Served on a brioche bun with fresh potato chips. 13.95

We unconditionally guarantee all food, beverages & service. Substitutions welcome. For parties of 8 or more, an 18% gratuity will be added to your check. Please feel free to increase or decrease this gratuity at your discretion.

SEAFOOD

We are proud to support our Alaskan Fishermen & are committed to sustainable fisheries.

ALASKAN MACADAMIA SALMON *
ALASKAN salmon, pan seared with macadamia nut crust, orange rum glaze, sweet cilantro infused oil and pineapple ginger relish. Jasmine rice and braised greens. 25.95

HERB CRUSTED ALASKAN HALIBUT *
Coated with basil pesto & spent grain bread crumbs, garlic mashed potatoes, roasted tomato vinaigrette tossed seasonal greens. 34.95

SEARED AHI TUNA *
Pepper rubbed, jasmine rice, wasabi aioli, soy mustard, housemade bean sprout kimchee & cilantro oil. Served rare. 25.95

ALASKAN ROCKFISH *
Seared with CAJUN spices, succotash, cilantro, avocado, tomatillo salsa, shaved radish. 23.95

FRESH CATCH *
We work with our network of FISHERMEN to bring you the freshest seasonal catch. Ask your server what we selected for you this evening.

BERING SEA KING CRAB LEGS
ALASKAN king crab steamed to order. Drawn butter, grilled asparagus. ½ lb. 31.95 Full lb. 46.95

BRICK OVEN PIZZAS

Our pizza dough is handmade each morning using an old world rye flour starter and allowed to slowly rise and proof for 48 hours. We bake our pizzas in our brick oven at 600°F for a superior crisp and tender crust.

FRESH MOZZARELLA AND TOMATO
House made marinara, fresh mozzarella, roma tomato, garlic and fresh basil. 11.95

PEPPERONI
Zoe's handcrafted pepperoni, house made marinara topped with our 5 cheese blend. 12.95

WILD MUSHROOM AND TRUFFLED ARUGULA
Cambozola and goat cheese, wild mushroom medley, caramelized onion, roasted garlic, baby arugula and white truffle oil. 13.95

BREWER'S PIE
Zoe's spicy coppa and pepperoni, Italian and Andouille sausage, crisp bacon and fresh mozzarella with house made marinara. 14.95

DOUBLE SAUSAGE MUSHROOM
Spicy Italian sausage and Andouille, caramelized fennel, oyster mushrooms, fresh mozzarella and house made marinara. 12.95

** These items are cooked to order & may be served raw or undercooked. Consuming raw or undercooked meats, poultry, seafood, shellfish or eggs may increase your risk of foodborne illness.*

DESSERTS

ORIGINAL PEANUT BUTTER PIE*
Chocolate cookie crust, creamy peanut butter filling, GUITTARD chocolate ganache, chocolate sauce. 7.95

FLOURLESS CHOCOLATE TORTE
A silky flourless chocolate torte, served with port poached cherries & a sweet cream. 7.95

CRÈME BRÛLÉE*
Traditional vanilla custard, crackling sugar crust. 7.95

WORLD FAMOUS BREAD PUDDING*
Vanilla custard, apples, currants, caramelized pecans, Yukon Jack sauce. 8.50

DREYER'S GRAND ICE CREAMS
French vanilla or the flavor of the day. 4.50

MOCHA CHEESECAKE
Freshly made in house with chocolate mousse, bourbon caramel sauce and raspberry puree. 7.95

BOTTLED BEER

BUCKLER NON ALCOHOLIC BEER 4.50
NEW GRIST GLUTEN FREE PILSNER 5.95
OMISSION GLUTEN FREE PALE ALE 5.95
ANGRY ORCHARD CRISP APPLE CIDER 6.95
SEATTLE CIDER CO. SEMI-SWEET HARD CIDER 8.95
WYDER'S DRY PEAR HARD CIDER 7.95

NON ALCOHOLIC BEVERAGES

LEMONADE 3.50

SAN PELLEGRINO
Plain or orange. 3.50

BLACKBERRY BASIL LEMONADE
Lemonade, blackberries and fresh basil. 4.50

SPARKLING EARL GREY PALMER
Earl Grey tea, lemonade, simple syrup and honey. 3.95

BLUEBERRY CRUSH
Blueberries, pineapple & cranberry juice, soda, fresh mint. 4.50

MOJITO
Traditional, raspberry or pomegranate. 4.50

ITALIAN SODA
Raspberry or pomegranate. 4.50

HOUSE BREWED ROOT BEER
Rich & full bodied, with sarsaparilla, sassafras & just a hint of vanilla. Natural cane sugar. 3.95

HOUSE BREWED CREAM SODA
Creamy with big vanilla flavors & natural carbonation. Natural cane sugar. 3.95

HOUSE BREWED GINGER BEER
Smooth drinking with flavors of spicy ginger balanced by the sweetness of natural cane sugar. 3.95

FRESH BREWED KALADI BROTHERS COFFEE
BrewHouse blend, deep roasted by KALADI BROTHERS of ANCHORAGE; rich & full flavored. 2.95

Please be aware that our restaurant uses ingredients that contain all the major FDA allergens (peanuts, tree nuts, eggs, fish, shellfish, milk, soy & wheat).

"ALASKA'S CRAFT BREWERY"

BREWED IN ALASKA BY ALASKANS FOR ALASKANS

OUR FLAGSHIP BEERS

MAKE-A-WISH® WITH LEAD DOG WHITE *Pint 5.95 Half Pint 3.95*
Alcohol: 5.35% by volume. Starting gravity: 12.60 Plato (1.050 S.G.).

BLONDE *Pint 5.95 Half Pint 3.95*
Alcohol: 4.76% by volume. Starting gravity: 11.0 Plato (1.044 S.G.).

AMBER *Pint 5.95 Half Pint 3.95*
Alcohol: 5.67% by volume. Starting Gravity: 14.25 Plato (1.058 S.G.).

INDIA PALE ALE *Pint 6.50 Half Pint 4.50*
Alcohol: 6.35% by volume. Starting Gravity: 15.50 Plato (1.063 S.G.).

BAVARIAN HEFEWEIZEN *Pint 5.95 Half Pint 3.95*
Alcohol: 5.00% by volume. Starting Gravity: 12.50 Plato (1.050 S.G.).

OATMEAL STOUT *Pint 6.50 Half Pint 4.50*
Alcohol: 5.61% by volume. Starting Gravity: 16.00 Plato (1.065 S.G.).

RASPBERRY WHEAT *Pint 6.50 Half Pint 4.50*
Alcohol: 4.76% by volume. Starting Gravity: 11.00 Plato (1.044 S.G.).

IMPERIAL BLONDE Snifter 6.95 Half 4.75
Alcohol: 9.00% by volume. Starting Gravity: 20.00 Plato (1.083 S.G.).

SPECIALTY/SEASONAL BEERS

CASK INDIA PALE ALE Pint 6.95 Half Pint 4.95
Alcohol: 6.35% by volume. Starting Gravity: 15.50 Plato (1.063 S.G.).

NITRO CREAM ALE *Pint 6.50 Half Pint 4.50*
Alcohol: 4.42% by volume. Starting Gravity: 11.50 Plato (1.066 S.G.).

GERMAN STYLE RYE ALE *Pint 6.95 Half Pint 4.95*
Alcohol: 5.40% by volume. Starting Gravity: 12.65 Plato (1.052 S.G.).

RED *Pint 6.50 Half Pint 4.50*
Alcohol: 6.38% by volume. Starting Gravity: 16.50 Plato (1.068 S.G.).

BLACK IPA *Pint 6.95 Half Pint 4.95*
Alcohol: 7.00% by volume. Starting Gravity: 16.50 Plato (1.068 S.G.).

RAZZ IPA *Pint 6.95 Half Pint 4.95*
Alcohol: 5.92% by volume. Starting Gravity: 15.00 Plato (1.057 S.G.).

CITRUS IPA *Pint 6.95 Half Pint 4.95*
Alcohol: 7.12% by volume. Starting Gravity: 16.50 Plato (1.068 S.G.).

DOUBLE IPA *Snifter 6.95 Half 4.75*
Alcohol: 9.00% by volume. Starting Gravity: 20.50 Plato (1.091 S.G.).

JIM BEAM BELGIAN QUAD Snifter 7.50 Half 4.95
Alcohol: 10.21% by volume. Starting Gravity: 22.00 Plato (1.092 S.G.).

2013 OAK AGED EISBOCK Snifter 7.50 Half 4.95
Alcohol: 10.00% by volume. Starting Gravity: 24.00 Plato (1.100 S.G.).

BOURBON BELGIAN DARK Snifter 7.50 Half 4.95
Alcohol: 8.10% by volume. Starting Gravity: 18.55 Plato (1.076 S.G.).

2016 BIG WOODY BARLEYWINE Snifter 7.50 Half 4.95
Alcohol: 10.06% by volume. Starting Gravity: 27.00 Plato (1.113 S.G.).

"BARREL TO BAR"

We have found these wonderful wines and bring them to you on tap. It's a great way to enjoy a quality glass or bottle of wine and the carbon friendly packaging is great for the environment. Enjoy!

	glass	liter
RIESLING		
Milbrandt COLUMBIA VALLEY 14	8.95	41.95
PINOT GRIS		
Acrobat OREGON 14	8.95	41.95
CABERNET SAUVIGNON		
Liberty School PASO ROBLES 10	8.95	41.95
MALBEC		
Terra Rosa MENDOZA, ARGENTINA 14	9.50	43.95

WHITE WINES

	glass	bottle
WHITE ZINFANDEL/ROSE		
Beringer CALIFORNIA	6.95	25.95
M.Chapoutier Rose Belleruche COTES-DU-RHONE 14		34.95
CHARDONNAY		
Chateau Ste. Michelle COLUMBIA VALLEY 14	8.95	33.95
Joel Gott Unoaked MONTEREY/SONOMA/NAPA 14		37.95
Sonoma-Cutrer RUSSIAN RIVER VALLEY 13	12.95	49.95
Catena MENDOZA, ARGENTINA 13		49.95
PINOT GRIS		
Benton Lane WILLAMETTE VALLEY 14		36.95
Archery Summit Vireton WILLAMETTE VALLEY 13		40.95
TORRONTÉS		
Alamos SALTA, ARGENTINA 14		28.50
RIESLING		
Schloss Vollrads QbA RHEINGAU, GERMANY 14		38.95
SAUVIGNON BLANC		
Nobilo, MARLBOROUGH, NEW ZEALAND 14	8.95	33.95
Cottat Vieilles Vignes SANCERRE, FRANCE 14		39.95
GEWÜRZTRAMINER		
Hugel ALSACE, FRANCE 10		38.95
MERITAGE		
Conundrum, CALIFORNIA 13	12.95	59.95
SPARKLING		
Chandon Fresco Brut CALIFORNIA NV	10.95	
Scharffenberger Brut MENDOCINO COUNTY NV		39.95
Moët & Chandon White Star CHAMPAGNE, FRANCE NV		59.95
Bollinger Special Cuvée CHAMPAGNE, FRANCE NV		74.95

RED WINES

	glass	bottle
MERLOT		
Oxford Landing SOUTH AUSTRALIA 14	7.50	28.50
Angeline NAPA VALLEY 14	11.50	43.95
Desert Wind WAHLUKE SLOPE 11		36.50
Wild Horse CENTRAL COAST 13		33.95
L'Ecole Nº 41 COLUMBIA VALLEY 11		49.95
CABERNET SAUVIGNON		
SledgeHammer CALIFORNIA 13	9.95	37.95
Amavi Cellars WALLA WALLA VALLEY 11		48.95
Mount Veeder NAPA VALLEY 12		52.95
Donedei COLUMBIA VALLEY 10		64.95
ZINFANDEL		
Temptation CALIFORNIA 12	8.95	33.95
Seghesio SONOMA COUNTY 14		49.95
RED		
Marietta Christo Lot #2 CALIFORNIA		39.95
SANGUINETI MAESTRO TUSCANY, ITALY 13		38.95
Château Lyonnat LUSSAC ST-ÉMILION, FRANCE 10		47.95
MALBEC		
DiSeño MENDOZA, ARGENTINA 14	8.50	31.95
Achaval Ferrer MENDOZA, ARGENTINA 13		49.95
TEMPRANILLO		
Ramón Bilbao RIOJA, SPAIN 11	9.95	37.95
SHIRAZ/SYRAH		
Yalumba Y Series SOUTH AUSTRALIA 13	8.95	33.95
Langmeil Hangin' Snakes AUSTRALIA 12		40.95
Charles Smith Boom Boom COLUMBIA VALLEY 13		36.95
GRENACHE/SYRAH		
Owen Roe Sinister Hand YAKIMA VALLEY 14		49.95
PINOT NOIR		
Montpellier CALIFORNIA 13	7.50	28.50
ERATH OREGON 14	10.95	41.95
Villa Mt. Eden Bien Nacido SANTA MARIA VALLEY 09		37.95
Chehalem Three Vineyard WILLAMETTE VALLEY 12		54.95
Goldeneye ANDERSON VALLEY 12		69.95

DINNER MENU

MARCH 3RD - 16TH

AROUND TOWN

IDITAROD
4th Avenue / March 5th

RUNNING OF THE REINDEER
4th Avenue / March 5th

2016 FUR RENDEZVOUS
City-wide / February 26th - March 6th

ANCHORAGE SYMPHONY'S "PARADE & PROCESSION"
ACPA / March 5th

ANCHORAGE SYMPHONY ORCHESTRA
Family Concert
ACPA / March 6th

DAVID SANBORN
ACPA / March 12th

GROWLER TUESDAY

64 oz. of Pure Pleasure!
These crazy prices are only available on Tuesdays and do not include Growler Glass fee of $5.00

6.00 GROWLERS FOR OUR CRAFT BEERS

11.00 GROWLERS FOR OUR HIGH GRAVITY BEERS

NEW - LIMITED SPECIAL RELEASE GROWLER STYLE AND PRICE VARY WEEKLY

GLUTEN FREE & VEGETARIAN MENUS NOW AVAILABLE

Twitter

GBrewHouseAK

907 274-BREW (2739)

737 WEST 5TH AVENUE, ANCHORAGE AK 99501

www.GlacierBrewHouse.com

GENERAL MANAGER *Will Warren*

EXECUTIVE CHEF *Jolene Langreck*

COCKTAILS

CLASSIC FAVORITES

THE HONEST MARTINI
SVEDKA vodka or Tanqueray gin, olives. 9.95

LONG ISLAND ICED TEA
Our classic Long Island, with rum, vodka, gin, tequila, triple sec, fresh lemon sour, cola. 9.95

DARK & STORMY
The Kraken Black Spiced rum, lime, housemade ginger beer. 9.95

MAKER'S MARK OLD FASHIONED
Maker's Mark, Fee Brothers Indian Orange bitters, orange, cherry, sugar, soda splash. 9.95

BLOODY MARY
SVEDKA vodka, housemade Mary mix, BREWHOUSE Blonde Ale, pickled green bean & red cherry pepper. 9.50

CLASSIC MOJITO
Cruzan White rum, fresh mint, soda. 9.50

BARREL AGED DOUBLE RYE MANHATTAN
House aged for three months in American oak barrels. High West Double Rye whiskey from Park City, Utah, Vya sweet vermouth & Fee Brothers Whiskey Barrel-Aged bitters. 11.95

MARGARITAS
Served with Lunazul Blanco tequila, fresh sweet-&-sour and a splash of BREWHOUSE Blonde.
- **ORIGINAL** 9.95
- **ORANGE-POMEGRANATE** 10.95
- **THREE AMIGOS** Lunazul Blanco tequila, Jim Beam Black bourbon, New Amsterdam gin. 10.50

MULES

MOSCOW MULE
SVEDKA vodka, ginger liqueur, lime sour, housemade ginger beer. 9.95

PEACH MULE
SVEDKA Peach vodka, ginger liqueur, lime sour, white peach puree, housemade ginger beer. 9.95

MANGO PINEAPPLE MULE
SVEDKA Mango Pineapple vodka, ginger liqueur, lime sour, housemade ginger beer. 9.95

BREWHOUSE SPECIALTIES

SNOW COSMO
Absolut Kurant vodka, white cranberry juice, lime sour. 9.95

LEMON DROP
Svedka Citrus vodka, fresh lemon sour. 9.95

MAI TAI
Cruzan rum, tropical juices, orange curacao & a healthy float of The Kraken Black Spiced rum. 9.95

WHISKEY SOUR
Maker's Mark bourbon, lemon sour, fresh lime, fresh orange. 9.95

SWEET TEA
Sweet Tea vodka, fresh mint & fresh lemon sour. 9.95

ELDERFLOWER PIMM'S FIZZ
Pimm's liqueur, St-Germain, fresh lemon sour, soda. 9.50

SANGRIA
Red wine, blackberry brandy, triple sec, fresh orange & lime, splash of soda. 8.95

CLASSIC COSMO
Svedka Citrus, triple sec, fresh lemon-lime sour, cranberry. 9.95

SAKE-TINI
Pineapple ginger infused sake, gin, lemon sour. 9.50

FIGURE 3.6
This menu provides a great example of some of the many headings a menu planner can employ.
Reprinted with permission of Glacier BrewHouse.

customers to choose the specific components from a larger selection of meats and cheeses, work well in certain operations, like wine bars or microbreweries. Whether this movement evolves into a broader trend or stays boutique remains to be seen; however, it is not inappropriate to list cheese and/or charcuterie as a separate heading on a menu.

Beverages

Establishments with numerous beverage offerings often locate their alcoholic drinks on a separate menu. However, those with few or no alcoholic options tend to list their beverages in a section of the main menu. The heading may be entitled "Beverages" or "Drinks." Even those restaurants with extensive lists may opt to include their wines by the glass on the main menu or to pair certain drink choices with each entrée. Pairing a beverage with each dish encourages those who may be intimidated by wine or beer lists to order an alcoholic beverage. By-the-glass listings also encourage sales to those parties who cannot consume a full bottle of wine in a single sitting. If an operation specializes in certain cocktails, those should be included on the main menu (or at least on a table tent) to help increase beverage sales. A menu is only effective as a marketing tool if it lists the products management wishes to sell.

For those operations that do not serve alcohol, a beverage heading on the main menu is essential. It should include a selection of cold and hot beverages, including juices, coffee, hot tea, iced tea, sodas, still and sparkling waters, milk, and any specialty drink creations. Just because a restaurant does not serve alcohol does not mean that its beverage selection must be boring. A nonalcoholic spritzer made from cranberry juice and sparkling water, mango lassi, watermelon agua fresca, or even a simple raspberry iced tea can convert a basic beverage list to one that generates buzz in the community. In the case of homemade purees or fruit juices, a house beverage can even be an outlet for product utilization purposes.

While all of these menu sections are popular, it is important to emphasize that the heading names and menu items listed must support and make sense with the company's brand. A restaurant catering to a quick-dining clientele may list only "Appetizers," "Entrées," and "Desserts," while an upscale, leisurely paced restaurant might have a far more expansive number of headings. A prix fixe or table d'hôte menu might ignore all of the traditional headings and instead write "First Course," "Second Course," etc. or dispense with the labels entirely and simply separate the courses with asterisks or other visual dividers. When headings support the brand and the market's needs, guests have an easier time navigating the menu and a better dining experience overall.

Summary

The headings and menu items appropriate for a menu depend both on the business's concept and on the style of pricing. A menu may use à la carte, semi à la carte, table d'hôte, or prix fixe pricing. Numbers of headings and menu items listed impact both the quantity of courses most guests will order and the length of time it takes for customers to read through the menu. Balance and variety, both on the plate and across the menu, are critical elements to creating an interesting menu that will attract and retain customers. Variety and balance are applicable to ingredients, flavor, cooking technique, temperature, texture, color, shape, size, composition, and plate presentation, though certain variables may be limited by the available kitchen equipment and desired work flow. While there are no absolutes when it comes to naming menu sections, there are certain headings that are more commonly used in the industry.

Breakfast menus often include beverages, à la carte items or sides, and entrées, which may be subdivided into eggs, omelets, griddle items, cereals, and house specialties. Lunch and dinner menus typically use similar terminology for both meal periods, though soups, salads, and sandwiches are often bigger sellers at lunch than they are at dinner. These menus may include some or all of the headings: appetizers, soups, salads, sandwiches, entrées, and sides or accompaniments. Desserts, cheeses, and beverages may appear on the main menu, on a separate menu, or, in the case of cheeses, not at all. Depending on the business concept, entrées may be categorized by cooking technique or by main ingredient. Alternatively, a menu planner may choose to name the headings numerically as in "First Course," "Second Course," etc. Whatever terminology is used, it must support the business's brand and concept.

Comprehension Questions

1. What are the four approaches to menu pricing described in this chapter that impact menu headings?

2. For what variables are variety and balance most relevant?

3. Under what circumstances might a business use the same ingredient (other than basic pantry staples) in multiple dishes? (List two possibilities.)

4. List three headings into which breakfast entrées might be subdivided.

5. List five common headings used for a lunch or dinner menu.

6. How do menu headings differ from a breakfast menu to a lunch menu?

7. How does a menu impact work flow in the kitchen? What can a menu planner do to prevent kitchen bottlenecks?

8. List two examples of ways in which a menu planner can control food cost through product utilization (i.e., use of scraps other than throwing them in the trash).

Discussion Questions

1. List some menu headings you have seen in a restaurant that are not among the traditional headings listed in the chapter.

2. Describe a restaurant (or other foodservice business) experience you have had in which the menu was not effective in your opinion. What aspect of the menu made it an unpleasant experience for you?

3. When dining out in a casual restaurant, how many menu items do you consider ideal to see under each heading? How would the number differ if you were dining at an upscale restaurant?

4. If you were to open your own restaurant, what pricing style would you prefer to utilize? Why?

5. Name three entrées that might generate scraps or leftovers through their production. Name the ingredients that would be left over and create a menu item (not an entrée) that could utilize those leftovers.

6. Describe in detail an original entrée of your creation. Make sure that it incorporates the concepts of variety and balance on the plate. Describe all of the ways in which the dish exhibits variety and balance.

Case Study

Imagine a chicken-themed restaurant (semi à la carte) where every single dish includes chicken in large portions. The menu headings are Appetizers, Soups, Entrée Salads, Sandwiches, and Entrées. There are no desserts, and the beverages, not listed on the menu, are not made from chicken (thankfully!). The menu includes about forty menu items.

The manager notices that there is significant loss in inventory spoilage and that the average check is slightly less than the cost of the average entrée. Wanting to reduce costs and increase revenue, the manager tasks you, the menu planner, with proposing changes to the menu. Given only the information you have, what changes would you make to the menu?

Capstone Project

Step 3: Building on the previous steps, write menu headings appropriate for your business concept. Describe the business's pricing approach as well. Create menu items for each heading on the main menu; you will work on additional food menus/headings (dessert menu, kids menu, etc.) in the next chapter.

Menu Styles and Headings II—
Beyond the Basics

INTRODUCTION

While restaurant breakfast, lunch, and dinner menus may be what most people think of when they hear the term "menu," menus span a much broader range of styles. All menus provide a listing of food available for service, but menus differ based on the market they serve and the type of dining experience they describe. Some menus, such as brunch or high tea menus, are designed for specific meal periods beyond the traditional three. Some cater to a narrowly focused market, such as children's menus or room service menus. A special occasion banquet menu may be used only for a single event and provide limited choices, if any. Ethnic or tasting menus are utilized by certain restaurants, but they do not necessarily follow the conventions of traditional restaurant menus. In short, the range of menus goes way beyond the traditional breakfast, lunch, and dinner versions.

It is important for a menu planner to understand the differences and nuances of each kind of menu. Although the menu planner for a business is often the chef or manager of that one business, a single company is sometimes called upon to create specialized menus for specific occasions. For example, a chef in a restaurant might create the main lunch and dinner menu, but if the restaurant owner wants to periodically provide catering or host special events in the restaurant for large groups, the chef must design menus for those purposes as well. Simply providing the standard dinner menu for a group of one hundred that has bought out the restaurant is a recipe for disaster. Hotels are classic examples of businesses that must offer various types of menus. A single hotel kitchen might service an upscale restaurant for three meals a day with brunch on Sundays, the hotel banquet halls, room service, afternoon tea, and a late-night lounge. The better a menu planner understands how these types of menus differ, the better shot she has of meeting the needs of both the guests and the business.

CHAPTER 4 LEARNING OBJECTIVES

As a result of successfully completing this chapter, readers will be able to:

1. Describe the characteristics of various menu types, including take-out, room service, cycle, noncommercial, banquet or special occasion, catering, brunch, ethnic, tasting, children's, lounge, high tea, and dessert menus.

2. Create a set of food items and headings for any of the aforementioned menu types that addresses the needs of both the customer and the business.

CHAPTER 4 OUTLINE

Similarities across Menus

Types of Menus
    Take-Out Menus
    Room Service Menus
    Cycle Menus and Noncommercial Businesses
    Banquet and Special Occasion Menus

Tasting Menus
Catering Menus
Ethnic Menus
Fusion and Small Plates Menus
Brunch Menus
Afternoon Tea Menus

Similarities across Menus

The complete range of menu types varies greatly, but there are some commonalities among all of them. All menus must cater to the needs and eating habits of the market or client. Sometimes the client is an individual who determines the menu for a larger crowd, as for a wedding or business meeting, but even then the menu planner should guide the client to select foods likely to appeal to the audience.

The rules of variety and balance play a role in all forms of menus, not just restaurant menus. For example, a banquet menu should vary the ingredients and cooking technique used for each course (unless, of course, the meal is sponsored by a food-related association like a beef council or a grill manufacturer). Nutrition plays a role as well, though it may be less of a focus for a single, special occasion event.

The naming conventions for menu headings may or may not resemble those of a traditional restaurant menu. For example, a catering menu may list options for appetizers and entrées, but it may also include headings such as "hors d'oeuvres" or business meeting "refreshments," as these types of services are common in a catering environment.

Types of Menus

Learning Objective 1

Describe the characteristics of various menu types, including take-out, room service, cycle, noncommercial, banquet or special occasion, catering, brunch, ethnic, tasting, children's, lounge, high tea, and dessert menus.

Learning Objective 2

Create a set of food items and headings for any of the aforementioned menu types that addresses the needs of both the customer and the business.

A discussion of a number of menu types and their unique concerns and characteristics follows.

Take-Out Menus

A take-out menu is a list of food products that may be ordered from a foodservice establishment, often a restaurant, for consumption off the premises. Some types of businesses, such as Chinese restaurants or pizza places, offer all of their food to go. Others do not offer take-out at all. The biggest concern with take-out foods is that there is no telling how long it will be before the customer consumes the food. Thus, anything offered on a take-out menu should hold up well over long periods of time with minimal quality loss. As many consumers will store the leftovers and reheat hot foods later, take-out menus should include foods that store and reheat well, too. Pulled pork barbecue with rolls on the side might be a good choice for take-out; poached eggs with hollandaise sauce would not.

Portability is another concern. Because customers (or delivery people) carry take-out food from the restaurant to another location, the food could easily be destroyed when jostled in a bag. A delicate plate presentation that collapses with the slightest movement is a poor choice for a take-out menu. Sandwiches work well as they can be eaten on the run. Plated foods are perfectly acceptable as long as they will remain attractive with some minor movement. Packaging helps to keep the food looking edible. Covered containers, sometimes with raised dividers for different components of the plate, can keep a dish from turning into a single, amorphous blob. Dishes that are designed to be a uniform mixture, such as stir-fries or tossed salads, work well as they eliminate the need for divided containers.

While some restaurants simply use their full restaurant menu for their take-out menu, there is no requirement to do so, though the menu headings typically match. A take-out menu should include only those choices that will represent the business well when taken off-site. A disappointed customer is less likely to return, even if the flaws in the food result from the purchaser's treatment of it. Take-out menus should be available both on paper and online so that customers can take the menus with them or look the menu up on a business's Web page. Many take-out operations today allow for customers to place orders not only by phone or in person but also electronically through a Web page or smart phone application. Some restaurants contract with a third-party business to receive orders and deliver them to customers; in those cases, the third party may post the restaurant's menu on its own Web page. Take-out menus are typically found in casual and fast-food restaurants, carryout-only businesses, and certain corporate foodservice operations.

Room Service Menus

The concerns with room service menus are similar to those for take-out menus. While a room service menu need not account for guests reheating the food, the food does need to be transportable and must hold its quality for at least twenty minutes. In a large hotel, the walk alone from the kitchen to a distant room could easily take ten minutes. The plate presentations cannot be too high, as most hotels use plate covers to help protect the food in transport. The presentations should not be too delicate, either, as even a highly trained waiter may bump into a careless hotel guest en route. The food should be palatable even if it is not piping hot or ice cold as room service food slowly inches toward room temperature on the walk from the kitchen. A beautiful risotto might gel into a single, solid mass by the time it reaches the guest. A warm apple pie a la mode might become pie with cream sauce after a ten-minute walk. There are ways to address these concerns, such as delivering the apple pie and ice cream separately, but the transportation issues must be considered as part of the menu development process.

When a hotel operates a full-service restaurant, the room service menu is typically not a duplication of the restaurant menu. It tends to be limited to just a few popular items in each category that change with the time of day. That said, a room service menu should include beverages, appetizers, salads, entrées, and desserts, except for the breakfast menu, which follows a traditional breakfast format. Room service menus should plan for guests of all ages, especially children, who may not want the normal adult fare. Hotel guests sometimes want food late at night, long after the restaurant has closed. Menu planners may wish to adjust the menu to offer only a few late-night snacks (wings, burgers, salads—lounge food) after a certain hour to eliminate the need for a large overnight kitchen staff. In such cases, the menu should include a menu heading like "Late Night," or something similar, for those items. Other hotels simply cut off room service after a certain hour.

Room service for breakfast is common in many hotels. Breakfast menu items should come under the broad heading "Breakfast" with standard breakfast menu headings below. (All other menu items may be listed under the broad heading "Lunch," "Dinner," or "All Day" with further heading subdivisions below.) When breakfast room service is offered, guests should have the ability to place the order the night before for a given arrival time in the morning. While evening room service customers are more likely to be guests who arrived late or just want privacy over a meal, users of room service for breakfast may be in a hurry in the morning. Placing the order the night before allows the guest to focus on getting ready for her day instead of wondering how long it will take for the kitchen to complete her order. Advance ordering also allows the kitchen to be more efficient in its planning. Breakfast room service menus should offer a range of juices and cold items (pastries, breads, cereals, etc.) with a few quick-service hot options so that delays due to cooking time are minimal.

Cycle Menus and Noncommercial Businesses

A cycle menu is one that rotates a series of menu items over a period of time. It could be as simple as serving spaghetti every Monday and meatloaf every Tuesday or as complex as creating a thirty-day cycle that repeats the more popular dishes within the same month but leaves others to return only once the cycle restarts. Cycle menus are common for captive audiences in such places as schools, corporate cafeterias, and hospitals, but they can also be used to rotate the specials in a restaurant. For example, a restaurant might decide to cycle its soup du jour, so that every Friday is clam chowder, every Saturday is beef barley, and so on.

Cycle menus help to balance the business's need for efficiency with the customer's need for variety. The most efficient foodservice operation would offer the same one dish every day. That way, the business could minimize inventory, staff, equipment, and training. Unfortunately, few people would come to such a restaurant, and for a captive audience, the monotony would be unappetizing and unhealthy. A captive market, such as college students, might want a new dish every day of the semester, but that would require a huge investment in inventory, training, and recipe development. A cycle allows for some balance between these two opposing needs.

BREAKFAST

Available 24 hours

Fruit and Fruit Juices

Freshly Squeezed Orange Juice   Small ....$3.95   Large $4.95

Apple, Cranberry, Grapefruit, Pineapple, Tomato or V8 Juices

Small.........$3.95   Large.........$4.95

Fresh Seasonal Sliced Ripe Melon $5.50

Stewed California Prunes..$4.75

Fresh Berries in Season $6.50

Sliced Bananas with Brown Sugar and Cream...................................$4.50

Seasonal Diced Melons, Fruits and Berries $6.50

Natural or Fruited Yogurt $4.95

Hot and Cold Cereals

Old Fashioned Oatmeal $6.50
Brown Sugar, Golden Raisins and Milk or Cream

Cream of Wheat with Maple Syrup and Milk or Cream $5.95

Selected Cereals $5.50
Corn Flakes, Rice Krispies, Raisin Bran, Granola, Special K or Frosted Flakes
With Bananas or Seasonal Berries...$6.50

Continental Breakfast

Choice of Chilled Juice, Breakfast Pastry, Sweet Butter and
Fruit Preserves, Coffee (Regular or Decaffeinated), Tea or Milk $10.95

Orders may be placed by dialing 88438. $5.00 minimum order. $2.00 In Room Dining charge, 18% gratuity and tax will be added.

FIGURE 4.1
This portion of a much larger room service menu illustrates the many menu item possibilities for in-room dining at a luxury hotel. Additional pages not shown include dinner, desserts, in-room hospitalities, and beverages.

Source: Peppermill Resort Spa Casino, Reno. Reprinted with permission.

BREAKFAST

The Peppermill Breakfast

Choice of Chilled Juice, Two Extra Large Eggs any style, Hickory Smoked Bacon,
Link Sausage or Grilled Ham Steak, Breakfast Potatoes,
Toast, Biscuits or Muffin, Sweet Butter and Preserves and
Coffee (Regular or Decaffeinated), Tea or Milk.................................. $17.50

Specialty Breakfasts

All Eggs and Omelettes are served with Breakfast Potatoes, choice of Toast, Bagel,
Biscuit or English Muffin with Sweet Butter and Fruit Preserves

Egg Beaters or Egg Whites available upon request

Two Extra Large Eggs any style $12.95
Choice of Hickory Smoked Bacon, Link Sausage, Grilled Ham Steak,
Canadian Bacon or Sliced Vine-Ripened Tomatoes

Classic Eggs Benedict $12.95
Twin Poached Eggs on Toasted English Muffin with
Canadian Bacon and Hollandaise Sauce
With Crabmeat... $15.95

Joe's San Francisco Special $12.95
Freshly Scrambled Eggs combined with Spinach, Ground Beef,
Sausage, Mushrooms and Onions, topped with Cheddar Cheese

Three Egg Omelette... $12.95
Select any combination of the following:
Bacon, Green Chiles, Spinach, Smoked Salmon, Mushrooms, Tomatoes, Ham, Bell
Peppers, Cheddar Cheese, Sausage, Onions, Jack Cheese

Corned Beef Hash.. $12.95
With Two Extra Large Eggs any style

Smoked Pork Chops and Eggs... $13.95
Served with Biscuits and Country Gravy

Breakfast New York Steak and Eggs $19.95
8 oz. Steak grilled to order

FIGURE 4.1   *(Continued)*

BREAKFAST

Chilled Smoked Pacific Northwest Salmon.....................................$15.95
Served with Red Onions, Capers, Sliced Egg and Bagel with Cream Cheese

From the Griddle
Selections served with Warm Maple Syrup and Sweet Butter

Crisp Belgian Waffle (5am to Noon)..$9.50
      With Seasonal Fresh Berries and Whipped Cream $11.50

Buttermilk Pancakes
Short Stack...$8.50
Full Stack...$9.50
Plain, Blueberry, Banana or Chocolate Chip

Cinnamon French Toast $9.50
Prepared with Banana Bread or Cinnamon Swirl

From Our Bakery
Selections served with Fruit Preserves and Sweet Butter

Freshly Baked Croissant...$4.95

Blueberry, Bran or Seasonal Fruit Muffin $4.95

Danish Pastry $5.50

Country Biscuits..$4.95

Toasted Bagel with Cream Cheese..$5.50

Toast...$3.50
Choice of White, Whole Wheat, Rye, Sourdough or English Muffin

Doughnuts
Each $1.50
Half Dozen..$8.75
Dozen $17.00

Orders may be placed by dialing 88438. $5.00 minimum order. $2.00 In Room Dining charge, 18% gratuity and tax will be added.

FIGURE 4.1   *(Continued)*

BREAKFAST

Side Orders

One Egg any style $2.95

Two Eggs any style $4.95

Egg Beaters $4.95

Hickory Smoked Ham, Link Sausage, Canadian Bacon
or Grilled Ham Steak $5.95

Breakfast Potatoes. $4.50

Corned Beef Hash $7.50

Sliced Vine-Ripened Tomatoes. $3.95

Biscuits and Country Gravy $7.95

ALL DAY DINING

Available 24 hours

Appetizers and Soups

Breaded Mozzarella with Marinara Sauce $9.95

Chilled Gulf Shrimp or Crabmeat Cocktail. $16.50
Zesty Cocktail Sauce, Wasabi Mayonnaise and Lemon

Crispy Fried Chicken Tenders $11.50
Served with Honey-Mustard or Barbeque Dipping Sauce

Asian Trio $11.50
Vegetable Spring Rolls, Chicken Potstickers and Steamed
Pork Dumplings with Ginger-Soy Dipping Sauce

Grilled Chicken Quesadilla. $11.25
Served with Pico de Gallo, Sour Cream and Guacamole

Spicy Buffalo-Style Chicken Wings. $10.95
Hot Wings served with Celery Sticks and Blue Cheese Dressing

Baked French Onion Soup. $7.50
With Sourdough Croutons, Swiss and Parmesan Cheese Gratinee

Freshly Prepared Soup of the Day. $6.50
Our Chef's finest served 11 a.m. – Midnight

Salads

Dressings include Blue Cheese, Thousand Island, Caesar, Ranch,
Honey-Mustard and Herb Vinaigrette

Peppermill Garden Salad $6.95
Crisp Seasonal Baby Greens with Tomatoes, Cucumbers,
Radishes, Carrots and Choice of Dressing

Cobb Salad. $14.95
Freshly Roasted Turkey Breast, Smoked Bacon, Avocado, Eggs,
Blue Cheese and Black Olives on Seasonal Greens

Orders may be placed by dialing 88438. $5.00 minimum order. $2.00 In Room Dining charge, 18% gratuity and tax will be added.

FIGURE 4.1 *(Continued)*

ALL DAY DINING

Available 24 hours

Fresh Fruit Fantasy $16.95
An array of seasonal sliced fresh Fruits and Berries, served with
Banana Bread, Honey-Yogurt Dressing and Cottage Cheese

Caesar Salad   Small. $8.95
                     Large. $11.95
Torn Hearts of Romaine tossed with Sourdough Croutons,
Parmesan Cheese and Caesar Dressing
         With Grilled Breast of Chicken. $13.95
         With Grilled Shrimp. $16.95

Seafood Mélange $17.95
Shrimp and Crabmeat tossed with Seasonal Greens, Tomatoes,
Avocado and Sliced Egg; choice of Louis Dressing or Herb Vinaigrette

Sandwich Selections

Served with choice of French Fries, Potato Salad or Cottage Cheese

California Clubhouse $12.50
Roasted Turkey, Hickory Smoked Bacon, Lettuce and Vine-Ripened Tomatoes

Traditional Hamburger $11.95
Half Pound Certified Angus Beef® Patty cooked to your order with
Vine-Ripened Tomatoes, Lettuce, Onions, Thousand Island Dressing and Pickle
Choice of Cheddar, Swiss, American or Blue Cheese . . . . add $1.00

Classic Grilled Reuben. $12.50
Thinly sliced Corned Beef piled high on grilled Rye with
Sauerkraut, Swiss Cheese and Russian Dressing

Deli-Style Sandwich. $11.95
Served with Vine-Ripened Tomatoes, Lettuce and Pickle
Choose from the following:

Pepperoni	Roast Beef	Cheddar Cheese
Smoked Ham	Roast Turkey	Swiss Cheese
Corned Beef	Tuna Salad	Jack Cheese

FIGURE 4.1   *(Continued)*

ALL DAY DINING

Available 24 hours

French Dip $12.95
Thinly sliced Roasted Beef served on French Roll with Beef Jus

New York Steak Sandwich $17.95
Served on Crisp Baguette with Sautéed Onions and Peppers

Traditional Grilled Cheese $10.50
Your choice of American, Cheddar, or Swiss Cheese on
Grilled White, Whole Wheat, Sourdough or Rye Bread

Patty Melt $12.95
Ground Beef Patty with American and Swiss Cheeses, Sautéed Onions and
Thousand Island Dressing on Grilled Rye

Grilled Chicken Sandwich $11.95
Marinated Grilled Chicken Breast with spicy BBQ Sauce,
Jack Cheese, Lettuce and Tomatoes

Grilled Veggie Sandwich $11.95
Grilled Mushrooms, Onions and Peppers, Avocado, Tomatoes,
Cucumbers, Lettuce, Jack and Cheddar Cheeses with Basil Pesto Mayonnaise

Orders may be placed by dialing 88438. $5.00 minimum order. $2.00 In Room Dining charge, 18% gratuity and tax will be added.

FIGURE 4.1 *(Continued)*

ALL DAY SPECIALTIES

Available 24 hours

Southern Fried Chicken $16.95
Served with French Fries, Biscuits and Honey

Penne Pasta with Steamed Vegetables. $15.95
Tossed with Fresh Basil, Tomatoes, Garlic and Olive Oil

16" Pizza. $19.50
We make our pizza dough and sauce fresh for authentic "pizzeria-style" flavor.
Please allow extra cooking time for your made-to-order pizza creation!
Choice of toppings:

Bell Pepper	Mushrooms	Italian Sausage
Onions	Tomatoes	Pepperoni
Black Olives	Ground Beef	Canadian Bacon

Grilled Pesto Chicken. $18.95
Pesto Marinated Grilled Chicken Breast served with
French Fries or Baked Potato and Fresh Vegetable

Golden Fried Shrimp $21.95
Served with French Fries, Cocktail Sauce and Lemon

T-Bone Steak (16 oz.) $32.95
Choice of French Fries or Baked Potato and Fresh Vegetable

FIGURE 4.1 *(Continued)*

How frequently the cycle repeats depends on the level of audience captivity and their length of stay. For example, a hospital has a highly captive audience but few of its patients may stay for more than a week. Such a hospital could easily operate a one-week cycle menu for its patients. A corporate cafeteria, on the other hand, will likely need a longer cycle with more frequent repetition of the most popular items. The businesspeople whom the cafeteria serves have some ability to leave the office to eat elsewhere if they get bored by the menu, but if served well by the cafeteria, many of them will remain frequent cafeteria patrons for the length of their employment.

In creating a cycle menu, the menu planner must account for all portions of the meal—the appetizers, entrées, sides, beverages, and desserts. In some cases, like a college cafeteria, all of the courses may be offered with multiple choices for each course; in others, like an elementary school cafeteria, only one course with limited choices may be offered. Either way, nutrition and general popularity are critical. When a captive audience usually or always eats from a single food provider, their physical health depends heavily on the food-service company. The food should provide a balance of nutrients both within a meal and across the entire cycle. However, the consumer gains no nutrition if she does not eat the food. Thus, the food must appeal greatly to the audience. Offering options may satisfy the customers' taste buds, but if only one selection is nutritious, the menu planner fails in her responsibility to serve the customers' nutritional needs.

A cycle menu should also account for product utilization. In fact, a rotating soup, omelet, quiche, or stir-fry of the day may allow the chef an outlet to use up leftovers on a schedule. If she knows that there is a set of ingredients or byproducts that build up over the week (bell pepper tops or turkey scraps, for example), the chef can plan to use them up via the cycle menu (possibly through a once-a-week bell pepper soup or turkey hash).

Cycle menus may or may not be printed for the guests to see. In a cafeteria setting, the customers may only learn the menu when they see the food on display, even though the kitchen staff has a copy of the menu behind the scenes for its own planning needs. Promoting the cycle to the target market is a much better option that keeps the customer base happy. If a scheduled meal is unappealing to a regular customer, it is better for that patron to know in advance and to plan an alternative than to suffer through an undesirable meal. When the choices in the cycle are all fairly popular, the printed menu can be a draw to attract business. For noncommercial operations, the cycle menu may be posted in print or listed electronically on a Web page. For commercial restaurants, the cycle rotation may be printed on the restaurant menu itself. For example, a restaurant that constantly advertises Wednesdays as prime rib night may attract a bigger crowd than it would by having servers wait until Wednesday to notify guests of the special. The cycle menu is not only a control and planning tool for the business but also a marketing tool to attract and keep loyal customers.

It should be noted that while cycle menus are quite popular in noncommercial operations, a noncommercial kitchen need not always resort to a cycle menu system. (A *noncommercial* foodservice business is one that services another organization whose mission is not food, such as a hospital, school, or museum.) The chef could vary the menu daily to take advantage of seasonal ingredients. Alternatively, the menu might be expansive but unchanging. For example, a corporate cafeteria that contains several stations including a large salad bar, a pizza station, a barbecue and grill station, and a sandwich station may offer enough variety on the menu that customers do not find it monotonous to eat there regularly. Such an approach works well for a large operation that services hundreds of guests daily, like a museum. When such a comprehensive menu is not feasible, a cycle menu usually offers the best approach.

Banquet and Special Occasion Menus

Normally defined simply as a "feast," a banquet is a culinary event that provides a sequence of courses, usually with little to no choice for the individual diner, though the courses could be served buffet style. The menu itself is typically determined by just one or two people—the actual client—in conjunction with the chef or a salesperson from the foodservice business. Banquets are often performed only for special, one-time events, such as a wedding or a business meeting, though the same menu could be repeated for a completely different audience. Consequently, nutrition is less of a concern unless it is expressed as a consideration for the group by the client.

Banquets follow a classic meal sequence, dependent somewhat on the number of courses being planned. A three-course banquet would usually offer an appetizer, entrée, and dessert, but the appetizer could be a soup, salad, or some more complex creation. The entrée could highlight any number of ingredients. A lengthier banquet menu might begin with a soup, progress to an appetizer, then a salad, then an intermezzo before finally arriving at the entrée. In this longer version, the appetizer is traditionally a seafood course while the entrée is meat-based. Of course, there are many variations to this traditional pattern. Europeans may prefer the salad after the main course. Vegetarians, obviously, would require that meat and seafood not play a role in any of these courses. A cheese course may follow the entrée, but cheese might have been part of a stand-up cocktail hour that preceded the sit-down meal. Dessert usually concludes the meal, possibly with a second treat of mignardise (bite-size sweets, such as chocolates, petit fours, or cookies) following a plated dessert.

A banquet of many courses can become tiresome to the palate and the stomach if the menu planner does not plan appropriately. To avoid palate fatigue, the menu planner should alternate light and heavy courses with an overall trend toward richer courses through the entrée.

Cycle 1 — Cont. Breakfast

	Sunday	Monday	Tuesday	Wednesday	Thursday	Friday	Saturday
Cereal	Whole-Grain Irish Oatmeal Irish Oatmeal Bar	Whole-Grain Irish Oatmeal Irish Oatmeal Bar	Whole-Grain Irish Oatmeal Irish Oatmeal Bar	Whole-Grain Irish Oatmeal Irish Oatmeal Bar	Whole-Grain Irish Oatmeal Irish Oatmeal Bar	Whole-Grain Irish Oatmeal Irish Oatmeal Bar	Whole-Grain Irish Oatmeal Irish Oatmeal Bar
Waffles	Waffles Vegan Waffles Waffle Bar Fixins'	Waffles Vegan Waffles Waffle Bar Fixins'	Waffles Vegan Waffles Waffle Bar Fixins'	Waffles Vegan Waffles Waffle Bar Fixins'	Waffles Vegan Waffles Waffle Bar Fixins'	Waffles Vegan Waffles Waffle Bar Fixins'	Waffles Vegan Waffles Waffle Bar Fixins'
Eggs	Cage-Free Hard-Cooked Eggs	Cage-Free Hard-Cooked Eggs	Cage-Free Hard-Cooked Eggs	Cage-Free Hard-Cooked Eggs	Cage-Free Hard-Cooked Eggs	Cage-Free Hard-Cooked Eggs	Cage-Free Hard-Cooked Eggs
Pars			Yale Bakery Granola		Yale Bakery Granola		
Fruit	Assorted Fresh Fruit Fresh Sliced Breakfast Fruit Tangelo Halves	Assorted Fresh Fruit Fresh Sliced Breakfast Fruit Rio Red Grapefruit Halves	Assorted Fresh Fruit Fresh Sliced Breakfast Fruit Cara Cara Orange Halves	Assorted Fresh Fruit Fresh Sliced Breakfast Fruit Rio Red Grapefruit Halves	Assorted Fresh Fruit Fresh Sliced Breakfast Fruit Tangelo Halves	Assorted Fresh Fruit Fresh Sliced Breakfast Fruit Rio Red Grapefruit Halves	Assorted Fresh Fruit Fresh Sliced Breakfast Fruit Cara Cara Orange Halves
Morning Sweet	Cinnamon Streusel Coffee Cake	Blueberry Oat Tea Bread	Yale & Hearty Chocolate-Chocolate Chip Muffins	Maple Pecan Buns	Vanilla Sugar Scones	Banana Nut Muffins	Orange Cranberry Tea Bread

Cycle 1 — Hot Breakfast

	Sunday	Monday	Tuesday	Wednesday	Thursday	Friday	Saturday
Cereal		Whole-Grain Irish Oatmeal Irish Oatmeal Bar Cream of Wheat	Whole-Grain Irish Oatmeal Irish Oatmeal Bar	Whole-Grain Irish Oatmeal Irish Oatmeal Bar Creamy Grits	Whole-Grain Irish Oatmeal Irish Oatmeal Bar	Whole-Grain Irish Oatmeal Irish Oatmeal Bar Cream of Wheat	
Eggs		Cage-Free Hard-Cooked Eggs Cage-Free Scrambled Eggs	Cage-Free Hard-Cooked Eggs Cage-Free Scrambled Eggs	Cage-Free Hard-Cooked Eggs Cage-Free Scrambled Eggs	Cage-Free Hard-Cooked Eggs Cage-Free Scrambled Eggs	Cage-Free Hard-Cooked Eggs Cage-Free Scrambled Eggs	
Waffles		Waffles Vegan Waffles Waffle Bar Fixins'	Waffles Vegan Waffles Waffle Bar Fixins'	Waffles Vegan Waffles Waffle Bar Fixins'	Waffles Vegan Waffles Waffle Bar Fixins'	Waffles Vegan Waffles Waffle Bar Fixins'	
Grill Place		Extra Thick French Toast	Multi-Grain Pancakes	Pain Perdu French Toast	Buttermilk Pancakes	Texas French Toast	
Breakfast Potatoes		Potato Hashbrowns	O'Brien Potatoes	Potato Scallion Hash	Red Bliss Home Fries	Potato Hashbrowns	

FIGURE 4.2

This one-week segment of a larger cycle menu at Yale University shows that cycle menus can be exciting, healthy, and delicious.

Source: Reprinted with permission of Yale Hospitality.

	Sunday	Monday	Tuesday	Wednesday	Thursday	Friday	Saturday
Breakfast Meat			Breakfast Ham		Lamberti Chicken Sausage Patties with Sage		
Pars			Yale Bakery Granola		Yale Bakery Granola		
Fruit	Assorted Fresh Fruit Fresh Sliced Breakfast Fruit Rio Red Grapefruit Halves		Assorted Fresh Fruit Fresh Sliced Breakfast Fruit Cara Cara Orange Halves	Assorted Fresh Fruit Fresh Sliced Breakfast Fruit Rio Red Grapefruit Halves	Assorted Fresh Fruit Fresh Sliced Breakfast Fruit Tangelo Halves	Assorted Fresh Fruit Fresh Sliced Breakfast Fruit Rio Red Grapefruit Halves	
Morning Sweet	Blueberry Oat Tea Bread		Yale & Hearty Chocolate-Chocolate Chip Muffins	Maple Pecan Buns	Vanilla Sugar Scones	Banana Nut Muffins	

Cycle 1	Sunday	Monday	Tuesday	Wednesday	Thursday	Friday	Saturday
Cereal	Whole-Grain Irish Oatmeal Irish Oatmeal Bar						Whole-Grain Irish Oatmeal Irish Oatmeal Bar
Waffles	Waffles Vegan Waffles Waffle Bar Fixins'						Waffles Vegan Waffles Waffle Bar Fixins'
Eggs	Cage-Free Hard-Cooked Eggs Cage-Free Scrambled Eggs with White Cheddar and Herbs Cage-Free Scrambled Eggs						Cage-Free Hard-Cooked Eggs Cage-Free Western-Style Scrambled Eggs Cage-Free Scrambled Eggs
Brunch							
Entrée	Pasta Primavera Quiche Lorraine						Chef's Choice Rigatoni Pasta
Grill Place	Vegan Sweet Potato Pancakes Chocolate Chip Pancakes						Chef's Choice Vegetarian Puff Pastry Tart with Mozzarella
Breakfast Meat	Niman-Ranch Nitrate-Free Hickory Smoked Bacon						Multi-Grain Pancakes Vegan Banana Pancakes
Breakfast Potatoes	Golden Home Fries						Niman-Ranch Nitrate-Free Hickory Smoked Bacon

FIGURE 4.2 *(Continued)*

	Sunday	Monday	Tuesday	Wednesday	Thursday	Friday	Saturday
Deli	Deli Bar Group 4 with Roast Beef, Cranberry-Almond Chicken Salad, Herbed Tuna Salad, Roasted Garlic Mayonnaise, and Roasted Pepper Hummus						Deli Bar Group 1 with Ham, Thai Curry Chicken Salad, Herbed Tuna Salad, Sriracha Mayonnaise, and Green Garbanzo & Cilantro Hummus
Fruit	Assorted Fresh Fruit Sliced Breakfast Fruit Tangelo Halves Greek Yogurt Bar with Housemade Granola						Assorted Fresh Fruit Sliced Breakfast Fruit Cara Cara Orange Halves Greek Yogurt Bar with Housemade Granola
Salad	Salad Bar Group 4: Greek and Spinach Deconstructed Salad						Deconstructed Salad Bar Group 1: Avocado Ranch and Blue Apple Deconstructed Salad
Morning Sweet/Dessert	Cinnamon Streusel Coffee Cake						Honey Walnut Cookies Chocolate Chip Blondies

Cycle 1	Sunday	Monday	Tuesday	Wednesday	Thursday	Friday	Saturday
Notes		*Pub Food*	*Mediterranean*	*Asian*	*BBQ*	*Taste of New Haven*	

Lunch

	Monday	Tuesday	Wednesday	Thursday	Friday
Clear Soup	Amish Chicken & Corn Soup	Vegetable Pistou	Vietnamese Chicken Noodle Soup	Turkey & Rice Soup	Mulligatawny Soup
Cream/Puree	Cheddar Cheese & Beer Soup	Cream of Cauliflower Soup	Sweet Potato Soup	Tomato Bisque with Cashew Cream	New England Clam Chowder
Entrée(s)	Roasted Buffalo Chicken Thighs made with Harvestland All-Natural Chicken	Greek-Style Sole with Lemons and Tomatoes	Coconut and Green Curry Pork made with Niman Ranch All-Natural Pork	Grass-Fed, Grass-Finished Beef BBQ Brisket Sandwich on a Brioche Bun	New Haven White Clam Pizza with Smoked Mozzarella

FIGURE 4.2 *(Continued)*

Vegetarian Entrée		Greenwheat Freekeh Meatballs in Apricot Sweet-and-Sour Sauce	Yale Creamy Macaroni & Cheese	Cheese Pizza
Vegan Entrée	Orecchiette with Broccoli Rabe & Vegan Gardein Sausage	Mai Pham's Tofu and Vegetable Stir-Fry Vegan Vegetable Potstickers with Ginger-Soy Sauce	Sweet Potato, Quinoa, and Mushroom Burger with Tomato Chutney	New Haven Greens Pasta
Grill Place	The Naked Hummel on a New England Hot Dog Bun with Variations Part I (Firecracker, Corn Dog, and Western Picnic) made with Local Hummel Hot Dogs Grass-Fed Hamburgers Grass-Fed Cheeseburgers All-Natural Harvestland Chicken Breast Sweet Potato & Black Bean Burger	Lamb and Feta Piadina with Sun-Dried Tomato Mayonnaise on Ciabatta made with All-Natural, Grass-Fed Lamb Grass-Fed Hamburgers Grass-Fed Cheeseburgers All-Natural Harvestland Chicken Breast Sweet Potato & Black Bean Burger	Chicken Banh Mi Sandwich made with Harvestland All-Natural Chicken Grass-Fed Hamburgers Grass-Fed Cheeseburgers All-Natural Harvestland Chicken Breast Sweet Potato & Black Bean Burger	All-Natural Harvestland Grilled Chicken Breast with Corn and Tomato Salsa Grass-Fed Hamburgers Grass-Fed Cheeseburgers All-Natural Harvestland Chicken Breast Sweet Potato & Black Bean Burger	Italian Sausage Hoagie with Onions and Peppers made with Lamberti Sausage Grass-Fed Hamburgers Grass-Fed Cheeseburgers All-Natural Harvestland Chicken Breast Sweet Potato & Black Bean Burger
Starch	Shoestring French Fries	Brown Rice with Green Garbanzos, Scallions, and Parsley	Jasmine Rice		
Vegetable	Steamed Broccoli Florets Roasted Acorn Squash	Sautéed Spinach with Garlic Roasted Golden Beets	Roasted Bok Choy Sesame Peas with Carrots and Peppers	Sautéed Super Slaw Roasted Cauliflower	Steamed Green Beans Roasted Harvest Vegetable Blend
Fruit	Assorted Fresh Fruit Honey Tangerine	Assorted Fresh Fruit Bartlett Pears	Assorted Fresh Fruit Clementines	Assorted Fresh Fruit Pink Lady Apples	Assorted Fresh Fruit Honey Tangerines
Deli Bar	Deli Bar Group 1 with Ham, Thai Curry Chicken Salad, Herbed Tuna Salad, Sriracha Mayonnaise, and Green Garbanzo & Cilantro Hummus				

Salad Bar Group 1: Avocado Ranch and Blue Apple Deconstructed Salad

FIGURE 4.2 *(Continued)*

	Sunday	Monday	Tuesday	Wednesday	Thursday	Friday	Saturday
Salads	White Bean Salad with Swiss Chard and Watercress Superfood Slaw with Apple Cider Vinaigrette, Pecans, and Golden Raisins Farro Waldorf Salad with Pepitas	Chickpea Salad with Sun-Dried Tomato Vinaigrette Brussels Sprout Salad with Oranges, Dried Cranberries, Walnuts, and Parmesan Quinoa Salad with Dried Cherries, Radicchio, and Almonds	Lentil Salad with Mustard Vinaigrette Massaged Kale Salad with Soy Vinaigrette Thai Peanut Salad	Green Garbanzo Salad with Black Beans and Lime-Cilantro Vinaigrette Peruvian Corn Salad Spicy Tabbouleh Salad	Gigante Bean Salad with Butternut Squash and Dried Cherries Marinated Broccoli and Cauliflower Salad Ancient Grains Salad with Apples and Grapes		
Dessert	Peanut Butter Cookies Homemade Brownies	Cranberry Oatmeal Cookies Frangipane Bars	Chocolate Chip Cookies Vegan Ginger Almond Cupcakes with Chocolate Icing	Toffee Cookies White Chocolate Blondie	Gingersnap Cookies Lemon Coconut Oat Bars		
Misc		Housemade Blue Cheese Dipping Sauce			Corn and Tomato Salsa		
Cycle 1	Sunday	Monday	Tuesday	Wednesday	Thursday	Friday	Saturday
Notes	*Sunday Dinner*	*German*	*Italian*	*French*	*Latin/Caribbean*	*English Pub*	*Southern/Cajun*
Soup	Chef's Choice Soup	Amish Chicken & Corn Soup Cheddar Cheese & Beer Soup	Vegetable Pistou Cream of Cauliflower Soup	Vietnamese Chicken Noodle Soup Sweet Potato Soup	Turkey & Rice Soup Tomato Bisque with Cashew Cream	Mulligatawny Soup New England Clam Chowder	Cream of Mushroom Soup
Entrée(s)	Yankee Pot Roast made with Grass-Fed, Grass-Finished Beef	Herb-Crusted Niman Ranch All-Natural Pork Loin with Port Wine Reduction Sauce	Lemon-Herbed Chicken Breast made with Harvestland All-Natural Chicken	Harvestland All-Natural Chicken Thighs Baked with Herbs	Lime & Cilantro Carne a la Planche made with Grass-Fed, Grass-Finished Beef	Chicken Tikka Masala with Harvestland All-Natural Chicken	St. Louis-Style Pork Ribs made with Niman Ranch All-Natural Pork
Vegetarian Entrée	Corn Casserole	Flatbread with Caramelized Onions and Gouda	Eggplant Parmesan	Carla's Spinach Ravioli with Sage-Butter Sauce			Baked Cheese Grits
Vegan Entrée	Wild Mushroom Chili	Braised Lentils with Kale	Cannellini Beans with Wilted Greens	Vegan Gardein Chicken Provencal	Black Beans and Rice Peruvian Vegetable Stew with Quinoa	Vegetable Biryani Baked Vegetable Samosas	Vegan Black-Eyed Pea and Chili Casserole

(Soup through Vegan Entrée rows grouped under **Dinner***)*

FIGURE 4.2 *(Continued)*

67

Grill Place/ Street Foods	All-Natural Harvestland Grilled Chicken Breast with Cranberry-Apple Chutney Grass-Fed Hamburgers Grass-Fed Cheeseburgers All-Natural Harvestland Chicken Breast Sweet Potato & Black Bean Burger	Chicken Schnitzel made with Harvestland All-Natural Chicken Grass-Fed Hamburgers Grass-Fed Cheeseburgers All-Natural Harvestland Chicken Breast Sweet Potato & Black Bean Burger	Bucatini all' Amatriciana Grass-Fed Hamburgers Grass-Fed Cheeseburgers All-Natural Harvestland Chicken Breast Sweet Potato & Black Bean Burger	Herb & Honey Grilled Wild Alaskan Sockeye Salmon Grass-Fed Hamburgers Grass-Fed Cheeseburgers All-Natural Harvestland Chicken Breast Sweet Potato & Black Bean Burger	All-Natural Jerk Chicken Skewers with Mango Drizzle and Rice and Beans Grass-Fed Hamburgers Grass-Fed Cheeseburgers All-Natural Harvestland Chicken Breast Sweet Potato & Black Bean Burger	Beer-Battered Fish with MSC Certified Wild Cod Grass-Fed Hamburgers Grass-Fed Cheeseburgers All-Natural Harvestland Chicken Breast Sweet Potato & Black Bean Burger	Cajun Chicken Sandwich with Onion Jam & Remoulade with Harvestland All-Natural Chicken Grass-Fed Hamburgers Grass-Fed Cheeseburgers Sweet Potato & Black Bean Burger
Starch	Red and Gold Mashed Potatoes	Spaetzle	Golden Jewel Blend	Rice Pilaf	Roasted Sweet Potatoes with Lime	Shoestring French Fries	Bourbon Yams
Vegetable	Steamed Green Beans Roasted Parsnips and Carrots	Steamed Brussels Sprouts Roasted Cauliflower	Steamed Broccoli Raab Roasted Radicchio with Balsamic Vinegar	Steamed Green Beans with Tarragon Roasted Butternut Squash	Roasted Green Squash Steamed Carrots	Sautéed Spinach with Garlic Smashed Peas with Minted Butter	Sautéed Spicy Kale Honey-Roasted Carrots
Fruit	Assorted Fresh Fruit Gala Apples	Assorted Fresh Fruit Honey Tangerine	Assorted Fresh Fruit Bartlett Pears	Assorted Fresh Fruit Clementines	Assorted Fresh Fruit Pink Lady Apples	Assorted Fresh Fruit Honey Tangerines	Assorted Fresh Fruit Bartlett Pears
Salads	Salad Bar Group 4: Greek and Spinach Deconstructed Salad	White Bean Salad with Swiss Chard and Watercress Superfood Slaw with Apple Cider Vinaigrette, Pecans, and Golden Raisins Farro Waldorf Salad with Pepitas	Chickpea Salad with Sun-Dried Tomato Vinaigrette Brussels Sprout Salad with Oranges, Dried Cranberries, Walnuts, and Parmesan Quinoa Salad with Dried Cherries, Radicchio, and Almonds	Salad Bar Group 1: Avocado Ranch and Blue Pear Deconstructed Salad	Lentil Salad with Mustard Vinaigrette Massaged Kale Salad with Soy Vinaigrette Thai Peanut Salad	Green Garbanzo Salad with Black Beans and Lime-Cilantro Vinaigrette Peruvian Corn Salad Spicy Tabbouleh Salad	Gigante Bean Salad with Butternut Squash and Dried Cherries Marinated Broccoli and Cauliflower Salad Ancient Grains Salad with Apples and Grapes
Dessert	Brownie Walnut Pudding Sundae Bar	Vegan Cardamom Pear Cake with California Olive Ranch Olive Oil	Lemon Pound Cake	Un"beet"able Cake	Tres Leches Cake	Apple Crisp	Carrot Cake with Cream Cheese Icing
Misc						Housemade Tartar Sauce	

FIGURE 4.2 (Continued)

68

The lighter courses—broth soups, simple salads, sorbet intermezzos—work both as a palate cleanser to give the taste buds a rest and as a calorie break on the stomach. Portion sizes should remain small throughout the banquet so that the guests do not "run out of room" before reaching dessert.

The number of guests at a banquet and the style of service greatly impact what the menu planner can recommend to the client. Other than the first course, which can be set down at the table before the guests arrive, the courses must be quick to plate and serve when a large crowd is planned. For this reason, some companies recommend Russian service for a banquet. In Russian service, the food for an entire table is placed on a single platter, and the server transfers it to the guests' plates at the table. This style of service reduces the amount of table space needed in the kitchen for plating and divides the plate-up work among the servers. Russian service provides the best shot at serving all of the tables at the same time. If the menu planner chooses to go with American service (plated in the kitchen), the chef may need several teams of people to plate the same dish simultaneously, which requires significant table space, or the use of a conveyor belt.

When a banquet menu offers guests a choice within a course, the number of options should be limited to three or fewer. Too many choices slow service and require a larger inventory of ingredients. With fewer dishes to prepare, the kitchen can cook the food in bulk and speed the meal along, a critical element in a banquet during which no table progresses to the next course until every table has been served the previous course. Some operations expedite the process by requiring guests to pre-order their entrée choices, usually as part of their RSVP to the client. This way, the kitchen can better prepare its mise en place and have the food ready on time in the proper quantities. Coded place cards on the table make the process even faster, as servers deliver the correct meal to each guest without having to ask what each person ordered.

A special occasion menu need not be served banquet style. A restaurant may create a special menu just for a holiday and serve its guests American style. However, many of the rules of banquet menu creation still apply. The menu should adhere to an overarching theme and should follow a traditional course sequence. The number of choices between courses should be limited to reduce the amount of inventory left over when the restaurant returns to its regular menu the following day. Finally, because the meal is a one-time event, nutrition is less of a factor than is adhering to the theme of the day—a holiday, a cultural event, a winery providing the drinks, or a single-ingredient theme, such as pork. A special occasion menu can be served buffet style; buffets and their unique concerns are described in Chapter 9.

It should be noted that hotels, country clubs, and other operations that do a lot of special events often refer to their catering menus as "banquet" menus. To avoid confusion, this text will reserve the term "banquet menu" for the final menu experienced by the guests at a special event. "Catering menu" is the term that will be used to reference the extensive list of options (food, beverage, and more) from which a client selects the ultimate banquet menu. Catering menus are covered later in this chapter.

Tasting Menus

A tasting menu is usually a lengthy gustatory experience in which the guest submits to the chef's recommendations for course selection and sequence. Tasting menus may be as small as five courses or may run over twenty courses. Regardless of the number of courses, the total quantity of food can only go so high before guests become uncomfortably full. Larger numbers of courses require smaller portion sizes, possibly of just one or two bites.

Tasting menus are most commonly found in restaurants with extremely talented chefs. They may follow a classic banquet course sequence, but because of the small portion sizes, a tasting menu may appear to be an ongoing series of appetizers. As with banquet menus, the best tasting menus provide a periodic palate cleanser, which may be a salad or sorbet or may instead be a light, acidic course not all that different in appearance from the other courses. Short tasting menus and banquet menus may appear to be quite similar, but the client heavily influences a banquet menu while the chef completely controls a tasting menu and rarely offers guests choices other than to accommodate allergies

Hotel Winneshiek
Holiday party Menu 2015
<u>Plated Dinner $29</u>

Salad:

Spinach and Radicchio- pomegranate, Pistachio, Red wine Honey
Vinaigrette

Entrée Choices:

Salmon Filet with Crimini Mushrooms, Capers, and Mascarpone.
Served with- Jasmine wild rice blend and seasonal vegetables.

Sirloin Steak with Roasted Garlic-Bourbon Sauce, Bacon Jam.
Served with Garlic Mashed potatoes and seasonal vegetables.

Saffron Risotto with Smoked Gouda, Fried Leeks, and Basil Oil

Dessert:

Lingonberry-Almond Macarons

Chocolate Macarons

FIGURE 4.3

This hotel restaurant created a banquet menu for a holiday party.

Source: Reprinted with permission of Hotel Winneshiek.

and other dietary restrictions. Banquets typically support a larger event, like a wedding or conference; tasting menus are 100 percent about the food and dining experience. In both cases, menu headings are rarely used; course separations are denoted through spacing or the use of asterisks.

Because tasting menus are rare indulgences for most diners, guests often wish to take a copy of the printed menu with them to remember the experience. Thus, tasting menus should be printed on durable paper but without permanent covers that the restaurant would reuse for other guests. Chefs may wish to personalize the menus by signing them or by listing the date and name of the party. In some restaurants, a tasting menu is only offered to a small subset of the evening's patrons, usually to a small party that reserves a special room or a table in the kitchen. Tasting menus are generally expensive to produce, so they command high prices. To justify the price, a tasting menu should show off the best talents and innovations of the chef. Because guests want to feel that they've had a series of original dishes and not the same course over and over again, primary ingredients should never be repeated across courses in a tasting menu.

While most restaurants cannot offer a full tasting menu, some cater to the trend in small ways by offering tasting flights as an option for a single course. These flights allow customers to try multiple foods or drinks without committing to a full-size portion of any one item. Some guests use flights to help decide which food or drink to purchase on future visits. Examples of culinary flights include cheese boards with small tastes of several cheeses or a dessert course with a sampling of several miniature desserts. Beverage tastings, such as a flight of beer or wine, are also popular for guests who wish to sample more than one drink. As with full tasting menus, portion sizes on flights should remain appropriately small. For food, each item in the flight may be a mere one to two bites; for beverages, a 2-ounce pour of wine or beer allows for flights of four to five beverages without seriously impairing guests.

KITCHEN MENU

jonah crab cucumber, green mango, coriander

ravioli black trumpet mushrooms, ash, celery root

wahoo asparagus, hen yolk, fines herbs, caper

pork belly red cape beans, chimichurri, cocoa

sweetbreads sunchoke, black kale, bacon

beef english pea, kennebeck potatoes, rutabaga, green garlic

chocolate marshmallow, caramel, peanut

VEGETABLE MENU

beets walnuts, blue cheese, watercress, sherry vinegar

ravioli black trumpet mushrooms, ash, celery root

cauliflower golden raisin, chickpea, piquillo pepper, eggplant

hen egg rye, english pea, morel mushroom

jerusalem artichoke maroon carrot, fennel, chickweed

maitake steel cut oats, sea greens, yeast

parsnip walnut, cream cheese, caramel

seven course menu | 95 cheese course | 12 beverage pairings | mkt

FIGURE 4.4

This tasting menu highlights the talent of TV celebrity chef Bryan Voltaggio and showcases his support of agriculture local to his restaurant in Frederick, MD.

Source: Chef Bryan Voltaggio, VOLT Restaurant. Reprinted with permission.

Catering Menus

Caterers, which include standalone catering companies, hotel and country club catering departments, special event sites, and sometimes even personal chefs, accommodate the needs of a client to service a larger group. Caterers may supply a banquet, a buffet, a cocktail reception, or simply a bunch of sandwiches dropped off on disposable platters. Caterers range from inexpensive to extremely pricy, and their job is to meet the needs, no matter how unusual, of a guest whose needs are not met simply by going to a restaurant. At the higher end of the spectrum, caterers make dreams come true.

Catering can be done on-premise or off-premise, meaning respectively that the guests may come to a catering hall next to the caterer's kitchen or to a location to which the caterer must transport the food. Hotels and country clubs are examples of on-premise caterers. Many of the companies advertised explicitly as caterers are often off-premise caterers. Because caterers must adapt to a wide range of clients with vastly different needs, a catering menu is an enormous menu from which the client picks to create the event or banquet menu. The client may choose from dozens or hundreds of choices to create the shorter menu that the event attendees see.

Because a catering menu is never executed in its entirety at one event, variety is critical, but balance is not. It is perfectly acceptable for a caterer to list twenty chicken entrées on a catering menu, from which the client will pick one. That said, chicken should not be the only option for an entrée or the client is likely to seek out another caterer. A catering menu often includes menu headings not seen on other menus. Caterers often offer hors d'oeuvres as part of a reception prior to a main meal; thus, "Hors d'Oeuvres" is usually its own heading on a catering menu. *Hors d'oeuvres* are simply one- or two-bite items that guests can navigate easily while holding a drink in one hand. They should rarely require utensils other than a toothpick or perhaps a spoon on which a single bite rests. They should also not be messy to consume, or guests will end up with food all over their clothes. Other menu headings unique to catering menus include "Snacks" and "Carving Stations."

Full-service caterers—as opposed to caterers who only do drop-off, disposable trays of food—should have the ability to provide buffet, American (plated), or Russian (platter) service. The buffet might include carving stations. Consequently, the prices on a catering menu differ from the way prices are written on other menus. Prices may be listed by the piece (for hors d'oeuvres), by weight or volume (for buffet salads or soups), or per person (which lets the caterer determine how much food to supply). When a catering menu sells its food per person for a buffet, the portion sizes should be planned such that the food does not run out. After all, if the client paid for twenty people to eat, the buffet cannot run out of food before all twenty have had their fill. Services such as having a bartender, carver, or server(s) are often charged separately.

Because the client ultimately selects the event menu from the catering menu, it is up to the chef or salesperson to guide the client to make good choices. This is very much a give-and-take exchange. If a client wishes to offer three entrées, all beef, at her party, the chef or salesperson should encourage her to pursue greater variety. However, if the client describes the attendees as cattle ranchers in town for a conference, the plethora of beef may be appropriate. The chef could recommend a set banquet menu in which each course contains some beef instead of congregating all of the beef into a single course. In the end, if the chef or salesperson and the client understand the attendees' needs and the caterer's capabilities, the menu is easier to determine. The client will almost always request a written (in print or online) catering menu from which to choose, but a caterer should anticipate requests for items that are not listed on the catering menu. Once the caterer executes a new dish effectively for one event, the menu planner may add it to the comprehensive catering menu. Ultimately, the catering menu should include everything that the company is capable of providing and wishes to sell again.

Catering menus, unlike most other menus, go beyond the straightforward listing of food and drink options. Clients pursue caterers rather than restaurants because they want specific services (not just food) that a typical restaurant cannot provide. Thus, a catering package (sometimes called a banquet package) includes options for tables, chairs, cloths, decorations, number of servers, floral arrangements, photography, room rentals—in short, anything that the customer might need for the event—for a fee. For example, rather than ordering one hundred cocktails for a party, a client might order a full bar for which she pays for the bartender, the physical bar setup, and the amount of alcohol consumed at the event. Some services are provided by caterers through their in-house staff; others are contracted out for a percentage. For example, a caterer might agree to manage all of the details surrounding purchases from a florist, and a percentage of the florist's fee gets added to the client's bill to cover the caterer's time. While most people think of a menu as dealing only with food and drink, a full-service catering menu includes a much broader range of services from which a client selects to create her personalized event.

Catering Policy:

Menu Selection:

To ensure complete customer satisfaction, **all food and beverage selections must be finalized no later than fourteen business days prior to the event.** When all details have been finalized, a written banquet contract (or revised contract, if one has already been signed) will be submitted for approval. A signed copy of the revised form must be returned to the sales department no later than seven business days prior to the event.

Guarantees:

Final guaranteed attendance numbers must be given to the sales department no later than seven business days prior to the event, upon which your contract will be updated and you will be sent a revised copy for approval. A signed copy of the revised form must be returned to the sales department. The guaranteed number may not be reduced after this time, and any increases to this number will be subject to the prior approval and authorization of the sales department. If a final attendance count is not received seven business days prior to the event, the sales department will consider the tentative guarantee (submitted at the time of booking) as the final guarantee.

Additional Fees/Charges:

All food and beverage items are subject to a 20% service charge as well as applicable taxes. Other case-specific charges are listed within the menu for specialized services.

Room Assignments:

Event room assignments are based upon the number of anticipated guests. We will do our best to honor your original assignment request; however we reserve the right to reschedule your room assignment based upon attendance and other business needs.

Proposals/Custom menus:

Proposals are available for any event, booked or inquiry, free of charge. We can send you a quote based on menu selections you have chosen, or help you create a menu to fit your event. Customized items/menus are available upon request, with prior approval from the Chef. Ask a sales associate today and make your event one to remember!

FIGURE 4.5

This section of a much larger catering menu shows the format typical of a catering menu.
Source: Reprinted with the permission of Jonathan Morrow.

<u>Hors D'oeurves</u>
Price per serving, quantity varies – see descriptions
Per Person Pricing ($18.00 min.)

Inn at Carnall Hall policy is that hors d'oeurves selection must match guest count.

Gourmet cheese tray, assorted crackers, fruit	5.00
Goat Cheese and Braised Shiitakes on Herbed Crostini	3.00
Brie and Fruit Salsa on Herbed Crostini	3.50
Assorted olives, pickled vegetables and cured meats platter	4.00
Pork and vegetable Roll with sweet chili dipping sauce	3.50
Tomato Bruschetta with Herbed Crostinis	2.50
Button mushrooms stuffed with garlic, herbs and cheese	3.00
Cucumber with cream cheese and smoked salmon	5.00
Deviled Eggs	3.50
Chef's Choice Chicken Salad served on mini-croissant	4.50
Miniature Crab Cakes with chipotle aioli	3.50
Coconut Shrimp with sweet chili dipping sauce	6.00
Bacon Wrapped Dates stuffed with fig cream cheese	4.25
Chicken Skewers (choice of sauce): Roasted Red Pepper Cream Jamaican Jerk	3.50
Beef Skewers (choice of sauce): Ginger Soy Dijon-Maple	4.00
Smoked Salmon Mousse on herbed crostini	4.00
Southwest Corn Dip served with Tortilla Chips	3.50
Five Cheese Spinach and Roasted Garlic Dip served with herbed crostinis	3.50
Baby Spinach, Feta and Roasted Garlic Hummus served with crostinis	3.50
Grilled chicken and roasted red pepper quesadilla with sour cream and salsa	3.00
Bacon Cream Cheese Jalapenos with chipotle-raspberry sauce	3.50

FIGURE 4.5 *(Continued)*

Jumbo Shrimp Cocktail with homemade cocktail sauce	6.75
Meatballs (choice of sauce): Italian, Port Marinara, Shaved Parmesan Southern, Sweet Bourbon Glaze	4.50
Sliders (choice of): Cheeseburger with Tomato and Onion Cuban (Ham, Swiss, Pickle) with Spicy Mustard Southern Beef, Spicy Cheese Blend, Roasted Poblano Peppers and Onion	4.50
Miniature Grilled Cheese with peppered bacon on grilled sourdough	3.75
Caprese Skewers	4.00
Assorted Vegetable Tray with buttermilk dipping sauce	4.00
Fresh Fruit Tray with yogurt dip	4.50

Hors D'oeurves: Carving Station Price Per Person

Herb encrusted Prime rib served with horseradish-chive sauce and caramelized onions	10.00
Brown Sugar rubbed Pork Loin served with spicy honey mustard and caramelized onions	8.00
Garlic Roasted beef tenderloin served with sauce béarnaise and caramelized onions	12.00
Add Rolls	1.00

Desserts: price per person

Raspberry white chocolate cheesecake	2.75
New York style cheesecake	2.50
Moist chocolate cake with dark chocolate ganache	2.75
Vanilla cake with dark chocolate ganache	2.25
Carrot cake with cream cheese icing	2.75
Red velvet cake with cream cheese mousse	2.50
Lemon tarts	2.50
Peanut Butter Pie Tarts	2.75

FIGURE 4.5 *(Continued)*

Dinner Served:

All served dinners include bread and butter. Choose from one soup or salad, up to three entrées and up to two desserts. For groups larger than 25 we must have a preorder. There will be an additional $5 charge per plate for ordering upon arrival.

Bread and Butter

Chef's choice fresh baked bread and whipped butter

Soup

Chef's choice

Salad

House Salad: Mixed field greens, Roma tomatoes, red onions, shredded carrots and Ella's house vinaigrette.

Caesar Salad: Chopped romaine, grated parmesan, croutons and Caesar dressing

Spinach Salad: Baby spinach, mandarin oranges, red onions, toasted walnuts and strawberry-balsamic vinaigrette

Entrée

14 oz. Ribeye Grilled Ribeye, Savory Bread Pudding, Seared Asparagus and Horseradish-Chive sauce	46.00
8 oz. Beef Tenderloin Grilled Beef Tenderloin, Garlic Whipped Potatoes, Seared Asparagus and sauce Béarnaise	44.00
Ahi Tuna Sesame Encrusted Ahi Tuna, Radicchio and Napa Cabbage Slaw, Tomato and Sauce Gribiche	42.00
Atlantic Salmon Pan Seared Wild Salmon, Herbed Quinoa, Sautéed Broccolini, Lemon-Peppercorn Beurre-Blanc	40.00
Blackened Catfish Baked Arkansas Catfish, Grilled Scallion, Shiitake Risotto, Lemon Butter sauce	32.00
Pork Tenderloin Brown sugar glazed Pork Tenderloin, Caramelized Apples, Garlic Whipped Potatoes, Grilled Asparagus, Cognac Cream Sauce	36.00
Chicken Piccata Breaded Chicken Breast, Linguine, Roma Tomato, Artichoke Heart, Caper, Lemon-Butter Sauce	32.00
Chicken Marsala Pan Seared Chicken Breast, Garlic Whipped Potatoes, Grilled Asparagus, Sweden Creek Shiitake Marsala	32.00
Pasta Primavera Chef's Choice Pasta, Garden Vegetables, White Wine Cream sauce	26.00
Add Grilled Chicken	32.00
Add Sautéed Shrimp	34.00
Eggplant Parmesan Breaded Eggplant, Chef's Choice Pasta, Port Marinara, Mozzarella, Parmesan	26.00

FIGURE 4.5 *(Continued)*

Dessert

White chocolate crème brulee

Raspberry white chocolate cheesecake

N.Y. style cheesecake with strawberry coulis

Chocolate mousse tort with raspberry coulis

Chocolate Peanut Butter Pie

Granny smith apple crisp with caramel sauce

Fruit cobbler

Homemade gelato or sorbet

Dinner Buffet:
Per Person Pricing ($28.00 min; 16 person minimum)
Inn at Carnall Hall policy is that buffet item selections must match guest count.

Soup and Salads
Chef's Choice Soup	3.00
Ella's House Salad	3.00
Mixed Field Greens, Roma tomato, Red Onion, Shredded Carrot and House Dressing	
Caesar Salad	4.00
Chopped Heirloom Romaine, Grated Parmesan, Crostini and Caesar Dressing	
Spinach Salad	3.00
Baby Spinach, Seasonal Berries, Red onion, Toasted Almonds and Strawberry-Balsamic Vinaigrette	

Entrée Options: Carved price per person
Prime Rib	10.00
Herb encrusted Prime Rib served with horseradish-chive sauce and caramelized onions	
Pork Loin	8.00
Brown Sugar rubbed Pork Loin served with spicy honey mustard and caramelized onions	
Beef Tenderloin	12.00
Garlic Roasted beef tenderloin served with sauce béarnaise and caramelized onions	
Add Rolls	1.00

Entrée Options: Buffet
Hazelnut encrusted Salmon with Lemon-dill cream	9.00
Seared Chicken Breast with Sweden Creek Shiitake Marsala	7.50
Baked Arkansas Catfish with Lemon Butter sauce	7.50
Mozzarella Herb Chicken Breast with Roasted Red Pepper Cream sauce	6.50
Pasta Primavera with Garden Vegetables and White wine Cream sauce	6.00
Chicken Piccata with Roma Tomatoes, Artichoke Hearts, Capers, and Lemon-butter sauce	7.00
Breaded Eggplant over Linguine with Port Marinara, Mozzarella and Parmesan	7.00
Sautéed Tiger Shrimp over Linguine with Cajun White Wine Cream sauce	9.00

Sides:
Roasted Garlic Whipped Potatoes	3.50
Sweet Potato Casserole with Sweet Pecan Topping	4.00
Long Grain Wild Rice	3.00
Pasta with Garlic Herb Butter	3.50
Sweden Creek Shiitake Risotto	4.00
Roasted Vegetable Medley	3.50
Steamed Broccoli with Parmesan	3.50
Grilled Asparagus	5.00
Green Beans & Caramelized Onions	4.50
Fresh Baked Bread with Whipped Butter	3.00
Medley Seasonal Fruit	4.50

Dessert:
White chocolate crème brulee	6.00
Raspberry white chocolate cheesecake	6.00
N.Y. style cheesecake with strawberry coulis	6.00
Chocolate mousse tort with raspberry coulis	6.00
Chocolate Peanut Butter Pie	6.00
Granny smith apple crisp with caramel sauce	6.00
Fruit cobbler	6.00

FIGURE 4.5 *(Continued)*

Ethnic Menus

Ethnic menus are similar to their traditional counterparts except that they tend to follow the trends and traditions of the culture they represent. Menu heading names and sequences, menu items, styles of presentation and service, and even levels of variety and balance all adhere to the norms of the presented culture. For example, a Tuscan restaurant might opt to use only four menu categories—antipasta, pasta, main course, and dessert—as this provides the traditional meal sequence of Tuscany. Chinese restaurants divide their menus by each dish's main ingredient—chicken, beef, pork, seafood, vegetable, etc.—so the guests may order a variety of dishes that are traditionally served family style at the same time for all of the diners to share. Tapas (Spanish) and mezze (Middle Eastern) restaurants, in which guests choose a variety of small plates to create a full meal, are gaining in popularity as both allow for a wide sampling of foreign flavors. Dim sum (Chinese) is similar in that it allows for lots of small tastes, but with dim sum, the food is brought around on carts where customers see the food before deciding to order it from the cart. All of these examples of ethnic menus illustrate how ethnic restaurants impact not only the menu items but also the sequence of courses and approach to ordering and eating.

Ethnic restaurants offer guests a chance to experience another culture's dining experience, not just its food and drink. The food, the décor, the employee uniforms, and the style of service all work to enhance this experience. The menu itself may include descriptions of the cultural and culinary traditions of the country. Such text can increase sales and facilitate a dining experience that the guests cannot find at another nearby restaurant. An Ethiopian restaurant, for example, can explain on its menu the traditional use of injera—a flat, spongy bread—for picking up small pieces of stewed food as an alternative to the fork. This menu might also describe an Ethiopian coffee ceremony and thus drive coffee sales either at the end of the meal or in the afternoon between traditional meal periods. Guests unfamiliar with Ethiopian cuisine will find themselves both educated and reassured as they experiment with the dining style of another culture. Perhaps most important from a business perspective, the more authentic the dining experience, the higher the prices the restaurant can command on its menu.

Fusion and Small Plates Menus

One trend in American restaurants over the past few decades is the fusion of American and foreign culinary traditions (though one could argue that this is the essence of American cuisine through its entire history). Early in the trend's evolution, fusion meant strictly the combination of American and foreign ingredients and flavors to create entirely new dishes in a non-ethnic setting. The entire menu or only certain dishes might be fusion. More importantly, a restaurant could pull inspiration from different cultures on the same menu. Unlike an ethnic restaurant which highlights a single culture, a fusion restaurant might include a Peruvian-inspired dish alongside one influenced by Thai cuisine and a third created with Russian ingredients. Fusion cuisine continues to thrive, but until recently the menu and headings usually followed a traditional American pattern of dining.

Today, some American restaurants are experimenting with fused dining patterns as well. Long common in certain ethnic restaurants—see the previous discussion on tapas, mezze, and dim sum—a few restaurants are offering a menu comprised mainly of small plates with a few large ones, often big enough to serve an entire table a substantial portion. The small plates trend allows guests to create their own tasting menu from a semi à la carte restaurant menu. The portion sizes are usually larger than the one to two bites commonly found on a chef-driven tasting menu, but guests are encouraged to share the small plates among the table. This approach allows everyone at the table to get a bite or two of many dishes while exercising control over which items to select and how many dishes to order. Unlike a prix fixe tasting menu, the small plates trend also lets guests decide how much they would like to spend. The inclusion of a few large dishes allows guests to close the non-dessert segment of the meal with something more substantial than a small taste while still sharing among the table.

The small plates trend comes with few rules. The menu can adhere to a single cuisine or be a fusion of multiple cultures. Consequently, the dining room décor may reflect one or more cultures, or it may retain a neutral feel—sometimes upscale, sometimes not. The menu planner for a small plates menu often divides the small plates under several headings, but as the plates can come to the table whenever the kitchen has one ready, there is

ambar.
Balkan Cuisine

BALKAN EXPERIENCE $49
(unlimited small plates & drinks)

*add mixed grill selection for 10$ per person
*must be enjoyed by entire table

MEAT MEZZE 3 for 18$

GOVEĐA PRŠUTA.....8
beef prosciutto

DIMLJENI SVINJSKI VRAT.....8
smoked pork neck

PEČENICA.....8
pork file

KARLOVAČKA.....8
beef / pork salami

JAGNJEĆA KOBASICA.....8
lamb salami

KULEN.....8
spicy salami

KAJMAK BAR comes with bread

ŠUMADIJA KAJMAK.....7
not aged milk skim spread

ZLATIBOR.....7
aged 3-6 month

SMOKED SALMON.....9
capers / dill / onion / lemon

STRAWBERRY.....7
crispy prosciutto / micro basil

SPICY CRAB.....10
ajvar / cilantro / pickles chili

CHEF'S TASTING.....13
šumadija / smoked salmon spicy crab

SPREADS comes with bread

URNEBES.....6
aged cow cheese/ajvar/chilli

AJVAR.....6
rosted pepper / eggplant / garlic

GARLIC BEANS.....5
onion/dry roasted pepper/paprika

HUMMUS.....5
paprika / olive oil

SMOKED TROUT.....6
pickled jalapeno / cilantro/mayo

CHEF'S TASTING.....12
urnebes / smoked trout / hummus

HOUSE BAKED PIES

MEAT - pita sa mesom.....8
crispy phyllo / beef and pork garlic yogurt

CHEESE - pita sa sirom.....7
crispy phyllo / cucumber yogurt / roasted red pepper sauce

FLATBREADS

WHITE - pizza sa sirom.....8
kajmak / cured aged cow's chesse fresh herbs truffle paste / olive oil

PORK - pizza sa prasetinom.....9
slow cooked pork / pickled onion

MUSHROOM - pizza sa pečurkama..9
shiitake, crimini, button oyster mushrooms / arugula / cheese

SOUP & SALAD

VEAL SOUP - teleća krem čorba.....7
root vegetables / creme fresh

ZUCCHINI SOUP - čorba od tikvica..7
potato / sundried tomato

BALKAN SALAD - šopska salata.....7
tomato / pepper / cucumber / onion aged cow cheese

SQUASH SALAD - zelena salata.....9
mixed greens/panko-crusted mozzarella crispy bacon / pomegranate dressing

RED QUINOA SALAD.....9
grilled corn / pomegranate heirloom tomato / lettuce / balsamic

ORGANIC SLAW - slatki kupus.....7
mixed organic cabbage/carrot/radish organic vinaigrette

MARINATED THREE PEPPERS....6
spicy / mild / cheese / garlic organic vinaigrette / chives / parsley

VEGETABLES

GRILLED ASPARAGUS - špargle.....8
veloute / crispy prosciutto / pumpkin quail egg

**BRUSSELS SPROUTS
WITH BACON**-prokelj sa slaninom..8
lemon & garlic yogurt

CABBAGE CASUELA - podvarak.....7
braised cabbage / dry pepper/yogurt

AMBAR FRIES - krompirici.....6
aged kajmak / chives / homemade spice

**ROASTED MUSHROOM
CREPES**- šumske pečurke.....8
red pepper emulsion/béchamel / gouda

LEEK CROQUETTE.....6
ajvar emulsion / panko crust

GRILLED SEASONAL VEGETABLES..6
red & yellow peppers / green squash red onions / eggplant

MEAT & POULTRY

TARTARE STEAK - tartar biftek.....13
pork "cracklins" / sundried tomato butter pickled vegetables / onion / capers

HAM & CHEESE CREPE - palacinka....9
gouda / tartar sauce / panko bread crumps

ALMOND-CRUSTED CHICKEN.....8
walnut / green apple / chive / wasabi mayo

**BACON & PEANUT
PORK TENDERLOIN** - svinjski file.....10
miso-mustard tarragon / mashed potato

CHICKEN KEBAB - pileći kebab.....8
kajmak sauce / pickled onion

BALKAN KEBAB - ćevapi.....9
beef & pork / marinated onion/kajmak

LAMB AND VEAL KEBAB - šiš ćevap..10
spicy ajvar sauce/pickled jalapeno

AMBAR BURGER - pljeskavica.....11
beef & pork / urnebes / lettuce / tomato

STUFFED SOUR CABBAGE - sarma...9
potato mash/pork belly/rice/yogurt

SLOW COOKED PORK-trgano prase..10
yukon potato mash / cabbage slaw

STEAK & FRITES - goveđi stek.....10
aged kajmak/house fries / peppercorn

VIENNA SCHNITZEL - bečka šnicla...10
crispy veal/tartar sauce

SUMMER PEPPER- paprikica.....12
stuffed with root vegetables / beef & pork

SAUSAGES

BEEF & PORK - prebranac.....8
baked beans/onion/roasted pepper

LAMB & VEAL - jagnjeća kobasica.....8
red&yellow bell peppers / onion garlic eggplant / chili flakes / tomato

SPICY PORK - gurmanska kobasica......9
green peas and root vegetable stew

SMOKED PORK - dimljena kobasica.....7
homemade mustard sauce

SEAFOOD

DRUNKEN MUSSELS - dagnje.....8
rakija / garlic / capers / lemon / somun

**GRILLED CALAMARI
WITH GREMOLATA**-grilovane lignje..9
fresh herbs / diced pepper / lemon

SESAME CRUSTED SALMON-losos.....10
horseradish sauce/spicy eggplant/arugula

SHRIMP SKEWER-gamberi...10
prosciutto/asparagus/pepper spicy sesame aioli

MEDITERRANEAN BRANZINO....10
tomato / garlic /spinach / baked tomatoes

MIXED GRILL SELECTION

MIX MEAT PLATTER - mesano meso...32
pork loin / sausage / kebab / chicken / burger potato fries / urnebes spread

SEA FOOD PLATTER - morski tanjir......34
salmon / mussels / shrimp skewer/grilled calamari branzino / organic slaw

DRINKS
*all rail mix drinks included

COCKTAILS		WINE	BEER
SARAJEVO OLD FASHIONED.....11	MOJITO.....9	HOUSE SPARKLING.....8	YUENGLING.....6
POMEGRANATE COLLINS.....9	MANGO LEMONADE.....9	HOUSE RED.....7	BIP BELGRADE.....6
MARGARITA.....9	BERRY DAISY.....9	HOUSE WHITE.....7	

Consuming raw or under cooked meats, poultry, seafood, shellfish or eggs may increase your risk of food borne illness. Please inform your server of any food allergies.

FIGURE 4.6

This Balkan menu incorporates cuisine-specific headings and authentic foreign terminology, common characteristics of an ethnic menu.

Source: Ambar Restaurant. Reprinted with permission.

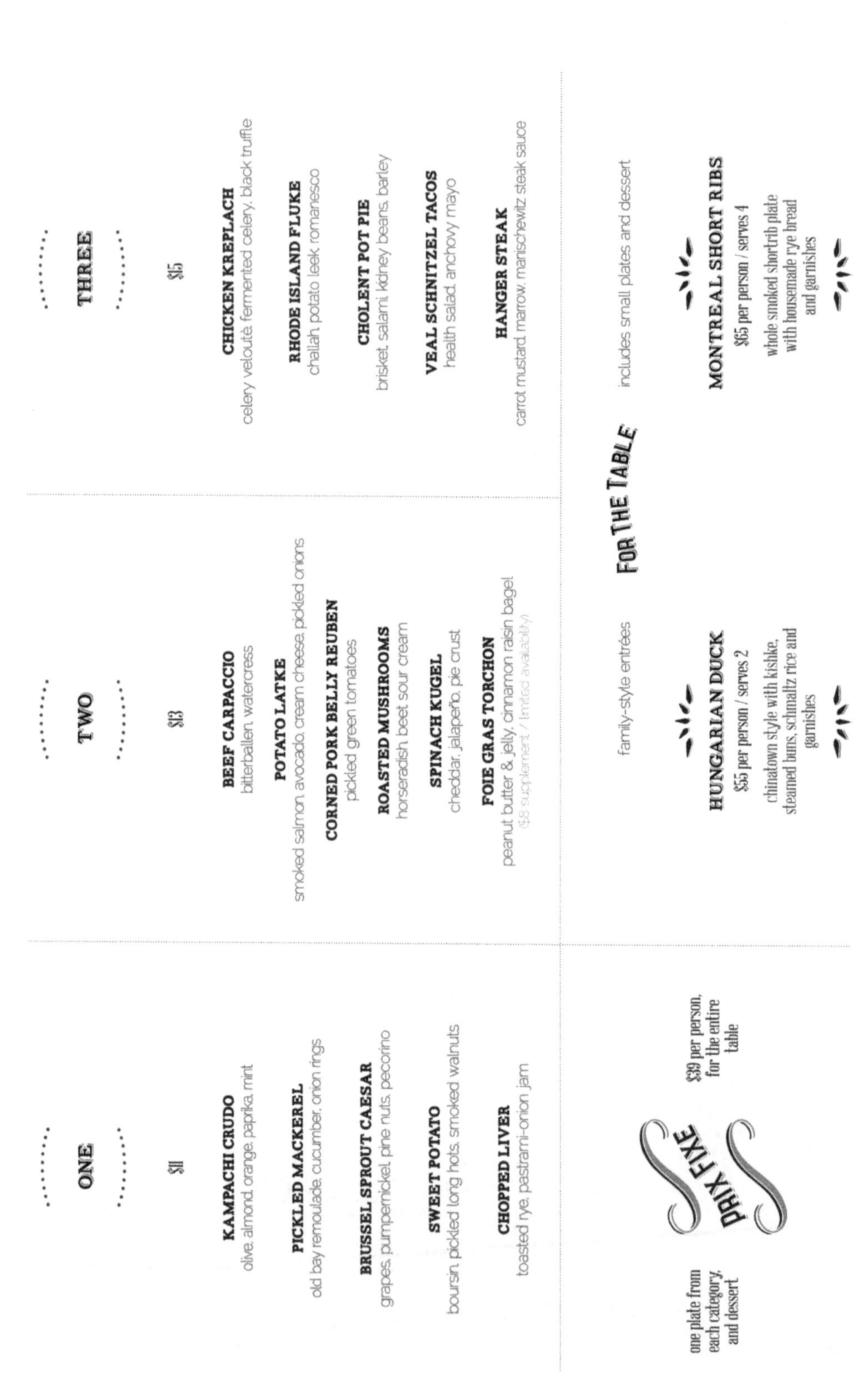

ABE FISHER

ONE

$11

KAMPACHI CRUDO
olive, almond, orange, paprika, mint

PICKLED MACKEREL
old bay remoulade, cucumber, onion rings

BRUSSEL SPROUT CAESAR
grapes, pumpernickel, pine nuts, pecorino

SWEET POTATO
boursin, pickled long hots, smoked walnuts

CHOPPED LIVER
toasted rye, pastrami-onion jam

TWO

$13

BEEF CARPACCIO
bitterballen, watercress

POTATO LATKE
smoked salmon, avocado, cream cheese, pickled onions

CORNED PORK BELLY REUBEN
pickled green tomatoes

ROASTED MUSHROOMS
horseradish, beet sour cream

SPINACH KUGEL
cheddar, jalapeño, pie crust

FOIE GRAS TORCHON
peanut butter & jelly, cinnamon raisin bagel
($8 supplement / limited availability)

THREE

$15

CHICKEN KREPLACH
celery velouté, fermented celery, black truffle

RHODE ISLAND FLUKE
challah, potato leek romanesco

CHOLENT POT PIE
brisket, salami, kidney beans, barley

VEAL SCHNITZEL TACOS
health salad, anchovy, mayo

HANGER STEAK
carrot, mustard, marrow, manischewitz steak sauce

❦ PRIX FIXE ❦

$39 per person, for the entire table

one plate from each category, and dessert

FOR THE TABLE

includes small plates and dessert

family-style entrées

HUNGARIAN DUCK
$55 per person / serves 2

chinatown style with kishke, steamed buns, schmaltz rice and garnishes

MONTREAL SHORT RIBS
$65 per person / serves 4

whole smoked shortrib plate with housemade rye bread and garnishes

FIGURE 4.7

This menu illustrates a format common for a small plates menu and allows for prix fixe or semi à la carte dining, guest's choice.

Source: Reprinted with permission of CooknSolo Restaurants.

COCKTAILS

$12

THE ABE FISHER COCKTAIL
beefeater, dolin dry, dolin blanc, dill, pickle juice

THE SUBJECT OF SOME REGRET
vodka, blood orange, honey

IN A PINCH
tequila, cucumber, salt, alpine artemisia

BEFORE IT'S TOO LATE
brandy, coriander, clove, lemon

EASY RIDER
gin, orange, bonal gentiane quina

YESTERDAY, TODAY AND AMARO
wild turkey rye, cynar, avena amaro, benedictine

MIND GAMES
scotch, zucca amaro, amaretto, lemon

SOFT DRINKS

$3

MAPLE–CARAWAY RICKEY

CUCUMBER–DILL SHRUB

GINGER LIME SODA

WINE

$12/glass - $50/bottle (750ml)

PARELLADA
pares balta, penedes, nv

SAGARNO
sarasola sagardoa, astigarraga, nv

PINOT GRIS
king estate, willamette valley, 2014

MELON DE BOURGOGNE
chateau de la dimerie, muscadet sevre et maine, 2014

SAUVIGNON BLANC
shinn estate vineyard, long island, 2014

SEMILLON
si vintners, margaret river, 2014

GEWURZTRAMINER
banyan, monterey county, 2014

CHARDONNAY
pintupi 9, mclaren vale, 2014

NEGRETTE ROSE
lionel osmin, fronton, 2014

GAMAY SAINT ROMAIN
domaine des pothiers, cote ronnaise, 2013

GRIGNOLINO
montalbera, asti, 2013

BLAUFRANKISCH
shooting star, yakima valley, 2012

NEBBIOLO
adelina, adelaide hills, 2011

TEROLDEGO ROTOLIANO
lechthaler, alto adige, 2013

CANNONAU
caladu, jerzu, 2012

TEMPRANILLO
vega sauco, toro, 2013

BEER & CIDER

AMSTEL LIGHT
amsterdam, holland, 3.5% $6

BRASSERIES KRONENBOURG PILSNER
strasbourg, france, 5.0% $6

SOLE PALE ALE
emmaus, pa 4.9% $5

BELL'S TWO HEARTED IPA
kalamazoo, mi 7.0% $65

CIDRE FERMIER BRUT
brittany, 2013 (750ml) 4.5% $8/36

EVES CIDERY AUTUMN GOLD CIDER
van etten, ny 2014 8.5% (750ml) $40

HANSSENS GUEZE
dworp, belgium, 6.0% $22

BROUWERIJ BOCKER OUD BRUIN
bellegem, belgium 5.5% $12

SMUTTYNOSE ROBUST PORTER
hampton, nh 6.2% $6

FIGURE 4.7 (Continued)

COFFEE & TEA

Rival Brothers French Press 4
Harney & Sons Teas 5

SCOTCH

Famous Grouse 10
Johnnie Walker Black 12
Chivas Regal 12 yr 12
Chivas Regal 18 yr 16
Glenkinchie 12 Lowlands 15
Aberlour 16 yr Speyside 17
Springbank 18 yr 38
Talisker 10 yr 15
Bruichladdich Rockside Farm Islay 16
Ardbeg 10 year Islay 14
Laphroaig 10 Islay 14

WHISKEY

Crown Royal 11
Still Waters 1•1•1 12
Jameson 11
Redbreast 12 year 15
Knappogue Castle Twin Wood 16 yr 18
Jack Daniels 10
Buffalo Trace 12
Maker's Mark 12
Old Grand Dad 10
Wild Turkey 101 Rye 12
Michter's US 1 Rye 13
Rittenhouse Rye 13
Masterson's 10yr Rye 18

BRANDY

Landy VSOP 13
Pierre Ferrand 1840 15
Paul Beau VSOP Grand Champagne 20
Germain Robin Coast Road Reserve Brandy 15
Domaine d'Esperance 'XO' Bas Armagnac 23
Boulard 'XO' Calvados 22

DESSERT

$9

BACON AND EGG CREAM
maple custard, chocolate foam

FLOURLESS CHOCOLATE CAKE
pineapple, toffee, malted cream cheese

HONEY TART
green apple, walnut, bee pollen

PRALINE BABKA
hazelnut brittle, orange zest

AMARO

$12

S. Maria al Monte Amaro
Zwack
Fernet Branca
Nonino Amaro
Caffo Vecchia Amaro del Capo
Meletti Amaro
Nardini Amaro
Amaro Fratelli Ramazzotti
Luxardo Amaro Abano
La Vigne di Alice 'Nina'
Averna Amaro
Lucano Amaro
Domenico Sibona Amaro
Campari
Amaro Montenegro
Cynar
Ettore Zucca Rabarbaro
Cappelletti Elisir Novasalus

FIGURE 4.7 (Continued)

RESERVE WINES

SPARKLING & WHITE

PINOT BIANCO contadi castaldi lombardy. nv	74
CHARDONNAY domaine buronfosse. cremant du jura 2012	66
CHARDONNAY lelarge pugeot ier cru champagne. nv	91
PINOT NOIR vincent couche cuvee chloe. champagne. nv	111
PINOT NOIR ROSE gruet truth or consequences. nv	60
GAMAY DE CHAUDENAY ROSE le sot de l'ange. touraine. 2014	68
SAUVIGNON BLANC scarbolo. friuli 2014	64
GRUNER VELTLINER weingut johann donabaum wachau. 2014	72
RIESLING nik weiss. mosel 2014	60
CHARDONNAY de wetshof. robertson 2013	73
CHARDONNAY domaine buronfosse. cotes du jura 2011	85
CHENIN BLANC a.a. badenhorst. swartland. 2011	134

RED

PINOT NOIR steele. santa barbara county. 2011	80
PINOT NOIR domaine serene 'yamhill cuvee'. willamette valley 2011	148
ST. LAURENT weingut strehn. mittelburgenland 2013	64
MALBEC bodegas benegas. mendoza. 2010	74
DOLCETTO scarpa. monferrato. 2010	63
CINSAULT chateau musar. bekaa valley. 2001	187
CABERNET FRANC bow & arrow. willamette valley. 2014	88
MERLOT il fauno di arcanum. tuscany. 2011	85
MOURVEDRE/SHIRAZ first drop. barossa valley. 2011	74
CABERNET SAUVIGNON dunham cellars. walla walla valley. 2012	118
SAGRATINO DI MONTEFALCO azienda leonucci umbria. 2010	112
MOURVEDRE chateaux pradeaux. bandol. 2009	125

DESSERT

SEMILLON chateau rieussec. sauternes. 2006 (375ml)	115
SEMILLON la fleur d'or. sauternes. 2011 (375ml)	68
FURMINT puklus pinceszet 3 puttonyos. tokaj 2007 (500ml)	68
FURMINT kiralydvar 6 puttonyos. tokaj 2003 (500ml)	178
FURMINT dobogo 6 puttonyos tokaj 2007 (500 ml)	145

FIGURE 4.7   (Continued)

RESERVE WINES

SPARKLING & WHITE

PINOT BIANCO contadi castaldi lombardy. nv	74
CHARDONNAY domaine buronfosse. cremant du jura 2012	66
CHARDONNAY lelarge pugeot ier cru champagne. nv	91
PINOT NOIR vincent couche cuvee chloe. champagne. nv	111
PINOT NOIR ROSE gruet truth or consequences. nv	60
GAMAY DE CHAUDENAY ROSE le sot de l'ange. touraine. 2014	68
SAUVIGNON BLANC scarbolo. friuli 2014	64
GRUNER VELTLINER weingut johann donabaum wachau. 2014	72
RIESLING nik weiss. mosel 2014	60
CHARDONNAY de wetshof. robertson 2013	73
CHARDONNAY domaine buronfosse. cotes du jura 2011	85
CHENIN BLANC a.a. badenhorst. swartland. 2011	134

RED

PINOT NOIR steele. santa barbara county. 2011	80
PINOT NOIR domaine serene 'yamhill cuvee'. willamette valley 2011	148
ST. LAURENT weingut strehn. mittelburgenland 2013	64
MALBEC bodegas benegas. mendoza. 2010	74
DOLCETTO scarpa. monferrato. 2010	63
CINSAULT chateau musar. bekaa valley. 2001	187
CABERNET FRANC bow & arrow. willamette valley. 2014	88
MERLOT il fauno di arcanum. tuscany. 2011	85
MOURVEDRE/SHIRAZ first drop. barossa valley. 2011	74
CABERNET SAUVIGNON dunham cellars. walla walla valley. 2012	118
SAGRATINO DI MONTEFALCO azienda leonucci umbria. 2010	112
MOURVEDRE chateaux pradeaux. bandol. 2009	125

DESSERT

SEMILLON chateau rieussec. sauternes. 2006 (375ml)	115
SEMILLON la fleur d'or. sauternes. 2011 (375ml)	68
FURMINT puklus pinceszet 3 puttonyos. tokaj 2007 (500ml)	68
FURMINT kiralydvar 6 puttonyos. tokaj 2003 (500ml)	178
FURMINT dobogo 6 puttonyos tokaj 2007 (500 ml)	145

not a standard sequence or set of terminology for the headings. Some operations pace the meal so that only one plate arrives at a time while others may deliver two or three at once.

No one knows for certain whether the small plates trend will continue to expand or not, but it does satisfy some major trends in America today. With the prevalence of food in the media, more people want to experience new culinary creations and exciting ingredients. The opportunity to taste 5–10 dishes in a single sitting satisfies that craving more than the traditional appetizer-entrée-dessert sequence can. Additionally, while families and groups of friends continue to eat out in restaurants frequently, they lose the experience of sharing the same foods that once took place daily around the dinner table. The small plates restaurant accommodates both of these market needs by encouraging sharing while providing portions small enough that a table can order a smorgasbord of dishes. As with all foodservice operations, if the menu's fare and style of service continue to meet the needs of the market, the business will continue to offer that type of menu.

Brunch Menus

Typically offered only on weekends, brunch is a meal served across the late-breakfast and lunchtime period, and as such it usually offers foods traditionally associated with both meals. A brunch menu often lists heavier breakfast foods alongside lunch salads, sandwiches, and entrées. Because people usually treat brunch as a substitute for two meals, the menu items may be richer and more substantial than one usually sees on a basic breakfast menu. The headings may be numerous for an extensive menu or as basic as "Breakfast Fare" and "Lunch Fare" for a small menu.

A simple brunch menu often includes omelets, poached-egg dishes, fancy versions of pancakes, waffles, and French toast. It may also include heartier breakfast meat dishes, such as steak and eggs or corned beef hash. Lunch options can range from entrée salads to hot sandwiches to simple entrées. Desserts are typically offered, too, and should be listed under their own heading or on a separate menu. A fancier brunch may be served buffet

beverages

fresh squeezed lemonade $5

"mock"goddess $6
green tea, cucumber, arugula, lime juice, jalapeño

cocktails
$14
caffe trieste
kraken rum, espresso, vanilla, egg white, & angostura bitters

green goddess
green tea infused vodka, cucumber, arugula, jalapeño, absinthe tincture rinse

quixote
city of london gin with aperol, honey, grapefruit, & gingerbeer

bloody maria
tequila with red harissa, ancho chili, plum tomatoes, smoked paprika & horse radish

market bellini
bubbles with guava & citrus

winter's bark
tequila with blackberries, orange, licorice tincture, arbol chile & mescal

FIGURE 4.8
This creative brunch menu boasts both breakfast and lunch offerings as well as cocktails.
Source: Sample menu only; items and pricing subject to change. Reprinted with permission of a.o.c.

brunch

omelette with tahitian squash 15
green harissa, avocado, queso fresco, fried potatoes & toast

wood-oven baked eggs 16
chickpeas, cavolo nero, tomato confit, feta & sumac

grilled asparagus with polenta 15
winter vegetables & soft egg

spanish fried chicken & cornmeal waffle 16
jamon butter & maple syrup

vanilla bean french toast   15
brown-butter bourbon, apples, pecans & mascarpone whip

a.o.c. brioche 14
melted gruyère, frisée, prosciutto & sunny-side up egg

duck confit hash 18
wild mushrooms & poached eggs

hanger steak & eggs 25
roasted baby artichokes, potato & tapenade

two eggs any style 13
bacon, fried potatoes & toast

market fruit 6 vande rose bacon 5 fried potatoes 4

grilled blueberry bread & lemon butter 5

grilled toast, market jam & butter 4 side of fries 5

available

until

3:00

charcuterie

jamon serrano 11

prosciutto di parma 12

lomo & two chorizo 10

coppa & soppressata 10

marinated olives 6

marcona almonds 8

bacon-wrapped dates & parmesan 9

a.o.c. bread 2

artisanal cheese
(please see our daily cheese menu)

focaccias

tomato confit, mozzarella, spicy soppressata & lemon 15

manchego, jamon, arugula, walnut & date 16

young broccoli, burrata, bagna cauda & cipollini onion 15

focaccia sandwiches *(salad or fries)*

brussels sprouts, cavolo nero, radicchio,
balsamic & burrata 16

roast turkey, mozzarella, green harissa,
avocado & castelvetranos 17

pork confit, braised cabbage, mustard vinagrette &
dandelion 17

the a.o.c. burger 17
manchego, romesco aïoli & balsamic onions

salads

citrus, ricotta salata, arugula & green harissa 15

market lettuces, basil green goddess, avocado & radish sm 13/ lg 16
add chicken +3, add shrimp +6

chicories with apples, pears, walnuts & fourme d'ambert & maple vinaigrette sm 13/ lg 17
add chopped chicken +3, add shrimp +6

flaked albacore salad with lemongrass sambal, raw bok choy & mizuna 18

spinach salad with mustard grilled chicken, bacon lardons, soft egg & breadcrumbs 18

plate lunch

farmer's lunch: winter vegetables, muhammara & chickpea purée, burrata & grilled toast 17

vintner's lunch: rillettes, cheese, cured meat, pickles, roasted grapes & grilled toast 18

maine lobster and shrimp roll, toasted bun & french fries 25

a 3% charge is added to all checks to cover the cost of full health care benefits for our employees.
thank you for supporting a healthier & happier restaurant staff.
if you would like this charge removed, please let us know.

*Note: Consuming raw or undercooked meats, poultry, seafood, shellfish,
or egg may increase your risk of foodborne illness*

FIGURE 4.8 *(Continued)*

style to allow guests to sample a wider range of foods in a single sitting. A buffet brunch may include displays of breakfast breads, fruits, salads, egg dishes, potatoes, and cured pork alongside grand presentations of chilled shellfish and cured or smoked seafood, chafing dishes full of hot entrée components (meats, starches, and vegetables), carving stations with multiple large roasts, and tables groaning with desserts.

Unlike on a basic breakfast menu, alcoholic drinks are traditional components of brunch menus. Champagne, mimosas, and Bloody Marys are common, but opportunities for creativity abound in this area. All beverages, alcoholic and nonalcoholic, should be marketed heavily on the main menu under their own headings. Because of the propensity for people to wake up late on weekend mornings (after late Friday and Saturday nights out), to dine late after church services, or to lounge around a bar all day watching sports, restaurants may offer brunch on weekends starting as early as 9:00 A.M. and continuing until the restaurant converts over to its dinner menu. Brunch, especially Sunday brunch, is quite common in fancier establishments, including hotels and country clubs.

Afternoon Tea Menus

Like brunch, tea (the meal, not the beverage) is reserved for a time between traditional meal periods. Tea is normally served mid-to-late afternoon and can function as either a snack or a light meal. Some foodservice operations serve tea only on weekends and holidays while others, especially high-end hotels, provide the service daily.

Often thought of as an English tradition, tea may celebrate the foods of England or the foods of Asia, where tea is also a popular beverage. The traditional English afternoon tea includes a range of sweet pastries, scones, and tea sandwiches, which are simple sandwiches that usually have a main item on crust-free bread or biscuit but without the addition of lettuce, tomato, or other garnishes common on large sandwiches. Tea sandwiches and pastries are usually no more than two bites in size. Scones may be larger and served with jam, lemon curd, and/or clotted cream. The popular way to present these delights is on a multitiered tray from which the entire table dines, though some establishments provide each guest her own tiered tray.

During afternoon tea, both hot tea and alcoholic beverages are traditionally offered. Multiple tea choices should be highlighted on the main menu or on a separate menu. They are typically served in pots rather than by the cup; in fancier establishments loose-leaf teas are used. Sherry, wine, and champagne are common alcoholic offerings for a tea. Some guests may treat afternoon tea as their evening meal, but most tea patrons use it as a bridge to stave off hunger between a light lunch and a late dinner.

Because tea (the beverage) is the centerpiece of this meal and guests usually get the full complement of edibles listed, the menu headings for the drinks may be more extensive than those for the food. A menu planner could list all teas under the heading "Teas," but for larger menus she could have separate headings for black tea, green tea, oolongs, and tisanes. Alcoholic drinks should come under their own heading.

Lounge Menus

Some people translate lounge menus as bar food. A lounge is an environment in which people can relax before, during, or after dinner, usually for drinks and accompanying snacks. Most lounges offer full menus following the pattern of appetizers, entrées, and desserts, but the purpose of the food is generally to accompany the alcoholic drinks, not the other way around. Consequently, lounge menus tend to offer larger numbers of appetizers and more casual entrées than the average restaurant might provide. Desserts are usually limited in number unless the business focuses on liqueurs and other after-dinner drinks.

The items on a lounge menu are typically high in protein, fat, and salt. These nutrients serve a purpose beyond flavor in a bar or lounge. Salt makes people thirsty, so menu planners include salty foods to encourage the sales of beverages. However, alcohol, consumed too quickly, causes customers to go quickly from comfortable to inebriated. Protein and fat slow the rate at which the stomach empties and thus the speed at which alcohol is absorbed into the body. They give a person a chance to process some of the alcohol in her system before getting walloped with the full impact of her total alcohol consumption. Fried

TEA SANDWICHES

CUCUMBER & WATERCRESS ON BRIOCHE
Creme Fraiche | Herbs | Heirloom Tomatoes | Toast Point

CURRIED EGG SALAD ON TOASTED NAAN
Madras Curry Cream

LOBSTER PROFITEROLE
Lobster | Light Truffle Mayonnaise | Fresh Dill

SMOKED SALMON CREPE NAPOLEON
California Caviar | Farm Fresh Herb Cream Cheese | Cucumber

STEAK AU POIVRE ON BRIOCHE
Roasted NY Steak | Cracked Black Pepper Aioli | Petite Green Beans
Frisse | Tomatoes

TEA SANDWICHES AVAILABLE FOR CHILDREN:

BOSTON LETTUCE WRAP
With Carrots & Hummus

SMOKED TURKEY & CHEESE ECLAIR

ORCHARD APPLE WEDGES
With Nutella

SCONES

APPLE CINNAMON & TAHITIAN VANILLA BEAN
Served with:
Apricot Preserves | Raspberry Preserves | Homemade Lemon Curd
Devonshire Cream

TEA PASTRIES

BAKED CHOCOLATE TART

BROWN SUGAR CORNMEAL CAKE
With Maple Icing

CITRUS PANNA COTTA
With a Black Pepper Blueberry Compote

PISTACHIO CRÈME FILLED SHORTBREAD

RASPBERRY CURD MERENGUE TART

Cocktails
$12

APPLE CIDER MIMOSA
Champagne | Apple Cider | Cinnamon & Brown Sugar
Non-Alcoholic: $7

EARL GREY MINT JULEP
Maker's Mark Bourbon | Cold Brew Earl Grey Tea | Simple Syrup
Mint Leaves

GINGER SPICED APPLE
Dewar's White Label Scotch | Fresh Squeezed Lime Juice | Simple Syrup
Apple Cider | Ginger Beer
Non-Alcoholic: $7

GOOSE AUTUMN FIZZ
Grey Goose Vodka | Grand Marnier | Pomegranate Juice | Sour Mix
Sparkling Water
Non-Alcoholic: $7

WILLARD'S AUTUMN GIMLET
Bombay Sapphire Gin | Fresh Squeezed Lime Juice | Pear Puree

CHAMPAGNE

MOET & CHANDON IMPERIAL BRUT
$16

VEUVE CLICQUOT YELLOW LABEL BRUT
$25

Afternoon Tea

TEA IS LIKE WINE; THE WAY IT IS PRODUCED, THE HARVESTING TIME AND ITS LEAF SHAPE ALL LEND THE TEA ITS PARTICULAR TASTE, WHILE CLIMATE AND SOIL CREATE ITS CHARACTER. WE ARE PLEASED TO HAVE YOU JOIN US FOR AFTERNOON TEA IN PEACOCK ALLEY AT THE WILLARD INTERCONTINENTAL.

$49 per adult / $22 per child *(3-12 years of age)*

TEA SELECTIONS
THE WILLARD INTERCONTINENTAL PROUDLY SERVES RONNEFELDT TEAS.

BLACK TEAS

WILLARD CUSTOM BLEND - SHANGRI-LA
A great black tea with the mysterious Babaco fruit with its aromas of pineapple, kiwi and plum.

ASSAM
Assam is a strong malty black tea with a multitude of golden tips. Rich in aroma with a pleasantly rounded finish, Ideal for those who enjoy a classic strong English black tea.

EARL GREY
A tea blend with a distinctive citrus flavor and aroma derived from the addition of oil extract from the rind of the Bergamot orange which adds a fragrant citrus fruit flavor.

DARJEELING
Often called the "champagne of teas", this classic summer flush Darjeeling is well balanced, astringent and carries gentle floral notes.

MARSALA CHAI
Chai is the word for tea in many languages but in India it means a special blend of Assam black tea and a famous range of exotic Indian spices.

ORANGE OOLONG TEA
A traditional Chinese Oolong melded with the fruit liveliness of ripe orange.

GREEN TEAS

JASMINE GOLD
Delicate jasmine blossoms diffuse their gentle fragrance over a summer picked China green tea.

MORGENTAU
A unique combination made of rich Senca green tea, the flower petals from exotic fruits and subtle mango & lemon fruit flavors.

HERBAL INFUSION

HERB & GINGER
A highly aromatic infusion packed with herbs and other feel-good ingredients, including ginger, lemongrass, licorice and lemon verbena for energy and freshness.

MINT & FRESH
The relaxing cool flavor of mint is accented with the notes of fresh lemongrass.

VANILLA ROOIBOS
The much loved South African herbal infusion is full bodied and touched with the richness of creamy vanilla.

WHITE TEAS

PAI MU TAN & MELON
Withered in the sun, this handcrafted, white-leafed tea has a delicately flowery and sweet aroma, further enhanced with the essence of melon.

FIGURE 4.9

This afternoon tea menu illustrates the kind of food and beverage offerings expected at a quality afternoon tea.

Source: Menu provided by The Willard InterContinental Hotel and reprinted with permission of IHG. © 2016 IHG.

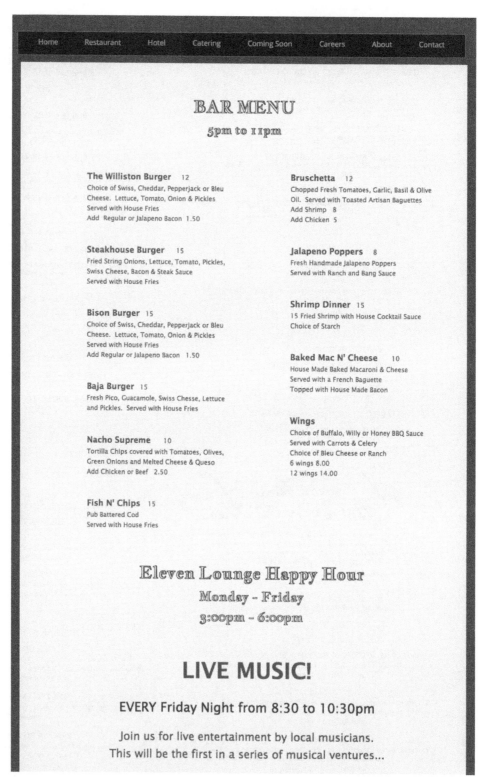

FIGURE 4.10

This section of a hotel lounge menu illustrates the kinds of food typical for a lounge menu.

Source: Reprinted with permission of Eleven Restaurant and Lounge.

appetizers, nachos and other cheese-heavy snacks, burgers, and chicken all make excellent lounge menu options. Fancier operations may list steaks and seafood as well. This is not to say that a lounge cannot offer a salad or a light entrée, but the vast majority of the listings on a lounge menu should be protein- and calorie-rich.

DESSERTS

Sundae Afternoon in New England
maple walnut ice cream, cranberry sorbet
maple syrup, maple cream cookies
and sugared cranberries 11

Mocha Hazelnut Semifreddo
hazelnut sweet crumbs, chocolate feuilletine
and espresso sauce 12

Warm Apple Tart
Calvados ice cream 11

Butterscotch Pudding
cocoa crisp and Chantilly cream
bittersweet chocolate sorbet 8/11
gluten free

Pear and White Chocolate Bread Pudding
crème anglaise and Chantilly cream 11

Cookie Plate
for here or TO GO 6/9

House-Made Ice Cream & Sorbet
with cookies 6/9

Chef's Selection of Cheese
6/per selection
served with honey, candied walnuts,
house made jam, crackers and breads

Liquid Desserts

First Frost
whipped cream vodka, house-made Irish cream,
Godiva white liqueur and cream
with cookies 15
without cookies 12

House-Made Irish Cream 11

FIGURE 4.11
This dessert menu provides balance and variety in its menu items.
Source: Chef Ris Lacoste and Pastry Chef Jonni Scott. Reprinted with permission.

Dessert Menus

A dessert menu is a separate document from the main menu, which may or may not have a dessert heading. Many mid-range to high-end dining establishments opt to list desserts solely on a dessert menu. While such an approach does not assist with the marketing of dessert early, it has many advantages.

A dessert menu provides plenty of space for a menu planner to describe delectable creations for the diner. The extra space also allows for the marketing of dessert beverages, from coffees to dessert wines to after-dinner cordials. Psychologically, having a separate menu to introduce a course suggests to the guest that this is an essential component to the meal, not simply another menu heading relegated to the corner of the main menu. With a dessert menu, the guest is handed a list from which to choose, but the only options are dessert and after-dinner beverages. The guest may still decline to order anything, but the psychological pressure is to select something from the menu. When desserts are listed on the main menu, the guest can rest easy knowing that she has already done her job as a customer and purchased something (a main course); with a dessert menu, the guest has yet to order something from the new list of menu items and thus feels some small pressure to do so.

The sole food heading on a dessert menu is typically listed as "Desserts." As with other menus, the dessert menu should include variety and balance. Also, to merit its own menu, a dessert menu should offer at least six choices and may list many more. If a restaurant provides cheese as a dessert alternative, it is listed among the dessert options. Dessert beverages, on the other hand, may require several headings on the menu. Possible headings include ports, dessert wines, bourbons, scotches, brandies, liqueurs, and tea, coffee, and espresso drinks (with or without alcohol).

Some menu planners, upon discovering that desserts are not popular sellers in their restaurants, have begun experimenting with portion sizes. Rather than serve a full portion of dessert, a pastry chef can prepare mini-desserts of just one or two bites for a low price. These miniature treats help to encourage dessert sales to guests who arrive at dessert already stuffed. The concept can be expanded to allow for dessert flights or samplers for those guests who wish to have a couple of bites of every dessert on the menu. With creative strategies, a menu planner can make dessert an essential component of the dining experience for nearly every guest. Creating an effective dessert menu is the first step of that marketing approach.

Children's Menus

A children's menu is a must for those businesses that cater to families with young children. Many parents are tight on money and prefer not to spring for a full meal portion from which their kids will eat only three bites. When a restaurant chooses not to offer a separate kids' menu, it communicates to parents that children are not common patrons and are not easily accommodated. (This is not to say that such a restaurant would turn away a child but rather that the child is expected to behave like an adult and to order off the adult menu.) Children who get their own "special" menu tend to feel more welcome in a restaurant than they do if they are forced to act like adults.

A children's menu may include many headings, but it usually lists three—entrées, beverages, and desserts. Some children's menus place beverage and dessert choices without a heading in small type at the top of the menu when they are included in the price of the entrée, table d'hôte style. The kind of food offered on a kids' menu should be simple and child-friendly. Ethnic restaurants may offer less spicy, simplistic versions of their culture's dishes. Because their taste buds are extremely sensitive, children often prefer foods that are blander and milder than their parents' preferences—thus the reason for the popularity of chicken fingers, cheese pizza, and plain pasta on kids' menus. However, mild does not mean boring. Kids do quite well with quesadillas, beans and rice, carrots and other mildly sweet vegetables, and fruit. Mild meats, like chicken, are good protein sources, but so are cheese and seafood. Whatever the ingredient, the portion size should be small. Kids eat less food than their parents, and their parents do not want to pay for excessive portions.

The ingredients on a kids' menu should be served as separate components where feasible, so children can identify each of the ingredients easily. If a child with an aversion to peas finds one pea in a stew, she may dismiss the entire dish. However, given a plate of stewed meat, sliced carrots, and buttered peas, the same child could enjoy the meat and carrots and simply skip the peas. The separation of ingredients also helps parents to spot potential allergens. Because of the danger of allergic reactions, common food allergens should be listed clearly in any dish in which they appear.

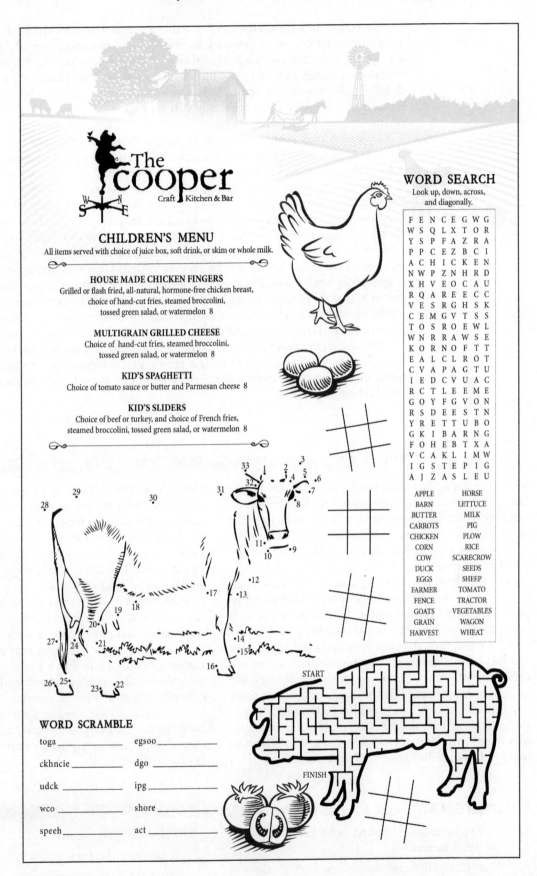

The cooper
Craft Kitchen & Bar

CHILDREN'S MENU
All items served with choice of juice box, soft drink, or skim or whole milk.

HOUSE MADE CHICKEN FINGERS
Grilled or flash fried, all-natural, hormone-free chicken breast,
choice of hand-cut fries, steamed broccolini,
tossed green salad, or watermelon 8

MULTIGRAIN GRILLED CHEESE
Choice of hand-cut fries, steamed broccolini,
tossed green salad, or watermelon 8

KID'S SPAGHETTI
Choice of tomato sauce or butter and Parmesan cheese 8

KID'S SLIDERS
Choice of beef or turkey, and choice of French fries,
steamed broccolini, tossed green salad, or watermelon 8

WORD SEARCH
Look up, down, across,
and diagonally.

```
F E N C E G W G
W S Q L X T O R
Y S P F A Z R A
P P C E Z B C I
A C H I C K E N
N W P Z N H R D
X H V E O C A U
R Q A R E E C C
V E S R G H S K
C E M G V T S S
T O S R O E W L
W N R R A W S E
K O R N O F T T
E A L C L R O T
C V A P A G T U
I E D C V U A C
R C T L E E M E
G O Y F G V O N
R S D E E S T N
Y R E T T U B O
G K I B A R N G
F O H E B T X A
V C A K L I M W
I G S T E P I G
A J Z A S L E U
```

APPLE   HORSE
BARN   LETTUCE
BUTTER   MILK
CARROTS   PIG
CHICKEN   PLOW
CORN   RICE
COW   SCARECROW
DUCK   SEEDS
EGGS   SHEEP
FARMER   TOMATO
FENCE   TRACTOR
GOATS   VEGETABLES
GRAIN   WAGON
HARVEST   WHEAT

START
FINISH

WORD SCRAMBLE

toga _____   egsoo _____

ckhncie _____   dgo _____

udck _____   ipg _____

wco _____   shore _____

speeh _____   act _____

FIGURE 4.12
This children's menu combines healthy, kid-friendly food with activities to occupy the children.
Source: Reprinted with permission of The Cooper Craft Kitchen & Bar.

Beverages on a children's menu should be simple but healthy. While soda might excite a child, most parents wish to see a selection of juices and milks instead. Fun, creative drinks are not the sole domain of adults, either. Hot chocolate with whipped cream and crushed peppermint candy can make a child's eyes sparkle at breakfast, and a virgin strawberry daiquiri may have greater appeal than a basic soda. When feasible, beverages for the youngest children should be served in a cup with a lid and a straw to avoid spills unless the parent or child requests otherwise.

Unlike an adult menu, a children's menu may double as an activity sheet to occupy the kids until the food arrives. Often, they are paper printouts with games or pictures that the kids can color with crayons supplied by the restaurant. If the kids are happy during the meal, the parents will be happy (and very likely to return). The food on a children's menu should be relatively quick to prepare. Servers should ask the parents whether they wish the child's dish to come out right away, which also helps to occupy the child. When a child eats her entrée during the parents' appetizer course, she is then in a position to color more, engage in conversation, or possibly taste her parents' food without the nagging pain of hunger to disgruntle her. For a more energetic child, dessert may be the only civilized option. Offering dessert, usually just a couple of choices listed on the main kids' menu, gives parents the chance to distract a child with sweets so that the parents can enjoy their main course (or their own dessert). As with the entrée, a child's dessert should be a smaller portion than the adult-size desserts. To keep kids (and their parents) as loyal customers, some menu planners include dessert in the price of the meal.

Pint-sized customers may not pay the bill or determine the tip, but they often are instrumental in deciding which restaurant a family patronizes on any given night. Providing a menu that meets their needs is a surefire way to develop a loyal customer base among this youthful market.

Summary

Specialty menus that go beyond the traditional breakfast, lunch, and dinner menus abound in the foodservice world. Most of these menus still adhere to the rules of variety and balance, and they all must address the needs of the intended market or client. The heading conventions may vary, but the menus continue to serve the needs of both the customer and the business. Takeout and room service menus focus on foods that transport well. Cycle menus repeat their menu items on a schedule. While cycle menus are used often in noncommercial businesses, they are sometimes utilized to plan specials for a commercial restaurant. Banquet menus offer a set sequence of courses with few choices; the options are constrained by the target audience or client and the need to serve everyone efficiently and at roughly the same time. Tasting menus are often elaborate gustatory experiences, but portion sizes must allow guests to make it through the entire meal. Catering menus list a plethora of options from which a client selects; the ultimate menu that the guests see at the catered event is a subset of the catering menu. Ethnic menus highlight the foods and cultural traditions of the represented culture. Fusion menus combine several cultural influences on a single menu; the small plates trend applies the tapas and mezze style of service to a wide range of cuisines. Brunch menus boast traditional foods from both breakfast and lunch while afternoon tea menus offer tea sandwiches and pastries along with hot tea or alcohol. A lounge menu provides food that pairs well with the consumption of alcohol in a bar environment. Dessert menus focus the guest's attention entirely on the dessert course's food and beverage offerings. Finally, children's menus attend to the food and often to the entertainment needs of a business's youngest customers to keep them happy and occupied so that their parents can enjoy their own meals.

Comprehension Questions

1. List two commonalities between traditional menus and other menus.

2. What characteristics should food on a take-out menu have?

3. When do many hotels begin taking orders for room service breakfast?

4. What is a cycle menu?

5. What two factors impact how often a cycle menu repeats?

6. List an example of a type of food in a restaurant that might be offered on a cycle.

7. How might a menu planner help guests avoid palate fatigue during a lengthy banquet?

8. As guests at a banquet must all be served the same course before any table moves to the next course, what style of service other than American service is often used at banquets?

9. How do catering menus differ from other types of menus?

10. What "course" is often listed on a catering menu but not on most other menus?

11. List five beverages commonly offered on a brunch menu.

12. List three kinds of foods typically served at afternoon tea.

13. What qualities should food on a lounge menu possess?

14. What function does a children's menu often serve other than providing a list of food and beverage choices?

Discussion Questions

1. Select a specific ethnic restaurant in your area. How does its menu differ from a traditional menu format?

2. Think of a time that you ordered take-out or room service. How well did the food meet your expectations? Was it an appropriate choice for take-out or room service? Why?

3. Think of two restaurants you have patronized—one that offers dessert on the main menu and one that presents a separate dessert menu. Which set of dessert options sounded better to you? Was one more effective than the other at encouraging you to buy dessert? Why?

4. Describe a favorite children's menu from your childhood. What made it your favorite? How often did you go to that restaurant as compared with others that your parents chose?

5. Select one of the types of menus (other than catering) listed in the chapter. Create a menu (names of dishes only) appropriate for the menu type you selected. Explain why it works well as a model for that particular menu type.

6. Consider the trends of small plates and fusion cuisine. Do you think they will continue for the next ten to twenty years? Why/why not? What other trends do you foresee emerging in menus in the future?

Case Study

Analyze each of the menus included in the chapter. What does each menu do that differs from a standard restaurant menu but makes it appropriate for the type of menu it is and the clientele or event it serves? Do any of the menus do something that impresses you? Recognizing that these menus originate from successful businesses across the country, select one menu that you believe would not work if transplanted to an existing business in your local community. What would need to change to appeal to the market served by the existing business near you?

Capstone Project

Step 4: Continue the process of writing menu items and categorizing them under menu headings appropriate for your business concept. Beverages should also be included if you wish to place them on the main menu. If appropriate, create a separate dessert menu, children's menu, or other specialty menu that makes sense for your concept. (Do not create a separate beverage menu yet as that will be the focus of the next chapter.) To prepare for the upcoming steps in the project, select ten dishes from across your menu, including one from each heading, and write recipes for those dishes.

CHAPTER 5

Beverage Menus

INTRODUCTION

The headings, menu items, and descriptions for a beverage menu are vastly different from those on a food menu but no less deserving of attention. Beverage menus are excellent opportunities for revenue and profit generation. Beverages usually require less labor to prepare and serve than food does, and they command huge profit margins. However, while beverages are considered essential components of a meal for most diners, a poorly written beverage menu can intimidate a guest and discourage beverage sales. A well-written beverage menu encourages guests to enjoy multiple or higher-priced beverages as part of the dining experience.

Not too long ago, "beverage menu" was synonymous with "wine list." Many of today's restaurants recognize that not all patrons are wine drinkers and that beverages of all types represent an opportunity to meet a guest's needs while increasing revenue. Depending on the business's concept and the target market's demographics and psychographic preferences, a beverage menu may highlight cocktails, liquor, wine, beer, or nonalcoholic drinks such as tea, coffee, juice, or water. When an establishment becomes known for an excellent beverage program, drinks can become as much a draw for business as the food and service are. Learning how to create a quality beverage menu that meets the needs of the business and the clientele is a necessity for any menu planner.

CHAPTER 5 LEARNING OBJECTIVES

As a result of successfully completing this chapter, readers will be able to:

1. List several beverage types and describe the breadth of options available for each type.

2. Create a wine menu that follows a common approach to wine-naming conventions and headings and supports a given restaurant concept.

3. Create a beer menu that reflects modern trends while supporting a given restaurant concept.

4. Create a cocktail and liquor menu that follows common menu item and naming conventions.

5. List the range of menu item options available for nonalcoholic beverages.

6. Describe the menu planner's role in supporting safe alcohol service.

CHAPTER 5 OUTLINE

Wine Menus

Learning Objective 1
List several beverage types and describe the breadth of options available for each type.

Learning Objective 2
Create a wine menu that follows a common approach to wine-naming conventions and headings and supports a given restaurant concept.

While modern beverage menus often include a range of alcoholic beverages, wine menus were for years the default option for any upscale restaurant. Because wine pairs well with food, wine lists continue to be popular in mid-range and high-end establishments, even if no other type of alcohol is served. Wine menus range from a single page of fewer than twenty options to bound books with several hundred listings.

As with every other type of menu, a wine menu must support the company's concept and appeal to the target audience. For example, a casual lounge that focuses on inexpensive bar food and beer and liquor sales may have a short wine list with inexpensive options for those consumers who only drink wine. An expensive French restaurant may opt to focus mainly on pricy French wines with only a few cheaper options. A wine list that includes only expensive options is likely to sell less wine overall, but the problem is magnified when the food and wine are at very different price points. Generally speaking, less expensive restaurants should offer less expensive wine choices, but even extremely expensive operations should have available at least a couple of affordable wines. No matter what the price point, guests should always be able to find wine by the glass that costs less than the cost of an entrée.

Wine menus should provide variety across several variables including grape type, region, color, body, and vintage. The New World wines of North and South America, Australia, and Africa are typically labeled by grape type; European wines are usually identified by region. Finally, any producer can create a wine and give it a proprietary name based on neither grape type nor region. While a wine menu can list wines from any number of regions, at a minimum it should include local wines (in the United States that means in state, from neighboring states, or at least from somewhere in America) and wines from the same country as the cuisine being served. For example, an Italian restaurant in New York should include Italian, American, and, ideally, New York State wine options. A Greek restaurant in Texas may include Greek and American wines. Restaurants serving American fare may opt for a selection of American wines only. The logic behind these rules of variety is that Americans will want either the beverage traditionally served with that food or the local wines with which they are most familiar. These rules are only minimum guidelines for variety; a restaurant is always free to include wines from all over the world.

When determining which wines to include on the wine list, a menu planner should ensure that several whites and reds are included. Sparkling and rosé wines offer even greater variety but should not be considered a substitute for a healthy listing of reds and whites. The selection should include light, medium, and heavy wines to pair well with the range of light to heavy foods. Most of the wines should be dry with at least one semi-dry option to drink with the entrée. Sweet wines may be included to pair with dessert. Finally, because wine qualities depend in part on the weather during the grapes' growing season, the wines served should not all come from the same vintage or year.

Naming and Categorizing Wines

Because of the many variables that identify a wine, a listing on a wine menu should include the wine's producer, grape type, appellation (region), and vintage (or at least as much of that information as is available). Old World wines may not state a grape type, but connoisseurs of those wines are familiar with the grapes used in certain regions. Nonvintage wines will not provide a year. If the wine producer has given its wine a proprietary name, that name should be listed with other basic information available about the wine. Example 5.1 illustrates the several naming conventions.

The order in which the components of a wine's name are listed depends upon how the menu planner chooses to organize the wine list and to name the headings. There is no universal standard, but generally speaking, if a heading states the commonality among the wines under that heading, the commonality should not be the first thing mentioned for each listing. In fact, that variable may be eliminated entirely. The variable that most distinguishes each wine from the others under the same heading should be listed first. For example, if a wine list has a category entitled "Cabernet Sauvignon," a wine under that heading

---

EXAMPLE 5.1: Wine-Naming Conventions

Cabernet Sauvignon, Cakebread Cellars, Napa Valley, 2013	Named by grape type (cabernet sauvignon). Lists in order: grape, producer, region, and vintage.
Châteauneuf-du-Pape, Rouge, Château de Beaucastel, 2012	Named by region (Châteauneuf-du-Pape). Lists in order: region, color, producer, and vintage.
Joseph Phelps, Insignia, Napa Valley, 2012	Named by proprietary name (Insignia). Lists in order: producer, proprietary name, region, and vintage.

---

might be written as "Cakebread Cellars, Cabernet Sauvignon, Napa Valley, 2013" or simply as "Cakebread Cellars, Napa Valley, 2013." If the same wine were listed under the heading of "California" or "Red," then the grape type would lead the listing as "Cabernet Sauvignon, Cakebread Cellars, Napa Valley, 2013." In essence, wines named by grape type should list the grape type first, unless the grape type is stated in the heading. Similarly, wines named by region should list the region first unless the heading does that already. Proprietary names are rarely used as a heading, so they are often listed with the producer first, followed by the proprietary name. The vintage is usually listed at the end of the wine's name, although some menu planners choose to list the vintage first because the layout creates a natural column with each wine beginning with a four-digit year in its name.

No matter how a menu planner chooses to sequence a wine's name, if the wine list includes more than a dozen or so wines, it should provide a bin number for each wine. A bin number is simply a number given to a wine that corresponds to the number on the bin or container in which the wine is stored at the restaurant. Listing a bin number allows for the guest to order by number instead of by wine name. The use of a bin number helps to avoid communication errors, as some wines have similar names. Additionally, guests who are uncomfortable pronouncing the foreign words in a wine's name can simply provide the bin number without embarrassing themselves in front of their tablemates. When listed, bin numbers are usually placed in a separate column to the left of the wine names.

Just as there is no standard format for naming a wine, there is no universal approach to naming the headings on a menu. Some menu planners use grape types as headings; others use countries or regions. Still others divide the menu simply into sparkling, white, rosé, red, and dessert. Of course, these are not the only approaches. Wine menus can be intimidating to some customers, so some menu planners have taken the approach of categorizing wines by their body and flavor. In these cases a category heading might be "Light and Fruity" or "Crisp, Mineral-y Whites." Extensive wine lists at upscale restaurants often assume that guests know something about wine, so they tend to sort wines by country and then by grape type or region. One- or two-page wine lists in a casual, kitschy, or trendy restaurant are better suited to employ more innovative, user-friendly naming conventions.

Pairing Wine and Food

Upscale restaurants often have a sommelier to guide and advise diners in their wine purchases; at a minimum, the servers are trained to play this role. More casual restaurants may rely on the menu to do the job of pairing wines with food. Short wine lists can include brief tasting notes for each wine. An example of a brief tasting note might be "A crisp, dry, light-bodied white wine with hints of grapefruit and hay." Other menu planners take the liberty of listing a recommended wine for each entrée. For example, directly underneath a seafood stew, the menu might state, "Recommended pairing: Estancia Chardonnay" or simply "Pairs well with an American Chardonnay." There are conflicting theories as to the value of specifying a wine to pair with each dish. On the one hand, guests who are intimidated by wine may be relieved to see a suggested pairing and may order wine that they otherwise might have shunned. On the other hand, a guest who does not care for the recommended wine type may choose to skip wine entirely for fear that his preferred wine would not go with his chosen meal. The only way to know which theory makes sense for a given restaurant's audience is to test it. A menu planner might list recommended wine pairings for a month or two to see whether wine sales go up or down. The lessons learned from that data let the menu planner know whether to continue listing wine pairings or to remove them in the next iteration of the food menu.

To determine which wines go perfectly with which foods can require years of study. Fortunately, the best wine choice for a guest is partly based on his menu choice and partly based on his taste preferences. The best match for a dish might be a chardonnay, but if the guest only likes red wines, a lighter red wine would be the appropriate recommendation. The old mnemonic of red wines with red meat and white wines with white meat is far too simplistic, and it does not take into account guest flavor preferences. The better rule of thumb is to pair light-bodied wines with lighter foods and full-bodied wines with heavier foods. (Body is simply the weight or viscosity felt in the mouth. Just like the difference between skim milk and heavy cream, body can vary greatly even with wines of similar flavor profiles.) Body is important because a mismatch causes the wine to overpower the food or vice versa. When the food and wine align in body, the aftertaste of each remains perceptible while the other is consumed, and both interact to create pleasant new flavors. Only once the body of the wine is determined appropriately should the menu planner or server worry about pairing wine aromas or overtones to the food. Sweetness in wine does not always pair well with savory dishes, but semi-dry (slightly sweet) wine is an excellent choice for the strong flavors of smoke, piquant, or salt in food. Very sweet wines should be reserved for dessert.

While a wine menu should provide variety and balance in its listings, all of the wines should match appropriately with the food. An Indian restaurant that serves a lot of spicy food should devote some percentage of its list to semi-dry wines that pair well with heat. A restaurant that only serves seafood should focus almost exclusively on light and medium-bodied wines. When a restaurant menu runs the gamut from light to heavy dishes, the wine list should follow suit. However, even when a wine list is limited by the food choices, it should still offer variety. For example, a seafood restaurant's wine menu could include Sauvignon Blanc, Chardonnay, Riesling, Gewürztraminer, and Pinot Blanc as well as lighter reds, such as French Beaujolais or Italian Dolcetto. Similarly, the wine list might include wines from Australia, France, Italy, Germany, and several U.S. states. Simply because a wine list must match with a narrowly focused food menu does not mean that it cannot provide variety.

Portion Sizes

The most common format for a bottle of wine is a 750-mL bottle, which provides approximately five 5-ounce servings. Almost every wine list devotes a significant portion of its menu items to this format. However, not every table will want a bottle of that size. Some guests want only a glass of wine, while others want something in between. Operations that can support a large wine inventory should include several bottle sizes on their wine menu. A half bottle allows a table of two to share a bottle of wine without overindulging. It also gives guests a chance to order a small bottle for each course rather than selecting a single bottle to pair with multiple courses. Large-format bottles, like a magnum (1.5 L), allow large parties to share from a single bottle, which can make a special occasion feel even more special. When possible, an extensive wine list should include a few half-size and a few large-format bottles on the menu.

No matter how big or small the wine menu is, it should always include some wines by the glass. Some guests dine alone and only want a glass or two to drink. Some individuals in a party will prefer to select different types of wine (or other alcoholic beverages). Whatever the reason, wines by the glass sell very well and help to encourage wine sales. At a minimum, a restaurant should offer at least two whites and two reds by the glass—one light-bodied and one full-bodied of each color. Wine-centered establishments may list over a dozen different options by the glass.

The portion size for wine served by the glass is up to the establishment, but a 5-ounce portion of wine is considered standard. (Wine glasses are not intended to be filled to the top.) It contains approximately the same quantity of alcohol as a 12-ounce beer, which makes counting drinks for the purposes of safe alcohol service easier. Wine bars may give guests a choice among several smaller pour sizes to encourage the purchase of multiple

WINE

Reserve List Available

SPARKLING / WHITES	REDS

Bubbles Around the World

Emile Boeckel, *Rose*, Cremant D'Alsace, France NV — 14 / 56
Crisp and fresh with cranberry, pomegranate, and wild strawberry.

Poggio delle Baccanti, *Sparkling Red*, Naples, Italy 2014 — 13 / 52
Aglianico blend. Violets, black pepper, plum and boysenberry. Full and dark.

Valdivieso, *Chardonnay Blend*, Curico Valley, Chile NV — 9 / 36
With Semillon. Green apple, almond and white flower. Crisp, clean and dry.

La Serra, *Moscato D'Asti*, Piemonte, Italy 2014 — 11 / 44
Baked pear, marzipan and honeysuckle. Crisp with a sweet finish.

Peillot Montagnieu Brut, *Altesse Blend*, Bugey, France NV — 15 / 60
Macintosh apple, lemon citrus and brioche. Full bodied a long, fresh finish.

Aromatic Whites
Taste how these varietals differ between warm and cool climates

Juliusspital, *Scheurebe*, Franken, Germany 2014 — 12 / 48
Ripe Asian pear, pink grapefruit and honeysuckle on the nose and palate. Fruity and round with bright minerality on the finish.

Banyan, *Gewurtztraminer*, Monterey, CA 2014 — 9 / 36
Gardenia, tangerine, lychee and a hint of white pepper on the nose and palate. Crisp and dry with a fine minerality and a bright, dry finish.

Paul Anheuser, *Riesling Kabinett*, Nahe, Germany 2002 — 10 / 40
Notes of Clementine, orange blossom and wet stone on the nose and palate. Medium bodied with a hint of sweetness and a fruity finish.

Tasting flight of above **16**

Exotic Whites
Not your every day whites

Calabretta, *Ansonica*, Calabria, Italy 2013 — 10 / 40
Ripe peach, melon and lemon zest on the nose and palate. Medium bodied with a refreshing acidity and a hint of minerality on a dry finish.

Coenobium, *Trebbiano blend*, Lazio, Italy 2013 — 16 / 64
Blended with Malvasia and Verdicchio. Beeswax, fresh figs, white peach and sage on the nose and palate. Full and fresh with a dry finish.

Vera, *Arinto blend*, Vinho Verde, Portugal, 2014 — 10 / 40
Yellow peach and grapefruit, golden delicious apple and meyer lemon on the nose and palate. Bright with a lively minerality and a dry finish.

Tasting flight of above **17**

Chardonnaysiens
Old and New World versions of the classic Bourgogne white

Corvidae "Mirth", *Chardonnay*, Columbia Valley, WA 2013 — 10 / 40
Golden delicious apple, meyer lemon and a hint of tropical fruit. Medium to full bodied with bright acidity and a clean, refreshing finish.

Domaine Parisse Bois de Fée, *Chardonnay*, Saint-Véran, FR 2011 — 16 / 64
Honeysuckle, baked pear, lemon, & a hint of vanilla on the nose and palate. Medium bodied with a round mouthfeel & a long, lingering finish.

Sonoma-Loeb, *Chardonnay*, Sonoma County, CA 2013 — 15 / 60
Candied pineapple, butterscotch and lemon curd on the nose and palate. Full and round with rich mouthfeel and a refreshing finish.

Tasting flight of above **21**

Oak vs. Stainless
Taste how aging styles can make a difference with these dry whites

Savee Sea, *Sauvignon Blanc*, Marlborough, New Zealand 2015 — 12 / 48
Passion fruit, tangerine, key lime and sage on the nose and palate. Crisp and fresh with a bright acidity and a fruity finish.

Domaine de Bel Air, *Sauvignon Blanc*, Pouilly Fume, FR 2014 — 14 / 56
Hints of meyer lemon, gooseberry, fresh cut grass and wet stone. Light and crisp with a bracing mineraltiy and a zippy finish.

Lagaria, *Pinot Grigio*, Veneto, Italy 2014 — 10 / 40
Asian pear, honeydew melon, kaffir lime and beeswax on the nose and palate. Full and round with a dry and mineral driven finish.

Tasting flight of above **18**

Pinot Lovers Unite
Three different approaches to a traditional varietal

Transverse, *Pinot Noir*, Santa Rita Hills, CA 2013 — 14 / 56
Dark notes of black cherry, black currant, ripe strawberry & cherry cola on the nose and palate. Medium bodied with a mild acidity and a long, juicy finish.

Dom. Maurice Charleaux, *Pinot Noir*, Maranges, Burgundy, 2013 — 19 / 76
Pomegranate, bing cherry, tart raspberry and anise on the nose and palate. Light to medium bodied with a robust acidity and a dry, spicy finish.

Cooper Hill, *Pinot Noir*, Willamette Valley, Oregon 2014 — 16 / 64
Raspberry, cherry tart, strawberry preserves and hints of baking spice on the nose and palate. Light to medium bodied with mild acidity and a juicy finish.

Tasting flight of above **25**

Mountains to the Sea
Cruise the elevations of Europe

Foradori, *Teroldego*, Alto Adige, Italy 2012 — 18 / 72
Rich and dark with notes of black plum, bittersweet chocolate, licorice and earth on the nose and palate. Full bodied with mild tannin and a dry finish.

DeAngelis, *Montepulciano*, Abruzzo, Italy 2013 — 10 / 40
Maraschino cherry, raspberry, leather and spice on the nose and palate. Medium to full bodied with a fruity palate and earthy tannin on the finish.

Tami, *Frappato*, Sicily, Italy 2013 — 12 / 48
Ripe red cherry, strawberry, rhubarb and licorice on the nose and palate. Light to medium bodied with a dry, slightly tannic finish.

Tasting flight of above **20**

Spices and Berries
Spice up your palate or give it a kick of fruit

Autonom, *Grenache Blend*, Santa Barbara County, CA 2011 — 17 / 68
Blend of Syrah and Mourverdre. Candied cherries, black pepper, black plum on the nose and palate. Medium bodied with mild tannins and bright finish.

Brutocao, *Zinfandel*, Mendocino, CA 2011 — 12 / 48
Hints of clove, red plum, stewed raspberries and blackberry cobbler. Medium to full bodied with round structure and a long dry finish.

Valdevisio, *Carmenere*, Capachapoal Valley, Chile 2011 — 16 / 64
Fresh bell pepper, bittersweet chocolate, blackberry and black plum on the nose and palate. Medium bodied and juicy with mild tannin and a long finish.

Tasting flight of above **23**

Bordeaux Blends
Interpretations of the classic Bordeaux varietals from around the world

Reunion, *Malbec*, Mendoza, Argentina 2015 — 10 / 40
Red plum, ripe raspberry, red roses and tobacco on the nose and palate. Medium bodied with bright tannins and a chewy finish.

Chappelet, *Cabernet Blend*, Napa, California 2013 — 18 / 72
Blended with Merlot & Petit Verdot. Notes of blackberry, cassis, vanilla, bittersweet chocolate Full bodied with a beautifully balanced tannic structure.

Château Chaigneau, *Merlot Blend*, Lalande de Pomerol, BDX 2010 — 15 / 60
Blended with Cabernet Franc. Blackberry, black plum, cedar and anise. Medium to full bodied with moderate tannins & a dry finish.

Tasting flight of above **22**

Uninhibited Reds
Terroir driven varietals

Vino Pura de Uva Pipeño, *Pais*, Itata Valley, Chile 2015 — 13 / 52
Cranberry, raspberry, dried sage and coriander on the nose and palate. Medium bodied with mild tannin, mild acidity and a long earthy finish.

Maison Angelot, *Mondeuse*, Bugey, France 2012 — 12 / 48
Fruity on the nose and palate. Notes of tart red cherry, raspberry and plum. Hints of licorice and fresh black pepper. Medium bodied with a pleasant finish.

Lopez de Heredia "Vina Cubillo", *Tempranillo*, Rioja, Spain 2007 — 19 / 76
Pomegranate, rhubarb, red plum, tobacco and oak on the nose and palate. Full bodied with elegant tannin and a dry, relatively smooth finish.

Tasting flight of above **22**

FIGURE 5.1

This wine menu, with its many wines by the glass and available tasting flights, incorporates playful menu headings and user-friendly beverage descriptions.

Source: Reprinted with the permission of District®

tastings or flights. Given the choice between a set of three 2-ounce pours or a single 5-ounce glass, some customers will opt for the extra quantity and cost of the three-wine flight just to experience the variety. That said, the more common approach to wine service in the average restaurant is to offer only one size—usually a 5-ounce glass for table wines (but less for dessert or fortified wines, like port or sherry, when they are offered).

Beer Menus

Learning Objective 3
Create a beer menu that reflects modern trends while supporting a given restaurant concept.

Not all that long ago, a restaurant's beer menu would have been a short list of mass-produced beers divided between those on tap and those in a bottle. While this type of beer list still exists in many places, it is not the only approach to beer. Boutique, regional American beers abound and come in a range of styles. Beer consumers no longer think of beer as a product but rather as a set of products that includes lagers, ales, stouts, porters, and even more subsets of those types. In a world that produces Belgian tripels, German hefeweizens, and American pumpkin ales, it is too simplistic to assume that the only choice Americans want is between regular and light beer.

Like a wine menu, a well-done beer menu should display variety in type and location. Beer is made around the world, and an extensive beer list should include beers from a wide range of countries. American microbreweries, relatively small producers compared to the big-name international giants, are flourishing around the United States and are very much in fashion. At a minimum, the menu should include some local microbrews (and other American beers) and beers from the same country as the style of cuisine being served. In other words, a Belgian restaurant should list Belgian beers, a German restaurant should have German beers, and so on. Similarly, a beer list should include several types of beer styles. Beer can be brewed from different grains including barley, wheat, and oats. Beers also vary in the level of bitterness and hops. A menu planner should research the kinds of beer popular in the local area but recognize that there may be variation within a style. For example, if ales are popular in a given community, the beer list might include pale ale, India pale ale, blond ale, red ale, brown ale, golden ale, cream ale, and/or amber ale. The greater the number of choices, the more a restaurant becomes a destination for beer connoisseurs. Except for the most minimalist of beer menus, a menu planner should offer some bottled beer and some beer on tap.

Beer comes in a wide range of price points, too. As with wine, the price point for beer should align with the price point of the food on the menu. An upscale restaurant can offer high-end beers in 750-mL bottles, but an inexpensive bar should stick with cheaper beers on tap or in 12-ounce bottles or cans.

The headings and item descriptions used for beers on a menu depend greatly on the length of the beverage menu and the business's approach to beer. The menu might list all of its offerings under the single heading of "Beer" with an alphabetical listing of choices by producer or by country. Alternatively, the menu might divide the headings by style or by country of origin. As with wine, there is no universally accepted format, but a consumer should be able to find his preferred beer easily on the list. If the list includes a significant number of boutique beers that are not well known in the community, brief tasting notes for each beer may increase sales and help assuage guests' insecurity in ordering. Given the current interest in American microbrews, listing each American beer's city and state of origin makes good marketing sense. Additionally, beers around the world now vary greatly in their alcohol content. If a beer list includes beers outside the more common range of 4–6% alcohol, the menu planner should list each beer's alcohol by volume percentage (ABV%) on the menu.

When serving beer from a tap (portioning glasses from a larger keg), a restaurant has the flexibility of determining the portion size. A 12-ounce portion is considered a standard size for tracking alcohol consumed, though some places prefer to serve a pint. The type of glassware should support the brand of the business. German beer halls might use beer steins while upscale Belgian restaurants might have a different glass (supplied by the beer producer) for each beer they serve. Oversized portions (like a yard) should be reserved for specialty bars or drinking halls.

Listing suggested pairings for beer and food on a menu is acceptable, but this approach is less commonly done with beer than it is with wine. Microbreweries that also operate a

fresh draft beer

Red text denotes new beers added this week.
Underlined Beers denotes extremely limited supply.

NAME	STYLE	ABV	Gl./Pitcher/Growler
Sierra Nevada Bigfoot (Chico, CA)	Barleywine	9.6%	6.00 / 30.00 / 31.00
St Bernardus Prior 8 (Belgium)	Belgian Dubbel	8.0%	8.50 / 42.50 / 43.50
Goose Island Matilda (Chicago, IL)	Belgian Pale	7.0%	5.50 / 27.50 / 28.50
St Bernardus Abt 12 (Belgium)	Belgian Quad	10%	10.00 / 50.00 / 51.00
Delirium Tremens (Belgium)	Belgian Strong	8.5%	8.00 / 40.00 / 41.00
Duvel (Belgium)	Belg. Strong Pale	8.5%	6.50 / 32.50 / 40.00
Tripel Karmeliet (Belgium)	Belgian Tripel	8.4%	8.00 / 40.00 / 41.00
Blue Moon (Golden, CO)	Belgian Wit	5.4%	5.00 / 15.00 / 16.00
St. Bernardus (Belgium)	Belgian Wit	5.5%	6.00 / 30.00 / 31.00
4 Hands Alter Ego (St. Louis, MO)	Black Ale	5.5%	5.00 / 15.00 / 16.00
New Belgium 1554 (Fort Collins, CO)	Black Ale	5.6%	5.00 / 15.00 / 16.00
Schlafly Dbl Bean (St. Louis, MO)	Blonde	5.6%	5.50 / 16.50 / 17.50
Argus Ginger Perry (Austin, TX)	Cider	4.5%	6.00 / 30.00 / 31.00
Crispin Blackberry Pear (Colfax, CA)	Cider	5.0%	5.00 / 15.00 / 16.00
Corsendonk Dubbel (Belgium)	Dubbel	7.5%	7.50 / 37.50 / 38.50
Cuvee de Jacobins (Belgium)	Flemish Red/Sour	5.5%	11.00 / 55.00 / 56.00
Berbe Ruby (Belgium)	Fruit Beer	7.7%	10.50 / 52.50 / 53.50
Founders Mango (Grand Rapids, MI)	Fruit Beer	8.0%	6.00 / 30.00 / 31.00

Growlers are To Go Only - 4/13/16

fresh draft beer

Red text denotes new beers added this week.
Underlined Beers denotes extremely limited supply.

NAME	STYLE	ABV	Gl./Pitcher/Growler
Hofbrau (Germany)	Hefeweizen	5.4%	5.00 / 15.00 / 16.00
Ballast Point Dorado (San Diego, CA)	IPA (Imperial)	10%	5.50 / 27.50 / 28.50
Bell's Two Hearted (Kalamazoo, MI)	IPA	7.0%	5.50 / 16.50 / 17.50
Bell's Hopslam (Kalamazoo, MI)	IPA (Imperial)	10%	6.00 / NA / NA
Evil Twin Molotov (Brooklyn, NY)	IPA (Imperial)	13%	7.50 / 37.50 / 38.50
Founders All Day (Grand Rapids, MI)	IPA (Session)	4.7%	5.00 / 15.00 / 16.00
Green Flash Soul Style (San Diego, CA)	IPA (Tangerine)	6.5%	5.50 / 16.50 / 17.50
Green Flash West Coast (San Diego, CA)	IPA	8.1%	6.00 / 30.00 / 31.00
Hoptical Illusion (Patchogue, NY)	IPA	6.8%	5.50 / 16.50 / 17.50
Lagunitas IPA (Petaluma, CA)	IPA	6.2%	5.00 / 15.00 / 16.00
Nectar (Paso Robles, CA)	IPA	6.7%	5.00 / 15.00 / 16.00
New B. Citradelic (Fort Collins, CO)	IPA (Tangerine)	6.0%	5.00 / 15.00 / 16.00
New Holl. Mad Hatter (Holland, MI)	IPA	7.0%	5.00 / 15.00 / 16.00
Sierra Nev. Hophunter (Chico, CA)	IPA	6.2%	5.00 / 15.00 / 16.00
Ska Mandarina (Durango, CO)	IPA (Orange)	6.8%	5.00 / 15.00 / 16.00
Stone IPA (Escondido, CA)	IPA	6.9%	5.00 / 15.00 / 16.00
Schlafly Kölsch (St. Louis, MO)	Kölsch	4.8%	5.00 / 15.00 / 16.00
Lindeman's Framboise (Belgium)	Lambic	2.5%	7.50 / 37.50 / 38.50

Growlers are To Go Only - 4/13/16

fresh draft beer

Red text denotes new beers added this week.
Underlined denotes extremely limited supply.

NAME	STYLE	ABV	Gl./Pitcher/Growler
Lagunit. CitruSinensis (Petaluma, CA)	Pale Ale	7.9%	5.00 / 25.00 / 26.00
Schlafly Pale Ale (St. Louis, MO)	Pale Ale	4.4%	5.00 / 15.00 / 16.00
Scrimshaw (Fort Braggs, CA)	Pilsner	4.4%	5.00 / 15.00 / 16.00
Mark Twain Rambler's (Hannibal, MO)	Red	5.5%	6.00 / 18.00 / 19.00
Fitz's (St. Louis, MO)	Root Beer	0%	2.50 / 7.50 / 8.50
Abita Rye Pale Ale (Covington, LA)	Rye (Barrel Aged)	9.5%	5.50 / 27.50 / 28.50
Civil Life Rye Pale (St. Louis, MO)	Rye	4.5%	5.00 / 15.00 / 16.00
Perennial Saison De Lis (St. Louis, MO)	Saison (Chamomile)	5.0%	5.00 / 25.00/ 26.00
Prairie 3rd Anniv. (Tulsa, OK)	Saison (Raspberry)	8.0%	6.00 / 30.00/ 31.00
4 Hands Bonafide (St. Louis, MO)	Stout (Imperial)	8.5%	6.00 / 30.00 / 31.00
4 Hds Devils Invention (St. Louis, MO)	Stout	7.0%	5.50 / 16.50 / 17.50
Evil Twin More Jesus (Brooklyn, NY)	Stout (Imperial)	12%	9.00 / 45.00 / 46.00
Firestone Nitro Merlin (Paso Robles, CA)	Stout	5.5%	6.00 / 30.00 / 31.00
Guinness Nitro (Ireland)	Stout (Irish Dry)	4.2%	5.00 / 15.00 / 16.00
Lagunitas Cappuccino (Petaluma, CA)	Stout (Imperial)	9.2%	5.00 / 25.00 / 26.00
New Hol. Dragons Milk (Holland, MI)	Stout (Bourbon)	10%	6.00 / 30.00 / 31.00
Sth. Tier Crème Brulee (Lakewood, NY)	Stout (Imperial)	10%	6.00 / 30.00 / 31.00
Broadway Honey (Colombia, MO)	Wheat (Organic)	6.0%	5.00 / 15.00 / 16.00
O'Fallon 15 Anniv. (St Louis, MO)	Wheatwine (Aged)	10%	12.00 / NA / NA

Growlers are To Go Only - 4/13/16

All Pints of Beer are HALF-PRICE
All Domestics are $2.25
All Well drinks are $2.50
All House Wine is $1 off
Most Appetizers are HALF-PRICE

Monday - Friday 4-7pm (at bar only)

CICERO'S FALL BEER SCHOOL
Wednesdays - Two Classes;
5:30pm & 7:00pm

Fall classes are every Wednesday and are an hour long. They focus on one brewery each week. Guest instructors for the fall classes include; brewers, owners and other brand ambassadors. Come to class and learn about new beers and taste some classics as well. All beer school classes are free.

FIGURE 5.2

This extensive beer menu boasts a broad range of beer types and origins.

Source: Chad Jacobs of Cicero's Restaurant. Reprinted with permission.

world class beer samplers

A Taste of Hops - Are You a Hop Head?
Stone IPA - Magnum, Chinook, and Centennial.
Citradelic - Nugget, Crystal, Azzaca, Cascade, Citra, Chinook, Galaxy, Simcoe
Lagunitas IPA - Made with 43 Different Hops
New Holland Mad Hatter - Citra, Michigan-grown Cascade, Centennial
$10.00 (4 - 5oz Pours)

Missouri Beers - Drink Local
Perennial Saison De Lis - A Saison Brewed with Chamomile.
Mark Twain Rambler's Red - Keep Rambling on….
Schlafly Kölsch - Classic Golden Ale.
Civil Life Rye Pale Ale - GABF Gold Medal Winner!
$10.00 (4 - 5oz Pours)

Sweet & Sassy - Get your Sweet on and Stay Sassy!
Lagunitas Cappuccino Stout - Brewed with boatloads of roasted coffee
Ska Mandarina - Brewed with Sweet Orange Peels
Prairie 3rd Anniversary - Delightful Flavor and Aroma
Crispin Blackberry Pear - Juicy and Complex
$10.00 (4 - 5oz Pours)

Grab Bag - A Little of That, A Little of This
Founders Mango Mangnifico - Mango and a touch of Habanero
Mark Twain Rambler's Red - Keep Rambling on….
Sierra Nevada Big Foot - Cult Classic Beast od a Barley Wine
Prairie Anniversary - Saison Brewed with Raspberries.
$12.00 (4 - 5oz Pours)

Carry On Cabbie - You're Gonna Need a Cab
Abita Rye Pale Ale (9.5%) - Pale, Munich and Rye, Oh My!
New Holland Dragons Milk (10%) - Roasty Malt, Vanilla, Dancing in Oak
Ballast Point Dorado (10%) - Hop Heads Rejoice!
Evil Twin Molotov Cocktail (13%) - This Beer will Knock Your Tongue Off
$15.00 (4 - 5oz Pours)

what 's happening

Monday is Game Night

Play board games with your friends

Play Pass The Pigs at the bar for prizes.

Enjoy $5 off all pitchers
(From 7:00 - Close)

Beer school is every Wednesday at 5:30 and 7:00
Class is Free, Just Show Up

Tuesday is Family Night
KIDS EAT FREE 5:30 - 8:30
One meal with each adult meal purchased

bottles to share

*Here is a select menu of large format bottles that we've
been holding onto for you to enjoy with friends.*

Boulevard Rye on Rye   12% $20 (750ml)
*Two kinds of malted rye provide spicy sweetness, giving way to notes of caramelized wood
and the citrusy tang of Citra and Ahtanum hops before easing into a dry, lingering finish.*

Boulevard Saison Brett   8.5% $20 (750ml)
*A Saison based on Tank 7, dry hopped and bottle conditioned with various yeasts includ-
ing brettanomyces, a wild strain that imparts a distinct earthy quality.*

Sam Adams Tetravis   10.2% $8 (750ml)
*Bold & rich, this enveloping quad builds its force and character through interlacing lay-
ers of flavor. Its deep complexity begins with a molasses sweetness with notes of dark
fruits like raisins and figs but develops further with an undercurrent of tart spice from its
distinctive Belgian yeast for a truly transfixing brew...*

Sam Adams Thirteenth Hour 11.8% $8 (750ml)
*The 13th hour is the witching hour, and a time when strange brews can occur. With 13
ingredients, we combined the roasted chocolate and coffee flavors of a stout with the complex spicy character of a Belgian-style ale aged in oak for a deep, robust, and captivating
brew.*

reserve menu

Widmer Old Embalmer '13   10.2% $10 (750ml)
*Brewed with copious amounts of malts, 2013 version of Old Embalmer barleywine fea-
tures x-431 hops that lend earthy and floral qualities for a brilliant balance and velvety
finish.*

Stone Southern Charred '15 12.7% $28 (500ml)
*This oak bomb bursts on the palate with a well-rounded mixture of deep caramel, molas-
ses, hops and char plus hints of brown sugar, with bourbony influence amplifying the
beer's maltiness. Quiet. Confident. Arrogant*

Southern Tier Backburner 10.5% $12 (750ml)
*Brewed with blackstrap molasses and maple syrup, which give it notes of dried fruit and
rich grains.*

Uinta Birthday Suit '15 7.6% $20 (750ml)
*Cast aside inhibitions and dive into this year's Birthday Suit, a Sour Abbey Ale brewed
with plums and an authentic Belgian abbey yeast strain that flaunts complexity and
charm. A playful combination of sour tanginess and subtle dried fruit esters, this Sour
Plum Ale bares it all in honor of Uinta's 22nd Birthday.*

CICERO'S BEER SCHOOL

Free Class To Learn About & Sample Beer
Fall Semester - Wednesdays - 5:30pm & 7:00pm
Watch our class podcasts at:
www.cicerosbeerschool.com

bottle and can specials on beer school beers and more

NAME	STYLE	ABV	PRICE
Uinta Dubhe	Black IPA	9.2%	5.00
(Salt Lake City, UT)			
O'Fallon Smoked Porter	Porter	6.0%	4.00
(Maryland Heights, MO)			
Free State Ad Astra	Altbier	5.6%	3.50
(Lawrence, KS)			
Sudwerk Big DIPL	Imperial IPA	9.0%	7.00
(Davis, CA)			
La Trappe Wit	Wit Bier	5.5%	5.00
(Netherlands)			
Cismont. Blacks Dawn (16.9oz)	Imperial Stout	8.5%	7.00
(Rancho Santa Margarita, CA)			
Moorehouse Black Cat	English Dark	3.4%	7.00
(UK)			
UCBC Hopfen	Bavarian IPA	6.1%	6.00
(St. Louis, MO)			
UCBC Dorfbier	Munich Dunkel	6.1%	6.00
(St. Louis, MO)			

**Beer Feature of the Month
for March is Sierra Nevada**

Buy any New Holland Beer on
Tuesday and you get a free glass to
take home.

FIGURE 5.2   *(Continued)*

bottled beer

amber/red ale

- Red's / Ambers are balanced in flavor; not overly hoppy or malty. Its flavor profile has plenty of caramel malt, with a subtle hop finish.

NAME	ORIGIN	ABV	PRICE
4 Hands Centennial Reprise Red	St. Louis, MO	6.0%	5.00
Bell's Amber Ale	Kalamazoo, MI	5.8%	5.00
Local Opt. Morning Wood (16.9oz)	Chicago, IL	7.3%	8.50
New Belgium Fat Tire	Fort Collins, CO	5.2%	5.00

brown ale

- Browns are balanced with enough malt to make them sweet and a bit of hops to give it character. They are roasty and toasty on the palate.

NAME	ORIGIN	ABV	PRICE
Avery Ellie's Brown	Boulder, CO	5.5%	5.00
Big Sky Moose Drool	Missoula, MT	5.3%	5.00
Grand Teton Bitch Creek	Victor, ID	6.00	5.00
Newcastle	England	4.7%	5.00
Samuel Smith Nut Brown	England	5.0%	5.50
Rogue Hazelnut Brown Nectar	Newport, OR	6.2%	5.50

belgian, belgian style, trappist ale

- Belgian pale ales are crisp, a bit hoppy, with a nutty malt character. The aroma is clean, with spicy yeast notes.
- Belgian dubbles are rich and malty with mild hop bitterness.
- Belgian quadruples are very strong ales that are full bodied and very malty. They are sweet and typically strong in alcohol content.
- Trappist ales must be brewed in monasteries by monks. There are currently eight monasteries (six in Belgium, one in the Netherlands, and one in Austria) brewing beer that can call their beer trappist.

NAME	ORIGIN	ABV	PRICE
Abbey Monks (Dubbel)	New Mexico	6.7%	6.00
Abbey Monks (Tripel)	New Mexico	9.2%	6.50
Chimay Red (Dubbel)	Belgium	7.0%	8.00
Chimay Blue Reserve (Strong)	Belgium	9.0%	9.00
De Ranke XX Bitter (IPA)	Belgium	6.2%	6.50
La Trappe (Dubbel)	Belgium	7.0%	7.00
La Trappe (Quad)	Belgium	10%	8.00
Omm. 3 Philosophers (Quad) (750ml)	Cooperstown, NY	9.8%	12.00
Orval (Pale)	Belgium	6.2%	7.50
Rochefort 10 (Quad)	Belgium	11.3%	8.25
Unibroue Don De Dieu (Strong Pale)	Canada	9.0%	6.00
Unibroue La Fin Du Monde (Tripel)	Canada	9.0%	6.00
Unibroue Maudite (Strong)	Canada	8.0%	6.00
Unibroue Trois Pistoles (Strong Dark)	Canada	9.0%	6.00
Westmalle (Tripel)	Belgium	9.5%	7.50

bock

- Bocks are typically a bit higher in alcohol compared to other easy drinking lagers. They will generally be heavily malted with a little bit of sweetness. Bocks are usually lighted hopped, but can still be bitter.

NAME	ORIGIN	ABV	PRICE
Aventinus (Weizenbock, 16.9oz)	Germany	8.2%	7.00
Michelob Amberbock	St. Louis, MO	5.2%	4.00
Rogue Dead Guy (Maibock)	Newport, OR	6.5%	5.00
Shiner Bock	Shiner, TX	4.4%	5.00

FIGURE 5.2 *(Continued)*

cider

- Fermented Apples or other fruit. They tend to be light and crisp. Ciders can be flavored and can range from dry to sweet.

NAME	ORIGIN	ABV	PRICE
Ace Berry	Sebastopol, CA	5%	5.00
Angry Orchard Apple Crisp	Cincinnati, OH	5%	5.00
Argus Ginger Perry (Pear)	Austin, TX	4.5%	5.75
Crispin	Minneapolis, MN	5.0%	5.00
Crispin - The Saint (22oz)	Minneapolis, MN	6.9%	9.00
J.K. Scrumpy (16oz can)	Fiushing, MI	6.0%	6.50
Original Sin Cherry Tree	New York, NY	6.7%	5.50
Strongbow	England	5.0%	5.00
Woodchuck Granny Smith	Springfield, VT	5.0%	5.00
Woodchuck Pear	Springfield, VT	4.0%	5.00
Woodchuck Hopsation (Hopped)	Springfield, VT	6.9%	5.00

fruit

- Some Fruit beers are sweet, some are tart and others bitter. If you like cider, wine or other fruity drinks, try one. You'll be happy you did.

NAME	ORIGIN	ABV	PRICE
Lindeman's Pêche (Peach)	Belgium	2.5%	8.00
Sam Smith Apricot (22oz)	England	5.1%	8.00
Kasteel Rouge (Cherry)	Belgium	8.0%	6.25
Abita Purple Haze (Rasp.)	Abita Springs, LA	4.2%	5.00
Sea Dog Blueberry	Bangor, ME	4.7%	5.00
O'Fallon Wheach (Peach)	St. Louis, MO	5.1%	5.00
Magic Hat #9 (Apricot)	South Burlington, VT	5.1%	5.00

lager

- Characterized by a very clean, crisp feel on the tongue and on the finish. Slightly hoppy and slightly malty, but less complex than other styles. These beers are best on a hot summer day.

NAME	ORIGIN	ABV	PRICE
Anchor Steam	San Francisco, CA	4.9	5.00
Budweiser	St. Louis, MO	5.0%	4.00
Bud Light	St. Louis, MO	4.2%	4.00
Bud Select	St. Louis, MO	4.3%	4.00
Busch	St. Louis, MO	4.6%	3.50
Coors Light	Golden, CO	4.2%	4.00
Corona	Mexico	4.6%	5.00
Heineken	Holland	5.0%	5.00
Michelob Ultra	St. Louis, MO	4.2%	4.00
Miller Light	Milwaukee, WI	4.2%	4.00
Modelo Especial	Mexico	4.4%	5.00
Modelo Negra (Vienna)	Mexico	5.4%	5.00
PBR	Woodbridge, IL	5.0%	3.50
Peroni	Italy	5.1%	5.00
Red Stripe	Jamaica	4.7%	4.50
Rolling Rock	St. Louis, MO	4.6%	4.00
Sapporo Silver (22oz)	Japan	5.0%	6.00
Stag	Woodbridge, IL	5.2%	4.00
Stella Artois	Belgium	5.0%	5.00
Urban Chestnut Zwickle	St. Louis, MO	4.8%	6.00
Xingu (Black)	Brazil	4.7%	5.00

india pale ale (ipa)

- IPA's are dominated by hops, but many still have plenty of malt. Depending upon what stage the hops are added in the brewing process, you will have various effects on the beer; like bitterness, aroma, and general flavor.

NAME	ORIGIN	ABV	PRICE
4 Hands Divided Sky Rye . (Can)	St. Louis, MO	6.5%	5.00
4 Hands Resurrected (Can)	St. Louis, MO	6.5%	5.00
Evil Twin Molotov Lite (16oz Can)	Brooklyn, NY	8.5%	6.00
Goose Island IPA	Chicago, IL	5.9%	5.00
Odell IPA	Fort Collins, CO	7.0%	5.00
Odell Mrycenary	Fort Collins, CO	9.3%	6.00
Ska Modus Hoperandi (Can)	Durango, CO	6.8%	5.00
Lagunitas Maximus	Petaluma, CA	8.2%	5.00
Omission (Gluten Free)	Potland, OR	6.7%	5.00

pale ale

- Pale ales are moderately hoppy, creating a mild bitter beer using primarily pale malt. This beer finishes clean.

NAME	ORIGIN	ABV	PRICE
Boddington's (16oz)	England	4.7%	5.00
Deschutes Mirror Pond	Bend, OR	5.0%	5.00
Omission (Gluten Free)	Portland, OR	5.8%	5.00
Schlafly American Pale Ale (APA)	St. Louis, MO	5.9%	5.00
Sierra Nevada	Chico, CA	5.6%	5.00

pilsner

- German Pilsners taste crisp with smooth malt flavor and light hops.
- Czech Pilsners are light and tend to taste of sweet malt with hints of caramel. They also lean a little on the hoppy side.

NAME	ORIGIN	ABV	PRICE
Firestone Pivo Pils	Paso Robles, CA	5.3%	5.00
Kulmbacher	Germany	4.9%	5.50
Pilsner Urquell	Czech Republic	4.4%	5.00
Scrimshaw	Fort Bragg, CA	4.4%	5.00

FIGURE 5.2 *(Continued)*

porter

- Roasty maltiness in flavor and aroma. Flavor tends to be creamy and can be hoppy or not hoppy at all.

NAME	ORIGIN	ABV	PRICE
Arcadia Shipwreck (Bourbon Aged)	Battle Creek, MI	12%	12.00
Breckenridge Vanilla	Breckenridge, CO	4.7%	5.00
Deschutes Black Butte	Bend, OR	5.2%	5.00
Founders Porter	Grand Rapids, MI	6.5%	5.00
Samuel Smith's Taddy Porter	England	5.0%	6.00

saison/bier de garde

- Very Complex and fruity, in aroma and flavor. Earthy tones are typical. Yeast is usually present, with a notable spiciness.

NAME	ORIGIN	ABV	PRICE
Du Bocq Saison 1858 (25.4oz)	Belgium	6.4%	10.00
Prairie Standard	Krebs, OK	5.2%	5.50
Saison Dupont	Belgium	6.5%	8.00
Boulevard Tank 7	Kansas City, MO	8.5%	6.00
Crooked Stave Vieille Artisanal	Denver, CO	4.2%	9.00
Stillwater Cellar Door	Baltimore, MD	6.6%	5.50
Urban Chestnut Apotheosis	St. Louis, MO	5.3%	6.00
Goose Island Sofie	Chicago, IL	6.5%	5.50
Jolly Pumpkin Bam Biere (Sour)	Dexter, MI	4.5%	7.50
Jolly P. Bam Noire (Dark Sour)	Dexter, MI	4.5%	7.50
Jolly Pumpkin Oro De Calabaza	Dexter, MI	8.0%	8.50

sour / wild

- Sour beers are very diverse. Some are super sour, some are sweet and sour, some are funky, and others are very mild.

NAME	ORIGIN	ABV	PRICE
Boulevard Tell Tale Tart	Kansas City, MO	6.2%	6.00
Crooked Stave Colorado Wildsage	Denver, CO	7.2%	9.00
Duchesse De Bourgogne	Belgium	6.0%	8.00
Jolly Pumpkin Bam Biere (Sour)	Dexter, MI	4.5%	7.50
Jolly P. Bam Noire (Dark Sour)	Dexter, MI	4.5%	7.50
Monks Café (Flemish Sour)	Belgium	5.5%	7.00
New Belgium Snapshot (Wheat)	Fort Collins, CO	5.0%	5.00
Petrus Aged Pale	Belgium	7.3%	7.50
Prairie Funky Gold (16.9oz)	Krebs, OK	6.5%	11.00

Love sour beers? If so, we have a special treat for you. Three of the most sought after sours in the country for 2015.

Avery Insula Collibus - (9.7% abv) Strong sour aged in Bourbon Barrels for nine months and fermented with a small amount of cherries.

Avery Fortuna - (8.1% abv) Aged in Suerte tequila barrels for a salty and citrusy flavor.

Tectum et Elix - (5.5% abv) Featuring multiple yeast strains and fermented for nine months in Cabernet Sauvignon Barrels.

Single Bottles: $20   **Flight of All Three Avery Sours: $50**

scotch ale / wee heavy

- With a rich mouthfeel, Scottish ales are very malty in taste and aroma with little hop character.

NAME	ORIGIN	ABV	PRICE
Odell 90 Shilling	Fort Collins, CO	5.3%	5.00
Founders Dirty Bastard	Grand Rapids, MI	8.5%	5.00
Skullsplitter	Scotland	8.5%	6.00
Traquair House Ale (16.9oz)	Scotland	7.2%	9.50

stout

- "Strong Black Beer" stouts are the son of the porter and tend to have deep, dark roasty character. They can vary from dry to sweet, and weak to strong.

NAME	ORIGIN	ABV	PRICE
Dieu Du Ciel Peche Mortel	Canada	9.5%	7.00
Evil Twin Soft DK	Brooklyn, NY	10.4%	6.50
Evil Twin Yin	Denmark	10%	6.50
Great Divide Yeti	Denver, CO	9.5%	6.00
New Holland The Poet	Holland, MI	5.2%	5.00
Old Rasputin	Fort Bragg, CA	9.0%	6.00
Prairie Bomb!	Krebs, OK	14%	11.00
Samuel Smith Chocolate Stout	England	5.0%	6.00
Samuel Smith Oatmeal	England	5.0%	6.00
Young's Double Chocolate	England	5.2%	6.00

wheat / wit / weizen

- Witbiers are characterized by their orange peel and coriander flavor. The mouthfeel is dry and creamy, with a soft finish.
- Hefeweizens have yeast added to the bottles. They are unfiltered and have strong clove and banana flavor.
- Dunkelweizens are similar to hefeweizens except there is more malt, and less bitterness, resulting in a much darker final product.
- American wheat ales are very clean and crisp with a soft fruity aroma. Crisp balance with a little creamy texture from the wheat.

NAME	ORIGIN	ABV	PRICE
Avery White Rascal	Boulder, CO	5.6%	5.00
Ayinger Urweiss	Germany	5.8%	6.50
Blue Moon	Golden, CO	5.4%	5.00
Goose Island 312	Chicago, IL	4.2%	5.00
Hoegaarden	Belgium	4.9%	5.00
Leinenkugel Sunset Wheat	Chippewa Falls, WI	4.9%	5.00
Lil Sumpin' Sumpin'	Petaluma, CA	7.5%	5.00
New Belgium Snapshot	Fort Collins, CO	5.0%	5.00
Schneider-Weisse (16.9oz)	Germany	5.4%	7.00
Shocktop	St. Louis, MO	5.2%	5.00
Unibroue Blanche de Chambly	Canada	5.0%	6.00
Weihenstephan Hef. (16.9oz)	Germany	5.4%	6.50
Weihenstephan Dunkel (16.9oz)	Germany	5.3%	6.50

For an up to date list of our draft menu, visit:

www.ciceros-stl.com

FIGURE 5.2 *(Continued)*

miscellaneous

NAME	ORIGIN	ABV	PRICE
Bitburger (Non-Alcoholic)	Germany	0%	5.00
Grt. Divide Old Ruffian (Barleywine)	Denver, Co	10.2%	6.00
Kondrauer Hopster (Hop Soda)	Germany	0%	5.50
Not Your Fathers Root Beer	Chicago, IL	5.9%	6.00
Occulto (Tequila Beer)	St. Louis, MO	6%	5.00
O'douls (Non-Alcoholic)	St. Louis, MO	>.5%	5.00
Root Cellars Ginger Beer	Columbia, MO	5.3%	6.00
Root Cellars Root Beer	Columbia, MO	6.7%	6.00
Twisted Pine Billy's Chilies (Spicy)	Boulder, CO	5%	6.00

THIRSTY FOR KNOWLEDGE?

CICERO'S BEER SCHOOL
— EST. 2006 —

CICERO'S FALL BEER SCHOOL s

Spring Semester starts January 13th

Wednesdays - Two Classes;
5:30pm & 7:00pm

Classes are every Wednesday and are an hour long. They focus on one brewery each week. Guest instructors for the fall classes include; brewers, owners and other brand ambassadors. Come to class and learn about new beers

FIGURE 5.2   *(Continued)*

restaurant should provide such pairings, as their menus ought to create an opportunity to show off each beer with at least one food item. However, in the average restaurant most customers will order the beer they like based on personal taste preferences rather than on the food they have ordered.

Liquor and Cocktail Menus

Cocktails and other liquor-based drinks have become increasingly trendy in recent years. Some upscale restaurants give their head mixologists (bartenders) equal billing with the chef. The arena of mixology provides a huge opportunity for creativity. Unlike beer and wine, which are created in their entirety by another company (except at winery and brewery restaurants), a cocktail is designed and prepared by the restaurant's employees. Striving to make their cocktail menus stand out, some mixologists even create their own mixers from scratch. Because mixed drinks are trendy, a menu planner should consider boutique mixed drink offerings for any operation with a full bar.

A cocktail and liquor menu should include beverages based on a range of different liquor types. For example, unless a business promotes itself as a vodka bar, all of the cocktails should not be based on vodka. Typically, the menu should offer at least one mixed drink based on each of vodka, gin, rum, tequila, and whiskey. A more varied menu might have drinks from an even broader range of sources. A well-done cocktail menu also incorporates multiple flavor profiles (sweet, sour, and bitter drinks) and utilizes a range of glassware.

How a menu planner describes a drink on a cocktail menu depends greatly on the level of innovation of the drinks. If the menu includes only classic drinks, it is perfectly acceptable to list only the drink names. However, many operations are encouraging their mixologists to create unique cocktails and liquors available only at that business. Many mixologists create handcrafted infusions and syrups; they may even infuse a neutral vodka to create one-of-a-kind flavored vodkas or bitters for their specialty cocktails. Once a mixologist strays from the classics, the menu must include the list of ingredients in its drinks. Even with complex cocktails, the ingredient list is still pretty short. Cocktail descriptions work quite well as minimalist ingredient lists; there is no need to insert flowery additions such as "shaken with ice and strained into a chilled cocktail glass for your drinking pleasure." However, given the current trend toward artisan, handcrafted products, the menu should point out any ingredients that are house-made and the brand names of any premium liquors used.

There are several ways to present a cocktail menu. It may be placed on the inside cover of the food menu, the first pages of a comprehensive beverage menu, or a table tent. Signature cocktails should be heavily marketed wherever they are listed. Guests know that they can order common classic drinks when a full-service bar is on display, but the only way they'll know about a business's unique creations is if they see them in print or hear about them from a server.

Cocktails are not the only use for liquor. A restaurant can highlight a wide range of liquors of a given type. Usually, the type selected supports the business's brand and cuisine. For example, a Mexican restaurant might stock a dozen different tequilas; an Irish pub might list a dozen or more Irish whiskeys. Even lounges or bars with nondescript food choices can make themselves known for a broad selection of bourbons, scotches, or vodkas. The best way to promote these beverage options is through a menu listing each brand name, any special qualities such as age or flavoring, and the price for a shot. Bars that rely on guests to find the brand name on display behind the bar will lose sales from those guests who cannot see the bar clearly from their seats.

When writing the menu, a menu planner can list the cocktails under a single heading of "Cocktails" or create innovative headings. Extensive lists might simply state "Gin Drinks," "Rum Drinks," and the like in a serious establishment. More playful operations might incorporate headings like "Sweet and Fruity" or "Manly Drinks." When a menu highlights liquor by the shot, those are almost always categorized by the type of liquor ("Scotches," "Brandies," etc.). Liquor that is appropriate for after dinner should be highlighted on a dessert menu to encourage sales of liquor alongside or instead of dessert. After-dinner beverages that combine liquor with other ingredients, such as coffee, should also appear on a dessert menu to drive those sales.

- VODKA AMOUR -

TEXAS MULE*
TITO'S VODKA, LIME, JALAPENO,
HOUSE GINGER BEER

FOOL'S COLLINS
TITO'S VODKA, JUNIPER CORDIAL,
LEMON, TOPO CHICO

CYNDI LAUPER*
TITO'S VODKA, CINNAMON, LEMON,
CRANBERRY BITTERS

FRENCH 75*
GIN, LEMON, SUGAR, BUBBLES

ROYAL BEES KNEES*
GIN, LAVENDER HONEY, LEMON

GIN GIN MULE*
GIN, MINT, LIME,
HOUSE GINGER BEER

- GIN AMOUR -

CORPSE REVIVER #2
GIN, LILLET BLANC, COINTREAU,
LEMON, ABSINTHE RINSE

DEAR CHARLOTTE*
GIN, GALLIANO, GINGER HONEY,
GRAPEFRUIT, LIME

GIN & TONIC
BOMBAY SAPPHIRE EAST GIN,
HOUSE TONIC

ROSEMARY'S GIMLET
BOTANIST GIN, ST. GERMAIN,
GREEN CHARTREUSE, LIME

BARTON SPRINGS
OXLEY GIN, ALESSIO BIANCO,
ORANGE BITTERS

NEGRONI*
GIN, CAMPARI, SWEET VERMOUTH

SUICIDE KING
BOLS GENEVER, DRY CURACAO,
ALESSIO VINO CHINATO, EARL GREY

BIJOU
PLYMOUTH GIN, CARPANO ANTICA,
GREEN CHARTREUSE

-ADULT MILKSHAKES-

PÉCHÉ
ABSINTHE, CHERRY LIQUEUR,
VANILLA ICE CREAM

BANANAS FOSTER
DARK RUM, BANANE DU BRESIL,
VANILLA ICE CREAM

CAFE ALEXANDER
BRANDY, CREME DE COCOA,
ST. GEORGE NOLA COFFEE LIQUOR,
VANILLA ICE CREAM

- WHISKEY AMOUR -

NEW YORK SOUR*
BOURBON, LEMON, SUGAR,
RED WINE FLOATER

LIONS TAIL*
BOURBON, LIME, ALLSPICE DRAM,
ANGOSTURA BITTERS

TIED FOUR THIRD
BOURBON, AMARO MONTENEGRO,
GINGER HONEY, GRAPEFRUIT, LEMON,
MINT, ANGOSTURA BITTERS

FIG MANHATTAN
RYE, SWEET VERMOUTH, HOUSE
CHERRY VANILLA BITTERS, FIG FOAM

SAZERAC*
RYE, SUGAR, PEYCHAUD'S BITTERS,
ABSINTHE RINSE

VIEUX CARRÉ
RYE, COGNAC, SWEET VERMOUTH,
BENEDICTINE, PEYCHAUD'S &
ANGOSTURA BITTERS

PECHE'S OLD FASHIONED
PECHE'S SINGLE BARREL WHISKEY,
JERRY THOMAS BITTERS,
LEMON PEEL, SUGAR

RYET ON THYME (BARREL AGED)
REDEMPTION RYE, AVERNA, LICOR 43,
BLACK WALNUT BITTERS, THYME

- RUM/TEQUILA AMOUR -

DAIQUIRI*
RUM, LIME, SUGAR

DARK & STORMY*
RUM, LIME, HOUSE GINGER BEER

PAPA'S PARADISE
PAPA'S PILAR 24, BANANE DU BRESIL,
SPICED PEAR, LEMON, CINNAMON,
BLACK WALNUT BITTERS

POMME PIE 75
TEQUILA, ALLSPICE DRAM, LEMON,
AGAVE, BAKED APPLE BITTERS, BUBBLES

CUCUY
AITOS ANJEO, ART IN THE AGE SAGE,
FIG, XOCOLATL MOLE BITTERS

SINORITA
VIDA MEZCAL, ANCHO REYES,
LIME, CINNAMON, FIRE & DAMNATION
BITTERS, ISLAY MIST

SMOKE & CHOKE
VIDA MEZCAL, GRAN CLASSICO,
CYNAR, COCCHI DI TORINO

-BRANDY AMOUR-

PORCH SWING
COGNAC, ABRICOT DU ROUSSILLON,
LEMON, EARL GREY

CALVADOS SOUR
CALVADOS, LEMON, SUGAR,
CHINESE BITTERS, EGG WHITE

BELAFONTE
PIERRE FERRAND 1840, DOLIN DRY,
BANANE DU BRESIL, LICOR 43,
BAKED APPLE BITTERS

- ABSINTHE -

MATA-HARI 60 ABV
AUSTRIA, NEUTRAL GRAIN

PERNOD 68 ABV
FRANCE, GRAPE

KUBLER* 53 ABV
SWITZERLAND, NEUTRAL GRAIN

SAINT GEORGE 60 ABV
CALIFORNIA, GRAPE

TENNEYSON 53 ABV
FRANCE, SUGAR BEET

GERMAIN-ROBIN 45 ABV
CALIFORNIA, GRAPE

PACIFIQUE 62 ABV
WASHINGTON, NEUTRAL GRAIN

VIEUX CARRÉ 60 ABV
PENNSYLVANIA, NEUTRAL GRAIN

CLANDESTINE 53 ABV
SWITZERLAND, NEUTRAL GRAIN

DUPLAIS 68 ABV
SWITZERLAND, NEUTRAL GRAIN

VIEUX PONTARLIER 65 ABV
FRANCE, GRAPE

BUTTERFLY 65 ABV
SWITZERLAND, NEUTRAL GRAIN

LEOPOLD BROS 65 ABV
COLORADO, GRAPE

COPPER & KINGS ABSINTHE 65ABV
KENTUCKY, GRAPE

JADE CF BERGER 65 ABV
FRANCE, GRAPE

JADE 1901 68 ABV
FRANCE, GRAPE

JADE NOUVELLE-ORLÉANS 68 ABV
FRANCE, GRAPE

JADE ESPRIT EDOUARD 72 ABV
FRANCE, GRAPE

ABSINTHE/CHARTREUSE

BLOODY AFTERNOON
ABSINTHE ROUGE, BUBBLES

WORLD OF TOMORROW
MATA-HARI ABSINTHE, BENEDICTINE,
LEMON, HONEY, PEYCHAUD BITTERS

ABSINTHE GOD
MATA-HARI ABSINTHE, ORGEAT,
LEMON, EGG WHITE, BITTERS

FRAPPONI
KUBLER ABSINTHE, CAMPARI, ORGEAT

YELLOW BIRD
YELLOW CHARTREUSE, LEMON,
AMARO MONTENEGRO, WHOLE EGG

SILVER MONK
GREEN CHARTREUSE, LIME,
HONEY, EGG WHITE

PÉCHÉ
SINFUL COCKTAILS & CUISINE
AUSTIN ▶ TEXAS

FIGURE 5.3

This cocktail menu includes both classic and house-invented cocktails as well as a section focusing on straight absinthe.

Source: Reprinted with permission of Péché

Nonalcoholic Beverage Menus

Learning Objective 5
List the range of menu item options available for nonalcoholic beverages.

Alcoholic beverages get a lot of attention from menu planners because of the opportunity for significant revenue and profit margins. However, nonalcoholic drinks are extremely popular and most guests order at least one, even when they order alcohol as well. Most casual restaurants prefer to list their nonalcoholic options on the main food menu. Some may leave them off the menu entirely and simply allow the server to address requests for soda or juice. Most customers assume that sodas and juices are available even if they are not listed on the menu. Menu planners for businesses with significant alcohol programs may take this approach in order to drive sales of alcohol. However, nonalcoholic drink sales should not be taken for granted. They are fabulous opportunities for increased revenue and profit. Not all nonalcoholic beverage programs merit their own menus, but depending on the approach the restaurant takes, they may deserve their own page on a comprehensive beverage or dessert menu. Unless the menu planner wishes to highlight a particularly interesting set of beverages, the nonalcoholic drinks are usually listed under the single heading of "beverages," but any single beverage type could merit its own category heading if there are a large number of drinks from which to choose.

Cold Beverages

The push toward environmentalism and sustainability has taken some of the momentum out of sales of bottled water. A few trendy restaurants filter their own water (and charge for it), while others offer only tap water. However, boutique bottled waters still allow

NON-ALCOHOLIC	
CRANBERRY CRUSH: Fresh Cranberry, Lime, Club Soda	
APPLE CRISP: Sparkling Apple Cider, Thyme, Lemon	
GINGER SWIZZLE: Ginger Beer, Mint, Lime	
N/A-GRONI: San Bitters, Grapefruit, Club Soda	
COSMONOT: Pinot Noir Juice, Grenadine, Citrus	8.50
Hot Chocolate with Vanilla Marshmallows	6.50
Hot Greenmarket Apple Cider	5.50
Iced Tea or Passionfruit Iced Tea	5.00
Amanda Palmer (Iced Tea + Lemonade)	6.00
Single-Origin Cold-Brew Coffee, Irving Farm, New York	6.00
Sparkling Apple Cider, Duché de Longueville, France	8.50
Bitter Lemon Soda, Fever Tree, England	6.00
Tonic, Fever Tree, England	6.00
Ginger Beer, Fever Tree, England	7.00
Root Beer, Abita, Louisiana	5.50
Beer, Einbecker, Germany (0.3% alcohol)	8.00
Gewurztraminer Juice, Navarro, Anderson Valley, California	11.00
Pinot Noir Juice, Navarro, Anderson Valley, California	11.00

FIGURE 5.4

This highly creative menu shows that nonalcoholic beverage menus can be a draw of their own.

Source: Reprinted with permission of Gramercy Tavern.

foodservice operations a chance to sell a product that would otherwise be given away for free as tap water. Some guests maintain a preference for certain brands of bottled water and automatically choose that brand over tap water when it is available. Similarly, certain customers prefer sparkling water over still, so they opt for bottled sparkling water when it is offered. A restaurant with an extensive water menu should highlight it on a beverage list or on the main food menu. One that stocks only one brand of still and sparking water is better served by having the server push the sales orally upon greeting the table.

Most businesses that do not serve breakfast still stock orange and cranberry juice for the bar. Restaurants that accommodate children often serve pineapple and/or apple juice as well. When a foodservice establishment caters to young families, it should list its juice offerings on the main menu and/or on a children's menu. A restaurant that goes beyond this basic set of juice offerings should definitely showcase its selection on the main menu. Apricot, sour cherry, mango, and peach are but a few of the many juices that a restaurant could provide. In ethnic restaurants, these selections give the establishment a sense of authenticity. A Turkish restaurant with apricot nectar or an Indian restaurant with mango lassi (a yogurt and mango drink) on the menu differentiates itself from other restaurants that focus on food rather than on a complete dining experience. Finally, a juice menu does not require that each juice be served on its own. Mixed juice drinks with other ingredients such as spices, herbs, coconut milk, yogurt, or other garnishes make for interesting choices for those who do not or cannot drink alcohol.

Milk is a simple offering that is usually listed only in family-friendly restaurants. However, it is a common request from children. Options include not only whole, reduced-fat, low-fat, and skim milk but also chocolate and other flavored milks.

Sodas are one of the most popular cold beverages among nonalcoholic options. Usually, restaurants go with a single brand name and stock only that brand's line of products. In fact, Coke or Pepsi will often provide a free fountain dispenser in exchange for an exclusivity agreement. However, big brand names are not a requirement for soft drink options. Old-fashioned flavors and brands are seeing a small but steady resurgence. Cream, orange, cherry, or grape soda distinguishes a beverage menu from the competition, as do small-batch root beer and ginger ale. A few properties have taken to creating their own soft drinks using carbonated water and house-made syrups. These old-fashioned fountain drinks command high prices and convert an ordinary soda into something extraordinary.

Iced tea, iced coffee, lemonade, and other cold beverage creations allow for simplistic or creative menu items depending upon what the market will sustain. Iced teas come in a range of flavors and house-made versions can originate from black, green, or herbal tea infusions; fruit- or herb-flavored teas can be made from scratch or purchased. Iced coffee can also be offered as an alternative to iced tea. Additions of milk or flavored syrups can generate a wide range of cold coffee and espresso beverages. Lemonade is rarely served in more than a couple of versions, but it, too, can be made from scratch to create a house specialty. Besides, lemonade infused with mint and lemon verbena can sell for a much higher price than a menu listing of "lemonade."

All of these cold nonalcoholic beverage categories may appear under their own headings on the main menu. However, if a business's beverage program is significant, they may merit a separate beverage page or even their own menu. Listing a separate heading for iced tea (or any other type of beverage) would not make sense for just one or two offerings, but with a dozen or so possible choices, a menu planner might opt to separate out some beverage headings and highlight those drinks, particularly if the products are homemade and unique to the business.

Hot Beverages

While most guests will not order an alcoholic drink to accompany dessert, many will purchase tea or coffee. Not long ago, even the most upscale restaurants listed only a choice between regular and decaf coffee; several tea bags may have been presented in a tea box or other container. Today, some foodservice establishments treat these beverages as headings rather than as a single drink.

Teaism Menu *seasonal*
Penn Quarter

starters

Beet Salad *roasted beets, beet hummus, apple, romaine lettuce, goat cheese, and orange fennel vinaigrette.........6.00*

Kale Salad *shredded kale, romaine lettuce, pecans and Persian cucumbers, topped with creamy hemp dressing and fried onion.........5.50*

Shrimp Wontons *four wrapped shrimp with bean thread noodle salad and spicy chili dressing…7.00*

Exotic Mushrooms *sautéed trumpet, oyster & shiitake mushrooms, spinach and plum chutney.........6.00*

Coconut Miso Soup *miso and coconut milk with kabocha squash and shredded kale.........4.75*

Lentil Soup *hearty curried soup with cilantro and pappadum.........4.75*

entrees

** **Grilled Salmon** from Blue Circle ~ with Indonesian-style collard greens, and brown rice 13.75*

Chicken Curry *ABF, non GMO, local ~ marinated chicken in a Thai yellow curry with brown rice and a skewer of Brussels sprout, potato, carrot, shiitake, turnip, radicchio, and onion.........12.00*

Okonomiyaki *Japanese cabbage pancake, wasabi-okonomi sauces, and a choice of kabob:* **vegetable / chicken** *or* **shrimp** *.........12.00 / 13.00*

Palak Shalgam Curry *spinach, spices and tomatoes, fried turnips, brown rice, and coconut yogurt 11.00*

Three Beef Brisket Tacos *from Roseda Farm ~ corn tortillas, Korean brisket, cabbage slaw, chipotle salsa, crema and lime......12.00*

on bread

Korean Brisket Sandwich *from Roseda Farm ~ ciabatta roll, lettuce, Asian slaw, house-made gochujang sauce, Just Mayo, topped with fried onions 12.00*

** **Grass Fed Burger** from Roseda Farm ~ on house-made grain focaccia, lettuce, onions, pickled jalapeños, and Just Mayo, served with a side of Asian slaw / optional goat cheese 1.50 ....12.00*

Tempeh Burger *organic & local from Twin Oaks ~ on house-made grain focaccia, lettuce, onions, pickled jalapeños, and Just Mayo, served with a side of Asian slaw / optional goat cheese 1.50.........11.00*

** **Tea-Cured Salmon Sandwich** from Blue Circle ~ salmon house-cured in Lapsang Souchong, with lettuce, Asian slaw, pickled cabbage, wasabi mayo, kizami seaweed, on ciabatta roll.........12.00*

Fried Chicken Sandwich *ABF, non GMO, local ~ Japanese Panko fried chicken, lettuce, Asian slaw, pickled cucumber, with yuzo kosho mayo, on ciabatta roll.........12.00*

bentos

make choices ~ switch your bento sides ~we are flexible

Fried Chicken *ABF, non GMO, local ~ pickled cucumbers, sweet potatoes, roasted onions, brown rice, and our famous onion-mayo sauce.........12.75*

** **Baked Chilled Salmon** from Blue Circle ~ with a classic tare sauce, broccoli with walnut miso jam, sweet potatoes, roasted onions, and brown rice.........12.75*

Black Bean Cake *with togarashi mayo, pickled cucumbers, roasted turnips & broccoli with a miso walnut jam, and brown rice.........12.75*

** **Roll your own Handroll** from Blue Circle ~ tea-cured salmon, pickled cabbage, sheets of nori, and brown rice, with dipping condiments.........12.75*

* Consuming raw or undercooked foods may increase your risk of foodborne illness, especially if you have certain medical conditions.

We cook and bake with nuts and so the risk of cross-contamination exists.

soup as meals

Udon Noodle Soup ....12.00 / 13.00
fat noodles with fresh ginger broth, spinach, kabocha squash, broccoli & choice of **vegetables / chicken** *or* **shrimp**

* **Chicken Hot Pot** 13.00
rich chicken and red miso broth with pulled chicken, cabbage, kabocha squash, spinach and yuzo kosho

* **Ochazuke** ....10.00 / 12.00
Japanese rice and tea "soup", with your choice entree of **pickled plum / salmon** *or* **shrimp**

trash or treasure ...... 5.00 each

These menu items were developed to utilize product often wastED in restaurants.

Stir-fried Napa Cabbage Butts *with gochujang sauce*

Winter bread salad *with orange, roasted vegetables, sunflower seeds, and orange fennel vinaigrette*

sipping broths

served in a 16 oz. mug with cilantro, citrus & jalapeño garnish

Coconut Miso Broth 4.00

Chicken and Ginger Bone Broth 5.00

and other things

○ cold things .....

Asian Slaw 4.00

Pickled Cabbage 4.00

Seaweed Salad 4.50

Pipe Dreams **Goat Cheese** 2.75

Turnip White Miso Salad.........4.00

Beet-Chickpea Purée.........4.50

Kabocha Squash *with tare sauce* 4.00

* **Tea-Cured Salmon** 7.00

Sweet Potato Salad 4.00

Pickled Cucumbers 4.00

Persian Cucumbers *with orange vinaigrette*...4.00

Broccoli *with walnut miso jam*.........4.50

Roasted Beets *with orange vinaigrette*.........4.00

○ hot things .....

Broccoli Walnut Sauté 4.50

Indonesian Collards.........5.00

Coconut Sauteed Spinach.........5.00

Flatbread *with* **Plum Chutney** ...4.00

Lundberg **Brown Rice** 3.00

Veg Kabob 4.50

Chicken Kabob 7.00

Shrimp Kabob 7.00

choose your kabob sauce:
*gochujang
orange vinaigrette
wasabi mayo
togarashi mayo*

FIGURE 5.5

This menu showcases teas among other cold beverage options.

Source: Printed with permission of Teaism

breakfast entrees

breakfast served Mon - Fri 7:30 am - 11:30am
Sat & Sun 9:30 am - 2:30 pm

French Toast with organic pure maple syrup, stewed apples & cranberries
single slice ....6.00 double slice 12.00

Buckwheat and Hempheart pancakes with orange butter & organic pure
maple syrup (extra syrup $2.00) 9.50

Sourdough Waffle with orange butter & organic pure maple syrup 7.00

* **Okonomiyaki** Japanese cabbage pancake with a fried egg, turkey bacon,
and condiments 11.00

* **Cilantro Scrambled Eggs** organic eggs with ginger, cilantro & jalapeño 7.00
with **Tea-Cured Salmon** ....12.75 or **Aidells Chicken Sausage** 10.75

* **Egg Sandwich** cilantro scrambled eggs, chicken sausage or turkey bacon,
Asian slaw, on ciabatta roll 10.75

Tempeh Scramble organic & local from Twin Oaks ~ wild mushrooms, spinach,
and tare sauce, with flatbread.........9.25

* **Tea-Cured Salmon, Flatbread & Raita** 12.00

Aidells Chicken Sausage, Flatbread & Raita 9.00

Homemade Granola oats, pecans, coconut, raisins, dried blueberries & apricots,
honey, maple syrup & spices, served with milk or homemade yogurt 5.00

Irish Oatmeal with apricots, blueberries, flax seeds & toasted almonds 4.75

Birchermuesli grains, dried fruits & nuts mixed in homemade yogurt
& mango juice, topped with fruit..........5.25

breakfast sides

**Aidells Chicken
& Apple Sausage** 5.50

* **Tea-Cured Salmon** 7.00

Turkey Bacon 5.00

Apple Gingerbread 2.50

Ginger or **Carrot Cake Scones** 3.00

Flatbread with **Plum Chutney** 4.00

desserts

Made by 🍵 *Teaism*
for kayak cookies

Salty Oat Cookie 2.35

Chocolate Salty Oat Cookie 2.50

Chunky Chocolate Pecan Salty Oat Cookie 2.50

Mandelbrot twice-baked German cookie with pistachios & orange.........2.00

Cocoa Nib Cookie Trio .3.00

Hempheart Cookie 2.00

Hungarian Tea Cake 4.00

Coconut Rice Pudding ...4.00

Jasmine Creme Brulée ...4.50

Mochi Japanese sweet bean confection.....3.75

Chocolate Coconut Cake gluten-free cake
with rum caramel, served with gelato 5.75

Dolcezza Gelato or **Sorbet**...................4.25

afternoon tea served daily 2:30 to 5:30

Includes sweets & savories, tea and a glass of Prosecco. Ask for detailed menus
from our staff ....30.00 (or 25.00 without alcohol)

Dupont Circle
2009 R Street NW
Washington, DC 20009
202-667-3827

Lafayette Park
800 Conn. Ave. NW
Washington, DC 20006
202-835-2233

Old Town
682 N St. Asaph Street
Alexandria, VA 22314
703-684-7777

hot teas ~ 16oz. brewed cup

New to tea? Try a classic **black** tea - which has
the highest caffeine content:

Chai Indian spices, with milk & sugar.........3.00
Earl Grey with oil of bergamot 3.00
Keemun English breakfast base 3.00

Oolongs have a more complex leaf & are the
"champagne" of teas:

Formosa a classic 4.75

How about a lighter, more vegetal **green** tea?:

Dragon Well classic Chinese 3.00
Jasmine floral and Chinese 3.75
Sencha spinachy, Japanese 5.00

Trying to avoid caffeine? **Tisanes** are blends of
fruits, flowers and/or herbs:

Berry Beauty fruity with hibiscus 3.00
Lavender Lemon Mint 3.00

Feeling adventurous?!

Golden Dragon elegant black tea, rolled with
golden tips 3.75
Gen Mai Cha spinachy Japanese green tea
with toasted rice 4.00
Soba Cha buckwheat tisane 3.25

Check out our tea menu for the full list with
descriptions! They can be iced, too!

iced teas (slightly sweetened)

Today's Iced Black Tea 2.50

Moroccan Mint green tea
& organic mint 2.50

Today's Iced Tisane 2.50

Chai Indian spices, with milk & sugar.........3.00

cold drinks

Zhenzhou Pearls 3.40

Japanese Sweet Green Tea 2.50

Ginger Limeade 2.50

Chai Shake with cinnamon gelato 3.50

Lassi 3.50
our homemade yogurt drink ~ tamarind,
banana, orange, mango, green tea or plain

Pomegranate Juice with blueberry 4.75

Orange Juice or
Mango Juice Blend organic 3.00

Bottled Flat or **Sparkling Water** 2.25

Imli Cooler Indian tamarind drink 3.00

Fresh Ginger Ale 3.25

We also have BEER, WINE, SAKE & COCKTAILS!

www.teaism.com
follow us on twitter @TeaismATeaHouse
email catering@teaism.com for catering options

2/4/16

FIGURE 5.5   (Continued)

COFFEE & CHOCOLATE BEVERAGES

DILETTANTE CHOCOLATE OPTIONS
What's Your Chocolate Number?

EXTRA DARK 72 DARK 63 EPHEMERE® DARK 52 MILK 41 WHITE 31

HOT CHOCOLATE & MOCHAS

HOT CHOCOLATE, TALL, 3.75
Your choice of chocolate, steamed milk

MOCHA, TALL, 4.25
Your choice of chocolate, house espresso, steamed milk

VIENNESE COCOA, TALL, 3.5
Double-Dutched cocoa blend

DEMITASSE SPECIALTIES
Big Flavor in a Little Cup

CIOCCOBREVE™, 3.45
Your choice of chocolate steamed with half & half

ESPRESSO DOUBLE SHOT, 2.5
Our Hapsburg espresso blend

MOCHA VIZIO™, 3.75
Your choice of chocolate, espresso double shot

TURKISH COFFEE, 3.75
Our Persian-spiced cocoa, double shot of espresso

CHOCOLATE with SPIRITS

***CHOCOLATE TODDY, 10**
Dilettante Ephemere® hot chocolate, brandy

***MOCHA NUDGE, 10**
Espresso, Dilettante Ephemere® hot chocolate, Frangelico

***SALTED CARAMEL NUDGE, 10**
Dilettante Ephemere® hot chocolate, Dilettante Caramel Sauce, espresso, vodka, Bailey's Caramel, sea salt

DILETTANTE SIGNATURES

MEXICANO®, 3.75
Cinnamon-spiced cocoa, water

MEXICANO® MOCHA, 4
Cinnamon-spiced cocoa, espresso

VOLTAIRE™, 3.75
Brewed coffee, dark Viennese cocoa

CARAMEL MOCHA, 4.5
Steamed milk, espresso, Dilettante Caramel Sauce, milk chocolate

COPENHAGEN, 4
Brewed coffee, Dilettante Ephemere® hot chocolate, Persian spices

ESPRESSO & COLD DRINKS

ESPRESSO, 2	CHAI TEA LATTE, 3.75
AMERICANO, 2.75	CHOCOLATE MILK, 3.25
LATTE, 3.5	CHOCOLATE SODA, 3.75
CAPPUCCINO, 3.5	SAN PELLEGRINO, 3.75
DRIP COFFEE, 2.25	

WHOLE LEAF & HERBAL TEAS
Served in a Teapot
- 4.75 -

INDIAN SPICE	EARL GREY	PEPPERMINT
DARJEELING	GENMAICHA GREEN	CHAMOMILE
FORMOSA OOLONG	ROOIBOS	SPICED PLUM

Contains alcohol - Must be 21 years of age or older - Please have ID ready
Automatic 18% gratuity added to parties of 8 or more

FIGURE 5.6
This highly creative menu illustrates the possibilities of using hot chocolate and coffee as a major draw for customers.
Source: Reprinted with permission of Dilettante Chocolates, Inc.

Coffee shops sometimes provide coffees of different origins and roasting levels. A dark roast Ethiopian Yirgacheffe tastes vastly different from a medium roast Guatemalan Antigua. When a restaurant provides several types of coffees from various regions, a separate beverage menu or a page on the dessert menu is deserved. As most guests are not experts in coffee, tasting notes are highly appropriate for such a coffee menu. Usually, these tasting notes refer to the acidity levels and other flavor overtones. Sometimes a restaurant will serve coffees with different flavor additions, such as hazelnut or vanilla. Flavored coffees do not require the separate menu page that regional coffees do, as their tasting notes are incorporated into their names. Offering multiple coffees on a menu does not necessitate a bank of brewing machines. Individual ceramic filters or French presses allow a server to brew any type of coffee to order in individual portions, while insulated thermoses allow servers to brew coffee in batches and to hold each variety warm until needed.

Espresso drinks continue to gain popularity in restaurants. Lattes, cappuccinos, mochas, and espressos all command higher prices than brewed coffee and make an evening a little more special for the guests. Espresso drinks allow for flavored syrups, but they are also a common canvas for creating alcoholic after-dinner drinks. A cappuccino with sambuca or frangelico makes for an alcoholic drink that goes well with dessert yet does not seem out of place among guests choosing plain coffee for dessert. Alcohol and coffee combinations also allow for tableside presentations, which can drive up sales quickly for guests who crave the spectacle.

Tea, like coffee, comes in a wide range of styles. Types include white, green, oolong, black, and herbal, although any of these varieties can be expanded with the addition of other herbs, spices, or flavoring agents. Great variation exists naturally within each of these tea types. Sencha, dragonwell, and hojicha taste vastly different from one another even though all are green teas. Upscale businesses that cater to tea drinkers may stock teapots and strainers and serve loose tea, while others simply allow guests to choose a single tea bag from a selection for steeping in the guest's cup. The more interesting the choices are, the more likely guests are to order tea as a beverage. For those businesses that serve afternoon tea (the meal), a wide selection of teas is a must.

Hot chocolate is less common than tea or coffee as an after-dinner drink because its sweetness may seem like a sugar overdose alongside a dessert. However, hot chocolate can be a popular breakfast option, especially among children. Served with whipped cream or marshmallows, hot chocolate provides a sweet caffeine rush for those who do not care for the bitterness of coffee or the tannins of tea. Hot chocolate also makes a fun addition to brunch, where it may include additions of alcohol to flavor it. While hot chocolate rarely commands its own category on a beverage menu, it can come in white, milk, and dark chocolate varieties. As with the other hot beverage choices, a unique product in a given community is a draw for customers who wish to partake of that indulgence.

While coffee, tea, chocolate, and espresso drinks would normally be listed together or among other beverages, they may merit separate headings if the business offers enough variations of each. That said, alcoholic versions of any of these drinks should be listed separately and should state the alcohol that has been added. To do otherwise is to run the risk that a child or teetotaler will order an alcoholic drink. Whether listed on the main food menu, a dessert menu, a comprehensive beverage menu, or their own menu page, hot beverages belong on the menus in most foodservice operations.

Special Concerns over Alcohol

Learning Objective 6
Describe the menu planner's role in supporting safe alcohol service.

Beverages, including alcoholic ones, can be a valuable addition to a meal, but a guest's overconsumption of alcohol can be a serious threat to a business's survival. One intoxicated guest who gets into a physical fight at the property or kills someone in a car accident on the way home can bring down the company through third-party lawsuits. Alcohol may be fun, but it has its limitations and its dangers. There are in-depth programs, such as the ServSafe Alcohol training program, to provide managers and servers a thorough approach to serving alcohol safely; however, as safe alcohol service relates to the menu planner's role, the basics follow in this section.

To address the risks of alcohol overconsumption by guests, a menu planner should ensure that special pricing and drink creations do not encourage excessive drinking. Selling alcohol is fine, but allowing customers to drink and drink for little to no money is a bad idea. Alcohol should not be used as a loss leader (sold below cost to attract business in food or entertainment sales). When alcohol is sold cheaply, servers must take extra care to count drinks and to cut off any customers who have had too much. Menu promotions that advertise free drinks, bottomless pitchers, or contests for quantity drinking are a recipe for disaster.

The drinks that are listed on the menu should be moderate in size and should not hide huge quantities of alcohol inconspicuously. A 12-ounce beer, 5-ounce glass of wine, and 1½-ounce shot of 80-proof liquor all deliver roughly equal amounts of pure alcohol. In industry terms, they are all thought of as equivalent to one drink. When a recipe calls for 2¼ ounces of 80-proof liquor, that beverage is equivalent to one and a half drinks. A customer or server who attempts to count drinks will have difficulty if 7 ounces of wine are poured into a huge glass that hides the quantity. A guest might think of that as one glass of wine when it is closer to one and a half drinks. Cocktails may equate to one or two drinks, but more than that becomes excessive. An oversized cocktail, if equal to three drinks, would put a customer over the legal blood alcohol limit with a single beverage order. The best approach to controlling alcohol consumption is through proper portioning and moderate drink sizes.

However, foodservice operations that serve alcohol usually hope to generate a profit. The menu planner plays a critical role in facilitating that goal. A simple alcoholic drink may not cost much, but one that uses high-end or premium liquor, wine, or beer commands a much higher sales price. By making sure that a wine and beer list includes some premium choices, the menu planner helps to increase revenue and profits from those customers willing to purchase a higher-quality product at a higher price point. Cocktails work similarly. A drink listed as a "margarita" will not sell for as much money as one that lists by name a high-priced brand of tequila. Alternatively, when a guest places an order for a classic drink, the server can attempt to upsell the customer on the spot. *Upselling* alcohol means inviting the customer to select a premium liquor for use in the drink. For example, if the guest orders a gin and tonic, the server might respond, "Would you like that made with Tanqueray?" If a drink made with Tanqueray sells for more money than one made with the well brand, the server makes additional revenue for the business every time a customer says yes. Of course, the number of upscale products that the operation is able to store depends on the amount of inventory space available and the expected rate at which these premium products will sell. Still, having just a few for sale can increase overall beverage revenue tremendously. Total alcohol consumption is inherently limited by the amount guests can consume before becoming intoxicated. Increasing alcohol revenue is best done by encouraging the sales of premium products, not by persuading guests to consume more alcohol.

Non-Restaurant Menus

While most of this chapter has focused on beverage menus for restaurants, beverages are a critical component of nearly every dining experience and thus deserve a spot on other types of menus as well. Children's menus should include juices and milk. Lounge menus follow the guidelines of restaurant menus, with particular attention paid to providing an interesting alcoholic beverage selection appropriate for the market. Brunch and afternoon tea menus should offer traditional beverages classically paired with those meals. Dessert menus, too, should display both alcoholic and nonalcoholic beverage options on their pages.

Room service beverage menus should offer most or all of the nonalcoholic beverages available in the hotel's full-service restaurant (with the possible exception of drinks like cappuccino, which may not transport well). Room service drinks are usually delivered in sealed containers or carafes to keep the liquid from spilling. A hotel that normally serves soda from a dispenser may need to stock bottled sodas for room service use. Otherwise, the

BEER, SPIRITS AND MIXERS

Available 24 hours

Beer

Domestic	Bottle	$5.50

Budweiser, Bud Light, Coors, Coors Light, Michelob,
Miller Genuine Draft, Miller Lite or O'Douls

Imported and Microbrews	Bottle	$6.00

Corona, Sierra Nevada Pale Ale or Heineken

Spirits and Mixers

Mixers	$3.95

Pepsi, Diet Pepsi, Sierra Mist, Mug Root Beer, Tonic, Club Soda,
Ginger Ale

Bloody Mary	Liter	$15.00
Freshly Squeezed Orange Juice	Liter	$16.00
Margarita	Liter	$22.00
Juice (Apple, Cranberry, Grapefruit or Pineapple)	Liter	$11.00

Brandy and Cognac

Courvoisier	$95.00
Hennessy XO	$375.00
Korbel	$38.00
Remy Martin VSOP	$160.00

Scotch

Chivas Regal	$100.00
Dewars White Label	$85.00
Glenlivet	$120.00
J & B	$80.00
Johnny Walker Black	$130.00

Gin

Beefeater	$60.00
Bombay	$80.00
Bombay Sapphire	$95.00
Tanqueray	$85.00

Tequila

Jose Cuervo Gold	$65.00
Patron Silver	$110.00

Orders may be placed by dialing 88438. $5.00 minimum order. $2.00 In Room Dining charge, 18% gratuity and tax will be added.

FIGURE 5.7

These pages from a room service menu show the wide range of alcoholic beverages that can be offered for in-room consumption.

Source: Peppermill Resort Spa Casino, Reno. Reprinted with permission.

BEER, SPIRITS AND MIXERS

Available 24 hours

Liqueur
Bailey's Irish Cream $75.00
Grand Marnier $125.00
Kahlua $75.00
Tuaca $75.00

Vodka
Absolut $75.00
Grey Goose $110.00
Ketel One $80.00
Skyy Vodka $58.00
Smirnoff $46.00
Stolichnaya $80.00

Rum
Bacardi Light $50.00
Captain Morgan $55.00
Malibu Rum $50.00
Myers's Rum $70.00

Whiskey
Canadian Club $55.00
Crown Royal $83.00
Crown Royal Reserve $110.00
Jack Daniel's $70.00
Jim Beam $50.00
Seagram's 7 . . . .$42.00
Seagram's VO $52.00

FIGURE 5.7   *(Continued)*

bubbles will escape en route to the room. Hot beverages should be transported in insulated carafes to help them maintain their temperature. The alcoholic beverage room service menu may be more limited, but it should include several wines, beers, and liquors popular among guests. The beer and wine choices should span the range of styles and flavors. The liquor choices should include one popular brand of each major category of liquor (tequila, rum, whisky, scotch, brandy, etc.). Room service menus need not list cocktails and mixed drinks, only the liquors themselves. Guests who wish to have a specific cocktail may order the components separately and mix the drink to their personal taste in the room or purchase the cocktail in the hotel lounge. If prepared in a bar for room service delivery, a mixed drink served on ice will be diluted by the time it reaches the guest, and a chilled but strained drink will no longer be cold. Providing the liquor and mixers in bottles and allowing guests to mix the drinks in their rooms with ice provided by the hotel yields a better result for the guest (though some boutique hotels are now offering services in which a bartender comes to the room with mixers and ice and mixes the drinks for the guests). Many hotels offer a few alcoholic beverage options through minibars in each guest room, listed on a separate minibar menu; the guest is charged based on what bottles are removed from the minibar. Minibars typically stock only individual portion sizes of each beverage. For 750-mL bottles of alcohol or a broader set of alcoholic options, guests usually must order through the room service menu.

Take-out beverage menus follow similar rules to room service menus, but local laws may prevent restaurants from selling alcohol to go. As a rule, all take-out beverages should be sold in sealed containers so that they do not spill in transport. Unlike most other menus, a take-out menu may list large-quantity (party-size) beverages. For example, a pizza place may sell soda in 20-ounce, 1-liter, or 2-liter bottles on a take-out menu. For a room service

FROM OUR WINE CELLAR

Ask for wines available by the glass

Champagne & Sparkling Wines
Chandon Brut Cuvee, Napa..$50.00
Dom Perignon, Champagne...$425.00
Martini & Rossi Asti, Piedmont..$50.00
Moet & Chandon – White Star, Champagne...............................$95.00
Mumm, Napa, Brut Rose...$55.00
Schramsberg Blanc de Blancs, Napa......................................$78.00
Veuve Clicquot "Ponsardin" Champagne..................................$125.00

White Wines
Chardonnay
Beringer, Napa...$42.00
Cakebread, Napa...$90.00
Far Niente, Napa...$110.00
Ferrari Carano, Sonoma...$70.00
Kendall Jackson Grand Reserve, California................................$65.00
Sonoma Cutrer Russian River Ranches, Sonoma.............................$48.00
Robert Mondavi, Napa..$60.00
Rombauer, Napa..$80.00

White Zinfandel, Riesling and Pinot Grigio
Beringer White Zinfandel, Napa..$29.00
Dillman Piesporter Goldtropfchen Spatlese...............................$42.00
Santa Margherita Pinot Grigio, Italy.....................................$60.00

Sauvignon Blanc
Cakebread, Napa...$54.00
Kenwood, Sonoma..$39.00

Orders may be placed by dialing 88438. $5.00 minimum order. $2.00 In Room Dining charge, 18% gratuity and tax will be added.

FIGURE 5.7   *(Continued)*

FROM OUR WINE CELLAR

Ask for wines available by the glass

Red Wines
Cabernet Sauvignon & Blends

Beaulieu Vineyard BV Rutherford, Napa	$65.00
Caymus, Napa	$180.00
Jordan, Alexander Valley	$120.00
Kendall Jackson, California	$55.00
Chimney Rock, Stags Leap District	$110.00
Cakebread, Napa	$165.00
Mount Veeder Winery, Napa	$85.00
Opus One, Napa	$525.00

Merlot

Duckhorn, Napa	$130.00
Ferrari Carano, Sonoma	$70.00
Kendall Jackson, Vintner's Reserve, Sonoma	$52.00
Pride Mountain Vineyards, Napa	$135.00
Raymond Reserve, Napa	$45.00

Pinot Noir & Shiraz

Wishing Tree Shiraz, Australia	$38.00
King Estate Pinot Noir, Oregon	$60.00

Our wine cellar carries an extensive selection, and we are the recipient of the coveted *Wine Spectator's* Best of Award of Excellence.

Please contact the Room Service Captain or Manager for vintages and other selections available.

Because the Peppermill Hotel Casino has been licensed by the State of Nevada to sell alcoholic beverages, no liquor, wine or beer may be brought into the Hotel for the purpose of hospitality entertaining without the prior knowledge of the Room Service Manager.

FIGURE 5.7   *(Continued)*

menu, a 20-ounce bottle might be the largest size available. If a beverage is sold by the cup, it should come with a tight-fitting lid.

Banquet menus should provide a very limited set of beverage options for guests. As banquets offer only one or two options per course, the beverages (often wine) can be paired with each course or one red and one white wine selected for the entire meal. Obviously, if the banquet is designed to highlight a particular beverage, that beverage should be served with each course. Nonalcoholic beverages should always be available for a banquet, even if an alcoholic drink is being highlighted. Water should be poured for every participant. Soda, tea, coffee, and juice should be available upon request. If the banquet provider is a hotel or other operation with full bar capability, the menu planner should work with the client in advance to determine whether to accommodate guests who want an alcoholic beverage not listed on the menu and what the additional cost would be. Fees for alcoholic drinks may be charged to the guest based on his consumption or to the event host based either on an upfront per person cost or on total usage at the event.

Cycle menus require beverage options that, like the food, address the nutritional needs of the audience. Sodas may be listed, but healthier alternatives of juice, milk, and water should also be included. Coffee and tea are common inclusions for adult markets. Alcoholic beverages are rarely appropriate for a captive audience but may make sense for a cycle menu that operates as part of a cafeteria or restaurant. Except for specialty drinks, such as an ethnic beverage designed to pair specifically with one ethnic recipe in the cycle rotation, the beverage component of a cycle menu does not usually rotate. It makes more sense to offer fewer juice, milk, and water options every day than to offer only pineapple juice one day, only grape juice another, etc. When people prefer a specific beverage for a given meal, they want it most days.

Catering menus should include an extensive set of options for customers. The caterer can purchase approximately what he needs for the event, and sealed bottles can be stored for a long time, assuming the caterer has the storage space available. Usually, caterers only sell full bottles, meaning that once the caterer opens a bottle, the client has purchased the entire bottle, even if only one drink is poured from it. Sometimes, the caterer gives the partial bottles to the customer; sometimes, the caterer keeps the excess. When the caterer is a hotel or restaurant that sells that bottle on its regular menu, it may charge the client per drink instead. If a client wants a beverage that is not on the catering menu, the caterer may agree to purchase it for the client under the condition that the client pays for the purchase. Because catering clients are a much broader market than the guests who visit a particular restaurant, the beverage offerings should be extensive. That said, the client should be guided to choose a fairly narrow selection of beverages to serve at the event.

The attendees at a single catered event are usually a very clearly defined market and their beverage preferences are known. If the client wishes to provide a cocktail hour, it is often sufficient to offer just one or two wines of each color, a couple of beers, and four or five different liquors with a few basic mixers and garnishes. Clients may want a full bar available, but they often reconsider once they are advised that they pay for six bottles if six guests each want a different brand of bourbon for their one drink. Under that scenario, all of the guests are usually perfectly happy just to have any whiskey available. The brands selected for a catered event should accommodate the client's budget and be popular choices for the market. For example, a super-premium vodka that none of the guests have heard of is less likely to satisfy the attendees than a cheaper one that they drink regularly. During the main meal, beer and wine are usually the alcoholic beverages served alongside nonalcoholic drinks. For adult-only events, soda and water may be the only nonalcoholic choices available, though mixers from the bar could also be served alone. If the caterer offered liquor during the cocktail hour, the client may want it available upon request through the meal or may insist that the bar close once the guests are seated. The ways that caterers charge for beverages mirror banquet beverage charging options.

As with traditional restaurant menus, the rules of safe alcohol service apply to all types of menus. Guests should be cut off once they have reached their alcohol limit; excessive consumption should not be promoted. Guests should never be allowed to self-serve alcoholic drinks. Nonalcoholic beverages should always be available, and water automatically provided to seated guests. Finally, as with all food and beverage menus, the most important factor from the menu planner's perspective is to ensure that the offerings meet the needs of the target market and the business.

Summary

Beverage menus include a wide range of both alcoholic and nonalcoholic offerings appropriate for the target market, the business's brand, and the meal period. Variety and balance make for a proper wine menu, which often lists wine by producer name, grape type, region, and/or vintage. Wines' headings may be categorized by color, grape type, region, or flavor profile. Some menu planners may include recommended wine and food pairings on the menu. Beer menus, like wine menus, should offer variety of region and style. The price points for the beer and wine listed should align appropriately with the business's food menu prices (cheap, mid-range, or pricy). Liquor and cocktail menus are printed in the food menu, on table tents, on a dessert menu, or as part of a larger beverage menu. While beer and wine listings may provide tasting notes, cocktails usually list only ingredients. Nonalcoholic beverage menus are just as important as alcoholic ones. Water, juice, milk, soda, iced tea, lemonade, coffee, tea, and other beverages are extremely popular and represent opportunities for additional sales. When these categories include creative or boutique products, nonalcoholic beverages can be as much of a customer draw as the alcoholic drinks. Because alcohol cannot be consumed safely in unlimited quantities, alcohol revenue should be driven through sales of premium products, not by promoting excessive consumption. Portion sizes for alcoholic beverages should be moderate. Finally, room service, take-out, banquet, cycle, and catering menus all require some special consideration when planning for their beverage offerings.

Comprehension Questions

1. List four variables that may provide variety and balance to a wine list.
2. List four bits of information that are normally included in the name of a New World wine.
3. What is a bin number, and why is it used?
4. What is the standard portion size for one drink of each for wine, beer, and 80-proof liquor?
5. List four different types of beer styles.
6. In an ethnic restaurant that serves beer, list the two countries from which at a minimum the beer options should be sourced.
7. How do cocktail menu descriptions differ from descriptions of other menu items?
8. If a menu planner does not list liquor drinks under a single heading of "Cocktails" or "Liquor," how might these drinks be categorized? List five possible headings.
9. List five categories of nonalcoholic beverages that might be found on a restaurant menu.
10. List one way that a menu planner or server can safely increase beverage revenue.

Discussion Questions

1. Consider two different beverage menus. One has eight pages of wine listings, two pages of beer listings, and two pages of cocktails. The other fits all of its alcoholic and nonalcoholic beverage offerings on a single page. Describe the restaurant for which each of these menus would make sense.
2. Do an Internet search to find a fairly extensive beer menu for a restaurant. What headings does the menu use to divide its beer offerings?
3. Imagine that you are a mixologist in an upscale restaurant. Think of three mixers (syrups, infusions, flavorings, etc.) that you could create in-house for use in your scratch-made cocktails.
4. Imagine that you are a menu planner for a boutique restaurant that makes all of its beverages from scratch. Create one soda, one flavored iced tea, one flavored lemonade, one juice beverage, and one espresso drink that you could prepare in-house but that cannot be purchased commercially as a ready-made product.
5. Create a beverage menu (item listings only) for a residential college dining hall.
6. Imagine that you are an off-premise caterer with a client who wishes to offer a cocktail hour before a sit-down meal at his private event. What advice would you give him for selecting beverages to serve at the cocktail hour and during the meal? If the event is a private party on the client's estate, how would you handle an attendee who has become intoxicated and wants to have another alcoholic drink?

Case Study

A small town bar/restaurant wants to jump on the trend of boutique cocktails, local wines, and American microbreweries to drive its alcohol sales. The manager hopes increased beverage sales will save the company, which currently loses customers every time it tries to raise its average entrée price over $12. The bar/restaurant has seats for about seventy customers. Currently, its top selling drinks are Budweiser and shots of its one brand of whisky. The manager, not particularly familiar with alcohol, goes online and decides to cut and paste other menus to create his comprehensive alcohol menu. As luck would have it, the menus he has copied are the same ones included in this chapter.

After three months with the new menu, the company goes broke with nearly 300 cases of alcohol in its storeroom. What did the manager do wrong? What approach would you have recommended to the manager to drive beverage sales?

Capstone Project

Step 5: Create a beverage menu consistent with your project's concept, target market, and menu. The beverage menu should include alcohol only if that makes sense with the concept. Additionally, write five recipes for various beverages on your menu. If the menu includes drinks with multiple ingredients, such as espresso and milk, at least three of those drinks should be selected for recipe creation. Single ingredient drink recipes can be as simple as the quantity of liquid poured, the glass type, and the service temperature.

CHAPTER 6

Standardized Recipes and Recipe Costing

INTRODUCTION

After determining the foods and beverages to include on a menu, the menu planner next turns to sales price determination. The prices that the customer sees on a menu are not picked willy-nilly from thin air but rather arise from a careful analysis of the operation's costs, the biggest component of which is the cost of each item sold—its food or beverage cost.

Many menu planners calculate each item's selling price directly from its food (or beverage) cost per portion. It is important to recognize that the true cost per portion for an item includes the costs for all of the consumables provided to the customer, even if some of those products are included "for free." While this chapter focuses exclusively on how to calculate a product's true cost per portion, it is merely a prelude to the ultimate goal of determining a sales price for each menu item. For ease of reading, this chapter explains costing concepts through food recipes, but the concepts apply equally to beverages. Both utilize recipes, and the cost per portion for each derives directly from the cost of the ingredients used in each recipe. When there is a difference between food and beverage costing, this chapter points it out.

CHAPTER 6 LEARNING OBJECTIVES

As a result of successfully completing this chapter, readers will be able to:

1. State the importance of using standard recipes and portion control.

2. Define the concepts of as-purchased, edible portion, and yield percentage.

3. Calculate a product's as-purchased quantity, edible portion quantity, or yield percentage given the other two variables.

4. Calculate a product's as-purchased cost, edible portion cost, or yield percentage given the other two variables.

5. Use a costing sheet to calculate a recipe's total cost.

6. Calculate an item's true cost per portion, including a spice factor and Q factor.

CHAPTER 6 OUTLINE

Standard Recipes and Portion Control

Learning Objective 1
State the importance of using standard recipes and portion control.

In order for a recipe costing process to be valid, a foodservice operation must utilize standard (or standardized) recipes. A standard recipe is one that is written in sufficient detail that each and every employee who uses it creates an identical product. Standard recipes account for the equipment, employee skills, purveyor products, and quality and quantity standards of the business where the recipes are prepared. They are always followed exactly by all employees and not thought of simply as guidelines. Finally, they deal with all aspects of food production, from ingredient preparation to portioning and presentation to storage of leftovers.

Standard recipes may be written down or communicated verbally through training. Specificity is critical. A recipe that gives the cook too much leeway is likely to waver greatly in production costs from day to day. For example, if a portion size for a swordfish entrée is listed as "one steak," the cook might serve one guest a 5-ounce steak and another one a 7-ounce steak. The costs for these two dishes differ significantly and make calculating a fair selling price nearly impossible.

Employees may measure portions by volume, by weight, or by count. A kitchen can employ measuring cups, ladles, scales, or even certain presentation dishes to control portion sizes. For example, a 6-ounce gratin dish cannot hold more than 6 ounces of product as long as the dish is not mounded above the rim. When an operation does not use standard recipes and portion control methods consistently, calculating a cost per portion becomes a fruitless activity that yields irrelevant information.

As-Purchased, Edible Portion, and Yield Percentage

Learning Objective 2
Define the concepts of as-purchased, edible portion, and yield percentage.

To calculate a recipe's cost accurately, it is important to understand the concepts of as-purchased (AP), edible portion (EP), and yield percentage (Y%). "As-purchased" refers to an ingredient in the form in which it arrives from the purveyor. For example, if a restaurant purchases its potatoes unprocessed, then the raw, unpeeled potatoes are the AP form. If the chef purchases frozen potatoes peeled and cut into French fries, then the precooked fries are the AP form. The key to understanding AP is that the kitchen has not processed the product beyond the form in which it arrived at the operation's door.

Edible portion is the form each product takes after it has been processed by the kitchen. For produce, "edible portion" refers to the trimmed and cut but not cooked product. For example, peeled and diced carrots for a glazed-carrot recipe or trimmed green beans are in their EP form. For meat (or poultry or seafood), EP may refer to the ingredient after it has been cooked. Whether EP meat is based on a raw or a cooked weight depends on how the product is advertised. A menu that states that its 6-ounce burgers are measured by their "precooked weight" employs an EP based on raw ground beef. However, a restaurant that advertises a sandwich with "4 ounces of sliced corned beef" refers to a cooked EP weight; the meat is sliced and measured after the corned beef has been cooked.

Learning Objective 3
Calculate a product's as-purchased quantity, edible portion quantity, or yield percentage given the other two variables.

Yield percentage is the tool for comparing the relative sizes between a product's AP and EP forms. An AP ingredient represents 100% of the weight of that ingredient. During processing, some of that ingredient's weight may be lost through peeling and trimming, or, in the case of certain meats, from water loss through aging and/or cooking. The percentage of product that remains is the ingredient's yield. When the same ingredient is processed the same way by individuals with similar skills, the percentage of product yielded remains fairly consistent over time. This allows a manager to utilize a yield percentage to calculate how much of a given ingredient will remain after it has been processed.

To calculate a Y%, a cook must weigh (or measure) an ingredient both before processing (AP weight) and after processing (EP weight). Using this information, the Y% is calculated as follows:

$$\text{Yield Percentage (Y\%)} = \frac{\text{Edible Portion (EP) Weight}}{\text{As-Purchased (AP) Weight}}$$

Example 6.1: A cook takes a 23-ounce rutabaga and trims and dices it down to 15 ounces. What is the yield percentage for rutabaga processed this way?

$$Y\% = \frac{EP}{AP} = \frac{15\,oz}{23\,oz} = 0.652 \text{ or } 65.2\%$$

Example 6.2: A business purchases a 19-pound boneless rib roast for dry aging. After weeks of aging, the roast now weighs 17.5 pounds. The chef trims off an additional 14 ounces of fat and unusable trim from the aged roast prior to cooking. Cooking the roast reduces the final cooked weight to 15 pounds. The 16-ounce portions served to the guest are cut from this cooked roast. What is the yield percentage for this prime rib?

The first step is to recognize that most of the information here is extraneous. Calculating Y% only requires EP and AP weights. The AP weight is given as 19 pounds. Because the servings are portioned from the cooked (and not the raw) roast, the EP weight is the weight of the trimmed and cooked roast, given as 15 pounds.

$$Y\% = \frac{EP}{AP} = \frac{15\,lb}{19\,lb} = 0.789 \text{ or } 78.9\%$$

It is important to note that for this formula to work both EP and AP must be expressed in the same units—all ounces or all pounds or all cups. Also, the result will be the Y% in its decimal form. To convert it to its percentage form, simply move the decimal point two spaces to the right and add the percent sign.

Given this equation, a manager can solve for any of the three variables (Y%, EP weight, or AP weight) given the other two. The equation can be expressed as a graphic formula as follows:

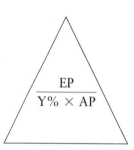

In this graphic formula, "EP" represents edible portion quantity, "AP" represents as-purchased quantity, and "Y%" is the yield percentage in decimal form. To solve for any of the variables, simply cover up the unknown one and follow the calculation depicted with the other two variables.

Example 6.3: Sliced, peeled cucumbers have a yield percentage of 84%. If a cook has to prepare 2½ pounds of peeled, sliced cucumbers for lunch, how many pounds of as-purchased cucumbers should she start with?

In this example, we know Y% (84% or 0.84) and EP weight (2.5 lb). We need to solve for AP. By covering up AP, we are left with EP ÷ Y%.

$$AP = \frac{EP}{Y\%} = \frac{2.5\,lbs}{0.84} = 2.98\,lbs$$

The cook should begin with roughly 3 pounds of cucumbers to yield 2.5 pounds of sliced, peeled cucumbers. It should be emphasized that in this formula Y% is always entered in its decimal form.

The concepts of EP, AP, and Y% apply equally to food and to beverage; however, in the case of beverages, the loss that creates a Y% of less than 100% stems from evaporation and spillage rather than from intentional trimming and peeling. To determine an accurate Y% for a beverage, a manager must closely track purchases and sold beverage quantities to determine what quantity, if any, is lost in the process of pouring drinks. Using the AP quantity purchased and the EP quantity sold, the manager can easily calculate the Y% from the aforementioned graphic formula.

The graphic formula applies to any product for which the loss or waste either has no value or has the same value as the rest of the product. For example, potato peel may be thought of as having no value (if it is thrown in the trash) or as having the same value as the rest of the potato if the peel is cut thick and used in a potato skin appetizer. However, the components of large cuts of meat, poultry, and seafood do not often work that way. A whole chicken, for example, costs one price per pound, but when broken into smaller cuts, the breasts, wings, thighs, and bones all have different values per pound because they would each cost a different price per pound if purchased separately. Determining an accurate cost per pound for a product in this situation requires a butcher's yield test. A butcher's yield test can be somewhat complicated to explain, but most cost control books provide thorough explanations of the process. Traster's *Foundations of Cost Control* (Pearson Education) provides an excellent description of the butcher's yield test and cooking-loss calculations. When a product does not require a butcher's yield test or cooking-loss test, its EP cost can be derived quite simply from its AP cost and Y% as described in the next section.

AP and EP Costs

Learning Objective 4
Calculate a product's as-purchased cost, edible portion cost, or yield percentage given the other two variables.

When a product is processed from an AP to an EP form, its effective cost per weight or volume changes as well. For example, whole onions might cost $1.00/lb, but if sliced, peeled onions have a 70% yield, then a chef needs to buy 1.4 pounds of whole onions to get a 1-pound yield of sliced onions. The cost for 1.4 pounds = $1.00/lb × 1.4 lb = 1.40. Thus, the cost for sliced, peeled onions is actually $1.40/lb, not $1.00/lb. This logic illustrates the difference between EP cost and AP cost. In this particular case, $1.00/lb is the AP cost and $1.40/lb is the EP cost.

Fortunately, calculating an EP cost is quite simple given an AP cost and a Y% for a given product. The equation to do so is as follows:

$$EP\$ = \frac{AP\$}{Y\%}$$

where "EP$" represents edible portion cost, "AP$" represents as-purchased cost, and "Y%" is the yield percentage in its decimal form. Both EP$ and AP$ are per-unit costs, meaning that they are written in terms of dollars per pound, ounce, cup, piece, etc. If the AP cost for a product is $30.00 for a 50-pound bag, the cost should first be divided to a cost per single unit (per pound, in this case). Thus, $30/50 lb translates to $30 ÷ 50lb = $0.60/lb. To enter $30 into the above equation without converting it to $0.60/lb first would not provide valuable information. Any cost per unit can be calculated by dividing the total cost by the total weight or volume. Mathematically, this is written as follows:

$$Cost\,per\,Unit = \frac{Total\,Cost}{Total\,Weight\,or\,Volume}$$

Example 6.4: What is the edible portion cost per pound for diced potatoes if the as-purchased potatoes cost $37.60 for a 40-pound box and the yield percentage for diced potatoes is 66%?

First, calculate the AP cost per pound.

$$Cost\,per\,Pound = \frac{Total\,Cost}{Total\,Weight} = \frac{\$37.60}{40\,lb} = \$0.94/lb$$

Now, it is possible to calculate EP$. Remember that the Y% of 66% is written as 0.66 in decimal form.

$$EP\$ = \frac{AP\$}{Y\%} = \frac{\$0.94/lb}{0.66} = \$1.42/lb$$

The edible portion cost for diced potatoes is $1.42/lb.

As with AP and EP quantity, the relationship between AP$, EP$, and Y% can be written in a single graphic formula as follows:

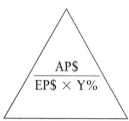

$$\frac{AP\$}{EP\$ \times Y\%}$$

As with the earlier graphic equation, simply cover up the variable you wish to determine and follow the mathematical instructions depicted with the remaining two variables.

Example 6.5: A chef has planned for an EP cost of $0.77/lb for her collard greens. The new purveyor supplies collards that are more closely trimmed of stem, so the yield percentage has changed to 91%. What price should the chef expect to pay (AP) for her EP cost to be accurate?

$$AP\$ = EP\$ \times Y\% = \$0.77/lb \times 0.91 = \$0.70/lb$$

In this example, if the chef pays $0.70/lb or less AP, then her expense on collard greens should remain within budget. If they cost more, she will be over budget on collard green costs.

While chefs use the AP, EP, Y% and AP$, EP$, Y% formulas for a variety of reasons ranging from calculating order quantities to determining target AP prices, the menu planner primarily needs them to calculate the EP$ for each ingredient. Using the EP$ = AP$ ÷ Y% formula, a menu planner can quickly determine the total cost for a given standard recipe in a foodservice operation.

Recipe Costing

Learning Objective 5
Use a costing sheet to calculate a recipe's total cost.

In most foodservice businesses, recipes are costed using the aid of a costing sheet (usually set up in a computer worksheet or as part of a POS system). Costing a recipe is the next step in determining the cost per portion for a dish on a menu. To begin the calculations on a recipe costing sheet, a menu planner must first know each ingredient's name and quantity, Y% and AP cost. The names and quantities (number and unit) for each ingredient are transferred to the costing sheet directly from the standard recipe. In most professional kitchens, recipe ingredients are written in EP amounts. The Y% comes from prior kitchen tests. While books are available to provide average yield percentages across the industry for various products, the more accurate information comes from a test of the product as it is prepared in the restaurant's kitchen. For example, if a book states that carrots have a Y% of 87%, but the cook who prepares the carrots consistently averages an 85% yield, then the 85% figure is the one to use. It is more accurate for this particular operation. Finally, the AP cost comes directly from the purveyor invoices. This data is typically entered into the costing worksheet in its raw format as a total cost per case or weight. The AP cost per unit for each ingredient can be easily derived from the raw information in a separate column. (The reason for a separate column is to make updates to the costing sheet easier in the future. If the computer worksheet is set up to conduct the calculations automatically, a person can transfer the new price per case or weight from a future invoice and allow the computer to do the rest.)

Chefs can purchase recipe costing software or utilize that function within their company's point of sales system; however, the costing process is not so difficult that it cannot be performed by hand or by creating one's own recipe costing program in an Excel worksheet. Either way, the chef or menu planner must enter the same starting information into the program for the computer to perform the calculations.

Table 6.1a depicts a sample recipe costing sheet with the known information entered. The information in the heading will be explained later in the chapter, as will the spice factor entries listed for salt and pepper.

Recipe: Chicken Chasseur					Spice Factor:	
No. of Portions: 12					Q Factor:	
Cost per Portion:			FC%:		Selling Price:	
Ingredient	Recipe (EP) Quantity (from Recipe)	Yield Percentage (from Kitchen Tests)	AP Cost (from Invoice)	Converted AP Cost	EP Cost	Extended Cost
Chicken breast, 5 oz., airline, prefab, frozen, indiv. pack	12 ea (60 oz)	100%	$31.45/24 ea			
Butter, unsalted	6 oz	100%	$64.40/36 lb			
Shallot, minced	2 oz	77%	$4.68/5 lb			
Mushrooms, button, trimmed, sliced	4 oz	94%	$8.25/3 lb			
White wine, dry	3 oz	100%	$5.50/750 mL			
Demi-glace	9 oz	100%	$0.18/oz (made in-house)			
Tomato, plum, concassé	8 oz	58%	$34.00/40 lb			
Tarragon, chopped	3 Tbsp	64%	$2.77/2 oz			
Salt	To taste	100%	Spice factor			
Pepper	To taste	100%	Spice factor			
Total						

TABLE 6.1a
Recipe Costing Sheet—EP Quantity, Y%, and AP$ Entered

The next step to costing a recipe is to convert the AP cost to units that match the EP quantity units listed in the recipe. For example, if a recipe requires 18 ounces of flour and flour is purchased by the pound, the AP cost must be converted from cost per pound to cost per ounce. If the units do not match, multiplying the two figures together provides useless information. Only an AP cost with a per dollar unit that matches the recipe EP unit is a useful figure.

Example 6.6: A recipe calls for 27 ounces of diced tomato. Tomatoes are purchased at $61.45/40-lb case. Convert the AP cost to useful units.

Since the EP ingredient is listed in ounces, the AP cost must be converted to dollars per ounce.

$61.45 ÷ 40 lb = $1.54/lb

$1.54/lb ÷ 16 oz/lb = $0.10/oz

The useful AP cost is $0.10/oz.

Many culinary school textbooks explain the process of converting units, so an in-depth discussion of how to convert units is not described here. For a more thorough description of the unit conversion process, reference Traster's *Foundations of Cost Control* (Pearson Education).

To make the AP costs on the costing sheet useful, the menu planner or other manager converts each entered AP cost so that its units match the EP units from the recipe. Table 6.1b illustrates this step in the process.

The next column in the costing sheet is "EP Cost." The EP cost is calculated with the equation EP$ = AP$ ÷ Y%. Recall that the Y% is always written in its decimal form in the equation. This computation is done for each ingredient using the converted AP cost (useful units). When an ingredient has a Y% of 100%, the EP cost will match the converted AP cost.

Recipe: Chicken Chasseur					Spice Factor:	
No. of Portions: 12					Q Factor:	
Cost per Portion:			FC%:		Selling Price:	
Ingredient	Recipe (EP) Quantity (from Recipe)	Yield Percentage (from Kitchen Tests)	AP Cost (from Invoice)	Converted AP Cost (AP Units Converted to Match EP Units)	EP Cost	Extended Cost
Chicken breast, 5 oz, airline, prefab, frozen, indiv. pack	12 ea (60 oz)	100%	$31.45/24 ea	$1.310 ea		
Butter, unsalted	6 oz	100%	$64.40/36 lb	$0.111/oz		
Shallot, minced	2 oz	77%	$4.68/5 lb	$0.059/oz		
Mushrooms, button, trimmed, sliced	4 oz	94%	$8.25/3 lb	$0.172/oz		
White wine, dry	3 oz	100%	$5.50/750 mL	$0.217/oz		
Demi-glace	9 oz	100%	$0.18/oz (made in-house)	$0.18/oz		
Tomato, plum, concassé	8 oz	58%	$34.00/40 lb	$0.053/oz		
Tarragon, chopped	3 Tbsp	64%	$2.77/2 oz (1 oz yields ¼ c chopped)	$0.346/Tbsp (Y% already accounted for in 1 oz = ¼ c)		
Salt	To taste	100%	Spice factor	N/A		
Pepper	To taste	100%	Spice factor	N/A		
Total						

TABLE 6.1b

Recipe Costing Sheet—AP Cost Converted to Useable Units

There are a couple of exceptions to this process that should be noted. First, when an ingredient is measured per "each," Y% is not a factor. For example, if a recipe asks for "4 large onions, diced," it does not matter how much of the onion is lost in processing. In the end, the cook is still left with four large onions worth of product. This logic is even more obvious with the example of shrimp cocktail. Assume a recipe for shrimp cocktail requires that a cook serve five large shrimp per customer. If the cook loses 20% of the weight through peeling and deveining five shrimp, it is irrelevant. She still has five shrimp left to serve to the customer. (If the shrimp were measured by the ounce for a recipe, the situation would be different. She would need to start with a larger weight of shrimp to pare down to the right number of ounces.) Another exception to the rule is for products that have undergone a butcher's yield test or cooking loss test already. These tests calculate an effective EP cost for the product (usually per ounce and per pound). In such an instance, the menu planner should simply utilize the EP cost from these tests and enter it directly into the EP cost column, adjusting it only so the units match the ingredient EP units. Finally, if a kitchen test conversion already factors in yield, then the EP cost should not account for yield a second time. This occurs typically when a chef must convert from weight to volume or vice versa for ingredients that are not mostly water. For example, if a chef determines that 2 ounces of fresh rosemary usually yields 6 tablespoons of chopped rosemary after stemming and chopping, then she can convert an AP cost in dollars per ounce to a useful AP cost in dollars per tablespoon using the formula 2 oz = 6 Tbsp. This formula has already accounted for the loss of the rosemary stems, so the Y% for rosemary should not be factored for a second time to calculate EP cost. In such a situation, the EP cost is the converted AP cost.

Recipe: Chicken Chasseur					Spice Factor:	
No. of Portions: 12					Q Factor:	
Cost per Portion:			FC%:		Selling Price:	
Ingredient	Recipe (EP) Quantity	Yield Percentage	AP Cost	Converted AP Cost	EP Cost - (Converted AP$ ÷ Y%)	Extended Cost
Chicken breast, 5 oz, airline, prefab, frozen, indiv. pack	12 each (60 oz)	100%	$31.45/24 ea	$1.310 ea	$1.31 ea	
Butter, unsalted	6 oz	100%	$64.40/36 lb	$0.111/oz	$0.111/oz	
Shallot, minced	2 oz	77%	$4.68/5 lb	$0.059/oz	$0.077/oz	
Mushrooms, button, trimmed, sliced	4 oz	94%	$8.25/3 lb	$0.172/oz	$0.183/oz	
White wine, dry	3 oz	100%	$5.50/750 mL	$0.217/oz	$0.217/oz	
Demi-glace	9 oz	100%	$0.18/oz (made in-house)	$0.18/oz	$0.18/oz	
Tomato, plum, concassé	8 oz	58%	$34.00/40 lb	$0.053/oz	$0.091/oz	
Tarragon, chopped	3 Tbsp	64%	$2.77/2 oz (1 oz = ¼ c chopped)	$0.346/ Tbsp	$0.346/Tbsp (Y% already factored into 1 oz = ¼ c)	
Salt	To taste	100%	Spice factor	N/A	N/A	
Pepper	To taste	100%	Spice factor	N/A	N/A	
Total						

TABLE 6.1c
Recipe Costing Sheet—EP Cost Calculated

Table 6.1c illustrates the step of calculating EP cost from the converted AP cost in the sample recipe.

Example 6.7: Calculate the EP cost for the shallots from Table 6.1c.

The shallots are listed in ounces but sell for $4.68/5 lb. They have a yield percentage of 77%.

First, convert the AP cost to useful units.

$4.68 ÷ 5 lb = $0.936/lb

$0.936/lb ÷ 16 oz/lb = $ 0.059/oz

Next, use the EP$ = AP$ ÷ Y % formula

EP$ = $0.059/oz ÷ 0.77 = $0.077/oz

Example 6.8: Calculate the EP Cost for the tarragon from Table 6.1c.

The recipe calls for chopped tarragon measured in tablespoons, but the tarragon costs $2.77/2 oz. The yield percentage is 64%, and the kitchen test reveals that 1 ounce of AP tarragon = ¼ cup chopped tarragon.

First, convert the AP cost to useful units.

$$\$2.77 ÷ 2 oz = \$1.385/oz$$

Since 1 oz = ¼ c, and ¼ c = 4 Tbsp, $1.385/oz is the same as $1.385/4 Tbsp.

Thus, the cost per tablespoon is as follows:

$$\$1.385 ÷ 4 Tbsp = \$0.346/Tbsp$$

To get the conversion 1 ounce = ¼ cup, the chef would have already stemmed the tarragon and kept only the chopped leaves. The loss (stem) has already been removed, and thus the yield percentage has already been accounted for. Consequently, the EP cost is the same as the converted AP cost. EP$ = $0.346/Tbsp.

With the EP costs determined, it is quite simple to calculate the extended cost (or extension) for each ingredient in the recipe. The extended cost is the cost that a single ingredient contributes to a recipe. When all of the extended costs for a recipe are added together, they represent a preliminary total recipe cost, pending any adjustments for spices or other add-ons.

To calculate an ingredient's extended cost, multiply the EP quantity by the EP cost. Mathematically,

$$\text{Extended Cost} = \text{EP Quality} \times \text{EP\$}$$

Since the units in the extended cost formula match, the result is simply a dollar figure (not dollars per unit).

Example 6.9: A chicken chasseur recipe calls for twelve (each) chicken breasts. The breasts have an EP cost of $1.31 each. What is the extended cost for the chicken in this recipe?

$$\text{Extended Cost} = \text{EP Quality} \times \text{EP\$} = 12\text{ea} \times \$1.31/\text{ea} = \$15.72$$

To calculate a preliminary total recipe cost, sum all of the extended costs in the recipe. Table 6.1d shows the sample recipe from the Table 6.1 series with the extended costs and preliminary total recipe cost calculated.

Recipe: Chicken Chasseur					Spice Factor:	
No. of Portions: 12					Q Factor:	
Cost per Portion:			FC%:		Selling Price:	
Ingredient	Recipe (EP) Quantity	Yield Percentage	AP Cost	Converted AP Cost	EP Cost	Extended Cost (EP Quantity × EP$)
Chicken breast, 5 oz, airline, prefab, frozen, indiv. pack	12 ea (60 oz)	100%	$31.45/24 ea	$1.310 ea	$1.31 ea	$15.72
Butter, unsalted	6 oz	100%	$64.40/36 lb	$0.111/oz	$0.111/oz	$0.666
Shallot, minced	2 oz	77%	$4.68/5 lb	$0.059/oz	$0.077/oz	$0.154
Mushrooms, button, trimmed, sliced	4 oz	94%	$8.25/3 lb	$0.172/oz	$0.183/oz	$0.732
White wine, dry	3 oz	100%	$5.50/750 mL	$0.217/oz	$0.217/oz	$0.651
Demi-glace	9 oz	100%	$0.18/oz	$0.18/oz	$0.18/oz	$1.62
Tomato, plum, concassé	8 oz	58%	$34.00/40 lb	$0.053/oz	$0.091/oz	$0.728
Tarragon, chopped	3 Tbsp	64%	$2.77/2 oz	$0.346/Tbsp	$0.346/Tbsp (Y% already factored into 1 oz = ¼ c)	$1.038
Salt	To taste	100%	Spice factor	N/A	N/A	S.F.
Pepper	To taste	100%	Spice factor	N/A	N/A	S.F.
Total (sum of extended costs)						$21.309

TABLE 6.1d
Recipe Costing Sheet—Extended Costs and Total Recipe Cost

Cost per Portion

The preliminary cost per portion is simply the total recipe cost divided by the number of portions that the recipe yields. The formula is written as follows:

$$\text{Preliminary Cost per Portion} = \text{Preliminary Total Recipe Cost} \div \text{Number of Portions in Recipe}$$

Example 6.10: A recipe has a preliminary total recipe cost of $21.309 and yields 12 servings. What is the preliminary cost per portion for this dish?

$$\text{Preliminary Cost per Portion} = \text{Preliminary Total Recipe Cost} \div \text{Number of Portions}$$
$$= \$21.309 \div 12 = \$1.776$$

It is important to note that this is strictly a preliminary cost per portion. The true cost per portion must first factor in any spice factor adjustment. For entrées in certain establishments, the Q factor must be taken into account as well.

Spice Factor

Learning Objective 6
Calculate an item's true cost per portion, including a spice factor and Q factor.

Spice factor and Q factor are simply short cuts for calculating a recipe's true cost per portion when not every single ingredient or item provided to a customer is included in the recipe cost calculation. Imagine trying to account for the cost of a small amount of salt and pepper used in a recipe. What if these seasonings are added "to taste"? How would a chef calculate the extended cost for these spices then? The simplest way to account for items added "to taste" or for ingredients like herbs and spices measured "by eye" is to utilize a spice factor.

A spice factor is a figure that represents the additional cost to a recipe for any ingredients not specifically listed with an amount in the recipe. Some chefs may choose to include a wide range of ingredients in the spice factor, while others will limit it solely to salt and pepper. The spice factor may include garnishes, herbs, spices, table seasonings (including items like ketchup and hot sauce), and even bread and butter that are provided to the customer "for free." These ingredients represent real costs to the business. Even though the customer does not pay for them directly, these costs should be included in the menu prices of all sold products.

The spice factor is always written as a percentage and it is applied equally to all menu items regardless of their level of seasoning. A chef may choose to use the spice factor for all herbs and spices, rather than calculating each one individually (like the tarragon in the sample chicken chasseur recipe). The same spice factor percentage would be used for both heavily and lightly spiced dishes. This approach spreads the cost of herbs and spices across all menu items rather than making the heavily spiced dishes more expensive. While this may seem unfair, most guests assume that the menu price reflects the main ingredients, not the spices. Many customers would have trouble paying as much for a saffron and cardamom chicken dish as they do for a simply grilled steak. Although saffron and cardamom are both very expensive spices, most customers would view these menu choices as the difference between chicken and steak, not between expensive spices and cheap seasonings. The spice factor applies the spice cost to all of the dishes, making the chicken a less expensive option than the steak.

To determine the spice factor for a foodservice operation, the chef or manager must first determine which ingredients will be included in the spice factor. Next, the chef must track the cost of all spice factor ingredients and all other ingredients over a period of time, usually one to six months. If one ingredient is sometimes considered a spice factor and sometimes considered a standard ingredient, the chef must determine how much of the cost goes toward the spice factor. For example, if a chef includes a fresh raspberry garnish in the spice factor but also prepares a raspberry tart, she must determine the amount of raspberry expense that went toward spice factor versus tart. Finally, the chef totals the cost of all of the spice factor items over the period and compares them to the total cost of the food purchases for the same period. The spice factor is calculated using the following formula:

$$\text{Spice Factor} = \frac{\text{Value of Spice Factor Items (Over a Period of Time)}}{\text{Value of Total Food Purchases (Over the Same Period)}}$$

The spice factor will always be a decimal and may be converted to a percentage by moving the decimal point two spaces to the right.

Example 6.11: In a restaurant, the spice factor items cost $3,150 over three months. During the same three months, all food purchases were $174,890. What is the spice factor for this restaurant?

$$\text{Spice Factor} = \frac{\text{Value of Spice Factor Items}}{\text{Value of Total Food Purchases}} = \frac{\$3,150}{\$174,890} = 0.018 \text{ or } 1.8\%$$

To adjust a recipe's preliminary cost per portion to account for the spice factor, simply multiply the preliminary cost per portion by (1 + spice factor in decimal form). Thus, if a company's spice factor is 1.8%, each preliminary cost per portion would be multiplied by (1 + 0.018) or 1.018 to get a spice factor adjusted cost per portion. For many restaurants, this is the true cost per portion for a dish.

Example 6.12: A restaurant has a spice factor of 2.3%. The chicken chasseur recipe has a preliminary cost per portion of $1.776. What is the cost per portion after adjusting for the spice factor?

$$\text{Spice Factor Adjusted Cost} = \text{Preliminary Cost} \times (1 + \text{Spice Factor})$$
$$= \$1.776 \times (1 + 0.023)$$
$$= \$1.776 \times 1.023 = \$1.82$$

The spice factor may be multiplied by a cost per portion or by a total recipe cost. Whether the cost per portion is calculated before or after the spice factor adjustment is irrelevant. The result will be the same.

Q Factor

While most restaurants use a spice factor, only some use a Q factor. In à la carte and semi à la carte restaurants, a customer must purchase each menu category separately. For those restaurants, each starch, vegetable, and other accompaniment is costed separately. When starches and vegetables are paired with a specific dish, their costs per portion are added to the cost per portion of the main item to yield a total cost for the dish. However, in some restaurants, the guest, not the chef, chooses the sides to pair with the entrée selection. In others, the purchase of an entrée includes a guest's choice of salad, soup, and/or dessert (or more). Q factor becomes a highly useful tool when the customer gets a choice of "free" add-ons.

The Q factor accounts for the cost of the add-ons that a customer may select. To determine the Q factor value for a restaurant, the chef or manager first calculates the cost for one serving of each of the possible add-ons on the menu. Next, the chef identifies the most expensive choices the customer could pick. This determination depends upon which headings the customer may choose from. For example, if a guest has a choice of salad, choice of soup, and choice of dessert, then the chef will note the most expensive salad, soup, and dessert. However, if the guest must choose between salads and soups for a first course, then only the most expensive of the soup and salad selection is relevant. The Q factor value is the sum of the costs of the most expensive add-on choices.

Example 6.13: Using the data in the chart below, determine the Q factor for this restaurant. With the purchase of an entrée, the guest may choose a salad, a soup, and a dessert. Bread and butter are automatic add-ons for entrées as well.

Add-On	Cost per Portion
House Salad	$0.78
Caesar Salad	$1.02
Chicken Noodle Soup	$0.49
Beef Barley Soup	$0.54
Ice Cream Sundae	$1.14
Molten Chocolate Cake	$0.99
Pecan Pie	$1.46
Bread	$0.15
Butter	$0.09

In this operation, the most expensive options that the guest may choose are Caesar salad, beef barley soup, pecan pie, bread, and butter. Note that the bread and butter are the only options in their heading, so they are selected by default. The Q factor is the sum of the most expensive choices that the guest may select, so Q factor is calculated as follows:

$$Q \text{ Factor} = \$1.02 \text{ (salad)} + \$0.54 \text{ (soup)} + \$1.46 \text{ (dessert)} + \$0.15 \text{ (bread)} + \$0.09 \text{ (butter)} = \$3.26$$

With a Q factor determined, the menu planner can simply add the Q factor to each of the entrée costs per portion (spice factor adjusted) to determine the true cost per portion. After all, if a steak entrée is calculated to cost $4.22 per portion, but the guest has the ability to add on another $3.00 worth of sides for no additional cost, then the real cost to the restaurant when a guest orders steak is $7.22 ($4.22 + $3.00).

Note that unlike the spice factor, which is *multiplied* times a cost per portion, the Q factor is *added* to the cost per portion.

Example 6.14: What is the true cost per portion for an entrée that costs $1.79 per portion in a restaurant that uses a Q factor of $2.11?

$$\text{True Cost per Portion} = \text{Cost per Portion} + Q \text{ Factor}$$
$$= \$1.79 + \$2.11 = \$3.90$$

Through the use of a Q factor, a restaurant accounts for the expense that a guest will generate if she orders the most expensive menu choices. If the guest picks less expensive options, the restaurant simply makes a greater profit off of that customer.

It is important to stress that the Q factor only deals with items that are added on to a meal "for free" *by customer choice.* Starches, vegetables, sauces, and garnishes that are predetermined by the chef to accompany an entrée are part of the entrée's preliminary cost per portion. If the menu planner costs this entrée and its partner components separately rather than in one costing sheet, then the per portion cost of the components must all be added together to get a base cost per portion for that entrée. For example, if a lamb chop with mint sauce costing $3.88 per portion comes with potatoes ($0.23 per portion) and asparagus ($0.37 per portion), then the preliminary cost for the lamb entrée is $3.88 + $0.23 + $0.37 + $4.48. The spice factor and Q factor adjustments (for additional "free" courses) would be based on this price.

In summary, after a menu planner calculates a recipe's total cost, she must still complete three more steps to determine the dish's cost per portion. Those steps are as follows:

1. Calculate preliminary cost per portion as total recipe cost ÷ number of portions
2. Adjust for spice factor by multiplying preliminary cost per portion by (1 + spice factor as a decimal). In restaurants that do not use a Q factor or for non-entrées, this is the true cost per portion.
3. Adjust entrées for Q factor by adding the Q factor to the spice factor adjusted cost per portion.

Recipe: Chicken Chasseur					Spice Factor: 2.3%	
No. of Portions: 12					Q Factor: $1.04	
Cost per Portion: $2.86			FC%:		Selling Price:	
Ingredient	Recipe (EP) Quantity	Yield Percentage	AP Cost	Converted AP Cost	EP Cost	Extended Cost
Chicken breast, 5 oz, airline, prefab, frozen, indiv. pack	12 ea (60 oz)	100%	$31.45/24 ea	$1.310 ea	$1.31 ea	$15.72
Butter, unsalted	6 oz	100%	$64.40/36 lb	$0.111/oz	$0.111/oz	$0.666
Shallot, minced	2 oz	77%	$4.68/5 lb	$0.059/oz	$0.077/oz	$0.154
Mushrooms, button, trimmed, sliced	4 oz	94%	$8.25/3 lb	$0.172/oz	$0.183/oz	$0.732
White wine, dry	3 oz	100%	$5.50/750 mL	$0.217/oz	$0.217/oz	$0.651
Demi-glace	9 oz	100%	$0.18/oz	$0.18/oz	$0.18/oz	$1.62
Tomato, plum, concassé	8 oz	58%	$34.00/40 lb	$0.053/oz	$0.091/oz	$0.728
Tarragon, chopped	3 Tbsp	64%	$2.77/2 oz	$0.346/Tbsp	$0.346/Tbsp	$1.038
Salt	To taste	100%	Spice factor	N/A	N/A	S.F.
Pepper	To taste	100%	Spice factor	N/A	N/A	S.F.
Total						$21.309
Preliminary Cost per Portion (Total Recipe Cost ÷ Number of Portions in Recipe) = $21.309 ÷ 12						$1.776
Spice Factor Adjusted Cost per Portion ((1 + SF) × cost per portion) or (1.023 × $1.776)						$1.82
True Cost per Portion, Q Factor Adjusted (SF adjusted cost per portion + Q Factor) = $1.82 + $1.04						$2.86

TABLE 6.1e
Recipe Costing Sheet—Spice Factor, Q Factor, and Cost per Portion Included

Table 6.1e shows the completed costing sheet for the chicken chasseur sample recipe. In this particular example, the Q factor covers the side dishes of which the customer gets a choice. If a vegetable and starch were specifically paired with this dish, those per portion costs would be added to the preliminary cost per portion for the chicken to get a preliminary cost per portion for the entrée. The spice factor and Q factor for the business are listed in the recipe heading, so the menu planner knows how to adjust the preliminary cost per portion. Once the true cost per portion is calculated, it is entered into the costing sheet's heading as well.

Summary

A menu planner must consider pricing as part of the menu creation process. Costing a recipe is the first step to calculating an appropriate menu price. Standard recipes allow the menu planner to assume that the recipe she costs is the recipe that is executed in the operation. Portion control is essential to keeping the costs accurate as well. Food is purchased in a form known as "as-purchased" or "AP." After it is peeled, trimmed, or otherwise processed, it is referred to as "edible portion" or "EP." The yield percentage represents the portion of food left as EP after processing from the original AP product. The AP and EP costs of a product can also be calculated using the Y%. With the standard recipe, Y%, and AP cost known, a menu planner can calculate the total cost of a recipe by converting the AP cost to useable units, calculating EP cost using Y%, determining the extended cost for each ingredient, and finally summing the extended costs. The menu planner uses the recipe cost and the number of portions the recipe makes to determine the preliminary cost per portion. The cost per portion must be adjusted using a spice factor to account for any spices or herbs that are not calculated directly in the cost of the recipe. If the dish being costed is an entrée that comes with "free" add-ons, a Q factor must be added to determine the true cost per portion for the dish. Only once the true cost per portion has been calculated for a dish can the menu planner determine its appropriate menu sales price.

TECHNOLOGY ASSISTANCE: SETTING UP A RECIPE COSTING TEMPLATE IN EXCEL

Costing recipes can be a time-consuming process, but if you create a model template in an Excel (or similar) worksheet program, you can reduce the workload significantly. By cutting and pasting the template, you'll be able to have the computer do most of the calculation work for you. Here's how in 10 steps.

1. In the first row, write out the costing sheet heading information. In cell A1 write "Recipe Name:" and plan on writing the actual name of each recipe in B1. In cell C1 write "Portions:" and plan on writing the number of portions each recipe makes in D1. In cell E1 write "Spice Factor:" and the business's spice factor as a decimal. In cell F1 write the number that is equal to 1 + spice factor. In cell G1 write "Q Factor" and plan on writing the Q factor in dollars in H1. In cell I1 write "True Cost per Portion". The true cost per portion will be calculated in the worksheet, but you will set it up to appear in cell J1. (See Table 6.2 on the following page to see how everything looks when entered properly.)

2. In the second row, write out the labels for each column to help you stay organized. You will need to separate numbers and units into their own columns so that the computer can calculate the formulas for you. If you wish, include in the labels where to find the information that must be entered. Those labels will be, in this order, "Ingredient Name," "Recipe (EP) Quantity," "Recipe (EP) unit," "Yield % (decimal format)," "AP$ dollars," "AP$ unit," "AP$ converted (dollars)," "AP$ converted (units—must match recipe unit)," "EP$ (dollars)," and "Extended Cost."

3. In the third row, enter two of the formulas that will be consistent for all recipes. In column I, write "=G3/D3" and in column J write "=B3*I3". In short, the formula in cell I3 is EP$ = AP$ ÷ Y%, and the formula in cell J3 is Extended Cost = EP quantity × EP$ (where the units match).

4. Copy and paste the formulas in I3 and J3 into the rows below. The computer should automatically adjust the formula to make it apply to the corresponding row. The formula should be copied into enough rows to account for your longest recipe, so if your longest recipe includes 12 ingredients, the formulas should be copied into the next 12 rows. (In Table 6.2, the formulas are copied for a sample six rows, rows 3–8.)

5. Find the cell in column I just below the last copied formula. (In Table 6.2, this is cell I9.) Label that cell "Total." In the cells below it, all in column I, write the following labels: "Preliminary Cost per portion," "SF adjusted cost per portion," and "True Cost per portion."

6. In column J, to the right of the label "Total," use the sum function to add all of the extended costs. The sum formula for a column is written as =sum(starting cell:ending cell). (For Table 6.2, this would be "=sum(J3:J8)".) This total is the total recipe cost.

7. In column J, to the right of the label "Preliminary cost per portion," write a formula that divides the total recipe cost (found in the cell one row above this one) by the number of portions the recipe makes (found in cell D1). This formula is written as =cell above/D1. (For Table 6.2, this would be "=J9/D1".)

8. In column J, to the right of the label "SF adjusted cost per portion," write the formula that adjusts the preliminary cost per portion (found one cell above this one) by the 1 + SF factor (found in cell F1). The formula is written as =cell above*F1. (For Table 6.2, this would be "=J10/F1".)

9. In column J, to the right of the label "True Cost per Portion," write the formula that adds the SF-adjusted cost per portion (found in the cell above this one) and the Q factor (found in cell H1). The formula is written as =cell above+H1. (For Table 6.2, this would be "=J11+H1.") Keep in mind that for non-entrée recipes and for recipes that do not use a Q factor, the Q factor value will be 0.

10. Link the True Cost per Portion at the bottom of the costing sheet to the heading for easier reading later. To do this, go to cell J1, which will show the True Cost per Portion, and enter =cell that contains the true cost per portion formula. (For Table 6.2, this would be "=J12".)

	A	B	C	D	E	F	G	H	I	J
1	Recipe name	(Name of recipe)	Portions:	(# of portion)	Spice factor (SF)	(1 + SF as decimal)	Q factor	(Q factor)	True cost per portion:	=J12
2	Ingredient name	Recipe (EP) Quantity	Recipe (EP) unit	Yield % (decimal format)	AP$ (dollars)	AP$ unit	AP$ converted (dollars)	AP$ converted (units must match recipe unit)	EP$ (dollars)	Extended Cost
3	From recipe	From recipe	From recipe	From kitchen test	From invoice	From invoice	Formula varies depending on AP and EP units	Same as column C	=G3/D3	=B3*I3
4									=G4/D4	=B4*I4
5									=G5/D5	=B5*I5
6									=G6/D6	=B6*I6
7									=G7/D7	=B7*I7
8									=G8/D8	=B8*I8
9									Total:	=sum(J3:J8)
10									Pre. cost per portion	=J9/D1
11									SF adjusted cost per portion	=J10/F1
12									True cost per portion	=J11+H1

TABLE 6.2

Creating a Recipe Costing Template in Excel

Once you have created the model recipe costing template, you can copy and paste it into a separate tab for each recipe or simply paste copies below each other on a single worksheet.

It is important to note the one calculation the template will not do for you. Column G, which adjusts the AP$ into usable units, requires a unique formula for each row. The formula cannot be copied and pasted because it will change depending on the units in columns C and F. You will need to write formulas based on your knowledge of unit conversions. For example, if you need to convert an AP$ from $/lb to $/oz, you will need to write a formula dividing by 16. (There are 16 ounces per pound.)

For the following examples, which illustrate how to create formulas for column G, assume the formula will be entered into cell G3 and apply to the ingredient and AP$ written in line 3 of the worksheet. The AP$ number in dollars is entered into cell E3.

Tech Example 6.1: The recipe calls for 12 ounces of onions and the AP$ is $35.20/50# bag. What formula should be entered into cell G3?

The AP$ must be converted to dollars per ounce. The information needed is that the product comes in a 50-pound bag, and there are 16 ounces in one pound.

The formula to enter in cell G3 is "=E3/50/16".

Tech Example 6.2: The recipe calls for 6 ounces of wine and the AP$ is $78.50/9L. What formula should be entered into cell G3?

The AP$ must be converted to dollars per ounce. The information needed is that the invoice price for the wine is for 9 liters, and there are 33.8 ounces in one liter.

The formula to enter in cell G3 is "=E3/9/33.8".

Tech Example 6.3: The recipe calls for 2 Tbsp of flour and the AP$ is $39.40/50#. What formula should be entered into cell G3?

Unfortunately, the menu planner cannot create the formula without additional information because flour does not convert easily between weight and volume like water does. Fortunately, a search online reveals that flour weighs 4.5 ounces per cup. (The menu planner could always conduct that measurement in the kitchen.) Also important to know is 16 oz = 1 lb and 1 cup = 16 Tbsp.

Here's the process in words. Divide the AP$ by 50 to get the price per pound. Divide again by 16 to get price per ounce. Multiply by 4.5 to get price per cup. Divide again by 16 to get price per tablespoon.

The formula to enter in cell G3 is "=E3/50/16*4.5/16".

Tech Example 6.4: The recipe calls for 2 pounds of zucchini, and zucchini costs $0.87/#. What formula should be entered into cell G3?

This is an easy one. Both the EP quantity and AP$ are written in pounds, and the price is for one pound, not for a case. The AP$ does not need any conversion.

The formula to enter in cell G3 is "=E3".

While time consuming to enter formulas this way, it is extremely helpful when keeping recipe costs up-to-date. Consider Tech Example 3. In the future, the price of flour may fluctuate, but the company is likely to continue to buy it in 50-pound bags. The other conversion formulas—ounces to pounds, ounces to cups, and cups to tablespoons—will not change. Once the formula is entered into cell G3, the menu planner can periodically enter the new price for a 50-pound bag of flour (from the invoice) into cell E3, and the recipe costing sheet will recalculate the cost per portion for that dish.

Comprehension Questions

1. What is a standard recipe, and why is it important for a foodservice operation to use standard recipes?

2. List three ways that a cook might measure serving portions to ensure proper portion control.

3. A bunch of carrots weighing 18 ounces is peeled, trimmed, and sliced prior to cooking. The prepped weight of the carrots is only 15 ounces. What is the Y% for this carrot preparation?

4. Diced turnip in a particular restaurant has a yield percentage of 88%. If a cook begins with 38 ounces of turnips, how many ounces of diced turnips should she expect to yield after processing?

5. A head of lettuce is prepped for use in a salad. The lettuce has a yield percentage of 79% and an AP cost of $0.84/lb. What is the EP cost per pound for this lettuce?

6. What is the EP cost for cherry tomatoes that have a yield percentage of 100% and cost $2.50/lb?

7. Complete the recipe costing sheet below and calculate the true cost per portion. The restaurant's spice factor and Q factor are listed in the heading. This dish is an appetizer and no add-ons come automatically with the dish.

Recipe: Calamari with Mango Salsa					Spice Factor: 2.1%	
No. of Portions: 8					Q Factor: $1.64	
Cost per Portion:			FC%: X		Selling Price: X	
Ingredient	Recipe (EP) Quantity	Yield Percentage	AP Cost	Converted AP Cost	EP Cost	Extended Cost
Calamari, cleaned, sliced	4 lb	91%	$12.81/5 lb			
Rice flour	8 oz	100%	$4.22/5 lb			
Mango, peeled, diced	14 oz	54%	$8.45/10 lb			
Red onion, peeled, diced	3 oz	88%	$23.97/50 lb			
Jalapeno, seeded, diced	1 oz	84%	$2.38/lb			
Cilantro, chopped	½ bunch	100%	$0.59/bunch			
Salt	To taste	S.F.	S.F.	S.F.	S.F.	S.F.
Pepper	To taste	S.F.	S.F.	S.F.	S.F.	S.F.
Total						

8. An entrée has a preliminary cost per portion of $3.12. It comes with a choice of soup or salad, bread, and dessert. If the restaurant uses a spice factor of 3.4% and a Q factor of $2.25, what is the true cost per portion for this dish?

Discussion Questions

1. If a restaurant does not use written recipes, how might it still employ standard recipes?

2. No cook measures products perfectly. For a steak that is supposed to be 10 ounces, what is an acceptable variance (weight plus or minus 10 ounces) that you would consider appropriate for portion control purposes?

3. The chapter mentioned that products portioned by count (by "each") have a 100% yield percentage even if they lose weight in trimming. List three products that might be portioned by count and describe the dish in which they would appear that way.

4. If you were in charge of costing recipes for a business, would you use a spice factor or cost every ingredient separately? Why?

5. Imagine that a restaurant serves bread to every table, whether they order entrées or only appetizers. If the restaurant does not charge for the bread directly, how should it be accounted for—using spice factor or Q factor? Why?

6. Describe a restaurant with which you are familiar that likely uses a Q factor. What items would the Q factor probably cover?

7. Some restaurant chefs choose to simplify the costing process by costing only the center-of-the-plate item (the steak, the chicken breast, etc.) and adding on a value, either as a percentage or dollar amount, to account for all of the accompaniments. What are the pros and cons to this approach? In what types of restaurants would this approach not work? What concept (discussed in this chapter) might help a restaurant account for all of its costs when costing only the center-of-the-plate item?

Capstone Project

Step 6: Using the recipes you created for your food and beverage menu items in earlier steps, create costing sheets for each of those recipes. Yield percentage information can be obtained through yield percentage guides or through your own hands-on tests with ingredients. Prices should ideally come from purveyor guides (provided by the instructor), but supermarket or Internet pricing that you research will also work. (A good way to get an estimate for wholesale prices from retail prices is to reduce the retail, non-sale price by 30%.) If you cannot locate pricing or yield percentage information for a specific ingredient, ask your instructor for help. You may cost your recipes on paper or using a template you have created on the computer.

CHAPTER 7

Menu Pricing

INTRODUCTION

The ultimate goal of costing recipes is to determine an appropriate selling price for the items listed on the menu. If the price is too high, the business will lose customers to other restaurants. With too low a price, the establishment will not maximize profits, and it may not bring in enough money to cover its costs. This chapter will not rehash the process of calculating the true cost per portion for a dish, which was covered in Chapter 6, but determining an item's selling price almost always starts with the item's true cost per portion—referred to as "food cost" or "beverage cost" in this chapter for the sake of expediency.

The menu planner begins by using one of several methods to calculate a tentative menu price for a menu item from its food cost (or beverage cost). He then modifies the price even further to account for customer psychology, product differentiation, and other variables. When the product being sold is an all-you-can-eat buffet, a prix fixe or table d'hôte menu, or noncommercial dining experience, other factors further impact the ultimate price listed on the menu. Through a thorough approach to menu pricing, the menu planner can create a menu that sells well, appeals to the target market's price sensibilities, and maximizes profits for the business.

CHAPTER 7 LEARNING OBJECTIVES

As a result of successfully completing this chapter, readers will be able to:

1. Calculate a preliminary selling price for a menu item using one of several pricing strategies.

2. List several factors that impact the final price written on a menu.

3. Describe the role that customer psychology plays in menu pricing.

4. Determine an appropriate sales price for buffet, prix fixe, table d'hôte, and noncommercial offerings.

CHAPTER 7 OUTLINE

Menu Pricing Strategies

There is no single best approach to determining a menu price for a given operation. Some businesses do well focusing on food cost percentage while others begin with a menu item's prime cost. Many of the menu pricing strategies discussed in this section are appropriate for à la carte or semi à la carte menus. (Other types of menus are examined later in the chapter.) Which method to utilize depends on the business's brand, the menu's food and beverage options, and the management's philosophy toward cost control.

That this chapter follows one on costing recipes suggests that menu pricing is a strictly linear process moving from recipe costing to price determination. In truth, the menu planner may jump back and forth between costing, pricing, and recipe modification to generate an effective menu. Menu prices for a given menu heading should vary within a fairly narrow range. For example, if entrée prices range from $16 to $20, guests will focus on the menu items rather than on the prices. If the prices instead range from $6 to $35, customers are more likely to choose their entrées based on price. A menu planner who finds that his preliminary prices span too wide a range may go back and modify the recipes to adjust their costs per portion. Some menu planners may opt to leave the recipe costs alone and simply modify the preliminary menu prices to shrink their range. Either way, the final menu prices must fall within an appropriate zone to appeal to the target market. For instance, if the business's vision is to appeal to budget-conscious customers in search of high-value, low-cost items, the final menu prices should all support that goal. Any menu prices that do not appeal to the target audience will likely sell poorly and possibly reduce revenue overall.

Food Cost Percentage Pricing Methods

The most popular approach to determining a preliminary menu price is the *food cost percentage method*. With the cost per portion for a recipe and a given food cost percentage, the menu planner simply employs the following formula:

$$\text{Sales Price} = \frac{\text{Food Cost}}{\text{Food Cost \%}}$$

In the formula, "Food Cost" is the true cost per portion for the menu item, and "Food Cost %" is a predetermined percentage written in its decimal form. The word "Food" may be substituted with "Beverage" to calculate preliminary sales prices for drinks.

Example 7. 1: What is the preliminary sales price for a dish that costs $3.22/ portion if the restaurant uses a food cost percentage of 31%?

$$\text{Sales Price} = \text{Food Cost} \div \text{Food Cost \%}$$
$$= \$3.22 \div 0.31 = \$10.39$$

Example 7. 2: Given a beverage cost percentage of 18.5% and a cost per portion for a bottle of beer of $0.89, what should a bar charge for the beer using the food cost percentage method?

$$\text{Sales Price} = \text{Beverage Cost} \div \text{Beverage Cost \%}$$
$$= \$0.89 \div 0.185 = \$4.81$$

The food cost percentage formula is quite simple. The real-world challenge is determining an appropriate food cost percentage. Average food cost percentages vary widely in the industry. High-end restaurants may use a 20% food cost percentage while fast-food establishments may go as high as 40%. Most often, a business experiments with a food cost percentage around 30% and then adjusts the percentage after a few months—once some historical, financial data has been collected—to improve the business's profitability.

When a foodservice business already has some historical data and a budget in place, it may use the *overhead-contribution method* to determine an appropriate food cost percentage. The amount of money collected from a menu item's sale pays for the cost of the item itself and a portion of the additional overhead required to run the business—salaries and wages, rent, utilities, etc. Viewed collectively across a month or year, revenue collected from food and beverage sales covers the cost of the food and beverage sold and the overhead expenses; any remaining money goes toward profit. Mathematically, food and beverage costs + overhead costs + profit = 100% of the sales revenue.

If a manager is working from a fairly accurate budget or from historical data, he can calculate the percentage of sales that goes toward profit and overhead expenses. Since all that remains from sales is food and beverage cost, the remaining percentage is the food (and beverage) cost percentage that should be used in the sales price = food cost ÷ food cost % formula. This is how the process looks mathematically:

1. Contribution Margin % $= \dfrac{(\text{Overhead Costs} + \text{Profit})}{\text{Sales}}$

2. Food Cost % $= 100\ \% - \text{Contribution Margin }\%$

   (Note: Convert contribution margin from its decimal to its percentage form first.)

3. Sales Price $= \dfrac{\text{Food Cost}}{\text{Food Cost \% (in Decimal Form)}}$

Example 7. 3: A restaurant uses the overhead-contribution method to determine its menu prices. If the budget plans for $850,000 in overhead expenses, $1,400,000 in sales, and a profit of $50,000, what should the menu charge for an entrée with a cost per portion of $2.88?

1. Contribution Margin % $= \dfrac{(\text{Overhead} + \text{Profit})}{\text{Sales}}$

   $= \dfrac{(\$850,000 + \$50,000)}{\$1,400,000} = 0.643 \text{ or } 64.3\%$

2. Food Cost % $= 100\ \% - \text{Contribution Margin \%}$

   $= 100\% - 64.3\% = 35.7\% \text{ or } 0.357$

3. Sales Price $= \dfrac{\text{Food Cost}}{\text{Food Cost \%}} = \dfrac{\$2.88}{0.357} = \$8.07$

The restaurant should use a food cost percentage of 35.7%, and the menu should charge $8.07 for the entrée.

Because the overhead-contribution method references the budget as a whole, the food cost percentage that it calculates must be applied equally to all food (and beverages) in the business. However, this is not always the best approach to maximizing a company's profits. Most price-sensitive customers assess a restaurant's affordability based on the entrée prices. After all, entrées are what most people order in the average restaurant, if they order only one thing. Appetizers, alcoholic drinks, and desserts, on the other hand, are considered add-ons that the budget-conscious customer may not choose to purchase. A savvy menu planner might prefer to keep the entrée prices low to attract customers while inflating the prices of other menu items to increase profit.

The *Texas Restaurant Association (TRA) Method* uses food cost percentages to calculate menu prices, but unlike the overhead-contribution method, it allows for different food cost percentages for each menu category. The menu planner still calculates the total percentage of sales that overhead expenses represent, but he decides for each menu heading how much of the menu price should go toward profit. For example, assume that a budget shows that 65% of all sales goes toward the coverage of overhead expenses. If the menu planner decides that entrées should only make a profit of 5%, then using the overhead-contribution method's logic, 70% (65% + 5%) of the sales price goes toward overhead and profit while 30% (100% − 70%) is reserved to cover the cost of the food. The food cost percentage for entrées in this scenario would be 30%. However, the menu planner can then decide that appetizers should contribute a profit of 15% of their sales price. The combination of overhead and profit represents 80% (65% + 15%) of the sales price, which leaves only 20% (100% − 80%) to cover the food cost. The food cost percentage for appetizers becomes 20%. The TRA method encourages menu planners or other managers to select a different percentage for profit for each menu heading. Slow-moving items within a category may also merit a higher percentage profit than their counterparts to account for the proportionately larger share of inventory space and employee attention per sale that they require. Thus, items that slow down the production line and require a greater share of labor cost are assigned a higher profit percentage in the formula to justify the added cost and hassle of maintaining those items on the menu.

As with the overhead-contribution method, the TRA method is a tool to determine the food cost percentage that a menu planner uses to calculate a sales price from an item's cost per portion. Both methods ultimately conclude with the same sales price = food cost ÷ food cost% formula.

Example 7. 4: A restaurant uses the TRA method to price its menu items. If the overhead expenses for a business represent 71% of sales, and the management dictates that desserts should return 12% of their sales price as profit, how much should the menu planner charge for a dessert with a cost per portion of $0.73?

1. Overhead + Profit = 71% + 12% = 83 %

2. Food Cost % = 100% − (Overhead + Profit) = 100% − 83% = 17 % or 0.17

3. Sales Price = Food Cost ÷ Food Cost % = $0.73 ÷ 0.17 = $4.29

Prime Cost Pricing Methods

Food cost percentage methods assume that all items on the menu require roughly the same amount of labor to prepare. This is not always true. Imagine a restaurant that offers two dishes. Both cost the same ingredient-wise, but while one can be made in three minutes, the other requires twenty minutes of an employee's labor per portion. Should the customer pay the same for each dish? Should the additional labor cost be factored into the more time-consuming dish's price?

Prime cost is the combined total of food or beverage cost and labor cost. From a per portion perspective, labor is the direct labor cost required to prepare a single serving of the dish (or drink) and does not factor in the cost of other labor overhead (dishwashers, servers, managers, etc.). The direct labor cost does not come from a budget but rather from observation of the cooks preparing the food and knowledge of each cook's hourly wage. The direct labor cost for any task can be calculated by multiplying the cook's hourly wage by the number of hours (or fraction thereof) spent on that task. For example, if a cook earns $12/hour and spends 45 minutes (or ¾ of an hour) preparing 20 portions of a stir-fry entrée, then the direct labor cost for the 20 portions is $12/hour × 0.75 hours = $9. The direct labor cost per portion is $9 ÷ 20 portions = $0.45. Because cooks often multitask during their day, determining an accurate number of minutes that a cook spends on a given dish or recipe can be challenging. This method is best utilized when cooks are only responsible for one or two recipes or tasks each, as might be seen in a large-production, high-volume operation.

With a direct labor cost per portion for each dish, a manager can calculate the prime cost for each dish by adding the direct labor cost and the food cost per portion. The *prime cost method* generates a preliminary menu price by multiplying each item's prime cost by a price factor. The price factor starts off as an arbitrary figure, but with the accumulation of historical data, a menu planner can revise the price factor to make the menu more profitable. Mathematically,

1. Prime Cost = Direct Labor Cost + Food Cost
2. Sales Price = Prime Cost × Price Factor

Example 7.5: A restaurant uses the prime cost method and a price factor of 2.35. If a certain entrée has a food cost per portion of $2.73 and a direct labor cost of $0.36, how much should the restaurant charge for this dish?

1. Prime Cost = Direct Labor Cost + Food Cost = $2.73 + $0.36 = $3.09
2. Sales Price = Prime Cost × Price Factor = $3.09 × 2.35 = $7.26

The prime cost method more accurately accounts for direct labor cost, but customers may not perceive the value in the extra labor. Typically, guests are more aware of differences in ingredient costs than they are in labor costs. For example, a fairly complex chicken dish may require so much in labor cost that its prime cost approaches that of a low—labor/high—food cost steak. Still, many guests will question why their chicken costs as much as the steak; they simply will not connect the higher labor cost with the higher menu price.

The *actual pricing method* bases sales prices on each item's prime cost, but it generates a price divisor from the business's budget to generate the ultimate sales price. Similar to the TRA method, the actual pricing method begins by determining the percentage of sales that goes toward overhead and profit. Traditionally, the actual pricing method uses the terms *variable cost percentage, fixed cost percentage*, and *profit percentage*. Broadly speaking, variable costs (such as hourly worker wages or food costs) are those that fluctuate with sales, while fixed costs (such as rent or salaries) do not. In the case of the actual pricing method, the variable cost percentage does not include food and beverage costs or direct labor costs, as these are lumped under the heading of prime cost instead. Since 100% of sales goes to cover prime costs, variable costs, fixed costs, and profit, the percentage of sales available to cover prime cost can be thought of as 100% − (variable cost % + fixed cost % + profit %). This figure provides the price divisor used to calculate a sales price from a prime cost. Mathematically, the procedure is as follows:

1. Price Divisor = 100% − (Variable Cost % + Fixed Cost % + Profit %)

2. Sales Price = $\dfrac{\text{Prime Cost}}{\text{Price Divisor}}$

Remember that prime cost = food cost + direct labor cost.

Example 7. 6: A restaurant uses the actual pricing method to determine its menu prices. The budget shows a variable cost percentage of 21%, a fixed cost percentage of 33%, and a profit percentage of 5%. What should the restaurant charge for a dish with a food cost of $3.18 and a direct labor cost of $0.83?

1. Price Divisor = 100% − (Variable Cost % + Food Cost % + Profit %)
   = 100% − (21% + 33% + 5%) = 41% or 0.41

2. Sales Price = Prime Cost ÷ Price Divisor
   = ($3.18 + $0.83) ÷ 0.41 = $4.01 ÷ 0.41 = $9.78

The prime cost method uses a price factor while the actual pricing method uses a price divisor, but both rely on a menu item's prime cost as the basis for calculating its sales price.

Gross Profit Pricing Method

Pricing methods based on food cost or prime cost assume that a single factor or divisor will generate menu prices that are both within a narrow range and high enough to support the business's overhead expenses and profit goals. But what if that is not possible for a given foodservice concept? Consider the classic coffee shop. Customers willingly pay over $2 for a cup of coffee and even more for espresso drinks, knowing that the beverage cost is probably less than $0.30. Why don't customers accuse the operation of price gouging? Simply put, the overhead and labor expense percentages for a coffee shop are much higher than they are for a traditional restaurant. The majority of sales are beverage sales, so food sales do not cover much of the overhead costs. Consequently, the beverage cost percentage is extremely low.

While a low beverage or food cost percentage can generate prices high enough to cover a business's overhead and profit, such low percentages tend to magnify and exaggerate small differences in food and beverage cost. A drink that only costs an extra $0.05 may translate to a sales price of an extra $0.50 to $1.00. Such wide price variations for similar products are far more frustrating to customers than the low cost percentages. In such a situation, most customers will gravitate toward the cheapest option on the menu.

The better approach to menu pricing in this type of operation is the *gross profit method*. Gross profit is the money remaining from sales after deducting food and beverage costs. This money must cover all labor and other overhead. In an existing business, the manager knows roughly how many customers the business gets in a month and the total monthly overhead and labor expenses. Thus, the manager can figure out how much gross profit he needs to make from each customer to cover his monthly labor, overhead, and profit. As long as each customer pays at least this amount above and beyond the cost of the drink, the business will meet its profit goals. Mathematically, gross profit per customer is as follows:

1. Gross Profit = Total Sales (in a given period) − Total Food and Beverage Cost
(for the same period)

2. Gross Profit per Customer = Gross Profit ÷ Total Customers
(over the same period)

In a business, the budget may estimate the number of customers per month and the labor, overhead, and profit per month. Assuming the budget is accurate, the sum of the non-food and beverage expenses and the profit is the same as the gross profit, which must cover those costs. The gross profit per customer follows from this total gross profit calculation. From a budget gross profit per customer is calculated this way:

$$\text{Gross Profit per Customer} = \frac{\text{Total Overhead and Labor Expenses} + \text{Profit (in a Period)}}{\text{Total Customers (in the Same Period)}}$$

In this formula, the total overhead and labor expenses are simply the sum of all non-food and beverage expenses from the budget. This generates not a realized gross profit per customer but rather a necessarily minimum gross profit per customer to use for calculating menu prices in order to stay on budget.

Unlike the aforementioned pricing methods, the gross profit method *adds* a number to the food (or beverage) cost per portion. There is no multiplying or dividing involved. The formula to calculate a menu price using the gross profit method is as follows:

Sales Price = Food (or Beverage) Cost per Portion + Gross Profit per Customer

---

Example 7. 7: A coffee house uses the gross profit method to calculate its prices. From the operation's budget, the business expects to average 17,500 customers per month with average monthly expenses (excluding food and beverage costs) of $29,500 and a target monthly profit of $2,000. If a certain coffee drink costs $0.27 per portion, what should the menu planner charge for this beverage?

$$\text{Gross Profit per Customer} = \frac{\text{Total Overhead and Labor Expenses} + \text{Profit}}{\text{Total Customers}}$$

$$= \frac{\$29,500 + \$2,000}{17,500} = \$1.80$$

Sales Price = Beverage Cost per Portion + Gross Profit per Customer
= $0.27 + $1.80 = $2.07

Since the gross profit method adds rather than multiplies or divides the gross profit per customer to the food or beverage cost per portion, small differences in portion costs are not exaggerated. A customer, seeing that the prices fall within a narrow range, can ignore the prices and choose whichever beverage he prefers, while the manager knows that the customer will contribute the same amount of money toward the business's gross profit no matter what drink he ultimately purchases. The gross profit method is not ideal for all business models, but it is an excellent approach when food and beverage cost percentages are extremely low. Besides coffee shops, street food carts and certain types of bakeries might do well with this approach to pricing.

Base Price Pricing Method

Sometimes, a menu planner prefers to start not with the cost per portion for a dish but rather with the desired sales price and then to work backwards. This pricing approach usually emanates from a marketing orientation to menu pricing. In price-sensitive markets, menu planners recognize that customers will flock to a business at certain price points. The classic example is the "dollar menu" or "$0.99 menu" common in fast-food operations. Those businesses did not magically discover that certain products work out to a suggested selling price of $0.99. Rather, they began with the desired selling price and a target food cost percentage. Then, using the sales price = food cost ÷ food cost % formula, they calculated the maximum food cost per portion that an item on that menu could have. This approach is termed the *base price method*.

For the base price method, the food cost percentage formula is reworked to read:

$$\text{Food Cost} = \text{Sales Price} \times \text{Food Cost \%}$$

Example 7. 8: If a cafeteria chef must sell his entrées at a cost of $4.50 and hit a maximum food cost percentage of 32%, what is the maximum cost per portion for an entrée that he sells?

$$\text{Food Cost} = \text{Sales Price} \times \text{Food Cost \%} = \$4.50 \times 0.32 = \$1.44$$

Any operation could use this approach, and noncommercial foodservice businesses, such as corporate or school cafeterias, often do. They know that their customers or clients require a certain price point. In the case of federally reimbursed school meals, the foodservice provider receives only a certain amount of government money no matter the cost of the food they serve. Thus, the menu planners must develop recipes that fall below the maximum per portion food cost determined from the set sales price and the target food cost percentage.

Creating a recipe that hits a target food cost per portion is not as difficult as it might seem. Costs can be modified significantly through portion size adjustment. A meatloaf might switch from 5 to 4 ounces per serving. A turkey sandwich might drop from 3 ounces to 2.5 ounces of turkey per portion. Additionally, certain ingredients can be modified, removed, or added to the recipe. For example, the cost of a salad might drop significantly if the ¼ cup of oil-cured olives is reduced to three olives or removed entirely. Perhaps the chef will opt to switch to a cheaper variety of olive. If a recipe cannot be modified to fall below the food cost target without ruining the dish's quality and appeal, that recipe should be removed from the menu entirely.

Matching Competitors' Prices

One legitimate approach to price determination is simply to match the prices of competitors. A company with a product nearly identical to its competitor may fail to draw significant market share if it does not compete on price. Price-sensitive customers may not even consider patronizing a restaurant that does not meet or beat the prices of similar establishments in the area.

This pricing method works well from the revenue growth perspective but is extremely risky from the cost control and profit generation perspective. The menu planner or manager in one business rarely knows the cost structure of its competitors. One business may keep its costs artificially low by employing family members who donate their time. A large chain may get a better deal on purveyor prices than an independent restaurant can. Some businesses prefer to keep prices high but use a coupon or discount system to attract customers; a business that matches the prices but not the coupons will fail to draw customers away from the competition. Finally, to maintain a monopoly in the area, a business might attempt to temporarily reduce its prices below sustainable levels when a competing company opens nearby. They know they cannot do this for very long, but if a competitor attempts to match its prices, presumably that competitor will go out of business quickly from lack of profits. Then, the original business can return its prices to their original levels.

Generally speaking, matching competitors' prices works best only when paired with a second pricing strategy—typically the base price method. First, the menu planner matches a competitor's price for a given product. Then, he employs the base price method to determine a maximum food cost per portion for that dish. If the business cannot match the competitor's quality, quantity, and price at the same time, he may wish to distinguish his product from the competition in ways other than price.

Choosing the Right Pricing Method

There is no one best method for determining menu prices. Each strategy works well in different environments. Food cost percentage methods are easy to use and very popular, but the overhead-contribution and TRA methods require some historical data from the existing business—or at least an accurate budget—to be utilized effectively. Still, the basic food cost percentage method is an excellent starting point for a restaurant with a range of dishes that have within a single menu heading similar food costs per portion, comparable direct labor costs, and a food cost percentage that is not much lower than 20%. Prime cost methods work well when the direct labor cost for different dishes varies significantly.

The gross profit method is an excellent choice for businesses with exceedingly low food cost percentages and a market that typically buys just one item per visit. The base price method works well for noncommercial and fast-food operations. Matching competitors' prices is always a choice but should be utilized in conjunction with another method to ensure that such an approach is viable and profitable.

COMPREHENSIVE PRICING EXAMPLE

A restaurant, based in a downtown business district, opens for lunch only. Its menu focuses mainly on salads, sandwiches, and drinks although it also offers a small selection of appetizers and desserts. When the restaurant opened, it aimed for a 29% food cost and a 20% beverage cost. After 6 months (182 days), the manager has compiled the following data about the restaurant:

The manager is focusing on the sales price for the burger plate, which comes with fries and slaw.

The food cost (true cost per portion) has been calculated for the following items:

Total sales	$800,000	100%
Total overhead costs	$520,000	65% of sales
– Fixed costs	$144,000	18% of sales
– Direct labor costs	$88,000	11% of sales
– Other variable costs	$288,000	36% of sales
Profit	$40,000	5% of sales
Average guest check	$13.95	
Customers	315/day; 57,330 total	

TABLE 7.1a
Comprehensive Pricing Example Operational Data

Item	Cost per Portion
Burger and toppings	$1.69
Fries	$0.37
Slaw	$0.12
Total burger plate	$2.18
Soda	$0.10
Apple pie	$0.44

TABLE 7.1b
Comprehensive Pricing Example Costs per Portion

Part A: Using the food cost percentage method, what was the manager's calculated sales price for the burger plate before opening the doors (i.e., when the food cost percentage was 29%)?

$$\text{Sales Price} = \frac{\text{Food Cost}}{\text{Food Cost}\%} = \frac{\$2.18}{0.29} = \$7.52$$

Part B: Use the overhead-contribution method to determine what the food cost has been over the past 6 months, and then calculate the updated sales price for the burger plate.

$$\text{Contribution Margin}\% = \frac{(\text{Overhead Costs} + \text{Profit})}{\text{Sales}} = \frac{\$520,000 + \$40,000}{\$800,000} = 0.7 \text{ or } 70\%$$

$$\text{Food Cost }\% = 100\% - \text{Contribution Margin }\% = 100\% - 70\% = 30\% \text{ or } 0.3$$

$$\text{Sales Price} = \frac{\text{Food Cost}}{\text{Food Cost}\%(\text{decimal})} = \frac{\$2.18}{0.3} = \$7.27$$

Part C: The manager believes the burger plate should operate at a 5% profit to encourage sales of the full plate. However, the manager feels that side dishes, like the fries, should operate at a 20% profit. If the fries used the same 30% food cost approach as the full burger plate, a side of fries would sell for $0.37 ÷ 0.3 = $1.23. Using the TRA method, calculate a sales price for a side of fries that accounts for 20% profit on fries.

$$\text{Overhead} + \text{Profit} = 65\% + 20\% = 85\%$$

$$\text{Food Cost }\% = 100\% - (\text{Overhead} + \text{Profit}) = 100\% - 85\% = 15\%$$

$$\text{Sales Price} = \text{Food Cost} \div \text{Food Cost }\% = \$0.37 \div 0.15 = \$2.47$$

Part D: After observing the workers, the manager calculates that the direct labor cost to make the burger plate is $1.50. The manager adopts a price factor of 2.25 (only because a friend at another restaurant uses that price factor.) Using the prime cost method, calculate a sales price for the burger plate.

$$\text{Prime Cost} = \text{Direct Labor Cost} + \text{Food Cost} = \$1.40 + \$2.18 = \$3.58$$

$$\text{Sales Price} = \text{Prime Cost} \times \text{Price Factor} = \$3.58 \times 2.25 = \$8.06$$

Part E: Use the actual pricing method to calculate the burger plate's sales price. (Hint: The prime cost was already calculated in part D.)

$$\text{Price Divisor} = 100\% - (\text{Variable Cost }\% + \text{Fixed Cost }\% + \text{Profit }\%)$$

$$= 100\% - (36\% + 18\% + 5\%) = 41\%$$

$$\text{Sales Price} = \frac{\text{Prime Cost}}{\text{Price Divisor}} = \frac{\$3.58}{0.41} = \$8.73$$

Part F: The manager is curious about creating a package deal where customers pay one price to get the burger plate, a soda, and a slice of apple pie for dessert. He believes that nearly all of his customers will take advantage of that deal if he offers it. Believing that the restaurant will sell little else beyond these package deals, the manager decides to use the gross profit method to price the package. Using the gross profit method, what should the sales price be for the burger plate, soda, and pie package?

In this case, total food and beverage costs must first be calculated from the chart.

$$\text{Total Sales} = \text{Food and Beverage Costs} + \text{Overhead Costs} + \text{Profit}$$

Rearranging the formula,

$$\text{Food and Beverage Costs} = \text{Total Sales} - \text{Overhead Costs} - \text{Profit}$$

$$= \$800{,}000 - \$520{,}000 - \$40{,}000 = \$240{,}000$$

$$\text{Gross Profit} = \text{Total Sales} - \text{Total Food and Beverage Costs} = \$800{,}000 - \$240{,}000 = \$560{,}000$$

$$\text{Gross Profit per Customer} = \text{Gross Profit} \div \text{Total Customers} = \$560{,}000 \div 57{,}330 = \$9.77$$

The total food and beverage cost for the package is $\$2.18 + \$0.10 + \$0.44 = \$2.72$

$$\text{Sales Price} = \text{Food and Beverage Cost per Portion} + \text{Gross Profit per Customer}$$

$$= \$2.72 + \$9.77 = \$12.49$$

For comparison, if the sales price for the package were calculated using the food cost percentage method and a 30% food cost, the sales price would be $\$2.72 \div 0.3 = \$9.07$. This sales price, however, would impact total revenue in a severely negative way. Sodas and desserts often use a lower food cost percentage (or account for more profit using TRA terminology), which would drive the revenue up significantly if each item were purchased separately. Furthermore, the average check for the restaurant is $13.95. Assuming the burger is on the lower side of the restaurant's entrée prices, final sales prices will remain within a narrow range and still average around $13.95 using the gross profit method. A few additional à la carte purchases might drive the check average even higher. Using a straight food cost percentage method would create a wider range of prices for the package deals.

Part G: The manager likes the idea of the package deal and believes that using a single price for all deals will attract more customers. He believes the ideal price point is $12.95 (and that other beverage sales will keep the average check close to $13.95). Because the package includes a soda and dessert, he decides that all package deals must operate at a 25% food and beverage cost. Using the base price method, calculate the maximum food and beverage cost for a package deal. Then, determine the maximum food cost for any sandwich that can be included in the deal.

$$\text{Food (and Beverage) Cost} = \text{Sales Price} \times \text{Food (and Beverage) Cost \%} = \$12.95 \times 0.25 = \$3.24$$

The cost for the sandwich alone is the total cost minus the cost of the soda and the pie.

$$\text{Food Cost for Sandwich} = \$3.24 - \$0.10 - \$0.44 = \$2.70$$

Example Summary: The preliminary sales prices calculated for the burger plate alone were $7.27, $7.52, $8.06, and $8.73. The TRA method focused on non-entrée selections; the base price pricing method worked backward from a set price. The gross profit method could only be applied to the package deal in this example. Why? The gross profit method ensures that a set gross profit is made from each customer. Because customers in this restaurant presumably buy not only the burger plate but also beverages and sometimes desserts, adding the gross profit per customer to each menu item would inflate prices astronomically. The gross profit method works best when most customers order only a single item, like a beverage, or pay a single price for the meal, as in a prix fixe or table d'hôte restaurant. In this example, the package deal works like a table d'hôte menu.

There is no rule that says that a menu planner must use the same pricing approach for the entire menu. It is perfectly acceptable for a single restaurant to use a prime cost method for appetizers, a food cost percentage method for entrées, a gross profit method for beverages, and a base price method for desserts. Whatever strategy is employed, the menu planner should make sure that the end result will both appeal to customers and keep the business profitable.

Factors That Affect Menu Prices

Learning Objective 2
List several factors that impact the final price written on a menu.

While a menu pricing strategy generates preliminary sales prices for the items on a menu, those prices should not be placed on the menu without some modification first. The formulas provide target prices, but these prices could be viewed as minimum prices. Highly popular or unique items might merit a much higher sales price. Alternatively, the calculated prices may be approximations that the menu planner rounds to the nearest whole dollar. How a menu planner modifies the initial sales price calculation depends heavily on several factors.

Competition   Generally speaking, the more direct competition a restaurant has, the less flexibility the menu planner has to raise the sales price beyond the initial calculation. Direct competition differs from indirect competition though. Indirect competition comes from all other foodservice businesses. Direct competition only comes from similar foodservice concepts—like two pizza parlors or multiple Chinese take-out restaurants. When food, service, and atmosphere are similar in two nearby restaurants, then customers may perceive price as the only distinguishing factor. In such situations, the menu planner must keep prices as low as possible to attract business. However, since foodservice businesses sell more than just food—they sell service and atmosphere, too—a significant difference in only one of these factors may justify higher sales prices.

The less direct competition that a business has, the higher the menu planner may raise his prices above the preliminary sales price calculation. However, when prices become too steep for the product delivered, customers may opt for indirect competitors more regularly; for these customers, the kind of food and service provided is less important than affordability. In those rare instances where there is neither direct nor indirect competition, a foodservice business has a monopoly and can charge much higher prices than it otherwise would. People see this often in small turnpike rest areas and certain airports. There is no competition readily available, so a single business selling food and drink can gouge those few customers hungering for a drink or a bite to eat.

Price Sensitivity   If sales of a particular product change significantly when the sales price changes only slightly, that product is said to be price sensitive. The more price sensitive a product is, the less ability the menu planner has to increase the initial sales price calculation. In fact, he may even reduce the preliminary sales price slightly to drive up business dramatically. Price sensitivity depends heavily on competition and on how much people value a particular product over alternatives. For example, if people in a given city view lobster as a special occasion splurge that is not available at most restaurants, they are less likely to shun lobster because of a $2 price increase. However, if the lobster in a seaside town is present on every restaurant menu for the same low price as other entrées, guests in an establishment selling lobster for a much higher price will likely opt for one of the less expensive entrée choices.

Perceived Value   When customers believe that something has inherently higher value, they are willing to pay more for it than the sales price calculation might otherwise suggest. This value may be inherent to the product, such as a hundred-year-old bottle of rare wine, or it may be subliminally implied through the menu description. Some restaurants increase perceived value by naming the sources or provenance of their ingredients. Thanks to current culinary trends, dishes made with locally sourced or organic ingredients command a higher price because customers value those ingredients more. An ingredient's quality grade, such as prime versus choice beef, also impacts the perceived value and sales price when the grade is listed on the menu. However the operation chooses to direct the guests' attention to the value of its food, guests will gladly pay more for a dish they view as having a greater value than similar dishes with the same cost per portion.

Product Differentiation   A business that sells a product (food, service, and ambiance) identical to the competition's product is stuck fighting for customers based on price alone. However, a restaurant that sells a product unavailable anywhere else can charge almost whatever it wants for this unique experience. The more a business differentiates its products from the competition, the more flexibility the menu planner has in raising prices. Service and atmosphere can skew the acceptable selling price for a dish significantly. A menu can charge significantly more for a Caesar salad prepared tableside in a restaurant's rose garden than the average bar can charge for the same salad prepared in the kitchen. Similarly, three New York–style pizza places will battle each other by lowering prices, but a New York–style pizza, a wood-grilled boutique pizza, and a Chicago-style deep dish pizza are all very different products that just happen to share the name "pizza." If these pizzas were each found in only one of three nearby restaurants, the businesses could charge very different prices. Their products are highly differentiated.

A restaurant's or chef's trendiness in society also drives up prices. A famous chef can charge significantly more for a dish simply because customers will pay a premium to eat that chef's food. When a restaurant becomes the hot new thing that every foodie must try, the menu can charge much higher rates; customers will pay quite a bit for the ability to tell their friends they dined there. This rule applies even if some remarkably similar dishes are available elsewhere. An historic restaurant has similar appeal among tourists. The total experience for which the customer pays in trendy or historic restaurants goes well beyond the food. The experience is unique, and thus, highly differentiated.

In short, a menu planner can charge more for well-differentiated products with a high perceived value, low price sensitivity, and little competition than he can for similar menu items in a community where the items are not significantly different from the many competitors' products and the local market does not find them of high value.

Pricing Psychology

Learning Objective 3
Describe the role that customer psychology plays in menu pricing.

The exact price written on a menu can make a guest more or less comfortable paying that amount based simply on how the number looks. There are certain prices that Americans are used to paying, so they tend to gloss over these numbers and ignore their true value. In general, prices that end in $0.00, $0.25, $0.45, $0.49, $0.50, $0.75, $0.95, and $0.99 are more common and thus make menu readers more comfortable. If a menu were to list an item as $14.93 instead of $14.95, guests would likely notice the price and fixate on it more than they would the $14.95 price. Since the last thing a menu planner wants the guest to focus on is price, it is best to stick with the traditionally "comfortable" price endings.

Additionally, all menu prices communicate a subliminal message to the clientele. Prices ending in "9" suggest that the menu item is a bargain. While the difference between $4.99 and $5.00 is hardly significant, most people think of the two very differently. Many would say that $4.99 is cheap; it is not even a full five dollars. The $5.00 price tag, on the other hand, does not provide change from a five-dollar bill. Businesses that want their customers to think that they are a bargain tend to end their prices in nines. Fast-food $0.99 menus are classic examples.

Upscale establishments, on the other hand, want to communicate luxury and indulgence. They want their customers to feel that they are getting a top-dollar experience, which costs whole dollars, not pennies. Thus, high-end restaurants tend to use whole dollars for their prices. Mid-level restaurants often use prices that end in "0" or "5." These numbers suggest that the food is a value but not cheap.

Whether a menu planner rounds preliminary sales price calculations to numbers ending in "0," "5," or "9" depends heavily on the business's concept and the subliminal message the menu planner wishes to communicate about the establishment. For example, a preliminary price of $12.73 might be rounded to $12.75, $12.99, or $13.00 depending on the restaurant. It is important to note that most menu planners will round their sales prices up unless the price reduction is relatively small and delivers a big psychological boost. For instance, a calculated preliminary price of $1.01 might be rounded down to $0.99 to attract a bargain-hunting customer, but dropping a price of $1.33 down to $0.99 would be too severe a reduction. Such a drop would result in a very high food cost percentage for that one item. Since most foodservice businesses operate on low profit margins, rounding sales prices down significantly can easily lead to the complete evaporation of profits. Unlike supermarkets, which may advertise loss leaders (products that sell at very low prices to attract customers) to generate business elsewhere in the store, most restaurants can only sell

DINNER MENU
WINTER

GARDEN

Roasted Carrot Salad
toasted rye berries, caramelized goat cheese
chervil, maple vinaigrette
11

Wild Mushroom Soup
barley, leeks, vermouth, watercress
10

Belgian Endive Salad
pears, blue cheese, pecans
sherry vinaigrette
10

CHILLED

Peekytoe Crab Tartine*
toasted sourdough, lemon aïoli, winter radish
blood orange
17

Bison Tartare*
harissa aïoli, socca chips, cilantro
16

Day Boat Scallop Crudo*
green apple, shiso, chilies, scallion vinaigrette
17

Grilled Hudson Valley Foie Gras
medjool date pastilla, sunchoke, preserved lime
24

PASTA

Spaghetti Nero
prawns, mussels, octopus, fra diavolo, fines herbes
16/23

Sweet Potato Agnolotti
smoked sheep's milk cheese, walnuts
cippolini onion, balsamic vinegar
14/21

Heritage Wheat Tagliatelle
rose veal ragu, oregano
parmesan crusted sweetbreads
15/22

SIDES

Crispy Potatoes
tomato aïoli

Creamy Spinach
Lone Grazer cheese curds

Smoked Wild Mushrooms
salsa verde

All Sides 8

SEA

Sea Scallops*
black trumpet mushrooms, riso rosso
salsify, apple beurre blanc
30

Madai Snapper*
manila clams, savoy cabbage, charred leeks
bacon lardon
27

Lightly Smoked Steelhead Trout*
maple glazed brussels sprouts, rutabaga
citrus vinaigrette
28

LAND

Tamarind Glazed Pork Chop*
winter squash, peanuts, endive
puffed basmati rice
28

Dry-Aged Duck Breast*
swiss chard, beet, amaranth, braunschweiger
28

Dorothy's Pot Roast
mushroom confit, pommes aligot, rosemary broth
28
add foie gras 39

Grilled Millbrook Venison*
red cabbage, celery root, chestnut, black currant
32

CHEF AND OWNER / GAVIN KAYSEN
CHEF DE CUISINE / CHRIS NYE
GENERAL MANAGER / CATHERINE YOO

*CONSUMING RAW OR UNDERCOOKED MEAT, FISH OR OTHER PROTEINS CAN INCREASE THE RISK OF CONTRACTING A FOODBORNE ILLNESS

FIGURE 7.1

Whole dollar prices communicate a high-end, quality experience for this restaurant.

Source: Spoon and Stable. Reprinted with permission.

SIDES

Seasoned steak fries $1.50
Mashed potatoes $1.75
House salad small $3.25 large $6.25
Extra dressing or sauce $.50

Vegetable du jour $1.75
Coleslaw $1.00
Garlic bread $1.50
Guacamole $1.50

DESSERTS

Hockeytown Brownie Sundae
Rich fudge brownie topped with french vanilla ice cream & chocolate sauce $6.75

Apple Pie
Michigan apple pie served hot & finished with warm caramel sauce $6.25.
ala mode $7.75

Vanilla Ice Cream
with chocolate syrup $2.25

Chocolate Tuxedo Mousse
A moist chocolate crumb cake with layers of chocolate mousse and vanilla/chocolate swirl topped with whipped cream and a chocolate sauce drizzle $6.95

Old Fashioned Bread Pudding
Hockeytown Café's homemade bread pudding served warm with vanilla ice cream and rum sauce $6.25

BEVERAGES

Over 50 beer selections from around the world including 18 on tap!
Please refer to our table tents for current selections

Ask about our premium root beer & non-alcoholic beer selection

The Stanley Spiced Kraken Rum mixed with root beer and a hint of cream $6.25
Hat Trick A tropical blend of pineapple, banana and coconut Cruzan rums mixed with cranberry, OJ and pineapple juices $6.75
Face Off Absolut Mandrin, melon liquer, OJ and sour mix $6.25
Center Ice Captain Morgan, blue curacao, sweet sour mix, Sprite and garnished with lime $6.25
Playoff Blueberry Stolichnaya, Razzmatazz, a splash of Triple Sec and Sprite $6.75
"Red & White" Margarita Malibu Red, a hint of coconut rum & tequila, blended with the Taste of Florida juices over ice and finished with a splash of grenadine $6.75
Juice
Cranberry, pineapple, grapefruit, orange or lemonade
Non-Alcoholic Specialties
Wild Berry Breeze - A frozen combination of strawberry & raspberry
Squeeze Play - A frosty lemonade with a raspberry twist

SCORE WITH YOUR NEXT
GROUP EVENT! @

- Corporate and Group Outings
- Youth Hockey Events
- Birthday Parties and More!

313-471-3454

or visit hockeytowncafe.com

Follow us on

"...THE BEST PLACE IN TOWN

TO CATCH THE FACE-OFF, KICK-OFF OR TIP-OFF."

—THE DETROIT FREE PRESS

FIGURE 7.2

A menu with prices ending in "0" or "5" communicates value and a midrange price point.

Source: Olympia Entertainment, Inc. and Hockeytown Café

APPETIZERS   Kick off your meal with one of our great appetizers

HOCKEYTOWN Red Wings
Deep fried chicken wings tossed in our buttery Buffalo-style hot sauce. Served with bleu cheese dressing & celery sticks $7.25

Baked Spinach & Artichoke Dip
Creamy mixture of spinach & artichokes baked with mozzarella cheese. Served with tortilla chips $7.95

Loaded Potato Skins
Crispy potato skins with bacon, jack-cheddar cheese & green onions. Served with sour cream $7.95

Chips & Salsa
Crispy tortilla chips served with garden-fresh salsa $4.95

Cheese Quesadillas
Cheese-filled tortilla shells browned in light olive oil served with shredded lettuce, chopped green onions, tomatoes, sour cream & garden-fresh salsa $7.50 Add chicken $3.00

Mozzarella Sticks
Mozzarella cheese sticks served with marinara sauce or ranch dressing $6.25

Nachos Grande
Seasoned ground beef & tortilla chips piled high with green onions, tomatoes, shredded lettuce, black olives & shredded jack-cheddar cheese. Served with sour cream & garden-fresh salsa $9.95

Chicken Fingers Basket*
Crispy homestyle chicken fingers served with seasoned steak fries, celery sticks & your choice of BBQ sauce, honey mustard or ranch dressing $8.95

Cajun Beef Tips
Cajun seasoned sirloin tips tossed with caramelized onions & peppers served with bleu cheese coleslaw and garlic bread $10.95

Deep Fried Pepper Rings
Zesty fried banana pepper rings served with a BBQ-bacon ranch dipping sauce $6.25

Corned Beef Sliders
Corned beef topped with sauerkraut, Swiss cheese and Russian dressing served on a brioche with a side of bleu cheese coleslaw $7.95

FRESH SALADS   All salads are prepared to order

HOCKEYTOWN BBQ Chicken Salad*
Slices of grilled chicken breast tossed in BBQ sauce and served on a bed of iceberg lettuce with diced red onions, bacon, tomatoes, shredded jack-cheddar cheese & smokey ranch dressing $9.75

Fatoush Salad
Romaine, fresh mint, parsley, cucumbers, tomatoes and bell peppers served with a lemon-mint vinaigrette and toasted pita chips $7.95

Classic Caesar Salad*
With croutons, parmesan cheese & Caesar dressing $6.95. Add chicken $3.00 Add beef $4.00

Southwest Chicken Salad*
Chicken breast served on a bed of iceberg lettuce topped with black bean corn salsa, diced red onions, shredded jack-cheddar cheese, crispy tortilla strips & Mexican ranch dressing $8.95

Taco Salad
Fried tortilla shell filled with shredded lettuce & seasoned ground beef garnished with jack-cheddar cheese, diced tomatoes, green onions, black olives, sour cream & garden-fresh salsa $8.25

Michigan Salad
Mixed greens topped with Boursin cheese, Traverse City dried cherries, diced cucumbers, tomatoes, red onions & chopped walnuts served with a raspberry vinaigrette $9.95 Add chicken $3.00

Cobb Salad
With iceburg lettuce, chicken, bacon, cucumbers, tomatoes, red onions, hard boiled eggs & Gorgonzola Cheese and your choice of dressing $9.95

PIZZA

HOCKEYTOWN Deep Dish Pizza
Large Cheese Pizza $13.95   Small Cheese Pizza $9.95
Additional Toppings: Large Pizza $1.75   Small Pizza $1.00
Available toppings:
pepperoni, ham, Italian sausage, bacon, onions, green peppers, mushrooms, black olives, banana peppers, tomatoes, pineapple, extra cheese

Thin-Crust Pizza

BBQ Chicken Pizza
Topped with grilled chicken, red onions, bacon and sweet BBQ sauce $13.95

Buffalo Chicken Pizza
Topped with grilled chicken, Gorgonzola cheese, Buffalo sauce and crisp celery $13.95

Calzones

Meat Lovers
Bacon, ham, pepperoni, sausage & Boursin cheese $9.95

California Calzone
Fresh spinach, artichokes, parmesan cheese and grilled chicken $9.95

SANDWICHES

HOCKEYTOWN Buffalo Chicken
Fried chicken breast tossed in Buffalo sauce & served with lettuce, tomato & bleu cheese dressing on a sesame seed bun $9.50

Smoked Turkey with Guoda Cheese on Flatbread
Served with bacon, lettuce & tomatoes and a pesto mayo $9.95

Chicken Caesar Lawash*
Grilled sliced chicken breast wrapped in a flour lawash with Romaine lettuce, Caesar dressing & parmesan cheese $9.50

Hot Turkey Reuben
Shaved turkey breast stacked with homemade coleslaw, Swiss cheese & Russian dressing on grilled marble rye bread $8.95

Philly Cheese Steak or Chicken*
Juicy sirloin or chicken sautéed with onions & peppers. Served on a hoagie bun with Swiss cheese $8.95   Add sautéed mushrooms $.99

Bar-B-Q Pulled Pork
Boneless pork tossed in BBQ sauce & topped with homemade coleslaw served on grilled Texas toast $8.25

Corned Beef Reuben
Corned beef piled high & topped with Swiss cheese, sauerkraut & Russian dressing on grilled marble rye bread $9.25

Bar-B-Q Chicken Sandwich*
Grilled boneless chicken breast topped with BBQ sauce, cheddar cheese & bacon served on a sesame seed bun $9.25

Mesquite Grilled Chicken Salad
Mesquite rubbed chicken breast diced and tossed with sundried tomatoes, carrots, red onions and celery in a Southwest mayonnaise and served on grilled flatbread with lettuce and tomatoes $8.50

Italian Panini
Italian deli meat stacked with banana pepper rings, tomatoes, red onions and Provolone cheese $8.95

*Cooked to order, consuming raw or undercooked meat, poultry, seafood, shellfish or eggs may increase your risk of foodborne illness.

BURGERS   All burgers are prepared from seasoned fresh ground round (80/20), served on a sesame seed bun with seasoned steak fries & a pickle

HOCKEYTOWN Hockeytown Burger* – OUR HOUSE SPECIALTY!
1/2 pound of seasoned fresh ground beef served with lettuce, tomato, red onions & your choice of cheese - American, cheddar, pepper jack, Swiss or Provolone $9.95
add your own toppings: bacon $1.00; bleu cheese $.75; sautéed mushrooms $.50, sautéed onion $.50

BBQ Smoke House Burger*
With apple-smoked Bacon, caramelized onions, BBQ sauce & smoked cheddar cheese $11.95

San Fran Melt*
1/2 pound burger melt with pepper jack cheese, sautéed red onions & a Dijon mayonnaise sauce served on grilled Texas toast $9.95

Double-Stacked Black Bean Burger
Two black bean patties each topped with pepper jack cheese served on a sesame seed bun with lettuce, tomato & red onions $9.95

Michigan Cherry Burger*
Our famous 1/2 pound burger topped with Traverse City cherries & Boursin cheese and served with lettuce, tomato and red onions $10.95

Quesadillas Burger*
1/2 pound burger served in a tortilla shell, smothered with roasted Poblano peppers and a Mexican blend of cheeses served with tomatoes, scallions, sour cream & salsa $10.95

ENTREES   All steaks, pastas & salmon are served with garlic bread

HOCKEYTOWN Sizzler Steak*
Grilled 8 oz. sizzler served with whiped potatos, seasonal mixed vegetables $15.95
Additional toppings: sautéed onions $.99 sautéed mushrooms $.99
bleu cheese crumbles $.99

Fettuccine Alfredo*
Fettuccine pasta tossed in a fresh Alfredo sauce $10.95   Add chicken $3.00

Pan-Seared Salmon*
Pan-seared Atlantic salmon served with a medley of vegetables, mashed potatoes & a lemon-dill cream sauce $16.95

Rustic Penne Pasta
Penne pasta tossed with sautéed sweet Italian sausage, zucchini, yellow squash, peppers and onions in a pesto sauce $11.95

BBQ Baby Back Ribs*
Slow-cooked baby back ribs brushed with our house-made BBQ sauce served with coleslaw & seasoned steak fries. Half Slab $10.95 Full Slab $18.95

Grilled Chicken Breast*
Grilled chicken breast topped with Provolone cheese and smothered with sautéed green peppers, onions and mushrooms served with mashed potatoes $10.95

HOMEMADE SOUPS

HOCKEYTOWN Chili   **French Onion Soup**   **Soup Du Jour**
$3.95 Cup $4.95 Bowl $2.95 Cup $3.95 Bowl
Add to chili:
cheddar cheese $.50;
onions $.50; sour cream $.50

*Cooked to order, consuming raw or undercooked meat, poultry, seafood, shellfish or eggs may increase your risk of foodborne illness.

FIGURE 7.2   *(Continued)*

FIGURE 7.3

Prices ending in "9" communicate that the operation is a bargain as does the bundling of the wing combos.

Source: Dick's Wings & Grill. Reprinted with permission.

a small amount of food per customer—the amount that the guest can eat in one sitting. A loss leader crowds out profitable purchases that the customer would have otherwise made.

That said, it is a common approach in certain kinds of restaurants to "bundle" food into value deals that encourage most people to spend more money than they otherwise would. Such bundling need not give customers a huge bargain; a small price break is normally sufficient to boost sales substantially. For example, if a fast-food operation sells a burger for $2.00, fries for $1.50, and a soda for $1.00, each customer would have to spend $4.50 to purchase all three separately. Some customers might decide to save $1.50 and not purchase the fries. However, by offering a package deal that allows customers to purchase the entire meal for a price of $4.25, the business appeals to customers' bargain-hunting sensibility to drives sales. The restaurant may increase total revenue enough to make more profit over a month than it does without the price break. Small bundling discounts often go a long way to increasing sales of food overall.

Value pricing can also increase profit when an operation offers multiple sizes of a given product. For example, in those operations offering small, medium, and large sizes of beverages, the largest size is always a better deal per ounce than the smaller size. This persuades the customer to spend a little more money for the larger size. While this arrangement might seem to cut into profits, the only additional cost on a larger-size beverage is the beverage (and cup) cost; the increase in labor and overhead is insignificant. Thus, if the operation can add $0.25 to the selling price of the drink while adding only $0.05 to the beverage cost, the business makes an additional $0.20 profit by selling the larger size. (It should be noted

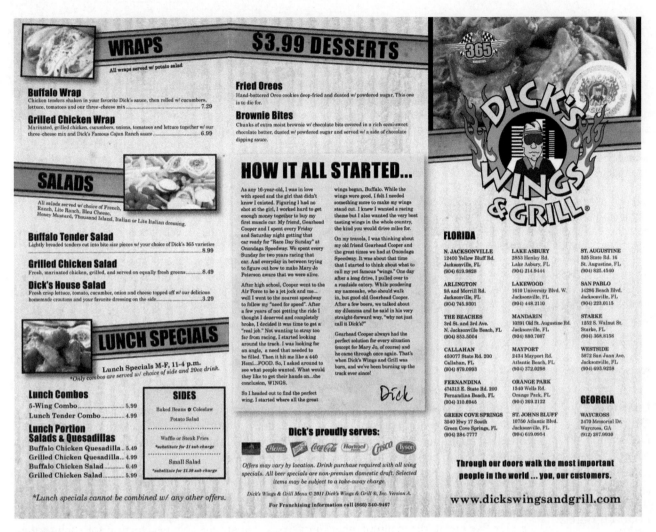

FIGURE 7.3 *(Continued)*

that this approach to upselling has become controversial in certain parts of the country as Americans battle with obesity. Consequently, there is an upper limit in most operations to the size of the product the market will tolerate when the largest size comes with an obscene number of calories.)

Finally, when trying to determine the exact selling price for a dish or drink, menu planners should keep in mind that for many customers there is a psychological price ceiling for a product. Above that point, sales will drop off dramatically. Thus, menu planners may only be able to set a price so high above a calculated sales price no matter how highly differentiated the product is. For example, a dry-aged 16-ounce cut of prime rib served in an elegant setting by tuxedoed servers might command a $40, $45, or even $50 sales price. However, at some point, guests will no longer tolerate a price increase. At $90, they will probably choose another entrée or go somewhere else to eat.

When the price ceiling for an item falls below the sales price calculated by the operation's standard pricing method, the menu planner has a particularly interesting challenge. Should the item be removed from the menu entirely? Not necessarily. A menu planner can leave the main item intact but reduce the food cost by substituting less expensive accompaniments; this approach works well, too, when a dish would otherwise fall well outside the price range for the menu's other dishes. Alternatively, if a specific menu item is the main draw for a large audience, the menu planner could leave that item's sales price artificially low (though still profitable) and increase the price for common add-ons (beverages, appetizers, sides, etc.) to make up the profit difference through sales of those other items. In short, there are few absolutes when it comes to setting a menu price, but the menu planner must always find a way to make the business profitable overall.

COMPREHENSIVE PRICING EXAMPLE CONTINUED

The earlier Comprehensive Pricing Example summary noted that the different pricing methods yielded four possible sales prices ranging from $7.27 to $8.73. How does the menu planner decide what price to put on the menu from this information?

First, the menu planner must know more about the restaurant's brand and the local competition than just these potential selling prices. In this particular case, the lunch-only restaurant offers fast and efficient table service. It caters to businesspeople who want a fast-casual meal for a reasonable price. They need service that can get them back to

the office in less than an hour, and this restaurant satisfies that need for them. The neighborhood includes many other restaurants serving sandwiches in the $7 to $8 range; many provide fast-casual service and sides with their sandwiches. Only two nearby operations include burgers on their menu. One is a fast food restaurant selling a burger and fries (no slaw) via counter service for $5.99; the other is an upscale steakhouse selling a much larger burger with fries and a mesclun salad in a leisurely environment for $18.

Given this information, the burger plate does not have a lot of direct

competition (due to differences in service styles), but it does have a good deal of indirect competition from the other sandwich operations. The restaurant can charge at least $7.50 for the burger as the table service differentiates it from fast food, but it cannot charge more than $8 without risking business lost to the other sandwich operations (with their $7 to $8 price range). With its fast-casual brand, the restaurant should stick with a price ending in "0" or "5." A price of $7.95 for the burger plate is appropriate. If there were more direct competition, $7.50 would be a better price.

Special Menu Pricing Situations

Learning Objective 4
Determine an appropriate sales price for buffet, prix fixe, table d'hôte, and noncommercial offerings.

While this chapter thus far has provided pricing strategies for the typical à la carte and semi à la carte menu, other types of menus may require a different approach. The adjustment is often minimal, but without at least a little tweaking, the menu planner may find that his menu prices do not cover all of the business's costs.

Prix Fixe　A prix fixe menu includes all of the courses on the menu for a single price. Typically, the customer has a limited selection for each menu category, but rarely do all of the options cost exactly the same per portion. When calculating an appropriate sales price for a prix fixe menu, the menu planner must first calculate the cost per portion for each of the menu choices. As with a Q factor calculation, the menu planner next determines the total cost to serve the entire menu if the guest orders the most expensive option for each course. For a new business, this sum becomes the food cost basis from which the sales price is derived. In an existing restaurant that is merely adjusting its menu prices, the menu planner may prefer to base the sales price on the average cost per person instead. The average cost per person is calculated by totaling the food costs for a month and then dividing by the number of guests that month. As long as the population continues to order the menu choices in the same proportions relative to each other, the average cost per guest will remain the same. Using the average rather than the maximum cost has both pros and cons. The average allows the restaurant to offer lower prices and thus to attract a larger audience. However, if the menu mix (percentage of each item sold) fluctuates and more people start ordering the most expensive options, the restaurant will lose money.

Example 7. 9: A prix fixe menu restaurant serves 1,230 guests in one month; the kitchen's food cost for that month is $26,000. If the menu planner uses a 27% food cost percentage and the standard food cost percentage pricing method, how much should the restaurant charge per person for the prix fixe menu?

$$\text{Average Food Cost per Guest} = \text{Total Cost} \div \text{Number of Guests}$$
$$= \$26,000 \div 1,230 \text{ guests} = \$21.14$$
$$\text{Sales Price} = \text{Food Cost} \div \text{Food Cost \%}$$
$$= \$21.14 \div 0.27 = \$78.30$$

Table d'Hôte   On a table d'hôte menu, the approach is similar to prix fixe pricing except that the menu planner can list different prices for each entrée choice. In this situation, the total cost per portion should be calculated using a Q factor in which the value of the Q factor is the sum of all the food costs per portion for all of the non-entrée courses. Thus, the Q factor might be the total cost per portion for the most expensive appetizer, soup, salad, bread, and dessert choices. This Q factor is then added to the cost per portion for each entrée choice. The sales price listed next to each entrée is calculated from the Q factor adjusted cost per portion for each entrée. Which sales price determination method to use still depends upon the menu planner's preference and the business concept.

Noncommercial Menus   A noncommercial operation, such as a corporate or school cafeteria, almost always uses the base price method for its menus. These businesses calculate a maximum food cost for their dishes and then adjust the recipes to fit the cost constraint. Often, the price that a noncommercial operation may charge for its food is set by the parent company (or by the government in the case of public schools). If the parent company subsidizes the foodservice business, that typically allows the menu planner to use a much higher food cost percentage than normal. In some instances, the cost of an entrée in a corporate cafeteria is set by the parent company, but other dishes, like dessert, are priced by the foodservice company. When this happens, the menu planner may use two different methods of pricing—a nonprofit base price approach for the entrées and a high-profit food cost percentage approach for the desserts.

Catering   In most restaurants, the sales prices on the menu must generate sufficient revenue to cover the food and beverage costs, labor, and overhead to run the business. Catering works differently. In most catering operations, the client pays separately for on-site staff. Rental equipment may be listed as an additional charge. In short, a catering menu typically works with a somewhat higher food cost percentage than a restaurant. The caterer effectively runs two revenue centers—one to cover the food cost, labor, and overhead of the office and commissary kitchen that preps the food and another to cover the cost of the front-of-the-house expenses, such as service staff, furniture, and linens. While the menu planner for a caterer may use a food cost percentage or prime cost approach to calculating sales prices, their percentages or factors are different from those typically used in a restaurant. Rarely would a caterer use a gross profit pricing strategy, as the number of customers served by a caterer will fluctuate significantly and unpredictably from week to week.

Buffets   Pricing a buffet is perhaps the most difficult challenge in all menu price planning. While most businesses derive their food cost per portion from a portion-controlled, standard recipe, buffets have no portion control at all. In an all-you-can-eat buffet, guests may continue to consume food until they can stuff no more into their mouths. Even a single-trip buffet cannot control how high the guest piles food onto the plate. And how is a menu planner to account for the fact that one customer may fill up on rice while another may choose to mound his plate with piles of lobster and crab? In a new establishment with no sales history, the menu planner must make a best guess based on how much of each dish he thinks the average customer will consume. He may need to factor in some loss from guests taking extra food that is left on their plates and additional food that never leaves the steam table but cannot be reused the following meal. The guess may be way off, but after a few days, the menu planner will have the historical data he needs to make an accurate sales price determination. With some history, the menu planner can calculate the total cost of food used each day or week, including any food that must be thrown out after the buffet is over. With this total food cost and the total customer count, the menu planner can calculate an average food cost per guest. The average food cost per guest = total food cost ÷ number of customers over the same period of time (just as with the prix fixe menu approach). This average food cost per guest should be the food cost basis from which the menu planner derives an appropriate sales price using one of the aforementioned pricing methods.

Summary

The purpose of employing a menu pricing technique is to generate preliminary sales prices within a price range that appeals to the target market while maintaining the business's profitability. The overhead-contribution and Texas Restaurant Association (TRA) methods are examples of food cost percentage pricing strategies. The prime cost and actual pricing methods factor the direct labor cost to produce a given dish into that dish's sales price. The gross profit method adds the same amount to each item's food cost to ensure that each guest contributes equally toward overhead expenses. Of course, a menu planner can always start with the menu price first, using the base price method, and work backward to create food cost parameters for each dish. While matching competitors' prices is a legitimate approach to menu pricing, it can carry additional risk unless paired with another pricing strategy. The preliminary menu prices generated from a menu pricing strategy should be further modified to account for competition, price sensitivity, perceived value, and product differentiation for the menu item and the business concept. Menu prices are next adjusted to make them psychologically comfortable for the guest. The ending digits in the price reflect the brand and image that the restaurant wishes to communicate to the guest. Package bundling and price ceilings may be taken into account as well. Alternate approaches to pricing may be required for prix fixe, table d'hôte, noncommercial, catering, and buffet menus to ensure that they are based on the proper food cost per portion.

Comprehension Questions

1. Using the food cost percentage pricing method and a food cost percentage of 32%, what is the preliminary sales price for a dish with a cost per portion of $1.36?

2. A restaurant's annual budget calls for $972,500 in overhead expenses, $1,634,000 in sales, and $88,000 in profit. Using the overhead-contribution method, calculate the preliminary menu price for a dish with a cost per portion of $3.62.

3. A restaurant uses the TRA pricing method. Overhead expenses represent 62% of total sales. If management decides that appetizers should return a 15% profit, what is the preliminary sales price for an appetizer with a cost per portion of $1.14?

4. Define the term "prime cost."

5. A café uses the prime cost pricing method and a price factor of 3.25. What is the preliminary menu price for a dish in this café with a food cost per portion of $1.68 and a direct labor cost of $0.22?

6. In a restaurant that uses the actual pricing method, variable costs (excluding direct labor cost) represent 24% of sales. Fixed costs are 37% of sales, and profit is targeted to be 5% of sales. What is the preliminary selling price for a dessert with a food cost of $1.10 and a direct labor cost of $0.67?

7. A coffee shop sees an average of 430 customers daily and budgets for an average of $650 in labor and overhead expenses daily. The owner wants to earn at least $50 profit daily. Using the gross profit pricing method, what is the preliminary menu price for a cappuccino with a cost per portion of $0.37?

8. Using the base price method and a food cost percentage of 35%, what is the maximum food cost that a chef may run for a dish with a sales price of $5.00?

9. Why is matching competitors' prices considered a risky pricing strategy?

10. List four factors that impact how much flexibility a menu planner has in adjusting preliminary menu prices.

11. A menu planner calculates a preliminary menu price of $9.94. What psychologically comfortable price should he list on the menu for a bargain-brand concept? What price should he list for a luxury establishment?

12. A roadside restaurant offers an all-you-can-eat buffet. Each month, the business averages 3,500 customers and runs a monthly food cost of $7,350. If the menu planner uses the food cost percentage pricing method and a food cost percentage of 36%, how much should the restaurant charge per person to eat from the buffet (preliminary menu price)? What price might the menu planner write on the menu if he wants to communicate "value" without seeming "cheap"?

Discussion Questions

1. The chapter states that to avoid a wide range of menu prices, the menu planner may go back to adjust recipes so that their preliminary sales prices fall within a narrower range. Why wouldn't a menu planner simply leave the recipes alone and just raise the lowest sales prices and drop the highest sales prices to narrow the final price range?

2. Describe the foodservice business concept you would open tomorrow, if you could. What pricing strategy listed in the chapter would you use? Why?

3. Typically, the base price method is used in fast-food and noncommercial operations. When might a midlevel or upscale restaurant use a base price approach?

4. Matching competitors' prices can be risky, but there is a benefit to factoring competitor pricing into one's own pricing structure. What is the risk of ignoring competitor pricing entirely when calculating menu prices?

5. Imagine that you wish to open a café on a strip that already has several restaurants offering relatively inexpensive café menus. What might you do to allow your operation to charge more and still attract customers? Provide at least four specific examples.

6. The chapter suggests that menu prices should end in 0, 5, or 9. Can you think of an example of a foodservice operation you have visited that does not follow this approach? What is your perception of the business and its pricing structure?

7. The chapter discussed value bundling of foods by referencing a typical fast-food model. Describe a situation (experienced or theoretical) where bundling could be applied to a midlevel or even upscale restaurant.

Case Study

An upscale destination restaurant in a small, historic town has very little competition and lots of business from customers looking for a romantic getaway. The chart that follows provides a snapshot of some of the business's financials over the course of the past year.

Number of customers	80/day, 29,200 annually	
Average check	$94.70	
Total sales	$2,765,000	100%
Total overhead	$1,885,000	68.2%
– Fixed costs	$632,000	22.9%
– Direct labor costs	$647,700	23.4%
– Other variable costs	$605,300	21.9%
Food and beverage costs	$688,500	24.9%
Profit	$191,500	6.9%

The restaurant aims for a beverage cost percentage of 22.0% and a food cost percentage of 27.5%. The chef would like to add a new dish to the menu—Duck Breast with Apples and Foie Gras, Sauternes Demiglace, Maple-Hubbard Squash Puree, Wilted Spinach, Rainbow Beet Confetti. The true cost per portion for this dish is $10.37. The direct labor cost for the dish is $5.12.

Using three different approaches, calculate preliminary sales prices for the dish. What sales price would you write on the menu and why? If the chef wanted to create a four-course prix fixe menu option, what information would you recommend he consider when determining the prix fixe menu items and the sales price for the prix fixe menu?

Capstone Project

Step 7: Using the completed recipe costing sheets from step 6, calculate preliminary sales prices for each of the costed dishes and beverages. Write a paragraph describing your selected pricing approach and your rationale for using that approach. Describe what type of psychological pricing strategy makes the most sense for your business concept and what level of competition you anticipate for your business. Finally, write your planned menu selling prices next to the corresponding dishes and beverages on your menu. For the remaining items on your menu, make up sales prices (as those items have not been costed), but keep the prices within a similar range to those items that were properly costed. Recognize that in the real world, the menu planner would cost all recipes, not just a select few.

CHAPTER 8
Menu Copy

INTRODUCTION

When customers arrive at a foodservice establishment, they do not necessarily know what they want to eat and drink. What they crave, consciously or subconsciously, is direction from the operation. For most restaurants, this requires an informative and persuasive menu.

Menus are the primary communication vehicle for almost every restaurant. They must address the questions that most customers have about the establishment. These questions go beyond "What is there to eat?" Guests wish to know how a dish is prepared, what the accompaniments are to an entrée, whether the food contains potential allergens, and many other bits of information. The simplest way to ensure that a customer has a positive experience at a restaurant is to provide her with the information she requires to order the food that will best meet her needs.

Menus must serve the needs of the business as well. A well-written menu operates as a marketing tool. It encourages sales of certain dishes and persuades customers to order more than just a single inexpensive entrée. *Menu copy* is the language or wording that appears on a menu; it encompasses both *descriptive copy*, which describes the menu items, and *institutional* or *boilerplate copy*, which provides the other information on a menu beyond descriptive copy. An effective foodservice business uses descriptive copy to both communicate information and influence customer decisions. As with menu item selection and pricing, menu item descriptions should appeal to the target market and underscore the operation's brand. As the typically brief menu descriptions for beverages were described in Chapter 5, this chapter will focus on menu copy for food items.

CHAPTER 8 LEARNING OBJECTIVES

As a result of successfully completing this chapter, readers will be able to:

1. Describe how a business's concept impacts the length of its menu copy.

2. Write descriptive copy that accurately communicates key information to a customer.

3. List the truth-in-menu representation categories and write a menu item description that adheres to the truth-in-menu standards.

4. Write descriptive copy that sells that dish persuasively.

5. List several uses for text on a menu beyond describing menu items.

CHAPTER 8 OUTLINE

160

Descriptive Copy That Communicates Information

Learning Objective 1
Describe how a business's concept impacts the length of its menu copy.

When writing descriptive copy for a given menu item, the menu planner must first consider the restaurant's concept and brand as well as the target market. The writing style must be appropriate for both. If the business is a quick-service operation in which customers can have lunch in less than thirty minutes, then the menu copy must be streamlined and easy to read. On the other hand, an upscale restaurant where diners expect to spend over two hours eating can provide lengthier menu descriptions.

Tone is as important as length to generate menu and audience alignment. A straightforward, no-nonsense operation that serves "serious" food to knowledgeable foodies may prefer descriptive copy that lists ingredients and cooking techniques with little embellishment. A casual establishment that stresses theme over food may emphasize that theme in its menu descriptions. For example, a sports bar may use sports terminology in the menu copy. A barbecue shack may incorporate country phrases or terminology. There is no one correct way to describe a dish, but the descriptive copy should match the style of the restaurant.

Example 8.1 illustrates how the same dish can be described in several ways to fit a restaurant's theme. Note that menu planners may locate the dish's name above the menu item description, to the left of the description, or embedded within the description. Separate titles for a dish make ordering easier, especially if there are multiple dishes with the same main ingredients—two chicken entrées, for example—but brief titles may cause the guest to skip over a more thorough and appealing description of the dish.

Example 8. 1: For a single dish, write three menu item descriptions for three different types of operations.

Concept 1: Upscale modern American restaurant with a straightforward approach to menu descriptions.

> *Hickory smoked **baby back ribs**, brown sugar–Maker's Mark glaze, maple-bacon baked flageolets, garlic-Tabasco collards*

Concept 2: A casual barbecue establishment that strives to make city folk feel like they're dining outdoors in the country.

> ***Cookie's Baby Back Pork Ribs***
>
> *Slow smoked over hickory and glazed with our brown sugar–bourbon barbecue sauce, these are the best dang baby backs this side of the Mississippi. Served with our chuck wagon baked beans and spicy stewed greens.*

Concept 3: A sports bar that incorporates sports into everything it does.

> ***End Zone Ribs**—Score seven ribs with this half rack of tender, smoked baby backs topped with our sweet and tangy end zone barbecue sauce. Don't pass up the sides of slow-cooked baked beans and collards. No penalty for excessive celebration.*

The descriptive copy should only use words that the majority of the target market is likely to know and to appreciate. For example, an upscale French restaurant serving the culinary cognoscenti can incorporate French terms in its menu copy in ways that a simple French café serving the local lunch crowd cannot. In an upscale restaurant, the menu planner may assume that most guests will understand and appreciate French culinary terms that describe a classic dish. In a casual café, diners rarely care about fancy terminology; they merely want to know what's in the dish they're ordering. Less familiar culinary jargon is more common in ethnic or upscale restaurants than it is in other types of foodservice operations.

Finally, while the wording used in menu copy can elicit an expectation of a certain level of quality, a spelling or other typographical error can instantly deflate those expectations. Top-notch restaurants do not communicate "flawless execution" when they cannot spell properly. Headings that are italicized or bold-faced must be consistently so. Multiple proofreaders should review all grammar, syntax, and punctuation to ensure that everything is written correctly before the menus are printed and distributed to the public. Sometimes, a spelling or grammatical error is included intentionally to go with a certain theme, but then the "poor writing" theme should be consistently used throughout the menu and obviously deliberate to the reader. In most cases, writing errors will make a guest feel that she is overpaying for anything but a cheap dining experience. After all, which sounds like it should command a higher price: "Shrimp and Salmon in a Lemongrass-Shiitake Broth" or "Shrimps and Slamon in a Lemongrass*Shitake Broth"?

Communicating the Facts

Learning Objective 2
Write descriptive copy that accurately communicates key information to a customer.

While the writing style and word choice for descriptive copy communicates the theme or brand of a restaurant, menu descriptions also express factual data about the dishes they describe. Guests inevitably have certain questions they wish to have answered in order to make an informed choice from a menu. If the menu planner omits that key information from a dish's description, a customer is less likely to select that option from the menu.

Perhaps the most important data to include in descriptive copy is the key ingredients for the dish. Beyond the dish's main components, menu planners should list ingredients that significantly impact the flavor. Guests with a distaste for certain flavors do not wish to be surprised by that flavor dominating a dish. Similarly, menu planners should list common allergens or dietary red flags that are otherwise hidden in a dish. For example, a customer with a dairy allergy will likely know that pasta Alfredo includes dairy, but if a bean soup is finished with sour cream, the customer will assume that the dish contains no dairy unless the menu states otherwise. Ingredients such as anchovies or shrimp paste in an otherwise vegetarian dish should be noted in the menu description so as not to mislead a vegetarian. If a chef uses a particularly rare or expensive ingredient, she should highlight that in the menu description to help sell the dish.

In addition to ingredients, guests typically want to know other facts about menu items, including accompaniments, portion size, and cooking technique. If the dish offers something special in terms of product quality, origin, nutritional value, or presentation, that should be noted in the descriptive copy as well. In short, guests do not want to be confused or misled by product descriptions. Menu item descriptions elicit images and expectations in a guest's mind. When the actual dish clashes with that expectation, the guest is likely to be disappointed. For example, a customer trying to watch her weight might choose a dish described as "lemon-scented salmon with cauliflower and rice" with the assumption that the dish will be low-fat and healthy. Her expectation will be shattered if the salmon arrives swimming in a lemon-honey glaze with a side of cauliflower tempura and fried rice. While the dish might taste delicious, it does not meet this guest's needs. A little more clarity in the descriptive copy in terms of cooking technique would address this problem.

Truth in Menus

Learning Objective 3
List the truth-in-menu representation categories and write a menu item description that adheres to the truth-in-menu standards.

While a poorly written menu description may confuse the guest, such an action is not illegal. However, lying on a menu constitutes false advertising and is illegal. Many localities have laws against false advertising, and some specifically address misleading language on menus. The National Restaurant Association outlines eleven areas for which menu planners should be extremely accurate so as not to engage in false advertising. These eleven categories are collectively referred to as the "truth-in-menu" or "accuracy-in-menu" representations, and menu planners should avoid violating these guidelines at all costs.

When the public or the government discovers a truth-in-menu violation, the result can be as minimal as a fine or as severe as customer loss of faith in the business's honesty and ethics, particularly once the news of the fraud gets out on the Internet and into the media. Guests want to get what they pay for. If they learn that a business lies about one product, they will assume that it misrepresents other products as well. To ease their concern about possibly being fleeced, many customers will spend their money elsewhere. Under the best circumstances, the business loses revenue and profit while it tries to win back customers; in other cases, the business loses so much money that it must close. The truth-in-menu categories are as follows:

WOODBERRY KITCHEN ⬡

FRIENDS AROUND THE TABLE　Woodberry Kitchen relies on long-standing relationships with the growers of the Chesapeake to provide the ingredients that nourish and delight our guests. At our table, you join us in supporting thoughtful agriculture that respects the abundance and traditions of the region while helping to ensure its future.

"IF YOU'RE AFTER GETTING THE HONEY / THEN YOU DON'T GO KILLING ALL THE BEES."
— *Joe Strummer*

SNACKS

One Straw Farm Popcorn　*Trickling Springs butter, J.Q. Dickinson salt, Snake Oil*	
Deviled Eggs　*Chipped ham, fish pepper*	
Smoked Rockfish Dip　*Spelt crackers*	
Onion Dip　*Potato chips*	
Kitchen Pickles	
Black Bean Dip　*Garlic oil, benne seed, herb, fish pepper, flatbread*	

CHESAPEAKE OYSTERS

Iced, on the Half Shell　*Mignonettes, cocktail, snake oil*　　18.
　　War Shores　*Medium brine, plump, vegetal finish, from Onancock, VA*
　　WK Strikers　*Sweet, medium brine, from Great Wicomico River, VA*
　　Rappicos　*Salty, medium brine, deep cup from Great Rappahannock River, VA*
　　Nassawadox Salts　*Salty bay oyster, from Nassawadox Creek, VA*
　　Battle Creeks　*Full ocean brine, plump, medium size oyster, from Tom's Cove, VA*
　　Shooting Points　*Full ocean brine, larger oyster, from Hog Island, VA*
Wood Roasted　　17.
　　Mason-Dixon　*Snake Oil, Trickling Springs butter*
　　Voyager　*Madeira cream, browned onions, city ham*
　　Bull Roast　*Fried short rib, sour cream, pickled peppers*
　　Gilded　*Crab imperial*

SOUPS & WARM PLATES

Woodberry Pantry Tomato Soup　*Adorable grilled cheese*	11.
Heirloom Squash Soup　*Toasted marshmallow, toasted pecans*	12.
Rockfish Collar Out of the Oven　*Charred cabbage, fish pepper honey, peanut romesco*	12.
Fried Oyster & Seaweed Noodles　*Egg yolk, 'Batch 13', city ham*	14.
Cabbage Wedge Out of the Oven　*Ginger dressing, radish, garlic & peanut granola, cilantro, benne miso*	14.
Slow Cooked Rabbit & Rigatoni　*Roasted mushroom, corn, mustard dressing*	16.
Tilghman Island Crab Pot　*Lump crab, house quark, fish pepper, toasts*	17.
Meatballs Out of the Oven　*Tomato sauce, whipped ricotta, toast*	16.
Fried Yellow Perch　*Carnival squash cilantro, mint, benne, garlic, sorghum dressing, peanuts*	12.
Seamless Ricotta Ravioli　*Lamb sausage, 'Batch 13', soft herbs*	16.

SUPPER

Winter Vegetable Pot Pie　*Celery root, parsnips, squash, whole wheat top*	24.
Wood Roasted Sweet Potato　*Carrots, radish, turnips, fried sunchoke, pepper sauce, miso, herbs*	20.
Cast Iron Chicken & Biscuit　*Buttered cabbage, carrot, herb pan sauce, honey butter*	28.
Middleneck Clams & Noodles　*City ham, garlic scapes, pepper flake, bread crumbs, herbs*	25.
PA Farmed Trout　*Carnival squash, sweet potato, smoked trout, celery root, apple, scaper herb butter*	31.
MD Rockfish Out of the Oven　*Carolina gold rice, fish pepper, MD crab, ham, put-up tomato dressing*	34.
Tavern Steak　*Fingerling sweet potatoes, beets, turnips, shallots, hunter sauce*	34.
Cape May, NJ Scallops　*Rye-sotto, mushrooms, put-up corn, ramp-peanut pesto, soft herbs, black garlic*	35.
14-oz. Ribeye　*Potato & cheddar gratin, WK steak sauce*	48.
Alsatian Sauerkraut　*Potatoes, apples, weiswurst, kielbasa, toulose, blood sausage, mustard cream*	32.

A side of...　　Buttered Cabbage　*Bacon* 7.　　　　　Potato & Cheddar Gratin 7.
　　　　Acorn Squash Out of the Oven　*Fish pepper honey* 7.

Consuming raw or partially cooked meats, poultry, seafood, shellfish, eggs or cheese may increase your risk of food borne illness.

FLATBREADS

Tomato Sauce　*'Caputo Bros.' melting curds, cheddar*	14.
Sweet Potato Flatbread　*Roasted garlic, brown onion, 'Allegheny', rosemary, honey*	14.
MD Blue Crab　*Cheddar, fish pepper, sweet potato, farm egg, herbs*	18.
Smoked Chicken　*Onion, put-up peaches, cheddar, salsa verde*	15.
Croque Monsieur　*Mustard cream, cheddar, pickled mustard seed, city ham*	15.
Lamb Sausage　*Sauerkraut, goldrush apples, Mountaineer*	15.
Slow Roasted Pork　*Barbecue sauce, Hawk's Hill cheddar, red onion*	15.

SALADS & COLD PLATES

Various Beets　*Apple butter, pickled mustard seed, pickled beets, rocket*	13.
Adolescent Greens　*Keys to the car, broken curfew*	13.
Kilt Kale　*Warm bacon dressing, shallot, 'Allegheny', cremini mushrooms*	14.
Goldrush Apple Salad　*'Monocacy Ash' dressing, radish, romaine, fried onion*	14.
Fried Oyster Chopped Salad　*Onion, cheddar, chipped ham, spicy ranch*	17.
Winter Vegetables　*Parsnip, radishes, beets, apple, sweet potato miso, benne*	15.
All Kale Caesar!　*Oy-chovie dressing, 'Allegheny', torn bread*	15.
Stretched to Order Mozzarella　*Wheatberries, put-up tomato jam, bread crumbs*	16.
Spicy Cheese on Toast　*Lebanon bologna, pickles, radish*	13.
Chicken Liver Spread　*Adorable toasts, blackberry jam*	12.
Raw Beef　*Verjus, J.Q. Dickinson salt, shallot, jalapeño mayonnaise, chips*	14.
Rainbow Chard　*Wood roasted parsnip, pickled green tomato, black garlic dressing, benne seed, fried sunchoke*	13.

CHEESE & CRACKERS

Farmstead Cheeses:　　16.
　　Cherry Glen 'Monocacy Ash'　*Quince paste; Boyds, MD*
　　Meadow Creek 'Appalachian'　*Toasted pecan butter; Galax, VA*
　　Doe Run 'St. Malachi'　*Blackberry jam; Coatesville, PA*

Our growers include: NEXT STEP ORGANICS, STEADFAST FARM, GREAT KIDS FARM, ONE STRAW FARM, COTTINGHAM FARM, REID'S ORCHARD, BLACK ROCK ORCHARD, DISTILLERY LANE CIDER WORKS, WHISTLE PIG HOLLOW, LIBERTY DELIGHT FARMS, SUNNYSIDE FARM, MANY ROCKS FARM, TUSCARORA ORGANIC GROWERS, TRICKLING SPRINGS CREAMERY, RETTLAND FARM, NEW MORNING FARM, BEILER'S HERITAGE ACRES, KNOPP'S FARM, SIDE BY SIDE FARM, WHITMORE FARM, BIG CITY FARMS, REAL FOOD FARM, MOON VALLEY FARM, HELP FROM ABOVE FARM, SASSAFRAS CREEK FARM, RICHFIELD FARM, PINE GROVE FARM, WILLOWDALE FARM, TOMATOES ETC. PRODUCE FARM, KARMA FARM, ZAHRADKA FARM, OAK SPRING FARM, LITTLE GUNPOWDER FARM *MD & PA Cheesemakers:* SHEPHERD'S MANOR CREAMERY, FIREFLY FARMS, HIDDEN HILLS DAIRY, HAWKS HILL CREAMERY, CAPUTO BROTHERS, CHERRY GLEN GOAT CHEESE CO., CHAPEL'S COUNTRY CREAMERY, P.A. BOWEN FARMSTEAD, MEADOW CREEK DAIRY, OTTERBEIN ACRES, CHARLOTTETOWN FARM, KESWICK CREAMERY: *Fresh, local, sustainable fish & shellfish:* WALTON SEAFOOD, RAPPAHANNOCK RIVER, THE GREAT WICOMICO OYSTER CO., WAR SHORE OYSTER CO., SHOOTING POINT OYSTER FARM, BARREN ISLAND, & TONY CONRAD

BRUNCH
10 a.m. to 2 p.m.
SATURDAY & SUNDAY

Spike & Amy Gjerde *Proprietors*

FIGURE 8.1

This restaurant uses ingredient-only descriptions to communicate a focus on quality food made from local ingredients. The listing of growers and suppliers reinforces that message.

Printed here courtesy of Woodberry Kitchen, Baltimore, MD

Quantity　When a menu states or implies a certain size or portion of food, the food provided to the guest must match that size. Thus, if a dish advertises "6 colossal shrimp," there must be six shrimp, all of a size that qualifies as colossal. "Extra large" portions must be larger than the standard portion size for a menu item. The biggest challenge for meeting the quantity requirement has to do with the weight of cooked foods. While it is easy to measure a sandwich with 4 ounces of sliced turkey breast, many entrées advertise a precooked weight for their meats and poultry. Unfortunately, a raw 12-ounce steak does not weigh 12 ounces after it is cooked to medium rare, and a well-done steak will weigh even less. The best way to accurately represent portion size on a menu for steaks, chops, and similar cuts is with a sentence somewhere on the menu stating that the measurements listed are for precooked weight. Those dishes for which this note is relevant can have an asterisk directing the customer to the clarifying statement.

Quality   While a menu planner may describe a dish as "outstanding" or "excellent," she must take care that industry terms with specific definitions are only used when they accurately describe the food being served. For example, beef can earn a grade of USDA prime, choice, or select (among others). If a menu calls its steak "prime," it cannot serve another grade of beef. (Note that prime rib refers to the cut, not to the quality grade.) Similarly, when a restaurant advertises grade AA eggs, the kitchen cannot serve grade A eggs. A menu planner should use terms that are not legally defined for the industry when she wishes to suggest that the food is of high quality but knows that the chef uses ingredients of varying or lower quality.

Price   The price listed on a menu is the price that the restaurant must charge. Any additional charges must be communicated to the customer. Common examples are "blue cheese dressing −$0.25 extra" and "add $0.50 for each additional pizza topping." Clubs or lounges must list cover charges or drink minimums if they are going to charge them to customers. Additionally, automatic service charges must be stated, such as "18% gratuity will be added to the bill of parties of 5 or more." In short, hidden fees may not appear on the bill without warning.

Brand Names   Major food companies have an interest in promoting and supporting their brand. Some invest millions of dollars in creating their brand, and they do not want it undermined by a sloppily run restaurant. Thus, if a menu or server suggests that one brand is being served, the restaurant may not substitute another brand. Examples of violations include filling bottles labeled Heinz with generic ketchup or listing Absolut in a drink description but using another brand instead. This is the reason that a customer may ask for "Coke" and hear the server reply, "Is Pepsi OK?" Were the server to simply nod and bring a glass of Pepsi, she would effectively imply that Coke is available for sale when it is not. The two colas are not interchangeable. These two soft drink powerhouses thrive by promoting brand loyalty and emphasizing the differences between the two brands. Offering a product that is substandard (and each believes the other's is substandard) under a different brand name undermines both products' brands. Brand-name food companies know this, and they sue for financial damages when they find a violation. When a brand name is listed on a menu or stated by a server (or customer), then that exact brand must be used.

Product Identification   When an ingredient is listed on a menu, that same ingredient must be used in the execution of the dish. This might seem obvious, but some restaurants regularly make substitutions without notifying customers. Substitutions may be necessary due to delivery shortages or price fluctuations, but customers have a right to know about the change. Often, an unethical chef believes that customers will not notice the difference. After all, what is the difference between a flounder and a Dover sole fillet? From the guest's perspective, about $30. If these two fish were fried and covered with a spicy remoulade, most guests would not be able to tell the difference, but then they should not pay for the higher-priced Dover sole only to get flounder. A switch from canola oil to peanut oil can cause an allergic reaction in guests who read a menu description as peanut-free. Allergic reactions can trigger not only a hospital visit but a successful lawsuit against the offending company. When substitutions are required, guests should be notified so that they can decide whether the change is acceptable to them.

Point of Origin   It is trendy in restaurants today to list the source of a dish's ingredients. In fact, some guests willingly pay a premium to support local farms through restaurant purchases. If a menu states that an ingredient comes from a specific place, then it must come from that source. An ingredient's source is easy to verify on case labels, packing slips, or invoices (both by a chef and by a lawsuit-happy customer). If the point of origin for a dish is likely to vary, the menu planner should consider alternatives to listing the source on the menu. Servers, chalkboards, and paper menu inserts all allow for daily information changes in ways that a printed menu may not. Of course, menu planners must also be able to distinguish between a point of origin and a place name that is simply the name of that food. For example, Maine oysters must come from Maine, but Manhattan clam chowder does not need to be made in Manhattan (or using Manhattan clams). The chowder is simply the name of a preparation style, just as French fries need not come from France. A menu planner must know the difference in order to ensure that she does not inadvertently list a point of origin for an ingredient that comes from somewhere else.

Merchandising Terms   Menu planners sometimes use terms to make their food seem better. Some are obviously exaggerations or opinions, such as "The Best Crab Cakes in Town." Called *puffery*, these claims which no reasonable person would interpret literally, need not be 100% accurate; for example, a "mile-high" cake should be tall but not literally one mile high. Other terms are easy to verify and should be accurate. "Made fresh daily" or "baked in-house" are merchandising phrases that help to sell products, but they must describe the product accurately. Bread that is "baked in-house" cannot be brought in fully baked from another source. "Made fresh daily" suggests that leftovers from the day before are not sold. The easiest way to determine whether a merchandising term must be accurate is to ask various people what a given term means to them. If they believe it is meant literally, then it must accurately describe the food being served.

Preservation   When an ingredient is listed in a menu description as having undergone (or not undergone) a method of preservation, then the ingredient used must match that description. For example, if pancakes come with "fresh strawberries," then canned strawberries are not an acceptable substitute. A chef cannot serve a wet-aged steak for one advertised on the menu as "dry aged." Terms such as fresh, frozen, canned, dehydrated, jarred, or bottled must accurately represent the foods being served.

Food Preparation   The words used to describe most cooking techniques have specific definitions. Steaming and boiling are not the same, so they should not be treated as interchangeable. If a menu describes broccoli as steamed, then boiled broccoli is not an acceptable substitute. Grilling and broiling are often similarly misstated on menus. A broiled steak should not be listed as a grilled steak simply because grilling is trendier and sounds better. In short, the cooking technique used in the kitchen must match the technique described on the menu.

Verbal and Visual Presentation   This category extends all of the aforementioned truth-in-menu guidelines to pictures and spoken words used in a restaurant. Just because a picture illustrating an eight-piece shrimp cocktail does not use the words "8 shrimp" does not exonerate the restaurant from serving only five shrimp. If a menu or menu board uses illustrations, those pictures must match the visual appearance of that dish when it comes out of the kitchen. Small variations, such as a slightly askew plate presentation, are acceptable, but obvious changes, such as the omission of a pickle or a different type of bread on a sandwich, are not. Words spoken by a server carry equal weight to the printed word or visual illustrations on a menu. Thus, if a server calls it butter, then butter must be served. When a guest asks whether a dish contains peanuts, the server's answer is effectively the restaurant's official answer. If the server does not know, she should find out before responding. A guest with a peanut allergy will likely sue a restaurant for passing off a dish as peanut-free when it contains peanuts. That the server made an error in describing the dish does not automatically excuse the business owners from liability in the lawsuit.

Dietary and Nutritional Claims   Dietary and nutritional claims are probably the least-used representations on menus because they present many potential pitfalls. While some chefs may think of terms such as "higher in fiber," "low fat," and "low sodium" as relative concepts based on one's sense of how food is typically prepared, these are actually highly technical and well-defined terms that have legal definitions. "Low fat," for example, is defined by the U.S. Food and Drug Administration (FDA) as "3 g or less per 100 g and not more than 30% of calories from fat."[1] Current definitions for FDA-regulated dietary and nutritional claims are available on the FDA's Food Labeling Guide web page, which may be accessed via the FDA's homepage at http://www.fda.gov. The other challenge with a dietary claim is measuring the accuracy of the claim in comparison to the food being prepared. For example, while a chain of restaurants may use strict standards to measure each ingredient in a recipe, single-unit operations may be somewhat more flexible with their employees. Allowing the line cooks to determine exactly how much butter or oil to use to sauté each dish can throw off an otherwise carefully calculated claim that the dish is low-fat. When nutritional claims are made on a menu for a specific dish, that dish must be executed exactly as described in the standard recipe. If someone were to send a random dish to a laboratory for analysis, the results must confirm that the dish meets the advertised nutritional requirements. While third-party laboratory analysis of a restaurant's food may seem unlikely now, such analysis will become more common in the near future. Per the federal 2010 health care law, chain restaurants nationwide with twenty or more outlets under the same brand name must post certain nutritional information in their restaurants. Enforcement of this federal regulation will not take effect until one year after the FDA has released its final rules on this segment of the law, but once in effect, the federal law will supersede local regulations on the subject. Every claim listed on a menu must be justifiable and provable if the restaurant is to avoid legal repercussions. Compliance requires standard recipes, strict recipe execution and portion control, and nutritional recipe analysis software or laboratory analysis for all chain restaurants to ensure that what gets printed on the menu matches what is served to guests.

For non-chain restaurants, the best approach to use when making a nutritional claim is to define the term on the menu. Some menus do this with little logos, such as hearts next to dishes that are heart healthy, and define the logo just once at the bottom of the menu. Others write the numerical nutritional information for each dish below the menu description. This approach tends to work better than using legally defined terminology, as most guests could not define those terms anyway. Symbols may also be used to highlight an endorsement rather than a specific dietary claim. For example, if a restaurant partners with the local diabetes association, it could highlight those dishes that have been approved by the association as "diabetic friendly." Such an approach allows the association (not the restaurant) to provide the dietary expertise while freeing customers from translating nutritional jargon on the menu. However, once a dietary claim goes into print on a menu, the operation must be able to prove the claim and the cooks must follow exactly the recipe that supports the claim.

Other legally defined terms may also appear on restaurant menus. "Organic," for example, is a legally defined term, and menu planners should not use it unless they can prove that a dish or ingredient meets the legal standard. Information on the USDA's "organic" certification program can be found by an "organic food" word search on the USDA's Food and Nutrition Information Center (FNIC) home page at https://fnic.nal.usda.gov. Another legally defined term, "grass fed," requires that "animals be fed only grass and forage with the exception of milk consumed prior to weaning. Animals certified under this program cannot be fed grain or grain by-products and must have continuous access to pasture during the growing season."[2] In 2015 and 2016, the FDA opened to the public a comment period on whether and how to define the term "natural"; food service operations may need to alter how they use the word "natural" in the future. For those operations that want to highlight the provenance of their ingredients, the better approach is simply to list the farms from which the ingredients come. If the farms are organic, customers for whom that is important will likely recognize the names of the farms. Other customers may simply assume that the farms produce high-quality ingredients—otherwise, why list them by name, right? Using legally defined terms can help a restaurant attract a certain customer base, but unless the menu planner can document compliance with the legal standards, those terms are best avoided.

Selling the Product

Learning Objective 4
Write descriptive copy that sells that dish persuasively.

While descriptive copy must communicate accurate information to the customer about what to expect from a dish, menu item descriptions serve a second purpose—selling the product to the guest. Some operations prefer to have their servers handle the sales pitch on menu items, but doing so leaves significant opportunity for error and loss of managerial control. An overwhelmed server may not take the time to push appetizers, desserts, or specialty beverages. While most customers will still order an entrée, the loss of

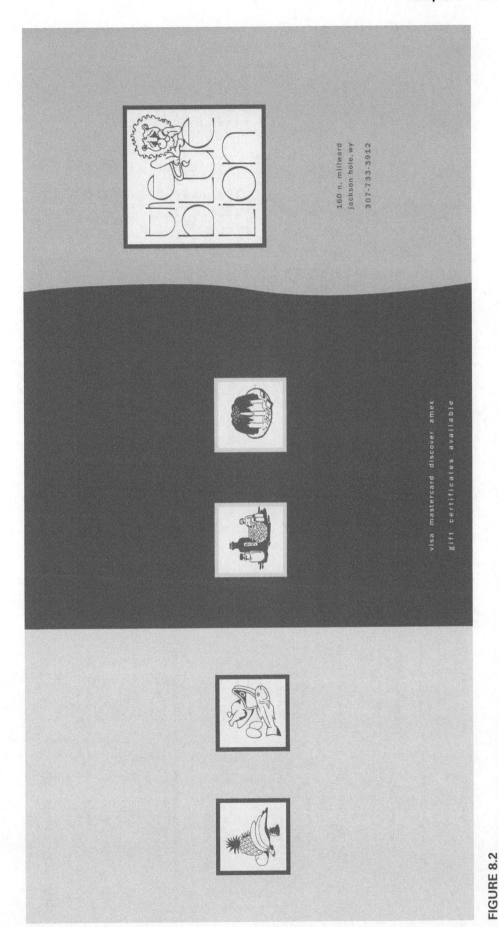

FIGURE 8.2

This menu illustrates a style of descriptive copy that focuses on ingredients, cooking technique, and presentation with additional adjectives as well.

Source: The Blue Lion. Reprinted with permission.

starters

please inform your server of any dietary or allergy restrictions we can accommodate

caesar salad
6.75
in place of dinner salad
4.75

french onion soup
au gratin
6.00

stuffed mushrooms
mushroom caps baked with a cream cheese, crab and courvoisier stuffing
10.00

buffalo ravioli
served over bolognese sauce
13.00

santa fe duck cakes
duck, red pepper, onion and southwestern spices, rolled in bread crumbs and sautéed until golden brown, served with chipotle mayonnaise
11.00

baked brie en croute
french brie brushed with dijon and layered with balsamic caramelized onions, wrapped in flaky puff pastry and baked until golden brown
10.00

thai seafood fritters
lobster, crab and shrimp rolled into a thai style dumpling, deep fried and served with a spicy soy sauce
14.50

grilled wasabi elk filet
elk shoulder tenderloin marinated with a mixture of fresh herbs, garlic, fish sauce and chile sauce, grilled rare, served sliced over seaweed salad and finished with wasabi vinaigrette
15.00

lighter fare

smaller portions of some of our favorites, salad a la carte

chicken marsala
sautéed all natural chicken breast with mushrooms, garlic and shallots, finished with a fresh basil and marsala wine sauce
16.50

organic king salmon
served with herb butter
25.50

please refrain from cell phone use while dining at the blue lion
no separate checks

---

all entrees include dinner salad with choice of bleu cheese, sesame vinaigrette, roasted red pepper vinaigrette or basil peppercorn dressing

meat entrees

roast rack of lamb
new zealand lamb rubbed with dijon mustard, rolled in seasoned bread crumbs and baked, served sliced with a peppercorn rosemary cream sauce and jalapeño mint sauce
42.50

beef tenderloin au bleu
sautéed painted hills ranch all natural beef tenderloin medallions finished with a crab, artichoke heart and brandy bleu cheese cream sauce
42.00

asian barbecued pork chop
16 oz. porterhouse pork chop, marinated and grilled, finished with a spicy asian barbecue sauce
27.00

grilled elk tenderloin
grilled to temperature, sliced and finished with a wild mushroom port sauce
41.00

cajun buffalo tenderloin
bacon wrapped buffalo tenderloin seasoned with cajun spices and grilled to temperature, finished with a raspberry cabernet sauce
44.00
grilled plain
42.00

mixed grille
grilled elk tenderloin, sliced and finished with a wild mushroom port sauce along with a grilled rainbow trout fillet, finished with herb butter
45.00

grilled beef tenderloin
bacon wrapped painted hills ranch all natural beef tenderloin grilled to temperature
40.00

poultry entrees

chicken frangelico
breast of all natural chicken encrusted with toasted hazelnuts, sautéed and topped with a frangelico mandarin orange cream sauce
19.50

chicken marsala
sautéed all natural chicken breasts with mushrooms, garlic and shallots, finished with a fresh basil and marsala wine sauce
22.50

health department warning! consuming raw or undercooked meats, poultry, seafood, shellfish, or eggs (such as hamburger cooked to order, sushi, oysters on the half shell or raw egg caesar salad) may increase your risk of foodborne illness, especially if you have certain medical conditions.

---

seafood entrees

please see tonight's specials for additional seafood entrees

sautéed salmon
sautéed organic king salmon served over a crab, spinach and roasted red pepper cream sauce and finished with basil infused olive oil
34.50

sautéed trout
fresh idaho rainbow trout sautéed with shrimp and finished with a curry leek cream sauce
28.00

seafood from the grill
organic king salmon 32.00
idaho rainbow trout 24.50

please choose from the following:
sun-dried tomato, basil and caper butter, pan blackened with cajun spices

green curry prawns
jumbo prawns simmered with tomatoes, snow peas and cilantro in a green curry sauce and served over jasmine rice
30.00

pasta entrees

southwestern shrimp linguine
shrimp sautéed with chorizo, artichoke hearts, red peppers, garlic and shallots tossed with linguine, and a southwestern tomato sauce and finished with cilantro, asiago and a mild artisan cheese
24.00
vegetarian style, with tempeh
19.00
(vegan style available by request)

risotto florentine
sautéed spinach, mushrooms, leeks and bacon served in a creamy white wine risotto, finished with fresh basil and asiago cheese
18.50
add grilled shrimp 24.50
add grilled chicken 21.50
add sautéed tempeh 20.50
(vegan style available by request)

buffalo ravioli
buffalo, mixed cheeses, portabella mushrooms, bell peppers, herbs and spices, wrapped in semolina egg pasta and served over bolognese sauce
29.00

FIGURE 8.2   *(Continued)*

sales from beverages and second or third courses can severely impact a company's revenue. It is best to use the power of the menu as a marketing tool and to allow servers to simply reinforce that message. (A few restaurants have begun experimenting with computer ordering systems at the table and allowing guests to order without the involvement of a server. In these types of operations, onscreen menus must fully take on the job of sales promotion.)

The biggest challenge to writing effective descriptive copy is to suggestively sell a dish without overdoing the sales pitch. Subtle suggestion works better than over-the-top descriptions. If a restaurant combines quality ingredients and creative flavor combinations, the menu description may need little more than a listing of the ingredients. Such menu copy may include ingredient sources or portion sizes, but extra embellishment is unnecessary. If a restaurant only serves standard fare that can easily be found elsewhere, then the sales pitch from the menu writer is critical to driving revenue. The text must make the food sound irresistible and encourage the guest to order a dish she might not otherwise order.

To avoid overdoing the sales pitch, the menu planner must keep in mind that a restaurant that is the best at everything does not need to crow about it; the public will find that out through online customer comments and restaurant reviews. These types of restaurants do very little in the way of selling a dish via descriptive copy. For all of the other restaurants in the world, customers want to know what the restaurant does best. Not every dish can be "the best you've ever tasted." If this were the case, the restaurant's reputation would precede it in the media. One or two signature dishes can be touted as "our specialty" or "the best in the city," but more than that just comes across as unbelievable. The remaining dishes on the menu should be described deliciously using seemingly objective language. Words that describe texture, flavor, size, and color come across as objective, but subjective words and phrases such as "awesome," "spectacular," "the best," and even "delicious" should be used sparingly. Table 8.1 compares menu item descriptions with an appropriate level of sales pitch to descriptions that seem so over the top as to be unrealistic.

Menu Copy That Sells Appropriately	Examples of Overkill
8 oz of tender choice filet with house-made béarnaise, local asparagus, and silken mashed Yukon gold potatoes	The most tender, flavorful filet mignon ever! This huge cut from USDA choice grade beef tenderloin is seared and roasted to your liking and paired with a super buttery, tarragon-kissed béarnaise sauce. We then serve it with a whopping pile of pencil-thin steamed and seasoned local asparagus, and the most creamy, lump-free mashed potatoes you've ever tasted—made from boutique, farm-raised Yukon gold potatoes.
These crab cakes are packed with 6 oz of Chesapeake Bay jumbo lump crab meat, seasoned with our own blend of spices, and coated in coarse brioche bread crumbs. No other filler necessary! Fried in butter and served with a side of piquant remoulade, these delicacies are the classic way to kick off your dinner in Baltimore.	Hon, you can't leave Baltimore without tasting our crab cakes. Made from local jumbo lump crab, these twin crab cakes are the sweetest, creamiest, most delicious appetizers on the bay. We coat them in brioche bread crumbs to provide that extra rich, golden brown coating you love in a crab cake, and fry them in butter to make them even more indulgent. Our chef's recipe cayenne-lemon-mayonnaise remoulade will wake up your taste buds so you can appreciate the sweet crab inside these must-have cakes. We swear you'll never find a better crab cake in your life.
Chocolate Orange Soufflé – Valrhona Guanaja 70% chocolate, Trickling Springs cream, orange blossom honey, and Gran Marnier. Blood orange garnish.	This lighter-than-air chocolate soufflé will send your mouth soaring to heaven with delight. We use only the best ingredients to infuse the dark, rich chocolate with the tangy sweetness of orange, so you can experience this awesome flavor combination. If this doesn't satisfy your chocolate craving, nothing will.

TABLE 8.1

Menu Descriptions and Overkill

Hunan Dynasty

皇朝飯店

World Famous Szechuan & Hunan Cuisine
Best Sushi on Capitol Hill

Serving Capitol Hill over Twenty Years
Private Banquet Rooms Available for
Parties & Conferences, Seating 200
Members of the House & Senate
Frequently Dine here

Tel: **(202)546-6161, 546-6262**
Fax:(202)546-4136

Free Delivery
Minimum order $12.00(Tax not included)

CHINESE FOOD & JAPANESE SUSHI

Open Hours:
Monday-Thursday 11:00am – 10:30pm
Friday 11:00am-11:00pm
Saturday 11:30am-11:00pm
Sunday 11:30am-10:30pm

Price subject to change without prior notice

PRSRT STD
US POSTAGE
PAID
WASHINGTON, DC
PERMIT #2228

**215 PENNSYLVANIA AVENUE, S.E.
WASHINGTON, D.C. 20003**

New Lunch Special
Monday – Friday: 11:00 am – 2:30 pm
Free Steamed Rice or Fried Rice, on Request.
Free Veg. Spring Roll

L1	Kung Pao Chicken	6.75
L2	Sweet and Sour Pork	6.75
L3	Hunan Beef	6.75
L4	Szechuan Beef	6.75
L5	Vegetable Combination	6.75
L6	String Bean Szechuan Style	6.75
L7	Beef w. Green Pepper	6.75
L8	Chicken Chow Mein	6.75
L9	Shrimp Chow Mein	6.75
L10	Moo Goo Gai Pan	6.75
L11	Sweet & Sour Chicken	6.75
L12	Roast Pork w. Snow Peas	6.75
L13	Chicken w. Snow Peas	6.75
L14	Chicken w.Black Bean Sauce	6.75
L15	Beef with Broccoli	6.75
L16	Chicken with Broccoli	6.75
L17	Szechuan Beef	6.75
L19	Szechuan	6.75
L20	Chicken w. Cashew Nuts	6.75
L21	Roast Pork w. Vegetables	6.75
L22	Hunan Chicken	6.75
L23	Chicken w. Garlic Sauce	6.75
L25	Beef w. Garlic Sauce	6.75
L26	Triple Delight	6.75
L27	General Tso's Chicken	6.75
L28	Orange Chicken	6.75
L29	Shrimp w. Broccoli	6.75
L30	Shrimp w. Vegetable	6.75
L32	Shrimp w. Cashew Nuts	6.75
L33	Scallops w. Vegetable	6.75

Bean Curd 豆腐類
Bean curd is a kind of vegetarian food, which contains mostly protein. The Human body can easily absorb this protein. Consuming bean curd regularly could lower your cholesterol and help to prevent high blood pressure and diabetes.

- Hunan Bean Curd (with pork extra $0.60) ... 6.50 7.95
- Kung Pao Bean Curd ... 6.50 7.95
- Bean Curd Szechuan Style (with pork extra $0.60) ... 6.50 7.95
- Bean Curd Mandarin Style ... 6.50 7.95
- Bean Curd with Mushrooms ... 6.50 7.95
- Bean Curd with Mixed Vegetables ... 6.50 7.95
- Bean Curd with Spinach ... 6.50 7.95

Noodles & Fried Rice 麵飯類
- Fried Rice (choice of: chicken, beef, pork or vegetable) ... 6.95
- Shrimp or Combination Fried Rice ... 7.25
- Lo Mein (choice of: chicken, beef, pork, or vegetable) ... 6.95
- Shrimp or Combination Lo Mein ... 7.25
- Vegetables Pan Fried Noodle ... 9.95
- Combination Pan Fried Noodle ... 11.95
- Stick Rice Noodle Singapore Style (curry flavor) ... 10.95
- Stick Rice Noodle Taiwan Style ... 10.95
- Healthy Brown Fried Rice ... 8.95
  (Choice of: shrimp, chicken, beef, pork or vegetable)

Thai Food
- Pad Thai (choice of chicken, beef, shrimp, veggie & combo) ... 9.95
- Red Curry (Choice of chicken, pork, shrimp and beef) ... 9.95

Chow Fun 炒河粉
- Chicken Chow Fun ... 8.95
- Beef Chow Fun ... 9.95
- Shrimp Chow Fun ... 10.95
- Combination Chow Fun ... 10.95

Appetizers 頭盤
- Crispy Spring Roll (2) ... 2.50
- Vegetable Spring Roll (2) ... 2.50
- Fried Wonton (6) ... 4.50
- Sweet & Sour Cabbage (cold) ... 4.95
- Pan Fried or Steamed Vegetable Dumpling (5) ... 4.95
- Pan Fried or Steamed Meat Dumpling (6) ... 4.95
- Fried Cheese Dumpling (6) ... 5.95
- Sweet & Sour Spare Ribs ... 5.95
- Bar-B-Q Ribs (4) ... 5.95
- Shrimp Tempura (4) ... 5.95
- Shrimp Toast (5) ... 5.95
- Beef on Stick (4) ... 5.95
- Pu Pu Tray (for 2) ... 9.95
  (Bar-B-Q Ribs, Cheese Dumpling, Beef Chocho, Spring Roll, Shrimp Toast)
- Noodle with Sesame Sauce (cold) ... 5.50

Soup 湯類
- Egg Drop Soup ... 1.75 3.50
- Wonton Soup ... 1.75 3.50
- Hot & Sour Soup ... 1.75 3.50
- Minced Chicken & Corn Soup (for 2) ... 5.95
- Vegetable Bean Curd Soup (for 2) ... 5.95
- Fresh Spinach with Bean Curd Soup (for 2) ... 5.95
- Minced Beef & Egg Flower Soup (for 2) ... 5.95
- Crabmeat & Chicken Soup (for 2) ... 5.95
- Asparagus Crabmeat Soup (for 2) ... 5.95
- Hot & Sour Seafood Soup (for 2) ... 5.95

Duck 鴨類
- House Duck Special ... 12.95
- Yu Ling Duck ... 12.95
- Roast Duck ... 12.95
- Crispy Duck ... 12.95
- Shredded Duck in Garlic Sauce ... 12.95
- Peking Duck ... (half)12.95 (whole)24.95

Chicken, Beef, Pork & Lamb
All Chicken & Pork Entree are Small $6.95, Large $8.95
All Beef & Lamb Entree are Small $7.95, Large $9.95
- Hunan Chicken/Pork/Beef/Lamb
- Sha Cha Chicken/Pork/Beef/Lamb
- Kung Pao Chicken/Pork/Beef/Lamb
- Chicken/Pork/Beef in Garlic Sauce
- Szechuan Chicken/Beef
- Moo Goo Gai Pan
- Chicken/Pork with Almonds
- Chicken with Cashew Nuts
- Sweet & Sour Chicken/Pork
- Chicken/Pork/Beef with Snow Peas
- Chicken/Pork with Bean Sprouts
- Moo Shi Chicken/Pork/Beef (Sm 2 pancakes, Lg 4 pancakes)
- Chicken/Pork/Beef/Lamb with Broccoli
- Chicken/Pork/Beef/Lamb with Black Bean Sauce
- Green Pepper Chicken/Pork/Beef/Lamb
- Chicken/Pork/Beef with Mixed Vegetables
- Chicken/Pork with Pineapple
- Mongolian Chicken/Pork/Beef/Lamb
- Beef with Vegetables
- Beef with Oyster Sauce
- Chicken Chow Mein
- Double Winter Beef
- Pepper Steak

Special Health Diet Dish
— By plain steamed with original flavor no M.S.G, salt and oil used —
You have to choose with seasoning sauce (white or brown sauce) on the side.

- 減肥素什錦 D1 Diet Combination with Vegetable ... 6.50 7.95
- 減肥素菜難 D2 Diet Chicken with Vegetable ... 6.95 8.95
- 減肥素干貝 D3 Diet Mix Veg. Sc-llop ... 9.95
- 減肥油棧蝦 D4 Diet Imperial Shr-p ... 8.50 10.95
- 減肥素豆腐鍋 D5 Diet Vegetarian Bean Curd ... 6.50 7.95

Chef's Special
- General Tso's Bean Curd ... 8.95
- General Tso's Chicken ... 10.95
- Orange Chicken ... 10.95
- Sesame Chicken ... 10.95
- Lemon Chicken ... 11.95
- Wonderful Flavors Chicken ... 10.95
- Triple Delight ... 10.95
- Sweet & Sour Delight ... 10.95
- Sauteed Fresh Spinach w/Black Mushroom ... 11.95
- Crunchy Crispy Chicken ... 13.95
- Crunchy Crispy Beef ... 13.95
- Orange Beef ... 14.95
- Jumbo Shrimp w/ Sesame in Lemon Sauce ... 14.95
- Crispy Prawn with Walnuts ... 15.95
- Happy Family ... 14.95
- House Salt and Pepper Shrimp ... 10.95
- House Salt and Pepper Chicken ... 10.95
- House Salt and Pepper Ribs ... 10.95

Seafood/Fish
- Szechuan Shrimp ... 8.50 10.95
- Hunan Shrimp ... 8.50 10.95
- Kung Pao Shrimp ... 8.50 10.95
- Jumbo Shrimp in Garlic Sauce ... 8.50 10.95
- Shrimp with Black Bean Sauce ... 8.50 10.95
- Imperial Shrimp ... 8.50 10.95
- Sauteed Shrimp with Cashew ... 8.50 10.95
- Shrimp with Vegetable ... 8.50 10.95
- Shrimp with Lobster Sauce ... 8.50 10.95
- Sweet & Sour Shrimp ... 8.50 10.95
- Shrimp with Snow Peas ... 8.50 10.95
- Shrimp with Broccoli ... 8.50 10.95
- Kung Pao Scallop ... 8.50 10.95
- Szechuan Scallop ... 8.50 10.95
- Scallop with Black Bean Sauce ... 8.50 10.95
- Scallop with Vegetable ... 8.50 10.95
- Scallop with Snow Peas ... 8.50 10.95
- Scallop in Garlic Sauce ... 8.50 10.95
- Seafood Combination ... 15.95
- Fish Filet with Mixed Vegetable ... 12.95
- Fish Filet with Black Bean Sauce ... 12.95
- Steamed Fish with Ginger & Scallion (Choice of: Sea Bass or Rock Fish) ... 22.95
- Human Crispy Whole Fish (Choice of: Sea Bass or Rock Fish) ... 22.95
- Sweet & Sour Crispy Whole Fish (Choice of: Sea Bass or Rock Fish) ... 22.95

Curry
- Curry Chicken with Potato ... 8.95
- Curry Beef with Potato ... 9.95
- Curry Shrimp with Potato ... 10.95
- Curry Triple with Potato ... 10.95

Vegetables
- Vegetables Combination in Hot Garlic Sauce ... 6.50 7.95
- String Beans Szechuan Style ... 6.50 7.95
- Eggplant in Hot Garlic Sauce ... 6.50 7.95
- Broccoli in Garlic Sauce ... 6.50 7.95
- Vegetables Combination ... 6.50 7.95
- Broccoli with Oyster Sauce ... 6.50 7.95
- Snow Peas & Water Chestnuts ... 6.50 7.95
- General Tso's Eggplant ... 6.50 7.95
- Orange Eggplant ... 6.50 7.95
- Sauteed Spinach ... 7.95

FIGURE 8.3

This take-out menu avoids menu descriptions entirely, which speeds reading through a lot of options.

Source: Hunan Dynasty.

Non-Restaurant Menus

When a menu planner creates a non-restaurant menu, such as a catering, banquet, or tasting menu, the rules on menu copy differ. The item descriptions must still communicate key ingredients, but selling the product may be less of a concern. When a catering menu is provided to a client through a salesperson, the descriptive copy should be limited, if only for space reasons. The salesperson can provide personal descriptions of the menu items and guide the client through the extensive menu options based on the client's needs. For upscale catered events, the caterer often provides a tasting experience, so the client can see exactly what each dish is like. Casual catering menus, like those provided by sandwich shops, may incorporate slightly more salesmanship, but usually the clients only pursue an establishment for catering if they are already familiar with the product.

Banquet menus can skip the salesmanship because the guests typically have no choice in courses. The purpose of descriptive copy on a banquet menu is to highlight potential problems for guests with allergies or dietary restrictions and to preempt some questions that the guests might ask the servers. The menu should sound delicious, but the guests receive the same set courses regardless, unless they express a dietary challenge. If the guests are required to select their entrées in advance, the menu description at the table is effectively moot.

Tasting menus and afternoon tea menus follow the same logic. If everything on the menu is included, then the menu needs only to describe, not to sell, the food. For this reason, afternoon tea menus tend to have more descriptive copy lines devoted to the tea (which the customer must select) than to the food (which is usually all-inclusive).

Noncommercial and take-out menus are often brief, too, but for a different reason. These types of menus are usually present in operations for which speed is an issue. Guests in a business's cafeteria want to order their food quickly, eat, and return to work. Customers that walk into a restaurant to place a take-out order do not want to wait any longer than necessary. In both cases, speed is essential. The longer the menu copy, the longer it takes for the guest to read the menu and place an order. The menu item descriptions should communicate the essential information, but they should do so in as few words as possible.

Children's menus follow a set of rules all to themselves. Because of the younger audience, the menu descriptions must employ easy-to-understand language. Sentences should be short and the main ingredients and common allergens should be the focus. Most children will not know cooking technique terms other than "fried" and "grilled," so the description should emphasize the ingredients and possibly the presentation. For example, a pancake that looks like a face made from berries, bacon, and whipped cream is a huge draw for the under-ten crowd; the presentation should be stated explicitly in the menu item description. That the dish is made from buttermilk pancakes, apple wood–smoked bacon, and local strawberries is irrelevant to a child; she only wants to know that it will arrive looking like a face. When a children's menu lists three or more components for each dish—think meat, starch, vegetable, and dipping sauce—the menu planner may wish to name each dish for a zoo animal or cartoon character. It makes ordering by name easier for the child. Additionally, when a child does not normally want to stop coloring to select from the menu, choosing between "Batman" and "Dora the Explorer" can hold the kid's interest just long enough for her to make that choice expeditiously.

History and Other Institutional Copy

Learning Objective 5
List several uses for text on a menu beyond describing menu items.

Menu items and their descriptions typically comprise the majority of text on a menu, but rarely are they the only words written on a menu. The menu is an opportunity to direct and enhance the guest's dining experience. Sometimes, the most exciting and unique part of a restaurant is its history; a description of that history on the menu expands the guest's experience beyond the food and service. If a famous person dined in the establishment, worked there, or currently owns it, that may be worth noting in the menu's institutional copy, especially if it is a draw for the clientele.

WELCOME TO THE FORT

It all began in 1961 when my mother, "Bay" (Elizabeth Arnold) wanted to build an adobe style home in the country outside of Denver, so my brother, Keith, and I could grow up in the country with clean air, horseback riding and fishing. My father (Sam'l P. Arnold) and mother were amateur historians. Bay was reading a book about Bent's Fort, a famous Colorado fur trade fort built in 1833, and saw a drawing in the book of this adobe castle on the plains. She turned to Sam'l and said, "Let's build an adobe castle like this!" At this time, they discovered this beautiful red rock property that was for sale and bought it in 1961.

They hired William Lumpkins, the top architect in adobe construction from Santa Fe, and he hired a contractor from Taos, New Mexico. With the help of a crew of 22 men from Santa Fe, we puddled over 80,000 mud and straw bricks, weighing 40 pounds each, to construct the main building. When the costs of construction exceeded the budget, the bank suggested that we put a business in the historic "Fort" we had built as our home. Sam'l turned to Bay and said, "You can cook!" and then she said to Sam'l, "Well, you can cook!" They redesigned the lower level to be the restaurant and the upper level as our living quarters. The Fort restaurant opened for business in February 1963.

That same year, we adopted a Canadian black bear cub named "Sissy" who lived at The Fort for 19 years. She was my pet bear, and died of old age.

What to serve in our Fort? Bay and Sam'l researched diaries of what the pioneers, mountain men and native Indian tribes ate along the Santa Fe Trail. As Bent's Fort was originally located near La Junta in Southeastern Colorado, the culinary influences of the Mexican and Spanish traders were also part of this amazing "fusion" cuisine served at Bent's Fort.

The Fort's staples have always been buffalo, elk and quail. Today we serve over 80,000 entrees of buffalo annually.

By exploring our rich Western cultural and culinary past, we reintroduce food trends of the 1800's, which create current trends of their own. We continue to be inspired by historic recipes and introduce new items to our menu.

Ask your waitperson to teach your group to do the Mountain Man Toast. You will find that it brings you "Shinin' Times" this evening. The word "restaurant" means to restore. Let us restore your soul as well as your stomach! A Hearty Welcome to my home. WAUGH! (Mountain Man lingo for "Right On!")

Holly A. Kinney

Holly Arnold Kinney, Proprietress

THE FORT'S PRIX FIXE DINNER SPECIAL

Enjoy Buffalo Prime Rib <u>exclusively</u> on Friday, Saturday, & Sundays.
Starts with a Fort Dinner Salad and freshly baked breads, then Buffalo Prime Rib served with buttery mashed potatoes with a hint of Horseradish, and seasonal vegetable, (horseradish upon request) and finished with your choice of our fresh Fruit Cobbler or The Fort's Famous Negrita for Dessert!
8 oz. portion for $39 or 12 oz. portion for $49 or 16 oz. portion for $59
Does not include Tax or Gratuity.

FIGURE 8.4

In addition to well-written descriptive copy, this menu includes institutional copy describing the restaurant's history and its commitment to local beef.

Reprinted by permission of The Fort Restaurant, Morrison, Colorado.

ENTREES SERVED WITH...

Fort Breads -A selection of pumpkin walnut muffins and dinner rolls.

Fort Dinner Salad - Seven crisp greens topped with pickled ginger, diced jicama and toasted pepitas. Add smoked duck for $4.

Dressing Choices: Chunky Maytag Blue Cheese, Herbal Damiana* House Vinaigrette, Buttermilk Ranch, Chipotle Honey or Balsamic Vinegar & Fine Extra Virgin Olive Oil
Reputed aphrodisiac herb

FROM THE PRAIRIE AND FOREST

All of The Fort's buffalo (bison) are from selected ranches in the Rocky Mountain Region

William Bent's Buffalo Tenderloin Filet Mignon-So Tender, it's like the First Kiss!

The most tender of all, choose from an 6-ounce or 8-ounce buffalo filet with seasonal vegetables and Fort potatoes. MARKET PRICE

Buffalo Sirloin Steak Medallions-A favorite of Kit Carson, who was commissioned to provide 1,000 lbs. of buffalo meat to Bent's Fort in the 1840's.

Full of flavor for the hearty appetite and served with seasonal vegetables and Fort potatoes.

Two 5-ounce buffalo sirloin medallions $42 or Three 5-ounce buffalo sirloin medallions $49

Kit Carson's 16-ounce Buffalo Ribeye Steak -Another of Kit's "favrits"!

Sink your teeth into a juicy 16-ounce Buffalo Ribeye steak, grilled to perfection and served with seasonal vegetables and mashed potatoes with a hint of horseradish, butter and cream. MARKET PRICE

Smoke House Buffalo BBQ Ribs-Bent's Fort's cook, Charlotte Green would approve!

Smoked buffalo ribs, slowly roasted and smothered in our tangy Jack Daniels barbecue sauce. Served with campfire beans and and mashed potatoes with a hint of horseradish, butter and cream. 1/2 rack (4) $36 full rack (8) $49

The Fort's Game Plate-Try them All! 🐾

Our most popular dish! A bone-in Elk chop, Buffalo sirloin medallion, and a grilled teriyaki Quail. Served with seasonal vegetables, and Fort potatoes, and wild Montana huckleberry preserves. $49

Add a side to any entree of an Elk Chop For $20, Buffalo Sirloin for $16, Duck Breast for $14, Lamb T-bone for $13, Buffalo Rib for $12, or Quail for $9.

🐾 Sissy Bear's paw print denotes a heritage recipe featured on The Fort's menu in the 1960s.

Regarding the safety of these items, written information is available upon request; Consuming raw or undercooked meats, poultry, seafood, shellfish, or eggs may increase your risk of foodborne illness. This item can be cooked to order.

FIGURE 8.4   *(Continued)*

COLORADO TERRITORY BEEF

William Bent, founder of the original Bents Fort in 1833 in southern Colorado, was also well known for raising high quality Colorado cattle on his ranch in the 1850's... we've searched out the best that Colorado Raised Beef has to offer and are now proud to provide you with what we are certain would make William Bent proud! Our beef is processed here in Colorado. Our Colorado beef is cared for by, hard working ranchers who take great pride in not just knowing and understanding how to raise world class cattle, but equally important to respect the environment and land. Our Colorado raised beef is as important to us as our chef and staff, who prepare the final touches to your carefully grilled steak. Our aged beef is truly a farm to table "Colorado Proud" process and with this pride in our Colorado and Western heritage, we proudly present our Colorado beef program. Waugh!

14-ounce Colorado Natural Beef NY Strip Steak
The marbling speaks for itself, tender, and rich with flavor! Served with seasonal vegetables and Fort potatoes. $54

"Tenderlips" Colorado Natural Beef Filet Mignon.- so tender it is like the first kiss!
6-ounce center cut beef filet grilled to perfection, served with seasonal vegetables and Fort potatoes. $42

Incorrect Steak - Frontiersman Dick Wootton's favorite steak and eggs
Our 14-ounce Colorado Natural Beef NY strip, topped with a blend of melted Mexican cheeses, New Mexican Dixon red chile sauce and a fried egg, served with seasonal vegetables and Fort potatoes. $56

Gonzales Steak Inspired by The Fort's wood carver Elidio Gonzales. 🐾
A 14-ounce Colorado Natural Beef NY strip, stuffed with New Mexican Hatch green chiles and topped with a freshly grilled chile pod, served with seasonal vegetables and Fort potatoes. $56

Have any Steak prepared **Incorrect Style** or **Gonzales Style** for an additional $4.

Add a side to any entree of an Elk Chop For $20, Buffalo Sirloin for $16, Duck Breast for $14, Lamb T-bone for $13, Buffalo Rib for $12, or Quail for $9.

*Regarding the safety of these items, written information is available upon request; Consuming raw or undercooked meats, poultry, seafood, shellfish, or eggs may increase your risk of foodborne illness. This item can be cooked to order.

FIGURE 8.4   *(Continued)*

FORT FAVORITES

Elk Chops St. Vrain.-Ceran St. Vrain was Bent's partner in the 1840's, when they were forming the Bent St. Vrain Company.
Two 4-ounce bone-in elk chops, grilled to perfection with wild Montana huckleberry preserves. Served with seasonal vegetables and Fort potatoes. $49

General Armijo's Colorado Lamb T-bones-He was known to steal your sheep and then sell them back to you in the 1840's!
Two spiced, 5 oz. Colorado Lamb T-bones, served with seasonal vegetables and mashed potatoes with a hint of horseradish, butter and cream. $35

Scottish Salmon*-Alexander Mackenzie, the Scottish explorer before Lewis & Clark would approve!
Fresh Scottish salmon from the North Sea, baked and served atop Rice Pilaf, with a Lemon New Mexican Red Chile Honey glaze. $35

Josefa Jaramillo's Vegetarian Tamales-Josefa was Kit Carson's beautiful wife!
Green Chile and Cheese Vegetarian tamales with New Mexican Red Chile gravy and Mexican crema on top. Served with homemade pinto beans, zucchini and tomatoes. $28

Shrimp Vera Cruz-From South of the Border-Delish!
Sautéed Shrimp with roasted peppers, Anaheim chile, roasted tomatoes and spices mixed together and served with coconut rice pilaf and pinto beans, served sizzling in a cast iron skillet. Like the first kiss! $38

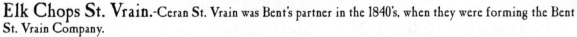

FROM THE YARD

Ancho Chile-Orange Duck-This is a favorite of hunters and duckmeat lovers...so tender and delish!
Two pan seared, tender duck breasts with an Ancho chile and Orange glaze. Served with seasonal vegetables and rice pilaf. $36

William Bent's Grilled Quail- Quail roamed the praires in the 1840's and was a favorite food of American Indians and fur trappers!
Teriyaki marinated quail served with wild Montana huckleberry preserves, seasonal vegetables, and Fort potatoes. Two -$28 Three-$36

Add a side to any entree of an Elk Chop For $20, Buffalo Sirloin for $16, Duck Breast for $14, Lamb T-bone for $13, Buffalo Rib for $12, or Quail for $9.

Regarding the safety of these items, written information is available upon request; Consuming raw or undercooked meats, poultry, seafood, shellfish, or eggs may increase your risk of foodborne illness. This item can be cooked to order.

FIGURE 8.4 *(Continued)*

AVAILABLE EXTRAS

President Jefferson's favorite Mac N' Cheese "Pudding"
He served this recipe at the White House in the early 1800's..............................$8
Ask your server to add Red Chile or Green chile to make your Mac n' Cheese Fort style!
Substitute any starch with President Jefferson's favorite Mac N' Cheese for $4.

Forest Mushrooms...$8

Red Chile French Fries...$5

Campfire Beans..$4

Seasonal Vegetables...$4

Chef's Selection Mashed Potatoes $4

Rice Pilaf...$4

Our Famous Sauces $4

Choose from: Hot or Mild Gonzales Green Chile
                Huckleberry Preserves
                New Mexican Dixon Red Chile Gravy
                Jack Daniels Barbecue

OUR STEAK GUIDELINE FOR DEGREE OF DONENESS

Rare - Warm/Cool center, bright red color throughout. (Juicy)

Medium Rare - Warm/Hot center, bright red center with pink outsides. (Very Juicy)

Medium - Hot center, bright pink throughout. (Juicy/Slightly Dry)

Medium Well - Hot center, light pink center. (Sometimes dry)

Well Done - Very hot center. (Dry)

Regarding the safety of these items, written information is available upon request; Consuming raw or undercooked meats, poultry, seafood, shellfish, or eggs may increase your risk of foodborne illness. This item can be cooked to order.

FIGURE 8.4   *(Continued)*

OUR COMMITMENT TO YOU

The Fort's a "scratch" restaurant. Making most all our cuisine we serve you from scratch, including salad dressings, sauces, and desserts. Whenever possible, we buy our produce and meats designated as all natural from local farmers and ranchers. Our seasonal, organic courtyard garden, has supplied our chard, arugula and herbs for your salad!

Our commitment to being "green" is not only good for Mother Earth, but fresh will always taste better and be better for you!

FIGURE 8.4 *(Continued)*

If a restaurant's concept needs explanation, a description of the concept on the menu may be appropriate. For example, if an Ethiopian restaurant opens in an area unfamiliar with the cuisine, the menu might describe how Ethiopians traditionally eat using their hands and pieces of injera (a flat, spongy bread) to pick up the food. A small how-to guide for using injera would put many customers at ease who might otherwise express concern over the lack of silverware on the table. Expounding on the culture of a cuisine can encourage sales, too. If a traditional Tuscan restaurant explains that in Tuscany guests typically order an antipasto, pasta, main course, and dessert, customers are less likely to order only pasta for dinner. If the restaurant concept is instead based on the provenance of the ingredients, that should be stated on the menu. Customers may appreciate the food (and the price they pay for it) more if they know that the chef's goal is to support local farmers and to use only local ingredients.

Long vignettes about a restaurant can enhance the dining experience, but they also slow the speed at which customers get through the menu. Thus, historical anecdotes or cultural information should only be included in the institutional copy if they add to the guest's experience. If there is excess space on a menu, unless additional text will make the guests more excited to dine there, the menu planner should fill the void with appealing and brand-appropriate photographs or illustrations. Alternatively, the menu planner may break up the extra space by adjusting the menu layout or font size.

While historical information is not a necessary component of a menu, pricing and food safety disclaimers are. The menu planner must always make space to provide the common "undercooked food" disclaimer on the menu. Not to warn people of potentially hazardous foods invites lawsuits from guests who get sick after ordering raw seafood or eggs over easy. The menu planner must also state automatic price adjustments, such as the addition of an 18% gratuity for large parties, on the menu to maintain fidelity with truth-in-menu guidelines.

Finally, as the menu is a marketing tool, the menu planner should consider promoting the business's other services on the restaurant menu. For example, if a restaurant offers catering or plans an upcoming special Valentine's Day dinner, that information may be stated in the menu copy. If the menus are laminated and not printed regularly, short-term announcements may be advertised through table tents or menu inserts instead. Other products for promotion might include on-site cooking classes taught by the chef, wine or beer dinners, upcoming special events or deals, or commercial products available for sale at the restaurant, such as jarred pickles or the chef's cookbook.

For casual and mid-level restaurants, it may be appropriate to advertise on the menu the business hours, address, phone, and web address for the restaurant. This type of information is essential for take-out menus but may also make sense for disposable dine-in menus that guests may take with them as mementos. Customers may store restaurant menus in their desks at work as a reminder to return to a certain establishment. Sometimes, they share these menus with friends and coworkers. The more data the restaurant lists on its menu about its hours, location, and contact information, the easier it is for a customer to decide to patronize that establishment.

Summary

The writing style for a menu item description must match the restaurant's concept and theme as well as appeal to the target market. Spelling and grammatical errors should be avoided unless that is part of the business's theme. Fundamentally, menu descriptions communicate information about a dish—its ingredients, portion size, cooking technique, nutritional value, presentation, accompaniments, and so on. The description should be clear and honest. Guests end up disappointed if they cannot understand the menu copy or if the description of the dish does not match what arrives from the kitchen. The National Restaurant Association lists eleven truth-in-menu categories to which menu planners should pay careful attention so as to avoid misrepresenting or falsely advertising the product being sold. The truth-in-menu categories are quantity, quality, price, brand names, product identification, point of origin, merchandising terms, preservation, food preparation, verbal and visual presentation, and dietary and nutritional claims. Menu planners should ensure that they use legally defined terms, such as "organic" or "grass fed," accurately as well. A well-written menu description not only informs the customer but also encourages her to buy the product. Selling the dish should align with the business's style and avoid hyperbole and exaggeration. Catering, banquet, tasting, and afternoon tea menus generally require less salesmanship in the descriptive copy than other types of menus do. Non-commercial and take-out menus often use brief descriptions to speed service while children's menus require simple wording that children can understand.

In addition to describing menu items, menu copy may describe historical or interesting facts about the establishment or information about the cuisine. Undercooked food disclaimers and automatic price additions must be stated somewhere on the menu. When space is available, the menu planner should consider promoting the restaurant's other services and noting its standard contact information. Properly done, menus become both a communication and a marketing tool for the business.

Comprehension Questions

1. What are the two primary functions of descriptive copy?
2. List the eleven truth-in-menu categories.
3. Go online to the FDA's *Food Labeling Guide*. Select one legally defined nutritional term. What is its legal definition?
4. List three things that a menu planner might write on a menu other than menu item descriptions.
5. A menu description states, "12 oz of grilled Montana prime strip steak served with Tabasco parsley butter and house-cured, fat-free cucumber pickles —$22.50." What truth-in-menu categories are applicable to this menu description? For each category you list, note how an unethical chef might violate this menu description's accuracy.
6. Briefly describe two different restaurant concepts. Create a dish that could be served in either place. Write two menu descriptions for the dish—each appropriate to its corresponding concept—that both inform and appropriately sell the dish. Be sure to note which description pairs with which restaurant concept.
7. Write a menu description for an item on a children's menu.

Discussion Questions

1. Should menu item descriptions be longer on a quick-service menu or on a fine-dining menu? Why? Is this what you have experienced in practice?
2. Think of a restaurant you have visited recently. How detailed was the descriptive copy? Did it fit the restaurant's theme? What drew you to the food you ultimately ordered?
3. Have you ever heard of or personally observed a restaurant violating a truth-in-menu representation? Describe the violation.
4. Have you ever felt misled by a menu description (even if the description was technically accurate)? Describe your expectations and the item that was actually served. What is your current perception of this establishment?
5. Think of a restaurant in your area (or in a nearby city) that could enhance the dining experience by providing a paragraph or two about the restaurant's history or about the traditions surrounding the cuisine. Write a paragraph or two that you feel would be appropriate for printing in that menu.
6. Imagine that you are a restaurant owner and that you want to write one over-the-top menu description to highlight one thing you serve. Which dish would you describe that way—the best seller, the slowest mover, your personal favorite, the chef's personal favorite, the most profitable, the least profitable, etc.? Explain your rationale.

Case Study

A restaurant opens in a tourist town right in the heart of the tourist attractions—museums, historic tours, and other sites. The owner decides to go with a "travel" theme since most of her customers will have traveled in from somewhere else. She creates a menu with eighty menu items representing all of the major cities, states, and regions around the United States.

The first page of the menu includes three paragraphs describing the theme and encouraging people to "sample the flavors of America." The descriptive copy is campy to create a fun environment. An example of one menu item description is "Potato skins: Try our amazing potato skins, traveling in from Idaho. These babies come loaded with cheddar cheese, bacon, onion, sour cream, guacamole, and salsa. They're better than good. They're Ore-Ida!" The rest of the descriptive copy is written in a similar style and length.

The restaurant opens to a good lunch crowd—smaller for dinner—but after a couple of months, business drops off significantly. The owner can't imagine why. What did she do wrong with the menu? What would you recommend she change? If she decides to stick with the original menu, what risk does she face?

Capstone Project

Step 8: Write menu item descriptions for all of the items on your menu in a style that is appropriate for the business concept. Additionally, select two to three images from the Internet or from other sources that might be appropriate to include on the menu. Write a paragraph of institutional copy appropriate for your menu concept that would enhance your guests' dining experience. Finally, write any other menu copy—food safety warnings, symbol definitions, automatic charge/ tip announcements, business address/hours/web page, etc.—that should appear on your menu. By the end of this step, you should have all of the information— menu headings, menu items, descriptive copy, prices, institutional copy, and images—that will appear on your final menu. Depending on how the layout process unfolds, you may not use all of this material, but having it readily available will speed and enhance the layout process.

References

1. http://www.fda.gov/Food/GuidanceRegulation/ GuidanceDocumentsRegulatoryInformation/ LabelingNutrition/ucm064911.htm. Accessed 25 April 2016.

2. https://www.ams.usda.gov/services/auditing/grass-fed-SVS. Accessed 26 April 2016.

CHAPTER 9

Unwritten Menus

INTRODUCTION

Restaurant menu descriptions play a vital role in both informing and marketing to the guest. But what about those instances when a printed menu is not utilized? In most restaurants, servers communicate daily specials orally. Buffets and cafeterias may not provide a printed menu to their customers at all; in these instances, the food must sell itself. Food that looks attractive on a buffet is likely to sell well while guests typically pass over unattractive dishes.

The visual appearance of the food on the buffet, the decorations added to the buffet, and the cleanliness of the buffet all contribute to a guest's perception of the buffet's appeal. An attractive and clean buffet draws lots of customers and sometimes persuades them to purchase larger quantities of food. A visually unappealing buffet results in excessive food cost as the food is unlikely to be consumed and instead will end up in the trash can. Knowing how to set up and arrange a buffet is essential for a menu planner. The buffet presentation plays the same role that menu descriptions do. They both underscore the brand and the theme of the business (or event), and they help to sell the product. That a menu is unwritten does not absolve a menu planner from achieving the communication and marketing goals that are normally performed via the written word.

CHAPTER 9 LEARNING OBJECTIVES

As a result of successfully completing this chapter, readers will be able to:

1. Describe how to market food visually on a buffet.

2. State the difference between an all-you-can-eat buffet and a cafeteria-style buffet.

3. Describe several possible layouts for buffet and cafeteria lines.

4. Organize food on a buffet to promote sales or to control costs.

5. List three ways caterers can charge based on a customer count guarantee.

6. Describe the role that servers play in communicating unwritten menu components.

CHAPTER 9 OUTLINE

Selling and Informing without a Menu

Buffet Layout

Buffet Food Arrangement

Guaranteed Guest Counts

Verbal Specials

Summary

Comprehension Questions

Discussion Questions

Case Study

Capstone Project

Selling and Informing without a Menu

As buffet operations do not always provide the customer with a printed menu, these businesses must inform customers about the food and encourage sales through other means. Printed placards and service staff can perform this function as effectively as a printed menu can. At a casual buffet or in a cafeteria line, large signs or small cards may be used to label each dish. Extremely casual operations typically employ larger signs with more information, so the guests need not interrupt the service staff with questions as frequently. The amount of information to list on the signs depends on the needs of the target market. For example, a college cafeteria may list only the name and key ingredients of a dish while a hospital cafeteria may include detailed nutritional information; both will likely list prices unless the buffet is all-you-can-eat. As guests can see and smell the food in front of them, the signs should inform customers about the dish but not waste space selling the dish with flowery language. These signs may be laminated index cards or printed 8½" × 11" pieces of paper inserted into clear plastic holders. Unless the buffet options never change, the signs are rarely permanent or high-cost.

Fancier operations often employ much smaller placards on their buffets, if they use signage at all. These labels simply provide the name of each dish and focus on the main items. Upscale businesses do not have less of a need to communicate with guests; rather, they tend to provide that service through human interaction. These types of buffets often have service staff available behind the buffet tables to greet guests and to answer any questions they may have about the food. Buffet staff use words to inform customers, but their actions help to sell the food. A buffet server must maintain the cleanliness of the buffet and replace platters that run low on food or that lose their attractive appearance. No matter how deliciously a sign or server describes a dish, it is difficult to overcome customers' negative perceptions of a dirty or unattractive display.

Learning Objective 1
Describe how to market food visually on a buffet.

So how does a business sell food on a buffet or cafeteria without the use of a persuasive menu description? In a word—visually. Any food placed on a buffet or cafeteria line must look colorful, fresh, and attractive. Wilted, damaged, or monochromatic food on a buffet simply does not sell well. Just as with an à la carte menu, buffet planners must plan for variety in color, shape, and texture both within each dish and across the entire buffet. Since customers can see all of the items on the buffet at the same time, not every dish can follow the same color scheme. If one dish uses orange and red julienne vegetables with a white fish, the platter next to it should provide a different set of colors and shapes, such as dark green spinach and golden brown meat. The only constraint to variety on a buffet that does not apply to an à la carte menu is that not all foods and cooking techniques are appropriate for buffet service. For example, fried food, which offers a crisp texture not easily achieved via other cooking techniques, loses its crisp quality rather quickly sitting in a chafing dish on a buffet. Thus, certain dishes and cooking techniques may not be appropriate for a buffet, even if they would otherwise increase the variety of the display.

Once a menu planner has determined what to include on a buffet to yield a stunning visual effect, the cooks and service staff must maintain the visual appeal of the buffet through the entire service. A dish that looks inviting when first placed on a buffet can become an eyesore just a few minutes and a few customers into a meal period. To keep a buffet looking appetizing, cooks should only send out small batches of food at a time and replace them regularly. Thus, rather than sending out enough food to serve the entire restaurant, the chef should prepare only enough to last fifteen to twenty minutes and then replace or refresh each dish regularly throughout the service period. Having fresh food on display at all times is critical to guests' enjoyment of a buffet, and in the case of a cafeteria, to how much money guests spend.

When replenishing a buffet, servers should not dump new food on top of old food. Not only will such an act turn off customers who see it, but the process is unsafe from a food sanitation perspective. The food at the bottom of the platter may end up sitting in the danger zone for hours and cross-contaminate the new food that regularly arrives on top of it. Instead, old platters, bowls, or chafing inserts should be removed from the buffet and replaced with new dishes that have been set up in the kitchen. Once a buffet dish has returned to the kitchen, the chef can determine whether it is appropriate to place any food remaining in the dish onto the next outgoing platter, to reserve it for employee meals, or simply to toss it in the trash. Frequently replenishing the buffet keeps the food looking fresh and the service platters clean. Additionally, hot food should be held hot and cold food held cold on the buffet. Chafing dishes (for fancy buffets) and steam tables (for casual cafeterias) maintain the heat and quality of the food they contain. Permanent buffet spaces often possess tables with the capacity to hold ice or to refrigerate hotel pan inserts, so cold food placed in them is held at a cold temperature. Off-premise caterers who must rely on portable equipment may not be able to place every cold dish over ice but certain highly perishable ones (think shrimp cocktail or cold lobster tails) should still be presented on ice. When a caterer or other food service provider does not have the ability to maintain food at the proper temperature on a buffet, it is that much more important that the food be rotated from the kitchen to the buffet every fifteen minutes or so.

In addition to the food placed on a buffet, service staff must also pay attention to the appearance and cleanliness of the buffet as a whole. As customers tend to spill food and disturb platter arrangements in the process of serving themselves, the staff must continually clean the buffet to maintain its quality appearance. Replacing older buffet platters with new ones allows the kitchen to refresh the original platters by wiping spills and replacing missing pieces of food from a composed presentation. Garnishes can help to distract attention from customer-disrupted platter arrangements, too. Garnishes on a platter should be colorful and arranged to one side of the platter (or bowl or chafing dish) so that customers do not disturb them while taking food. Ideally, they should relate in some way to the food they garnish, such as a bunch of oregano and colorful chiles for a bowl of black beans flavored with chiles and oregano. As long as the garnish remains visually appealing, guests are less likely to notice that the platter is no longer as perfectly arranged as it was when first placed on the buffet table. However, any garnish placed on a platter must be edible. Most guests will not attempt to eat a garnish, but occasionally a customer does. Eating the edible pansies from a platter's garnish, a customer may ruin the display, but he suffers no physical harm. Were he to consume poisonous daffodil flowers, however, the restaurant would have a lawsuit on its hands.

Inedible garnishes should only be utilized on the buffet table or guests' dining tables, not on the serving dishes. These table garnishes do not just provide visual appeal; ideally, they communicate the theme of the buffet or event in general. Thus, if the buffet is a BBQ theme, the table might be garnished with (clean) cowboy hats, boots, horseshoes, and lassos. Ice, tallow, or salt dough sculptures are dramatic table adornments that can be crafted to suit a theme, but even businesses without the staff and budget to create these sculptures

FIGURE 9.1

These two images show how ice sculptures not only provide beautiful table decoration but can also hold chilled food at the proper temperature.

Source: Ice Lab Ice Sculptures.

can greatly enhance a buffet with a few simple, inexpensive purchases, such as beads and plastic masks for a Mardi Gras party. General buffets without a particular theme might opt simply for flowers or other generic decorations. Unfortunately, expensive table decorations also present a theft opportunity for unscrupulous guests, so menu planners should either factor that expense into the cost of an event or train service staff to monitor these materials.

Many buffet planners use the buffet serving pieces themselves to enhance the visual appeal of a buffet. Extremely upscale operations may utilize only silver to communicate elegance to the guests. Other buffet planners may choose mirrors or decorative platters and bowls to lend visual interest to the buffet. Linens also add to a buffet's appeal. Various colorful cloths suggest whimsy and fun while a solid black or white display communicates formality and refinement. Height is an additional variable that contributes to a visually impressive buffet. Platters may be placed at an angle or at various heights by using risers (blocks or small dishes, often covered by cloths) to lift them off the table surface. Buffet businesses may stock tiered stands to allow for the presentation of several plates one above the other.

The shape of the tables offers yet another opportunity to vary a buffet. While a single straight line of rectangular tables can be decorated to enhance its beauty, a combination of rectangular, round, and serpentine tables adds another dimension of variety. Table shapes cannot be varied randomly as guest flow must be considered, but carefully arranged tables support both the aesthetic and practical needs of the guests.

Finally, buffets can offer one more level of variety to excite the guest—multiple styles of service. While most people think of a buffet as self-service from communal platters, a buffet can include some dishes that are portioned or prepared a la minute by an employee. For example, a carver may slice portions off a large roast at the buffet and present them to each guest. An omelet cook may prepare omelets to order for breakfast buffet customers. College cafeterias may have a cook, using portable burners at the buffet line, prepare stir-fries to order. This additional level of service helps to sell customers on a buffet purchase, especially when a restaurant wants to push much of its business to the buffet rather than to any available à la carte options.

In summary, buffets offer an opportunity to appeal to guests' visual senses. Variety in color, shape, texture, height, garnish, decoration, linen, table shape, and service style all help to make a buffet a visually stunning dining experience. Small signs or service staff may

FIGURE 9.2

This tiered buffet provides visual excitement through levels, colors, and creative serving pieces.

Source: Imijination Photography

FIGURE 9.3

This charcuterie and shellfish-themed buffet includes a carving station for prosciutto, which adds height while providing variety in service styles.

Source: Molly Peterson.

be required to inform customers about certain dishes and their ingredients, but when done right, the visual impact of a buffet sells the food as well as or better than the item descriptions included in a written menu. On a buffet, the menu and its functions still exist in unwritten form through the display of the many food choices presented for visual inspection by the customer.

Buffet Layout

Learning Objective 2
State the difference between an all-you-can-eat buffet and a cafeteria-style buffet.

By definition, a buffet is a display of food from which the customer serves himself. Within this simple definition are multiple variations, including the aforementioned buffet at which service personnel may portion or prepare to order some of the dishes on the buffet table. The two most common types of buffets are the all-you-can-eat buffet and the cafeteria. In the all-you-can-eat version, the business charges a single fee per person, and each customer may visit the buffet as many times as he wishes. Portion sizes on this type of buffet are nearly impossible to control, so an all-you-can-eat buffet is priced to account for the average amount and cost of food consumed. A cafeteria, on the other hand, charges each guest based on the type and quantity of food he selects. Cafeteria portions are either controlled by having each plate portioned—in advance or to order—by cafeteria workers or by weighing the food at the cash register and charging the customer per ounce of food (as is commonly done for cafeteria salad bar purchases).

Whether a buffet is all-you-can-eat or cafeteria style, there are some common challenges. One of the greatest is speed of service. All-you-can-eat buffets are often utilized at large catered events, such as weddings, where all of the guests hope to eat at the same time. If the guests are too slow in serving themselves, the first diner might be finished eating long before the last customer begins to pass through the buffet. Slow service leads to hungry, dissatisfied customers. Cafeterias run into a similar challenge. In an office or school cafeteria, many of the customers arrive simultaneously with a limited amount of time to eat. The longer they stand in line, the less time they have for the actual consumption of food. Customers who have a long wait are likely to purchase less food as they won't have time to eat more. Smaller purchases lead to less revenue and lower profits. Thus, cafeterias must speed service as much as possible.

Because buffet guests serve themselves some or all of their food, the best way to speed service on a buffet is through the buffet's layout. A guest in a restaurant with table service would be horribly inconvenienced if he had to wait for every prior customer to read through the menu and order before he was given the menu to read. Yet that is exactly the effect of a buffet with a single line. To make buffet service as efficient as possible for large parties, more than one guest ought to be able to take food at the same time. This means multiple buffet lines so that guests are not all funneled into a single line.

A single buffet line can generally serve fifty people efficiently within a short period of time. An event with more than fifty attendees requires a separate buffet for every fifty guests. There are two approaches to creating multiple buffets. The menu planner can set up identical buffet lines for every fifty people, or he can divide the menu choices among several buffets so that guests will find different options at each buffet table. There are pros and cons to each approach.

Multiple identical buffets allow guests to get the same items no matter which buffet they use. For a relatively small buffet selection, this is a great way to go. Customers will not waste time checking every buffet line to see whether there are better options at a different table. Additionally, even though such buffet lines may be all-you-can-eat, most guests will likely only need one pass through the buffet to taste all of the foods being served.

Menu planners must consider anticipated guest traffic flow to help determine the best location for multiple buffet lines. For 50–100 guests, a double-sided buffet line, starting at one end of the table and moving to the opposite end, may be the best approach. For 150–200 guests, the menu planner may consider having guests approach the middle of a

FIGURE 9.4

This simple buffet uses whole eggplants to lend visual interest to the buffet. The plates designate where on the buffet guests should start.

Source: Adam Barnes.

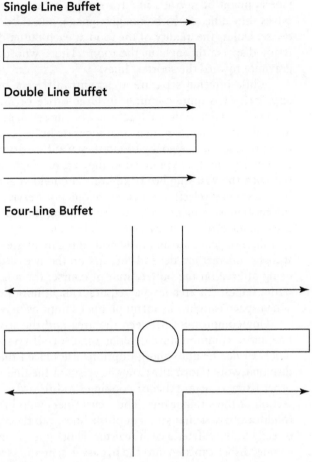

FIGURE 9.5
Sample buffet traffic patterns.

line of tables to pick up their plates and then head off in opposite directions. The key to communicating to guests the intended traffic pattern is simply the location of the plates; guests must grab a plate before moving to any other part of the buffet table. Furthermore, locating serving utensils on both sides of the table communicates to guests that they may use either side of the table to acquire their food. Figure 9.5 illustrates three possible guest traffic patterns at a straight-line buffet.

The type of buffet layout chosen depends partly upon how easily the kitchen and the guests can access the buffet. For example, a four-line buffet placed in the middle of a 200-person room makes sense only if the kitchen staff can easily get to those tables through the crowd. However, if the kitchen can only access the buffet tables when they are located around the perimeter of the room, then the menu planner should choose to lay out multiple double buffet lines along the sides of the room for easier replenishment of food. If the buffet has servers behind the tables to portion food for guests, then guests may only pass along one side of the buffet tables. To ensure that a buffet serves all guests as quickly as possible, the menu planner should locate the buffets for convenient access by both guests and kitchen staff and with enough lines that each line services only fifty people.

While multiple identical buffet lines work well for a moderate number of food selections, they are unwieldy options when there is an extensive buffet menu from which guests may choose. For example, an international gathering of 500 people may dine on a buffet highlighting foods from ten different countries. If each country were represented by only three dishes, that is still a thirty-item buffet. No guest could eat from thirty different dishes on a buffet, so the service line naturally slows as guests try to decide which dishes they will choose and which they will skip. A better approach is to make each cuisine (or two) a different buffet line and to locate the various buffet tables in different parts of the room.

Guests might be notified in advance that where they sit will determine from which buffet tables they dine, or, with enough signage, guests could choose to search out the food they desire. Unless the quality of the food at each buffet differs significantly, the guests will naturally disperse throughout the room. Those who do not care which cuisine they eat will gravitate toward the shortest lines.

While offering separate areas with different buffet options might seem an unusual approach, it is quite common in large office or museum cafeterias. The cafeteria might locate the salad bar in one location, hot entrées in another, pizzas at yet another buffet line, and cold sandwiches in their own separate buffet line. Just as guests skip through a written menu to find the category of food they want, customers at such a cafeteria jump directly to the line serving the type of food they crave. Each line may still provide multiple options, but with the vast number of options subdivided across different areas, customers choose from a smaller selection much more quickly. Service through an area layout is much faster for an extensive menu than is service using multiple identical straight-line buffets. However, menu planners must keep in mind that some guests will inevitably feel cheated that they did not get to see and taste everything in an area layout. Whether to use the area or the straight-line method depends heavily on the size of the group served, the number of dishes being offered on the buffet, and, of course, the amount of space available to arrange the buffet tables. An area layout requires much more floor space than a four-line buffet does. When space is tight, the menu planner's options may be similarly limited.

One compromise between the area and the straight-line buffet layouts is the bypass line, more common for cafeterias than for all-you-can-eat buffets. In the bypass line, all quick-service or grab-and-go options are placed flush along the straight buffet line. Any dish that would normally slow the speed of the line, such as portioning hot food entrées to order from a steam table or cooking food to order, is located in the bypass—an indented section of the straight line. Thus, customers who prefer to skip the individually portioned foods can bypass that segment of the line, grab their pre-portioned food items, and proceed directly to the cafeteria cash register. Those guests who want to wait for the more time-consuming dishes can step into the bypass indent and wait there without slowing the rest of the line. Figure 9.6 illustrates all three buffet layouts.

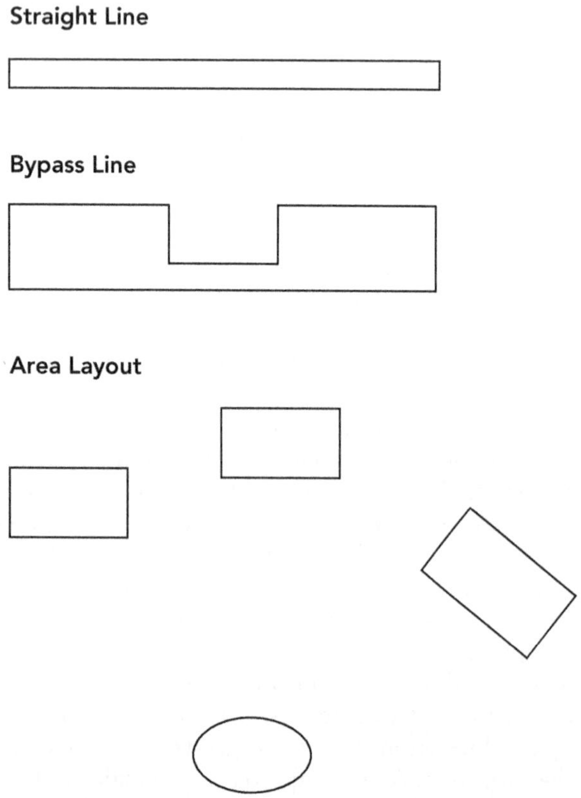

Straight Line

Bypass Line

Area Layout

FIGURE 9.6
Examples of buffet layouts.

Buffet Food Arrangement

Learning Objective 4
Organize food on a buffet to promote sales or to control costs.

While the layout of the buffet line impacts the speed of service, the menu planner arranges the food on the buffet line to control costs and to maximize profits. The theory behind food arrangement differs significantly for all-you-can-eat versus cafeteria buffets. An all-you-can-eat operation should be set up to encourage guests to select larger quantities of the less expensive dishes and smaller quantities of the more expensive ones. Since an all-you-can-eat buffet has a set price but no limit on consumption, the only way to control costs is to fill up guests on the cheaper items before they binge on the most costly dishes. If this type of buffet is set up incorrectly, the business's food costs will skyrocket. A cafeteria, on the other hand, charges for each bit of food sold. If the guest takes more food, the cafeteria generates more revenue and profit. Thus, a cafeteria should be set up to encourage multiple purchases and, ideally, purchases of the most profitable items.

If an all-you-can-eat buffet contains dishes that would normally be classified as appetizers, entrées, and desserts, then the courses should be set up in that order—appetizers first, entrées second, and, if included in the same buffet line, desserts last. This type of setup often occurs at upscale catering events that utilize buffets. Within each category, however, the food should be arranged so that the least expensive dishes within each category come first in the line and each subsequent dish is more expensive. The pattern repeats for each course. Most guests will take larger portions of the first few items they see in each category and have less room left on the plate by the time they get to the more expensive dishes.

Casual all-you-can-eat buffets, typically found in less expensive restaurants, need not follow the appetizers, then entrées, then desserts pattern, but if the buffet line does have a beginning and an end (i.e., not an area setup), the less expensive dishes should still come first. These operations sometimes put entrées, rather than appetizers, first, as they assume most guests will get the entrées no matter how full they are. Using this logic, the restaurant hopes that a number of guests, having already filled up on entrées, will skip appetizers (and possibly desserts) entirely. Because guests psychologically do not feel they have had a meal if they do not eat an entrée, they will not skip the entrée choices even if they have filled up on appetizers.

Whether the buffet is upscale or casual, desserts may be located in a separate area for the sake of speed. Many guests will only take dessert after they have eaten the savory offerings. Having them wait in the same line as people making their first pass through the buffet makes the line unnecessarily long. Having desserts on their own table with their own line and fresh plates allows guests who have already eaten their entrées to skip the main buffet and go directly to dessert without standing in line again.

Placing less expensive foods first in the buffet line helps to control food costs, but the approach is not foolproof. Thus, only the most upscale all-you-can-eat buffets (which charge exorbitant rates for their food) should include extremely pricy dishes. Typically, any dish that costs more à la carte for a single portion than the entire buffet does should not be included on the buffet. For example, if a restaurant offers a boiled shrimp entrée for $15 and the buffet only costs $12 per person, then boiled shrimp should not be included on the buffet. No matter how far down the buffet line the shrimp are located, guests will quickly recognize this as a bargain opportunity. They will order the buffet and fill their plates, multiple times, with piles of shrimp. This is particularly true if the rest of the dishes on the buffet are far less expensive than the shrimp are. For instance, on a seafood buffet full of lots of expensive dishes no single dish gets "rushed" by the guests, but the price is set to account for the higher food cost. The buffet costs more, but guests will find the buffet worth the price because of the many costly dishes. Were a restaurant to set up a buffet with only one expensive dish but price the buffet under the assumption that guests will flock to that dish, the customers would not view the buffet as a deal. They would, instead, order that one dish (or something else) off the menu. Shrimp, of course, are not the only example of a dish that would get hit hard by customers on a buffet; lobster, crab, lamb chops, and filet mignon would all suffer a similar fate, which is why they are rarely seen on an inexpensive buffet. Service staff should portion large roasts on a carving station to keep guests from cutting their own thick steaks. In general, while some foods will inevitably be more expensive than others, all of the dishes should fall within a similar price range on an all-you-can-eat buffet.

Unlike an all-you-can-eat buffet operation, cafeterias would love it if guests rushed their most expensive dish. Priced accordingly, a mad rush on shrimp might generate more profits than a surge in spaghetti sales. However, cafeteria guests typically are not looking for a fine dining experience (or they would probably search out a table service restaurant); value-priced dishes are often the best choices for a cafeteria.

When laying out the food on a cafeteria line, menu planners should organize the food in the order in which it would normally be eaten—appetizers first, entrées second, and so on. Beverages should be placed both at the beginning and the end of the cafeteria line to encourage sales of these high-profit items as much as possible. Some cafeterias locate desserts both at the front and the back of the line with the hope that some guests will take dessert before they realize how much food comes with the purchase of an entrée. Finally, all add-ons, such as portable, packaged snacks, should be located by the cash register. The cashiers have an opportunity to encourage the purchase of add-ons at the time of sale. Additionally, customers may decide to grab an extra snack for later while they are standing in line waiting to pay.

An area buffet layout may not follow any of the rules for the arrangement of food that a line layout requires. Guests may float from one table to the next in any order, and in the case of round tables, there may not be an obvious starting point and direction for guest traffic flow at each table. For cafeterias, signage helps to direct guests to each area, but guests may skip certain tables entirely, which limits a cafeteria manager's marketing opportunities. The only places that all of the guests will see are the entrance and the exit by the cash register. Thus, these two areas are prime marketing spots. Cafeteria managers should locate the items (or station) they most want to sell near the cafeteria entrance and place desserts and snacks as close to the cash register as possible. With an all-you-can-eat buffet, an area setup is the most difficult layout for controlling food costs. Consequently, it is absolutely critical that the costs of each dish in an area layout all-you-can-eat buffet are similar to each other.

Guaranteed Guest Counts

Learning Objective 5
List three ways caterers can charge based on a customer count guarantee.

Chapter 7 covered how to determine a per person price for a buffet. All-you-can-eat operations require calculating the average food cost per person as the basis for determining a sales price per person. Cafeterias, like most other foodservice operations, can determine a food cost per portion for each item and then price each dish accordingly.

Caterers face a significant challenge when it comes to calculating a sales price for their menus. Unlike other foodservice operations, caterers may have to lock in a per person price a year in advance with a client. Thus, menu planners for caterers have to anticipate future price fluctuations for ingredients. Additionally, a client may come in with a defined budget. In such cases, the caterer must provide *inclusive pricing*-that is, a price that includes tax and tip. Even when a client does not provide a budget, the caterer should still state in advance whether tax and tip are included in the price or will be added to the final bill.

Caterers have a particularly difficult challenge with buffets, which are almost always an all-you-can-eat format, as they must know how much food to prepare for a given event. Unlike a buffet restaurant, a caterer does not have a sales history for forecasting how many guests to expect on a given day or how much this particular group of diners will consume; estimating an average food cost per person becomes that much more difficult. Additionally, the caterer is beholden to the client to forecast how many guests to expect. Since most caterers cannot use the food from one party elsewhere, they aim to prepare just enough to satisfy all of the guests without running short on food. But what about a client whose prediction is way off? If extra guests arrive, can the client complain that the caterer should have had more food on the buffet? If only half of the anticipated guests show up, is the client permitted to pay only for those who attend, essentially forcing the caterer to eat the cost of the excess food? The best way to protect the interests of the caterer and the client fairly is through the use of a guarantee.

A *guarantee* (or guaranteed guest count) is the customer's prediction of how many guests the caterer should expect to serve. It is also the foundation upon which the caterer's food production and the client's price will be based whether or not the client's prediction is accurate. Caterers use their experience to determine how much of each dish to prepare per person for a catered event. For a plated banquet, the quantities may be embedded in the menu and the contract. For a buffet, the client, not knowing how much each guest will eat, simply expects the caterer to provide enough to satisfy all of the guests, no matter how heartily they eat. Fewer items on a buffet mean partygoers will consume more of each dish than they would with a much larger spread. Caterers are expected to adjust their production appropriately regardless of the menu or forecast guest count.

Because caterers have a brand and reputation to protect, they have an incentive to overproduce for a buffet so that the food does not run out. A client, knowing that a given caterer serves large portions, has an incentive to understate the guest count and pay for fewer guests under the assumption that there will still be plenty of food for the extra attendees. If the caterer does not feed all of the attendees, his brand is tarnished. If he overproduces significantly, his costs become exorbitant. The caterer naturally wants a guarantee that is accurate, but even an honest client cannot predict whether a guest will get sick last minute or decide to attend despite not replying to an invitation. Flexibility in a guarantee puts the customer at ease and helps to protect a caterer's brand, but too much flexibility precludes cost controls.

There are three ways that a caterer can treat a guarantee to ensure that he gets paid appropriately and protects the company's reputation while addressing unforeseen guest count fluctuations. While clients have the largest incentive to low-ball a guarantee with a buffet, all three types of guarantees apply equally to catered events no matter what the style of service. The first type of guarantee is a *minimum guarantee*. With a minimum guarantee, the client will pay for the number of guests stated in the contracted guarantee, even if fewer show up. If the guest count exceeds the guarantee, then the client will pay for the exact count up to a point. Typically, the caterer agrees to accommodate only some additional guests, usually 5%–10% above the count. The caterer prepares enough food for the 5%–10% buffer, and the client knows that if he has low-balled the guarantee too much, there will not be enough food for the guests. The caterer knows that he can charge for any additional guests that arrive but that at a minimum, he will collect a fee based on the guarantee.

The second type of guarantee is the *over/under* or *approximate guarantee*. Using this approach, the caterer allows for some flexibility in the client's guest count by charging as little as 5% below the guarantee and as much as 5% over the guarantee. To protect his reputation, the caterer prepares food for 5% over the guarantee so that the food does not run out. The client will not be penalized financially if the actual attendance falls slightly short of the guarantee. However, there is still a minimum charge below which the event's price cannot fall, and there is a maximum attendance above which the caterer will not accommodate. The client is incentivized to be as accurate as possible in his guarantee.

Finally, the third type of guarantee is the *exact guarantee*. As the name suggests, there is no flexibility in count. The client will be charged for the contracted guarantee, and the caterer will not accommodate any additional guests. This approach allows the caterer to control costs extremely well, but clients may be turned off by the lack of flexibility. This type of guarantee works best for small business meetings to which additional last-minute guests would not be invited and which all invitees are required to attend.

Verbal Specials

Learning Objective 6
Describe the role that servers play in communicating unwritten menu components.

Cafeterias and buffets are not the only examples of unwritten menus. Many restaurants with printed menus offer one or more daily specials. Sometimes these specials rotate on a cycle and are included in print on the menu. Other times, they are spontaneous creations based on available product and the chef's inspiration. These spur-of-the-moment inventions may be printed on a daily menu, written on a chalkboard, or placed on a menu insert, but for many restaurants, the easiest way to present them is through the server. As with written menus, the servers' oral descriptions must be accurate and sound delicious. In some operations, the kitchen requires the servers to taste the daily special before service so that they can answer questions about its flavor, ingredients, and presentation. Because a lengthy speech about a special will delay a server from other responsibilities, servers should keep their specials presentation brief. If the price of the special does not fall within the range of the regular menu prices, then it should be disclosed. Otherwise, the restaurant may opt not to have servers state the price of the special unless the guest asks.

Sometimes a guest initiates an off-menu request either by asking for a modification to a dish or by asking the chef to create something unique from components that may or may not appear on the menu. When a kitchen does accommodate such requests, the server must remain faithful to truth-in-menu rules and not misrepresent something that the kitchen prepares. The server should carefully record the guest's request and check with the kitchen to see whether it can be accommodated before making any promises to the guest. Even if the POS system allows for a special request entry, the server should follow up in person with the kitchen. If the kitchen does agree to prepare the off-menu dish, the server should confirm upon pick-up that the dish has been prepared as promised before delivering it to the guest. If the kitchen cannot accommodate the off-menu request, the server should communicate that to the guest as quickly as possible so that he can make an alternate selection from the menu.

Whether a dish is printed on a menu or not, the server has incredible power to influence the sales of certain dishes. Servers can provide personal recommendations and additional details for the items printed on the menu. When a menu provides minimalist, ingredient-only descriptions, the server has the opportunity to describe flavors, textures, and visual qualities for a given dish. A server who provides a menu description orally at the table operates as an unwritten menu and should complement rather than undermine the printed menu item and the operation's brand. Truth-in-menu rules prohibit the server from stating inaccurate information just to encourage a sale.

Whereas a printed menu markets to a general audience, the server can tailor spoken sales pitches to each individual guest. If a guest states a preference for a low-fat dish, the server can provide the best recommendation. If a guest wants to taste the specialties of the house, the server can guide the customer through that experience and menu selection. A printed menu offers upper management control of the message being communicated to the guests, but a server offers personalized attention that may increase sales and the quality of the guests' experience.

This personalized persuasion allows the server to upsell products to a guest. *Upselling* is the encouragement of a higher-priced or additional product to a guest who orders a standard one. For example, a guest might order a gin and tonic. The server could reply, "Would you like that made with Tanqueray?" If the guest says yes and the Tanqueray commands a higher sales price than the basic gin and tonic, then that is an example of effective upselling. The guest gets a higher-quality product, but he willingly orders it, which authorizes the higher charge. The restaurant ends up with more revenue, and the server presumably gets a higher tip based on a larger bill. Upselling need not be done solely on alcoholic drinks. In an Italian restaurant, if bread comes with an entrée for free, the server might ask if the guest wants garlic bread instead (which usually comes at a price). Indian restaurants, in which bread is not usually included, do the same thing when they ask a guest whether he would like naan with the meal.

Upselling is just one form of suggestive selling. Delicious menu descriptions, presented in writing or orally, are another example of suggestive selling. They encourage the guest to order something in particular. Suggestive selling can persuade a customer to choose one dish—perhaps a more profitable dish—over another through a simple server recommendation. A more powerful form of suggestive selling is to encourage the sales of additional courses. When a server greets a table, he might ask the guests whether they would like to start with an appetizer or some drinks. He can recommend dessert after clearing the entrée plates. The most effective way to suggestive sell is for the server to assume that the guest wants multiple courses and then to phrase his questions to the table accordingly. For example, rather than say, "Would you like an appetizer to start?" he might state, "Would you care to start with an order of our famous chicken wings this evening, or would you prefer one of our other spectacular appetizers?" The customer can always decline purchasing any appetizer, but some guests are inevitably persuaded to make the extra purchase through this form of questioning. Consider the difference between a server who hears a guest order a hamburger and states, "I'll put that right in for you," and one who instead replies, "Would you like cheddar or gorgonzola on your burger?" (upselling), followed by, "And would you care to start with a house salad, or are you looking to save room for dessert?" (suggestive selling). The second server may not convince every guest to make an additional purchase, but over the course of a meal, he will greatly outsell the first server. Suggestive selling and upselling by a server are excellent ways to extend the marketing and selling functions of a menu beyond the printed word.

Summary

When a foodservice business does not provide a written menu to the guest, it must sell the product and inform the customer in other ways. All-you-can-eat buffets and cafeteria lines are the most common examples of unwritten menu operations. Small signs or service staff inform the guests, but the food must sell itself visually. To keep food attractive, service staff must keep the buffet clean, replenish products frequently, and maintain the food at its proper temperature. The food itself must display variety in color, shape, and texture. Garnishes, table decorations, china, silver, centerpieces, and linen add to the appeal while variety in height and in table shape provide further visual spectacle. Buffets may be laid out in a straight line, bypass, or area setup; for large parties, multiple buffets may be identical or distinct to aid traffic flow. Food

should be arranged on a buffet either to control costs or to increase revenue. To control costs, place the less expensive foods near the front of the line or to the front of each "course." Cafeterias wish to increase revenue, so they should locate add-ons and beverages in prime locations where customers are likely to see them. Caterers utilize a guarantee to protect themselves from financial and reputation loss. The three types of guarantees are minimum, over/under, and exact. Servers also operate as unwritten menus when they present specials, accept off-menu requests, suggestive sell, or upsell at the table. Their work further markets the product to guests. There are many obvious differences between written and unwritten menus, but the foodservice business must inform customers and market its product regardless of the form the menu takes.

Comprehension Questions

1. List five things that a menu planner and/or chef can do to make the food on a buffet visually appealing.

2. List three things that a manager can do to make a buffet attractive beyond the food itself.

3. What is the difference between an all-you-can-eat buffet and a cafeteria?

4. List and describe three ways to lay out tables for a buffet.

5. How should a menu planner arrange the food for an all-you-can-eat buffet? Why?

6. In a cafeteria, which two locations should display add-ons?

7. List and define the three types of customer count guarantees commonly used by caterers.

8. Define suggestive selling and upselling.

Discussion Questions

1. Imagine that you are a server in a restaurant. Write out a brief introduction that you could present upon greeting a table that would include an example of suggestive selling.

2. List two examples of upselling that you have experienced in a restaurant—one that is done by a server and one that is simply written as an available option on a menu. Which one was more persuasive to you?

3. Imagine that you are catering an event (theme: your choice). Write out a list of twelve dishes that you would include on the buffet, keeping in mind that variety is essential. In what order would you arrange these dishes on an all-you-can-eat buffet with a straight-line layout?

4. If you were catering a buffet party for 1,000 people, how would you lay out the tables in the room? How many buffets would you have? Why?

5. As a caterer with a 1,000-person party, what type of guarantee would you use? How much food would you produce (in number of portions)? What are the pros and cons of using this particular guarantee method?

6. The chapter has referred to a cafeteria as a type of buffet. While a cafeteria sometimes includes a true buffet (like a salad bar sold by weight), not all of the items are completely self-service. Why is that? In your opinion, does it make a difference in how the cafeteria line is set up if the cafeteria is 100% buffet or not buffet at all? Why?

Case Study

A caterer has contracted with a client to provide a buffet for 200 people at a corporate event. The client wants to spare no expense on the food, so the menu includes crab cakes, filet mignon, lamb rib chops, and more. However, the client asks to cut any unnecessary expenditures from the event. The caterer, wishing to accommodate the client, agrees to keep the buffet to a single table, drop the number of servers to five, hold the number of bartenders to two, and reduce the on-site kitchen staff to two cooks.

The event is a disaster. Guests express frustration at waiting in line for so long to get their food. The line at the bar doesn't help. Even worse, by the time the last thirty people get to the buffet, the meat and seafood are completely gone. The caterer tries to appease the guests by cutting up some wheels of cheese that had been on display as table garnish, but the client is furious. The client believes he paid highly for the food and cannot understand why the caterer ran out. (The client doesn't complain at all about guests waiting in line.) The caterer, too, is baffled. He is sure he counted out 200 four-ounce portions of filet mignon, 200 three-ounce crab cakes, and 200 lamb rib chops. Because the food cost was so high, the caterer and the client had agreed in advance to an exact guarantee. The actual attendance was only 190, so the caterer cannot blame the client in this case. By the end of the night, the caterer had agreed to reimburse the client a significant amount of money for the debacle.

Where did the caterer go wrong in this situation? If the client wanted to keep the same budget, what could the caterer have done with the food to make it upscale but not run out?

Capstone Project

Step 9: Create a one-page training document for servers on how to market the menu to guests at the table. The document should include instructions for greeting guests, suggestive selling and upselling, and driving business to certain menu items. The document may include a sample script for servers to use. If your project includes a buffet, draw a floor plan of the dining room including the layout and location of the buffet; then, describe the layout of the food on the buffet including platter and table garnishes and signage. If your project does not have servers approaching guests at tables to market the menu, explain how and when marketing to the guest takes place and who performs the selling function. (As this step in the project is easy to execute, use this time as an opportunity to polish and refine any previous, incomplete steps. The next step in the project will be difficult to complete if all of the prior steps have not been fully completed.)

CHAPTER 10

Layout of the Written Menu

INTRODUCTION

With the menu items, headings, prices, and descriptive copy determined for a menu, the menu planner is finally ready to lay out and print the menu. In an era where people print documents at home all the time, this task might seem quite simple and straightforward. However, care and consideration must go into every detail of the process if the menu is to maximize its effectiveness. From the choice of paper and font to the layout of graphics and text, each decision has the potential to enhance or to undermine the guests' experience and the business's brand.

Menu design and printing can be performed by a professional menu designer and printer or by a menu planner with a little training and access to the right technology. Learning the considerations that go into menu layout and production allows the menu planner to perform the task in-house, if she chooses. Should she outsource the work, a knowledgeable menu planner will be able to communicate more effectively with the designer. Done properly, a printed menu can increase sales and subliminally direct customers toward the most profitable purchases. Poorly designed, a menu can turn off customers, persuade them to purchase less, and even encourage them not to return. As menus can take the form of menu boards, web page displays, and single-use pieces of paper, considerations for the layout of these types of menus are discussed as well.

CHAPTER 10 LEARNING OBJECTIVES

As a result of successfully completing this chapter, readers will be able to:

1. Lay out a menu to locate high-profit items where they are most likely to be sold in one-page, two-page, trifold, or multi-page formats.

2. Describe the factors menu designers must consider when selecting menu paper and font.

3. List several considerations for selecting a menu cover or page treatment.

4. State the pros and cons of contracting out the layout and printing of a menu versus doing the work in-house.

5. Calculate the quantity of menus to print for a restaurant.

6. Describe special concerns related to menu boards, electronic menus, and single-use menus.

CHAPTER 10 OUTLINE

Menu Size and Layout

Menu Construction
  Covers and Treatments

Printing In-House versus Printing Professionally
  Print Quantities

Other Types of Menus
  Web Menus

Summary

Comprehension Questions

Discussion Questions

Case Study

Capstone Project

Reference

Menu Size and Layout

Learning Objective 1
Lay out a menu to locate high-profit items where they are most likely to be sold in one-page, two-page, trifold, or multi-page formats.

The first decision a menu designer must make is to select the ultimate size of the menu. The standard size for copier or printer paper is 8½" × 11". Some establishments use this size of paper inserted into a cover for their menu. Others go several inches larger to allow for bigger print, more images, or possibly to squeeze the entire menu onto one or two pages. A dessert menu or table tent menu may be significantly smaller. However, a menu designer should consider the practicality of the menu when selecting the size. A menu that is too small may require a large number of pages, which slows guests in their ordering or encourages them to skip entire headings. An overly large menu may feel clumsy and knock over water glasses on the table. Menus that are comfortable to hold and read should be the goal. Because 8½" × 11" paper is the most common, defaulting to this size may result in cost savings, too.

The size of the paper determines the number of pages required for the menu, which in turn impacts the layout. A menu can be printed as a single sheet, as a two-page folio (possibly with content on the back cover), as a multipage book, or as a trifold in which the left and right sides close over a larger center page. Menus should always support the theme and concept of the restaurant. Thus, a quirky restaurant may have a nonrectangular menu or one that opens vertically rather than right to left, but a menu designer must keep in mind that nonrectangular menus cost significantly more to produce than do rectangular ones.

Whatever shape or form the menu takes, the pages should not be cluttered. Empty or "white" space at the margins and between listings makes the menu appear clean and orderly and gives the eye a moment to rest between lines of text. As guests need places to hold the menu without covering up text, and since reading a menu should feel less laborious than reading a book, a good amount of white space is essential on most restaurant menus. Some operations reserve as much as 50% of the menu for white space to maintain this uncluttered look, but the exact percentage of white space should reflect the theme and physical interior of the restaurant. A colorful restaurant with lots of graphics on the wall and a "busy" feel may wish to replace some (though not all) of the white space with thematic imagery and color to give the menu a similarly lively feel. When a menu has too much white space, the menu designer can include photos, drawings, text on the history of the building and owners, or information about the business and other services it offers. The designer must always include room for pricing policies or food safety statements to keep the restaurant in compliance with truth-in-menu and food safety regulations. The business's location, hours of operation, and contact information are optional for a sit-down establishment, but they are a must for a take-out menu.

When determining the location of certain menu items, designers should consider the menu's "hot zones." A hot zone is the location where a guest's eyes typically fall first—the location that all guests will see even if they only glance briefly at the menu to make a quick selection. Because Americans read from left to right and top to bottom, their eyes tend to settle on the upper half of a page and gravitate to the right. Thus, on a single-page menu, the hot zone is top center. On a two-page or multipage menu, the upper half of each right page is the hot zone. Finally, on a trifold menu, the hot zone is located on the upper half of the center page. (See Figure 10.1.)

Knowing the location of a menu's hot zone allows the menu designer to locate the items she most wishes to sell in the hot zone. Items there are likely to get additional attention from the guest and to garner a larger share of the business over time. Highly profitable items are best located in the hot zones.

Of course, menu items cannot be randomly moved throughout the menu just to put the most profitable ones in the hot zones. Menus are typically organized under headings listed in the order in which the courses are normally eaten. Thus, appetizers come first, soups and salads appear next, entrées follow, and desserts, if they are included on the main menu, come last (although small plate and other nontraditional menus allow for more flexibility with menu item location). When beverages are listed on the food menu, they may be placed at the beginning (common with cocktails) or at the end of the menu (more prevalent for soft drinks). Because the courses must come in a prescribed order, menu designers may experiment with font size and the location of images to get the most profitable items in a

FIGURE 10.1
Menu layouts and their hot zones.

heading to end up in the hot zone. If a heading falls completely outside of a hot zone, the designer at a minimum should place the items she most wishes to sell in the upper half of that menu category.

Another way to grab the customers' attention is through inserts or clip-ons. An insert is a page (usually the same size as the other menu pages) that is placed inside the menu but not bound to it. Because the insert is removable, the guest must hold and handle it separately to keep it from falling. This extra handling draws the guest's focus to the insert and to the menu items listed on it. A clip-on is a small piece of paper that provides a list of specials. It is usually attached or clipped on to the top of one of the menu pages. Because the clip-on does not lie flat on the main menu page, it, too, draws the attention of the guest. Clip-ons should never cover other menu items, as not all guests will lift the clip-on to see the options that lie beneath. Instead, the clip-on should be located over a visual image that contributes to the business's theme but is otherwise unnecessary. That way, if a clip-on is not used, the image, rather than a blank space, is visible to the customer.

Where the menu designer chooses to locate the price of each item greatly impacts sales. One cardinal rule is to keep the customers' focus on the product, not on the price. That is not to say that a menu can avoid listing the price, but the designer should not highlight, bold, or otherwise draw attention to a menu item's price. Similarly, menu items should not be listed in order of price (either highest to lowest or lowest to highest), as this pattern encourages guests to notice price differences in each subsequent menu listing. Some designers choose to list the price at the end of the menu description, so the reader must go through the entire description to get to the price. Others locate a dish's name on the left-hand side of a menu and the price in a column on the right-hand side. This approach informs the customers of the price but forces them to look away from the food listing if they wish to find out the price of a dish. Some guests may not look over at the prices at all.

Another approach to minimizing the impact of sticker shock on guests is to avoid listing prices in the format that most people associate with money. In most businesses, people see prices written as a dollar sign with a number, such as $9.95. Some research suggests that removing the dollar sign from the menu encourages customers to spend more than they otherwise would in a restaurant.[1] Listing the price as a plain number eases the impulse some people have to bargain shop every time they see a dollar symbol.

While some operations choose to emphasize their discount prices (think dollar menus), the menu designer should keep in mind that drawing a guest's attention to one price will make them consider all of the prices on the menu. Thus, a fast-food establishment that tries to make every purchase seem like a bargain—dollar menus, value meals, etc.—can successfully appeal to a price-sensitive market without undermining sales it might otherwise make. Were a table service restaurant to attempt to highlight a few discounted items, it would likely draw business away from other, more profitable sales.

Menu Construction

Learning Objective 2
Describe the factors menu designers must consider when selecting menu paper and font.

With the layout determined, the menu designer next selects the paper and typography best suited for the foodservice operation. When making these decisions, the menu planner should account for the market's demographics, dining room lighting, and legibility. To help support the overall guest experience, the menu planner should also consider the theme and feel of the establishment. A casual restaurant might use brightly colored paper with lots of photos on its menu, but to communicate a more serious food environment, an expensive restaurant would do better with fewer splashes of color and photos. The type of paper, kinds of images, and even the size and style of font project a certain experience to the consumer. That experience should always support the business's brand and concept.

In addition to choosing a paper's size, the menu designer selects the paper's color, weight, and texture. A designer can choose any color paper and font, but because of the contrast, the easiest to read is black lettering on a white background. A restaurant with a specific color theme might go with a similarly colored menu, but the paper should still be light and the writing dark. For example, a menu for a romantic, crimson-themed dining room might be printed on light pink paper with black lettering, but deep red paper would not provide sufficient contrast for ease of reading, especially in a dimly lit restaurant. Although black paper and white lettering do provide contrast, they are far more difficult to read than pages in which the light color is reserved for the background. Menu planners can utilize color to communicate holiday themes or cultural conventions—think red for Chinese New Year or orange for Halloween—but the most important consideration for selecting colors on a menu is the operation's theme and brand. If the dining room or operation's logo highlights a specific color, that color may be appropriate on the menu as a general background color or in boxes behind text to highlight certain dishes the restaurant wishes to promote. Otherwise, black and white work best for ease of reading, particularly in dining rooms that are not brightly lit.

A paper's weight and texture impact the guests' perception of the menu. Heavyweight (thick) paper communicates seriousness, while thin paper feels flimsy in the hands. Of course, the weight may be irrelevant if the menu is slipped into a larger cover or laminated, as the guest will be unable to tell the weight of the paper under such circumstances. A paper's texture can range from coarse and bumpy to smooth and glossy. The rougher paper feels like antique parchment, which feels more substantial in the hands; it also holds type well. A glossy paper, on the other hand, works well for photos. The coarse option is often better when the guest holds the paper directly without any covering, but again, the feel of the menu must support the restaurant's concept.

The font that a menu designer chooses should be easy to read but also suggestive of the business's brand. Roman fonts, which use straight lines and simple curves with few embellishments, are quite legible and communicate a classic or traditional feel. Sans serif fonts provide a sleeker, more modern approach. Some fonts are more common in different countries, so an ethnic restaurant may use a specific font to support the theme of the culture and food being served. Scripts and other nontraditional fonts are creative but difficult to read. It is best to reserve the suggestive but hard-to-read fonts for menu headings while utilizing the simpler fonts for menu items and descriptive copy. The business name, which customers already know when they sit down, is the best opportunity to communicate a brand through a font. As suggested earlier, the color of the type should be dark and highly contrasted with a light background.

The size of a font is as important as its style for readability. Many restaurants are dimly lit to create an intimate setting for the guests. While low lighting can make conversation and dining fun, it can make reading a menu challenging. Font size is measured in "points." The 11- or 12-point font of a computer word processor is easy to read in a brightly lit office but rather difficult to read in a restaurant setting. A slightly larger 12- to 14-point font is much easier for restaurant guests to read; menu headings should be even larger than that. Leading (pronounced LEHD–ing) refers to the space between lines of text. While many kinds of printed work can be easily read with little space between the lines of type, the low-level light of a restaurant setting calls for some additional space to aid reading.

The font size and style need not stay consistent for every word on the menu, but they should follow a clear visual hierarchy; that is, keep the same font size and style for words serving the same purpose. For example, menu headings ("Appetizers," "Entrées," etc.) are often larger and of a different font than menu items and descriptions, but all menu headings should use the same font. Menu item descriptions should similarly match each other's fonts. The use of bold and italic typeface should be limited so that they catch the customer's eye when they do appear. Other than its use in category headings, bold or italics is often used to highlight a dish's name (for ease of ordering) when the name is embedded within the menu description or to offset a policy or notice at the bottom of the menu. Otherwise, font adjustments should not be used. Overuse of bold, italics, and font variations creates a cluttered, disorganized menu that does not direct the gaze of the viewer effectively.

An effective way to highlight certain dishes without resorting to font changes is through colors, symbols, or boxes. Sometimes, a restaurant wishes to highlight its specialty. The menu designer can emphasize a particular dish simply by enclosing it in a box so that it is differentiated from the other dishes on the menu. The box may have a colored background to help the menu item stand out even more. Symbols are popular tools to point out dishes that conform to certain nutritional guidelines, that are particularly spicy, or that are specialties of the house. For example, a menu designer might place a heart symbol next to the low-fat, low-sodium options or a chile pepper next to the spicy ones. Alternatively, she might place a star or other symbol next to those dishes for which the restaurant is famous. When symbols are used, they should be defined at the bottom of the menu, but the use of boxes or shading designed to highlight a dish the restaurant wishes to sell needs no further explanation. It is important to note that highlights, boxes, and symbols can be overused. If everything on the menu is a specialty, then nothing is special. Menu designers get the best results when they only highlight a couple of dishes on each menu page.

Some menu designers use images to convey the business's brand or to sell certain products. Photographs of certain dishes help the customer to understand what a dish will look

FIGURE 10.2
Proper and improper variations in typeface.

Proper Use of Font Guides the Guest's Eye	Improper Use of Font Creates a Cluttered Mess
MEATS	**MEATS**
Dry-aged 14 oz **porterhouse** grilled over hickory wood and served with twice-baked potato and green beans	Dry-aged 14 oz **PORTERHOUSE** grilled over hickory wood and served with twice-baked potato and green beans
Seared twin **pork chops** stuffed with spinach and gruyere, topped with port wine-fig demiglace, and served with mashed sweet potato and braised cabbage	Seared twin *PORK CHOPS* **stuffed** with spinach and gruyere, topped with port wine-fig demiglace, and served with mashed sweet potato **and braised cabbage**

FIGURE 10.3

This menu uses color and photos to support its theme and the ship's wheel symbol to identify "pub favorites."

Source: The Pub Waterfront Restaurant.

FIGURE 10.4

This menu uses illustrations and black-and-white photos to support its 1930s–1950s theme, boxes to highlight certain dishes, and "ads" to promote other restaurants owned by the same parent company. In the restaurant, the menu is printed and folded to resemble a newspaper or "bulletin."

Reprinted with permission from matchboxfoodgroup.

FIGURE 10.4 *(Continued)*

like upon arrival, but menu planners must recognize that the food served must appear identical or nearly so to the depicted dish to avoid truth-in-menu violations. Menu photographs may portray things other than food, too. An ethnic restaurant might include a photo of the cuisine's country. An organic operation might show photos of the farms from which the ingredients are sourced. Some menu designers prefer black-and-white sketches or drawings, which are cheaper to print than color photos are, to elicit emotional responses that support the business concept. For example, a drawing of a cactus, a sombrero, and a map of Mexico might provide a sense of place in a Tex–Mex restaurant. A sketch of a school of fish or an oyster with a pearl might effectively reinforce the theme of a seafood restaurant. Whatever images are selected, the menu designer must ensure that they appear clearly on the printed menu. Blurred or difficult-to-interpret images add little to a menu and can frustrate or disorient a customer who cannot make out the image clearly.

Covers and Treatments

Learning Objective 3
List several considerations for selecting a menu cover or page treatment.

With the interior of the menu constructed, the menu designer must decide what cover or treatment, if any, the menu requires. Some businesses purchase permanent covers that allow for menu pages to be held inside and changed as desired. Others create menus in which the cover and content are affixed together; any change to the menu requires that the cover be reprinted as well. Still other establishments dispense entirely with covers and simply hand guests a single-page menu. Which approach the menu designer chooses depends on the company's brand and the relative permanence of the menu.

Menu covers come in a wide range of materials. Some are made of padded or synthetic leather while others are composed of hard plastic, wood, metal, or some other durable material. As with everything else related to menus, the cover should reflect the concept of the business. Leather is traditional for old-fashioned, high-end restaurants while metal may be used for a hip, modern, urban place. The front cover typically includes the business's name and logo, possibly with a slogan or other images. When permanent covers allow for multiple iterations of the menu to be rotated within, little else should grace the cover. This provides the restaurant flexibility in changing its operation without having to purchase new covers. For example, if business hours are printed on the cover, then the restaurant cannot change its hours without paying to produce new covers. Since non-paper covers are more expensive to produce than the rest of the menu, the less frequently they are replaced, the better. Permanent menu covers should be durable, stain-resistant, and easy to clean. Even if the content on a menu cover is accurate, it must still be replaced once damaged or stained. A dirty or torn menu reflects poorly on a restaurant, and it can turn off customers who might otherwise enjoy the establishment.

There are significant benefits to using a permanent menu cover that allows for printed pages to be placed inside. With a permanent cover, a soiled menu page can be easily replaced without having to purchase an entirely new menu. Similarly, the menu planner can inexpensively print a new menu in-house every day should the chef wish to adjust the menu. This helps to keep a business compliant with truth-in-menu regulations even when an ingredient is shorted on a delivery. In short, a permanent menu cover with inserts allows for flexibility without significant expense. Menu pages may be held in place at the corners or simply slid into a transparent cover, but changing the pages does not require changing the menu cover.

When a restaurant knows that its menu will not change for months at a time, the designer has the option of printing a menu of which the cover is a permanent part. In these cases, the cover and the first page inside the cover may share a single sheet of paper. Alternatively, the menu listings may begin on the cover itself. Typically, under these circumstances, the menu designer has the menu laminated. Lamination is a clear, plastic coating sealed around each page of the menu. It usually contains two back-to-back papers to generate a single double-sided menu page. Because lamination is highly durable and easy to wipe clean, laminated menus are popular in family restaurants where the menu does not change often but spills on the menu are common. The expense of lamination, however, does not make this type of menu cost-effective in operations that change their menus daily or weekly.

FIGURE 10.5

Permanent menu covers come in a wide range of materials, including these copper and wood, bamboo, and clear acrylic versions.

Source: Impact Enterprises, Inc.

Another approach to menu printing is to dispense with a cover entirely. Foodservice operations that can fit their menus on a single page may opt to print their menus without a cover. These menus may be laminated or not. They may be single- or double-sided. Without a cover to worry about, menu designers may include the restaurant's name and logo at the top of the first page or omit them entirely for space reasons. High-end operations with limited listings that change daily often prefer this style of menu. Using heavyweight, quality paper, the menu can be printed daily and handed to the customer without a cover. The menu designer may include the date at the top and permit guests to take the menu home with them as a memento and marketing tool. Should the restaurant wish to modify the menu for certain guests—to personalize a greeting at the top for a birthday party or to include only certain items for guests with dietary restrictions, for example—the task is as easy as adjusting the menu file on the in-house computer and hitting print. Such personalized attention can vault a restaurant from an above-average operation to a must-visit special occasion destination.

Printing In-House versus Printing Professionally

Learning Objective 4
State the pros and cons of contracting out the layout and printing of a menu versus doing the work in-house.

Once a menu has been laid out and the materials selected, the business's manager must decide whether the menus will be printed in-house or by a professional printer. Professional printers use high-caliber machinery that can produce crystal clear images in a range of colors. They are able to die cut menus into a range of shapes, if desired, and they can laminate menus as part of the service. Of course, professional printing costs money.

The greatest challenge to using a professional printer is that printers usually use specialized software for their machines. Thus, a menu planner might design a complex menu using Microsoft Publisher only to discover that the software is not compatible with the printer's software or that converting the document to the printer's software adjusts the layout and requires additional paid time from the printer. Professional menu designers and graphic designers usually use the same software that professional printers use. (The Adobe Creative Suite of applications is commonplace among designers and printers, but most printers also accept press-ready PDF files regardless of the application used for their creation.) Before investing the time in designing the menu layout on specific software in-house, the menu planner and designer should contact the printer to find out what file formats the printer accepts.

Because of the possibility of software compatibility error, the menu designer must confirm the accuracy of the printer's menu proof before authorizing the printer to print multiple copies. With the enormous opportunity for communication errors, the designer cannot simply assume that sending corrections to the first proof will result in a perfect menu. The designer must continue reviewing proofs until a correct one is achieved.

Professional menu designers are a valuable resource for restaurant employees unskilled in menu design. An experienced designer can make recommendations regarding paper, font, and layout that a chef or restaurant manager probably has not considered before. Professional designers are far more aware of the range of paper and font choices that exist. They are able to efficiently lay menus out electronically, whereas a restaurant professional may be more skilled with food than with a computer publishing program. Most can design the company's logo, letterhead, and business cards as well. Some companies, like MustHave-Menus (www.musthavemenus.com), provide templates for a restaurant to create its own menu, individualized design services, professional printing, web layout for a menu, and even online ordering platforms. For many foodservice operations, the cost of a professional menu designer is well worth the investment.

That said, a menu with a fairly straightforward design can be produced quite easily in-house. When a restaurant contracts with a professional printer, the cost is significant enough that the menus should last for several months. If a restaurant wishes to change its menu daily or weekly, it should print the menu in-house. In-house printing requires a high-quality laser or inkjet printer to ensure that the images and words print clearly. Menus printed in-house are typically done in black-and-white rather than in color, and they usually contain few, if any, images. These menus are almost always inserted into a permanent cover or handed to the customer without a cover; rarely would a restaurant laminate in-house. In-house printing still has costs in ink and paper, but these are far less expensive than asking a professional printer to reprint a menu daily to accommodate content changes. As long as a business is comfortable with a simple, straightforward menu with few images on a standard 8½" × 11" page, in-house printing is a highly cost-effective option.

Print Quantities

Learning Objective 5
Calculate the quantity of menus to print for a restaurant.

Calculating the number of menus to print depends heavily on the number of seats in the restaurant and on how long the menu is intended to last. Menus tear and stain over time, which requires that they be removed from circulation. Some guests take menus with them at the end of the meal. Employees may need a few copies to address questions of price or as training tools for new servers. While a restaurant that prints its menus daily may be fine with only enough menus to cover 25% of its seats, a restaurant that expects its menus to last for three to six months will need a much larger supply.

Typically, when a foodservice business has its menus printed professionally, it should plan on printing double or triple the number of seats in the dining room. As menus are damaged or stolen over time, the staff can pull from a backup supply to get through the future months. If a menu is only designed to last for a month, fewer copies are needed. However, if a menu is intended to last for over a year, it is still wise to stick with only enough to get through a six-month period—two to three times the number of seats. Menus must change periodically to account for market shifts and price fluctuations. A year's supply of menus may force the manager to choose between sticking with a menu that isn't generating sufficient profit after six months and throwing out clean, unused menus that are no longer effective cost control tools.

After estimating how many menus to print, the menu designer should inquire with the professional printer about price breaks for certain production quantities. Printing is usually priced per unit or per page with per-page discounts over certain quantities. Thus, a printer might charge $0.06 per page for 1–499 copies but $0.05 per page for 500 or more copies. In this example, if a restaurant calculates that it needs 480 copies, it makes more financial sense to order 500. Why? 480 × $0.06 = $28.80 while 500 copies × $0.05 = $25.00. It is cheaper to order the larger quantity even if the extras are simply thrown away. However, if the price break occurs at a much higher quantity than the business needs, the per-unit savings will not result in overall savings. For example, if a restaurant must order an extra 1,000 menus to save $0.02 per menu, the business will end up paying far more money for the printing only to end up with an abundance of out-of-date menus in less than a year.

To reduce the number of copies lost to theft, business owners should consider printing inexpensive copies of menus for customers to take with them, especially if the regular menus are costly to produce. Operations with significant take-out business, such as pizza parlors or Chinese restaurants, should have a large supply of take-out menus that are less expensive to print than the menus used for sit-down customers. Because these take-out menus are a marketing necessity to generate take-out business, these restaurants should print several thousand and encourage people to take them rather than hoarding a few to save on printing costs.

Other Types of Menus

Learning Objective 6
Describe special concerns related to menu boards, electronic menus, and single-use menus.

Not all menus follow the same rules as those for menus handed to customers in a sit-down restaurant. Take-out menus, for example, should be produced more cheaply, using less expensive paper than the identical menu for the same business's sit-down operation. Take-out menus may be done in color or in black-and-white, but the cost of printing should be balanced against the recognition that, for the most part, each copy of a take-out menu will be viewed by only one customer, and some will be tossed aside and never read by anyone. The best take-out menus are colorful, eye-catching, and appealing, but inexpensive enough that a restaurant can afford to give out hundreds per day.

Not all menus are designed to be printed and handed out to customers. A menu board is a large menu display, usually located behind an order taker in a restaurant with counter service. Menu boards can be professionally produced and printed like small billboards on hard plastic, or they can be blank slates on which restaurant managers affix plastic letters. A large chalkboard in a coffee shop is an example of a menu board, as are the panels in fast-food restaurants that are rotated in and out to show the menu offerings for a given meal period.

The moveable type and chalkboard versions allow for easy changes at no expense. A single small change alerts all customers to a new product or price, and since there are no other printed menus to change, there is no printing cost to make the change. Professionally produced boards do not have such flexibility, but they have a more professional appearance. They can include logos, photos, and a range of colors in clearly written type. Interchangeable panels, sometimes translucent and illuminated from behind, strike a balance between professional appearance and ease of modification. Because each panel only represents a small portion of the menu, one menu change requires the production of only one new panel, not the entire board. The panels may include logos, photos, and other information that is difficult to replicate on a chalkboard. Additionally, because the panels are easy to remove or rotate, breakfast menus can shift to lunch menus in a matter of seconds. With rotating menu boards, guests know exactly what is available at that moment based on what is displayed on the menu board behind the cashier.

One final variation of the menu board is the electronic display. Electronic displays can be simple, single-color text lines on a larger board (as one might see at a train station or airport) or complex images on screens, like those sometimes found at movie theater concession stands. Electronic displays combine a professional appearance with incredible flexibility. To change an electronic display, the menu planner need only make an adjustment to the computer program running the display. The screen modifies the display accordingly.

Menu boards of all forms are commonly employed at operations in which quick service is part of the brand. Thus, menu boards are typically designed to make ordering as quick and efficient as possible. Menu boards rarely include much in terms of menu item descriptions. In fast-food operations, they tend to offer bundled meals that can be ordered by number. Thus, a guest who can order "meal number 3" does not slow down the service line by ordering each separate meal item à la carte. These bundled options tend to be the most prominent and heavily marketed items on the menu to encourage higher revenue and faster service speed. Regardless of the type of operation, menu boards should be easy for customers to read while standing in line to place an order. When customers can read the menu board and decide on their orders before reaching the cash register, they do not inordinately slow down the service line for those behind them.

MOCHAS
[MOLTEN CHOCOLATE OR DUTCHED COCOA & ESPRESSO]
*AVAILABLE ICED

	TALL	GRANDE	X-GRANDE
*Ephemere Dark 52	3.90	4.15	4.50
Xtra Dark 72	4.15	4.65	5.00
Dark 63	4.15	4.65	5.00
Milk 41	4.15	4.65	5.00
White 31	4.15	4.65	5.00
*Viennese Mocha ALSO AVAILABLE SUGAR FREE	3.80	4.05	4.40
*Mocha Mexicano	3.90	4.15	4.55
Caramel Mocha	4.20	4.80	5.10

Signature SHOTS

	DEMITASSE
Espresso double shot	2.20
Mocha Vizio chocolate & espresso	3.30
Turkish Coffee spiced double	3.30
Cioccobreve creamy sipping chocolate	3.25

add an EXTRA SHOT
Ephemere Truffle Sauce .75   Molten Chocolate .85
Caramel Sauce .75   Espresso .75   Add Syrup .55

ESPRESSO & COFFEE
[CUSTOM BLENDED DILETTANTE COFFEE]
*AVAILABLE ICED

	TALL	GRANDE	X-GRANDE
Cappuccino	3.35	3.65	4.10
*Latte	3.10	3.80	4.10
*Caramel Latte	3.70	4.25	4.65
*Americano	2.35	2.75	3.00
*Fresh Brewed Coffee	1.80	2.15	2.45

HOT CHOCOLATE
[MOLTEN CHOCOLATE OR DUTCHED COCOA]

	TALL	GRANDE	X-GRANDE
Ephemere Dark 52	3.20	3.55	3.85
Xtra Dark 72	3.45	3.80	4.10
Dark 63	3.45	3.80	4.10
Milk 41	3.45	3.80	4.10
White 31	3.45	3.80	4.10
Viennese Cocoa ALSO AVAILABLE SUGAR FREE	3.10	3.45	3.75
Mexicano	3.20	3.55	3.85

TEA
[WHOLE LEAF & HERBAL]
AVAILABLE HOT OR ICED

	TALL	GRANDE	X-GRANDE
Spice Chai Latte	3.30	3.95	4.15
Whole Leaf Tea	2.05	2.40	2.45

ENGLISH BREAKFAST, GREEN, OOLONG, EARL GREY, JASMINE, BLACK ORANGE DECAF HERBAL- ROOIBOS, PEPPERMINT, CHAMOMILE

Ice Blended FRAPPES

	TALL	GRANDE	X-GRANDE
Ephemere 52 Mocha	4.70	4.95	5.20
Ephemere 52 Chocolate	4.55	4.75	5.15
Café Caramel	4.70	4.95	5.20
Caramel	4.55	4.75	5.15
Fruit	4.40	4.65	5.05

MANGO, RASPBERRY, PASSION FRUIT

COLD DRINKS

	TALL	GRANDE	X-GRANDE
Chocolate Milk [Ephemere 52]	2.95	3.35	3.65
Iced Tea	2.05	2.40	2.45
Italian Soda	3.55	3.70	4.40

SUBSTITUTIONS
Soy Milk .65   Rice Milk .65   Almond Milk .65

FIGURE 10.6
An example of a menu board.
Source: Dilettante Chocolates, Inc. Reprinted with permission.

Children's menus require another completely different approach to menu production because they are typically designed to be written upon. These menus should be prepared inexpensively as they are single-use items. Once a child colors all over one, it cannot be used again. While colorful children's menus are attractive, black-and-white photocopies which the child colors herself are equally, if not more, effective. In these cases, the design work for creating games and activities takes some doing, but once created, these menus can be photo-copied cheaply. The print savings are diverted instead to the cost of purchasing crayons.

Children's menus are not the only form of menu upon which guests write, however. Sushi restaurants often provide lists upon which customers write their order by marking order quantities next to each dish they wish to purchase. Room service menus work similarly, with places for guests to check off the dishes they want before hanging their order on their room's door handle. These menus can be printed as single-use copies, or they may be laminated for repeated use. Special wax pencils can be used to mark the laminated page; then, the page can be wiped clean after the order is served. (Note, because of the need for special pencils, the laminated versions are more appropriate for the sit-down sushi restaurant example than they are for room service menus.) While the laminated versions cost more to produce, fewer copies are needed. Single-use menus usually cost more over time.

Placemats in casual restaurants sometimes double as a menu. Because these are single-use items, they might call for inexpensive production. However, because the guest is staring at the placemat for quite a while at the table, most restaurants that use them put a little extra cost into the production of the placemat. To offset this cost, most sell advertising around the perimeter of the placemat and reserve the menu for the center. (Some places fill the placemat with advertising and use traditional menus for ordering.) The placemat as menu and advertising medium illustrates how creative restaurateurs cover the cost of menu printing when the opportunity makes sense with the brand.

High-end restaurants cannot avoid printing menus by selling advertising on placemats, but thanks to modern technology, a few now combine the menu and order placement process in a single piece of electronic equipment. In these technology-forward operations, small-screen portable computers are provided to the customer who reads the menu and places her order through the computer's touch screen. The upfront investment in the technology and subsequent replacement cost from theft or damage can be steep, but integrated into the restaurant's point of sales system, such an approach to menu production speeds service and reduces labor cost while allowing for extreme versatility. A menu planner who wishes to modify the menu daily or even hourly can do so with just a few keystrokes in the main computer system—no additional printing cost required. While not all customers feel comfortable ordering through a screen, as more Americans gain comfort with handheld technology, computerized menus may become more popular.

Web Menus

Thanks to the bounty of restaurant web pages, many diners can review a restaurant's menu from the comfort of home or work. For some operations, the menu listed on the company's web page is an exact copy of the print menu, usually in the form of a PDF file. For other businesses, the menu printed on the web page is designed solely for the web (though the content should not contradict the printed menu's text). There are pros and cons to each approach. A PDF version requires a customer download, which can be slow, but it is easy to store on one's own computer, to email to a friend, or to print out.

The specially designed web page menu allows for a wider range of features. In addition to faster access to the menu, web links may allow guests to jump to the menu heading of their choice. The web menu can include things that the corresponding printed menu does not, including nutritional information and a photo for each dish. Menu planners can easily adjust a web-based menu to list daily specials, too. However, knowing that, customers expect an online menu to be constantly updated and perpetually current and accurate. Menu planners who are comfortable creating web pages may design their operation's menu pages themselves. Others will hire a web designer or purchase an electronic menu template and platform to create their online menus.

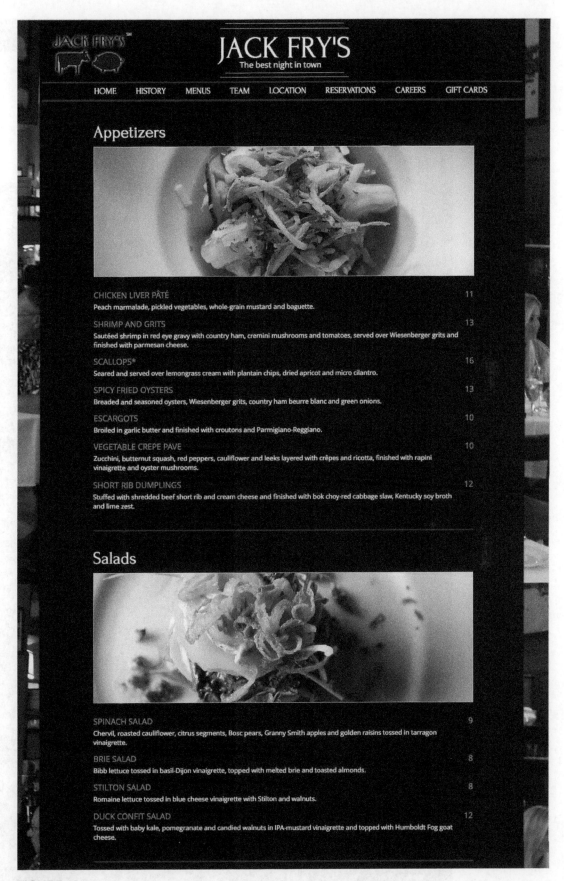

FIGURE 10.7

This menu is a web page on the restaurant's website.

Source: Stephanie Meeks and Jack Fry's Restaurant. Reprinted with permission.

Entrée

VEAL ROULADE 35
Rolled with spinach, prosciutto, mascarpone and Capriole goat cheese, encrusted with pine nuts, and served over sweet potato gnocchi with baby kale and sorghum-cider glaze.

SALMON* 28
Seared Scottish salmon with an almond and pistachio crust on wilted spinach and rice, finished with a tomato and chive beurre blanc.

PORK SHANK 33
Braised and served atop celeriac purée and purple potato-smoked bacon hash, finished with Porter jus and orange zest.

POLENTA TERRINE 25
Layers of polenta and fall squash purée, served with braised colllard greens and jalapeno-white cheddar mornay.

BEEF FILET* 44
Grilled tenderloin, asparagus, crisp fingerling potatoes and sage beurre blanc, topped with prosciutto and Parmigiano-Reggiano.

HALIBUT 34
Grilled and served over Tuscan white bean purée and cauliflower "couscous" with green cauliflower, chili oil, garlic-herb aioli and peperonata.

PORK CHOP* 29
Herb-encrusted center-cut loin chop with a compote of new potatoes, asparagus, smoked bacon and shiitake mushrooms in a rosemary-vermouth reduction.

DUCK* 30
Seared and sliced breast with green lentils, tempura haricots verts, bread-and-butter zucchini pickles, red pepper butter and pea shoot purée.

LAMB CHOPS* 41
Grilled Colorado lamb with potato au gratin, haricot vert and glace de viande.

JACK'S BURGER* 15
Black Hawk Farms ground chuck, caramelized onions, lettuce, tomato and habagardill pickle on brioche bun. Served with steak fries. Available with Gruyére or Tillamook cheddar. Add bacon or Stilton bleu cheese for $1.00

Executive Chef
McCLAIN BROWN

Sous Chefs
CALEB GUILLEN, JEFF HARMAN, DUNCAN WILLIAMS

PLEASE INFORM YOUR SERVER OF ANY FOOD ALLERGIES **** WE FRY IN PEANUT OIL****
CONSUMING RAW OR UNDERCOOKED FOODS MAY INCREASE THE RISK OF FOOD BORNE ILLNESS

Menu subject to change during special events.

Lunch, Monday - Friday
11am - 2:30pm

Dinner, Monday - Saturday
5:30 - 11pm

Dinner, Sunday
5:30 - 10pm

1007 Bardstown Rd
Louisville, KY 40204
info@jackfrys.com
T / 502-452-9244
F / 502-452-9289

Gift certificates available
in person and via telephone.

Reservations recommended for
any size party via telephone.

Meeks, LLC
dba Jack Fry's
Proprietor - Stephanie J. Meeks
General Manager - Brad Jennings

© 2014 by Antoine LaFramboise / B65

FIGURE 10.7   *(Continued)*

Vegetables & Such

Vegetable Carpaccio 8
Shaved veggies, caper, lemon, Parmesan

Arugula & Date Salad 9
Marcona almonds, gouda, celery, spiced orange vinaigrette

Roasted Parsnips 8
Miso, preserved lemon, togarashi

Roasted Asparagus 9
Shallot, pancetta, pickled mustard seeds

House Pita & Vegetable Purées 10
Chickpea, carrot, beet, pistachio dukkah

Smoked Potato 9
Crème fraîche, raclette, dill

Polenta & Spring Vegetables 12
Poached egg, ramp pesto, Parmesan

Bucatini 14
Black pepper, pecorino, asparagus, ramps

Ricotta Cavatelli 12
Beets, pistachio, pecorino

Celery Root Parmesan 12
Tomato porcini sauce, walnut, olive, spinach

*Housemade bread and butter
are available upon request.*

– – –

*During May, $2 from each pint of
Crooked Tree IPA sold will benefit the
Corktown STRUT arts festival*

Meat & Fish

Oysters (Half Dozen) 18
On the half shell, mignonette

Tuna Poke 21
Avocado, sesame, puffed rice

Beef Tartare 14
Grilled bread, tomato sauce, olives, herbs

Charred Octopus 14
Chickpea, basil-jalapeño pesto, saffron

Thai Mussels 12
Coconut milk, ginger, lemongrass, fried shallots

Parsley Root Casonsei 18
Lobster, lemon, chili, basil

Spanish Fried Rice 14
Squid, chorizo, lemon, aioli

Seared Quail 16
Yogurt marinade, carrot hummus, chickpeas, dates

Smoked Lamb Ribs 15
Agrodolce, yogurt, peas, lemon zest

Chorizo Sausage 12
White beans, marinated peppers

Celery Root Agnolotti 16
Short rib ragu, mushroom conserva

Lamb Ragu 16
Lumache, kalamata olives, leeks

Seared Swordfish 22
Green curry, sweet potato, herbs

Whole Trout 28
Fennel, fingerling potatoes, salsa verde

Beverages

Bottled Sodas 4
Mexican Coke, Abita Root Beer

Iced Tea or Diet Coke 2

Anthology Coffee 4
Nyangwe, Bourbon - Burundi

Espresso / Cappuccino . . . . . 3 / 4
Nyangwe, Bourbon - Burundi

Joseph Wesley Teas 3
*Dian Hong Congfu (black) & Shui Xian (oolong)
Gongfu Tea Service also available for $6/person*

Dessert

Cheese Plate . . . . Varies
Choice of 1, 2, or 3 w/ house crisps and preserves

Rice Pudding 8
Bay leaf, rhubarb, lemon cream, puffed rice

Pineapple Coconut Sundae 8
Cajeta, granola

Chai-Spiced Ice Cream Sandwich . . . 9
Dates, nuts, coconut yogurt

Chocolate Cream Puff 11
Hazelnut cream, white chocolate chili ice cream

Ice Cream 6
Selection varies daily

Sorbet 6
Selection varies daily

Selden Standard is grateful to work with the following farms and producers

Buffalo Street Farm • Clark Farms • Ferris Milling • Food Field • Geddes Farm • Guernsey Dairy • Holtz Farms • Hampshire Farms • Indian Brook Trout • Keep Growing Detroit
Mindo Chocolate • Rising Pheasant • S & S Farms • Salomon Gardens • Songbird Farm • Spirit of Walloon • Sunseed Farm • Tantre Farms • Victory Farms

SELDEN STANDARD

Dinner Menu

A Brief Word from the Government
Ask your server about menu items that are
cooked to order or served raw. Consuming raw or
undercooked meats, poultry, seafood, shellfish, or eggs
may increase your risk of foodborne illness

WWW.SELDENSTANDARD.COM

FIGURE 10.8
This menu was downloaded as a PDF from the restaurant's web page.
Reprinted with permission of Selden Standard

Consumers who email their friends the web address of a restaurant's online menu drive traffic to the company's web page. This peer-to-peer referral helps with the company's promotion and may expose customers to marketing on the website beyond the menu itself. The growth of social media (and its use by businesses of all sorts) has dramatically increased the number of customers whose first encounter with a restaurant is its website, which they find after clicking through links located on a blog or social media page. This trend means that more and more foodservice operations need to invest in professional-looking websites to survive. Web pages work best when a customer does not have to scroll way down the page to read the entire page. To fit compactly on a screen, web menus often require the customer to click on at least one link to get to the section of the menu they want to see. This approach to menu layout results in a professional, user-friendly web page menu, but also one that works better on a screen than it does in print. The cost to develop a web-based menu page is typically more than the cost to develop a PDF download version of a menu, but it is becoming increasingly common in today's plugged-in society. For those operations that want to cater both to the tech-savvy crowd and to those who prefer a printed menu, the best compromise is to offer a web-based menu and the option for downloading a printer-friendly version.

When a restaurant permits "off-site" ordering, the menu designer should consider allowing the process to occur through the business's website. Not that long ago, fax and phone orders were the only options for ordering off-site. Today, restaurant patrons can order through a company's web page or smart phone application. These online systems should be simple, intuitive, and easy to use. If an online ordering page is too difficult to navigate, customers will not use the system; the high-tech crowd may even choose another restaurant just for the convenience of ordering online. In most cases, restaurants hire professional web designers to ensure that their online ordering system operates properly and becomes a convenience rather than a hassle for customers. As with a foodservice business's web page, a frustrating, difficult-to-navigate online service can turn a theoretically positive benefit for the public into negative PR for the company.

Summary

Once the menu planner has all of the menu content in hand, laying out the menu is the next task. To do so, the menu planner or a menu designer selects the size and shape of the paper to yield the desired number of pages without making the menu too small or too cumbersome to hold. The items the business most desires to sell should be located in the menu's hot zones, the areas to which the eye is naturally drawn on a menu. Clip-ons and inserts also attract the guests' attention. Prices should be written and located to keep customers from focusing on pricing in their purchases. The paper's and font's color should provide high contrast for easy reading with a light background and dark text. Font size and style should similarly facilitate reading in dim lighting while supporting the business's concept. Judicious use of bold or italics can draw guests' attention to a few items on the menu; boxes and symbols work similarly. Images, such as photographs or illustrations, can further support the company brand while enhancing the guest experience.

Menu covers may be constructed from a range of materials and allow for new internal menu pages to be inserted as the menu changes. Some operations prefer to laminate menus to keep them clean and reusable for months. A menu designer can opt to dispense with covers entirely. Menus may be printed in-house or professionally. Professional printing costs more, but for complex designs with images, professional printing typically results in a higher-quality product. In-house printing is better when the menu changes often. How many menus to print depends on how long the menus are intended to last before they change and on the number of seats in the dining room. Ideal print quantities may vary from a portion of the dining room capacity to two or three times the number of dining room seats. Single-use menus, such as those for children, take-out, or room service breakfast, require greater print quantities, but the extra cost may be offset with cheaper printing quality or by using these menus as direct marketing pieces.

A menu board is far more expensive than a printed menu is, but only one menu is required to service all customers. Table-top electronic menus, which allow for menu flexibility and speed customer service, may become more popular in the near future. Web-based menus are extremely popular and excellent marketing opportunities, but they often require a different format than do print menus in order to appear user-friendly on the screen. If a company accepts orders electronically through its website, that ordering process should be easy to use as well. All menus should be designed to appeal to the target market and to support the company's image, but within those limitations, the creative possibilities for menu design are endless.

Comprehension Questions

1. Draw three examples of possible printed menu layouts and mark the hot zones on each menu.

2. List four ways to draw a guest's attention to certain menu items that are not located in a hot zone.

3. How can a menu designer write prices to keep the customers from focusing on price first?

4. Some printed documents are perfectly readable at 11-point font with no leading. Why would this arrangement not work for a printed menu?

5. List an example of a type of font that is easy to read. What kind of font is often difficult to read?

6. What qualities should a menu designer look for in a permanent menu cover intended to last for years? List three materials that would be appropriate for a permanent menu cover.

7. List one benefit to creating a laminated menu. When should a restaurant not laminate its menus?

8. List two reasons to use a professional menu designer and printer. What kind of restaurant would definitely want to print its menus in-house?

9. If a restaurant can accommodate one hundred guests in its dining room and it intends for its menu to last for six months, roughly how many menus should it have printed by a professional printer? (You may provide a range.)

10. Describe three styles of menu boards that a counter-service restaurant might use.

11. List three examples of single-use menus.

12. How does a web page menu typically differ from a printed menu?

Discussion Questions

1. Imagine that you are designing a permanent menu cover. What would you include on the front of the cover (if anything)? What would you include on the back of the cover (if anything)? Explain your answer and note two pieces of information you would not include on the cover.

2. A New Orleans–themed restaurant is decorated in purple, green, and gold—Mardi Gras colors. The menu planner wishes to have a creative menu that reflects the restaurant's concept. How would you recommend incorporating these colors and this concept into the menu? State one example of a bad approach to incorporating the colors into the menu.

3. A seafood restaurant has a large menu and a diverse market of customers. Among the menu options are three dishes that the owner wishes to highlight, as each appeals to a different segment of the market. The crab cakes are their most famous dish, and they have been highlighted in every restaurant review of the place. The heart-healthy poached scallops are intended to satisfy the older clientele. The broiled lobster is the most profitable dish on the menu. As the menu designer, you can use symbols, boxes, and hot zones on the menu. Which of these three techniques would you use for each dish? Why? (Recommend a different technique for each dish.)

4. You are a menu designer for a Mexican restaurant. You are trying to decide between laminated menus and menus with exposed paper inserts attached at the corners of a permanent cover. What information would you want to know to help you make an informed decision?

5. This chapter describes the possibility of menus displayed on a handheld or table-top screen and provided to customers to make their own selections— not particularly different from what many people do on a smart phone. What potential problems would you envision with such an approach to menus? (List three.) What steps or procedures could a manager take to address those problems?

Case Study

Online menus come in a wide variety of formats. Some allow for online ordering. Some use the web page menu to allow guests to jump to a specific menu heading. Others provide the complete menu on a single page or in a PDF download. Visit several restaurants' web pages to see how they present their online menus. For embedded online ordering, visit www.asiangourmetok.com. For links to menu headings from a main page, visit www.laristraaz.com. To see how a printed menu format differs from a web version, visit www.tedsbulletin.com; Ted's Bulletin's print menu is included in this chapter. (Keep in mind that all of these operations may change their menus and/or platforms between the dates of this text's printing and your visit to their website.) Locate a few other examples of online menus, including at least one for a restaurant where you have dined.

How do the different operations approach web menu formats? What are the pros and cons to each format? Why might a restaurant use a different format for its print menu versus its web menu? What does an operation's online menu format say about that business?

Capstone Project

Step 10: Lay out your menu using the menu copy, pricing, and, if appropriate, images created in the previous steps of the project. Items you wish to sell in the largest quantity should fall into the menu's hot zone. If appropriate for your concept, create separate dessert, children's, and beverage menus. The choice of font and color should be appropriate for your concept. Symbols and boxes may be used. If the desired menu paper and cover are not available, describe in a separate paragraph the paper color, weight, and texture; describe the cover design/material or paper treatment for the menu as well. Write an additional paragraph describing the format in which you would provide your menu on your operation's website and why you propose that format. Print the formatted menu on the desired menu paper or on plain white paper. Bring these finalized menus and content from all prior steps to the next class meeting for submission to the instructor and/or presentation to the class.

Reference

1. Yang, S.S., Kimes, S.E., & Sessarego, M.M. (2009). $ or Dollars: Effects of menu-price formats on restaurant checks [Electronic article]. *Cornell Hospitality Reports*, 9(8), 6–11. http://scholarship.sha.cornell.edu/chrpubs/169/. Accessed 2 May 2016.

CHAPTER 11

Evaluation: Menu Engineering

INTRODUCTION

Once a menu has gone to print and is ready for distribution to customers, menu planners consider the menu finished. But a menu is never a permanent fixture for a business. It is designed for a specific period of time. Like the food it offers, a menu has a shelf life, and once it has outlived its value, it must be created anew. A revised menu may be necessary to adapt to changing tastes or to update prices. Some restaurants change their menus seasonally while others do not adjust their menus for two or three years. The frequency with which a business modifies its menu depends in part on the business concept and in part on the stability of the customer market and ingredient prices. Over time, every foodservice business must change its menu to remain profitable.

Of all the information that a menu planner considers when updating a menu, the menu's profitability is perhaps the most important. Some items inevitably bring in more profit than others. However, removing less profitable items and adding high-margin ones is a simplistic and often unsuccessful approach to menu modification. Customers come to a foodservice operation in part because they like certain menu offerings. Removing low-profit, popular items

from a menu can result in a menu that makes more money per customer but brings in fewer customers; the result may be a less profitable business overall. Both popularity and profitability of menu items must be considered in tandem to maximize a foodservice business's profit.

After a menu planner evaluates a menu's performance, he can adjust the menu in many ways. Sometimes the best approach is to add and remove dishes entirely, but often a menu can be made more profitable through subtle changes to descriptive copy, sales prices, and menu layout. The process of analyzing a menu is fairly straightforward, but how to address each identified problem is completely up to the menu planner's professional judgment and experience. A good menu planner generates a profitable menu for a business's opening day. A great menu planner knows that even the best menu's profitability will wane over time and that the best way to maintain company profits is to evaluate and update a menu as it approaches the end of its useful life. Learning how to analyze a menu for popularity and profitability as well as how to use that information to modify a menu is a key requirement for any future menu planner.

CHAPTER 11 LEARNING OBJECTIVES

As a result of successfully completing this chapter, readers will be able to:

1. Perform a menu analysis to calculate each menu item's popularity and profitability.

2. Engineer a menu to increase the overall profitability of a foodservice business.

3. Describe the value of a point-of-sales system in menu engineering.

CHAPTER 11 OUTLINE

215

Menu Analysis

Periodically, every menu should undergo a review by a menu planner or a business's manager. Some menu items that seem like a good idea when a menu is first created lose their luster over time. There is not enough space on a menu to support menu items that do not contribute significantly to the business's profitability. Technically, the sale of a menu item does not generate profit; instead, it yields a contribution margin. The contribution margin of an item is its sales price minus its food (or beverage) cost. Mathematically,

$$\text{Contribution Margin} = \text{Sales Price} - \text{Food (or Beverage) Cost}$$

Every foodservice business has fixed costs and variable costs. The variable costs are those that increase with each sale. Food cost is an example of a variable cost since the business's food cost goes up as more food is sold. Fixed costs do not fluctuate with variations in sales. Rent, salaries, and insurance are examples of fixed costs, as they must be paid in the same amount each month whether the company serves one customer or one million customers. The contribution margin generated from the sale of each item goes first toward covering fixed expenses for the month, then toward building profit.

Depending on the size of a menu item's contribution margin, a dish may help a business pay off its fixed costs and generate profits quickly or slowly. For example, imagine a restaurant with two menu items—the first with a contribution margin of $1 and the second with a contribution margin of $10. It takes ten sales of the first menu item to cover as much fixed cost expense as the business earns from just one sale of the second menu item. Thus, foodservice managers refer to items with higher contribution margins as being more profitable than items with lower contribution margins.

Even if all menu items have the exact same food cost percentage, items with different food costs in dollars will have different contribution margins.

Example 11. 1: What are the contribution margins for a hamburger with a food cost of $1.25 and a steak with a food cost of $3.18 if both have sales prices based on a food cost of 30%?

First, calculate the sales price for each item using the formula

Sales Price = Food Cost ÷ Food Cost%
Sales Price (Hamburger) = $1.25 ÷ 0.30 = $4.17
Sales Price (steak) = $3.18 ÷ 0.30 = $10.60

Next, calculate the contribution margin.

Contribution Margin (CM) = Sales Price − Food Cost
CM (hamburger) = $4.17 − $1.25 = $2.92
CM (steak) = $10.60 − $3.18 = $7.42

In Example 11.1, even though the two items both have a 30% food cost percentage, the steak generates a contribution margin of $7.42 to cover fixed costs and profit while the hamburger only generates $2.92—a difference of $4.50. This business would make far more money in profit selling only steaks than if it sold only hamburgers.

However, rarely can a restaurant survive selling just a single product. Most sell a mix of items. The *menu mix* is an expression of the number of each item sold on a menu over a period of time. The menu mix is often stated in percentages, so each menu item is expressed as a percentage of total items sold.

A balanced menu mix in which menu items sell in equal quantities provides some benefits to a business. No single station is overly taxed with orders, and all of the ingredients in inventory move quickly with none languishing unused for a long period of time. However, a perfectly balanced menu mix is not necessarily highly profitable. Because each menu item generates a different contribution margin, increasing sales of those items with the highest contribution margins will increase the menu's overall profitability.

Menu Engineering is a system, invented by Michael Kasavana and Donald Smith, for analyzing each menu item's profitability and popularity against the average for all of the menu items and then adjusting the menu to increase overall business profit. Each menu item is scored as high or low profitability and high or low popularity. Once a menu planner knows how each item scores, he is better able to tweak a menu to make it more profitable.

The data used to conduct a menu analysis is easily compiled from sales records and recipe costing sheets. As a single unusual sales day skews the data, it is best to use sales and costing data over a period of several months, not days or weeks, to minimize the impact of any anomalies.

The process to conduct a menu analysis (as part of the menu engineering process) is complex, so the computations for calculating an item's popularity and profitability are described separately subsequently.

Popularity

The first step in conducting a menu analysis is to determine the relative popularity of each menu item. While it is possible to compare any item to any other menu item, the best comparison is between items from the same menu category. For example, almost everyone who patronizes a restaurant orders an entrée. If a menu planner were trying to decide which dishes to remove or to modify, would it be helpful to know that each entrée sells better than the best-selling appetizer? No. A menu planner would be foolish to constantly replace appetizers and leave the entrée selections alone in order to increase sales. Guests looking to eat a full meal will not stop ordering entrées to purchase appetizers instead, no matter how good the appetizers sound. A more valuable analysis compares entrées to other entrées and appetizers to other appetizers.

Whether to analyze each heading separately or to combine certain headings is completely up to the menu planner. This chapter uses the term "menu category" rather than "menu heading" as the menu planner may choose to treat multiple headings as a single category. For example, a menu planner may wish to treat the menu headings "from the sea," "from the land," and "from the air" as a single "entrée" category. Similarly, if a menu lists soups, salads, and appetizers under three different headings but customers generally only order only one starter before their entrée, then the menu planner should treat these three headings as a single category for analysis purposes.

To calculate whether a menu item is an above-average or below-average seller within its menu category, a menu planner must first determine the average number of each item sold within that category. To do so, the menu planner begins with a chart listing each of the menu items and how many of each are sold over a period of time—usually one or more months. Each menu category is analyzed separately. The average number sold is calculated by totaling the number of items sold in a category and dividing by the number of menu item listings in the category. The Table 11.1 series illustrates this process for a set of entrées.

Table 11.1a shows that there are seven entrées available for sale. Over the examined period, 6,025 entrées are sold. Calculating 6,025 (the total number of entrées sold) ÷ 7 (the number of entrées listed on the menu) = 860.7 (the average number of each entrée sold).

Menu Item	Number Sold
Chicken	1,380
Beef	1,092
Pork	881
Lamb	600
Salmon	905
Crab	746
Vegetarian	421
Total	6,025
Average number of each item sold (total ÷ number of offerings)	6,025 ÷ 7 = 860.7

TABLE 11.1a

Menu Analysis—Number of Each Item Sold

Having performed the calculation for the average number of each item sold, a menu planner can easily see whether a given menu item is an above-average or below-average seller for its category. However, a strict above- or below-average delineation is somewhat unfair for a measurement of popularity. For example, consider a menu in which the average number of each item sold is 400. Should a menu item that sells 401 units be considered popular while one that sells 399 units is considered unpopular? Mathematically, not every item can have above-average sales. A menu planner would make a serious error to change certain menu offerings with relatively equal sales quantities simply because some fall a couple of units below average and others fall a couple of units above average.

To change the focus from theoretical math to something statistically significant, the industry labels "popular" any item selling at a rate of at least 70% of the average number of each item sold. Thus, it is possible to have a menu in which all items are considered highly popular. Only those items with sales below 70% of the average number are considered to have low popularity.

Calculating the 70% industry standard is simple. To do so, multiply the average number of each item sold by 70% or 0.7. The resulting figure is referred to as the *popularity benchmark*. Any item with unit sales above the popularity benchmark is considered popular (high popularity) and any item with unit sales below it is labeled unpopular (low popularity). Table 11.1b shows the popularity benchmark for the menu presented in Table 11.1a and labels each entrée as high (H) or low (L) popularity.

In Table 11.1b, the popularity benchmark is the average number of each item sold $860.7 \times 0.7 = 602.5$. Any item that sells more than 602.5 units is labeled high popularity. Every item with sales below 602.5 is labeled low popularity. In this example, the lamb and the vegetarian entrées are the only two items considered to have low popularity.

Profitability

Identifying the popular and unpopular dishes is only the first step in the menu-analysis process. Menu planners must also determine whether a dish has an above-average or below-average contribution margin. A popular dish that is not particularly profitable is just as much of a problem as a highly profitable but unpopular dish. To calculate a menu item's relative profitability, the menu planner must first calculate each item's contribution margin. Recall,

$$\text{Contribution Margin} = \text{Item Sales Price} - \text{Item Food (or Beverage)}$$

Menu Item	Number Sold	Popularity (H/L) (Based on Number Sold above or below 602.5, the Popularity Benchmark)
Chicken	1,380	H
Beef	1,092	H
Pork	881	H
Lamb	600	L
Salmon	905	H
Crab	746	H
Vegetarian	421	L
Total	6,025	
Average number of each item sold (total ÷ number of offerings)	860.7	
Popularity benchmark (average × 0.7)	$860.7 \times 0.7 = 602.5$	

TABLE 11.1b

Menu Analysis—Calculating Popularity

Menu Item	Number Sold	Item Sales Price	Item Food Cost	Item Contribution Margin (Item Sales Price − Item Food Cost)
Chicken	1,380	$11.95	$3.47	$8.48
Beef	1,092	$19.00	$5.22	$13.78
Pork	881	$14.50	$4.51	$9.99
Lamb	600	$21.00	$6.29	$14.71
Salmon	905	$16.25	$4.88	$11.37
Crab	746	$19.00	$5.26	$13.74
Vegetarian	421	$9.95	$2.30	$7.65
Total	6,025			
Average number of each item sold (total ÷ number of offerings)	860.7			
Popularity benchmark (average × 0.7)	602.5			

TABLE 11.1c
Menu Analysis—Item Contribution Margins

Table 11.1c provides the sales price and food cost for each entrée from the Table 11.1a series. This information comes from recipe costing sheets and menu sales prices. The final column calculates each item's contribution margin. (The popularity column has been removed for ease of instruction and will be returned to the table later in the process.)

With the item contribution margin calculated for each item, the menu planner must next calculate each item's menu contribution margin, which factors in the number of units sold.

$$\text{Menu Contribution Margin} = \text{Item Contribution Margin} \times \text{Number Sold (for that Item)}$$

The menu contribution margins can be summed to determine the total menu contribution margin earned from the sales of these menu items over the period measured. This total menu contribution margin is the amount of money from the entire menu category (entrées, for the Table 11.1a series) that went to cover fixed expenses and profit during the period in question.

Table 11.1d illustrates the process of computing each item's menu contribution margin and the total menu contribution margin for these entrées.

There are a couple of things to notice from the menu contribution margin calculations in Table 11.1d. First, every single item contributes some money to cover fixed costs and profit for this operation. Thus, the purpose of menu analysis is not to determine which items are not profitable, as all of them are profitable to some degree, but rather to see whether there is a way to generate more profit from the menu as a whole. Second, there is not a direct correlation between the most popular items and their menu contribution margins, nor is there a direct correlation between the most profitable items and their menu contribution margins. This restaurant sells far fewer lamb than pork entrées, yet the lamb has a greater menu contribution margin. Additionally, the lamb has a much higher item contribution margin than the chicken does, but the more popular chicken generates a higher menu contribution margin than the lamb does. In short, to determine just how profitable a menu item truly is, a menu planner must consider both a menu item's popularity and its relative profitability.

Menu Item	Number Sold	Item Sales Price	Item Food Cost	Item Contribution Margin	Menu Contribution Margin (Number Sold × Item Contribution Margin)
Chicken	1,380	$11.95	$3.47	$8.48	$11,702.40
Beef	1,092	$19.00	$5.22	$13.78	$15,047.76
Pork	881	$14.50	$4.51	$9.99	$8,801.19
Lamb	600	$21.00	$6.29	$14.71	$8,826.00
Salmon	905	$16.25	$4.88	$11.37	$10,289.85
Crab	746	$19.00	$5.26	$13.74	$10,250.04
Vegetarian	421	$9.95	$2.30	$7.65	$3,220.65
Total	6,025				$68,137.89 (total menu contribution margin)
Average number of each item sold	860.7				
Popularity benchmark	602.5				

TABLE 11.1d

Menu Analysis—Menu Contribution Margins

To determine each menu item's relative profitability, the menu planner must first calculate the average weighted menu contribution as follows:

Average Weighted Menu Contribution = Total Menu Contribution Margin ÷ Total Number of Items Sold

Using the information in Table 11.1d, the average weighted menu contribution is $68,137.89 (total menu contribution) ÷ 6,025 (total number of items sold) = $11.31.

Finally, each menu item's contribution margin is measured against the average weighted menu contribution to determine its relative profitability. For example, from Table 11.1d, the item contribution margin for chicken is $8.48, below the average weighted menu contribution of $11.31. Thus, the chicken is labeled as having a low profitability. The item contribution margin for beef, on the other hand, is $13.78, well above $11.31, so beef is rated as highly profitable. Table 11.1e compares each item contribution margin to the average weighted menu contribution margin to categorize each dish as high or low profitability. The popularity column has been returned to the table to create a single summary menu-analysis chart.

As the process for conducting a menu analysis can be quite unwieldy for the novice menu planner, following is a summary of the steps to conduct a menu analysis.

Step 1: Using sales data, total the number of items sold in a given menu category. Then calculate the average number of each item sold utilizing the formula (separately for each menu category):

Average Number of Each Item Sold = Total Items Sold ÷ Number of Choices on the Menu

Step 2: Multiply the Average Number of Each Item Sold by 70% or 0.7 to yield the popularity benchmark.

Step 3: Label each menu item as high or low popularity based on whether its number of units sold is higher or lower than the popularity benchmark.

Menu Item	Number Sold	Item Sales Price	Item Food Cost	Item Contribution Margin	Menu Contribution Margin	Popularity (H/L)	Profitability (H/L)
Chicken	1,380	$11.95	$3.47	$8.48	$11,702.40	H	L
Beef	1,092	$19.00	$5.22	$13.78	$15,047.76	H	H
Pork	881	$14.50	$4.51	$9.99	$8,801.19	H	L
Lamb	600	$21.00	$6.29	$14.71	$8,826.00	L	H
Salmon	905	$16.25	$4.88	$11.37	$10,289.85	H	H
Crab	746	$19.00	$5.26	$13.74	$10,250.04	H	H
Vegetarian	421	$9.95	$2.30	$7.65	$3,220.65	L	L
Total	6,025				$68,137.89		
Average Number of Each Item Sold	860.7						
Popularity Benchmark	602.5						
Average weighted CM (total menu CM ÷ number of items sold)	$11.31						

TABLE 11.1e
Menu Analysis—Complete

Step 4: From recipe costing sheet and menu sales price information, calculate each menu item's contribution margin using the formula:

Item Contribution Margin = Item Sales Price − Item Food (or Beverage) Cost

Step 5: Calculate each item's menu contribution margin using the formula:

Menu Contribution Margin = Number Sold (for an Item)
× Item Contribution Margin (for that Item)

Step 6: Total all of the menu contribution margins for the category. Then, calculate the average weighted menu contribution using the formula:

Average Weighted Menu Contribution = Total Menu Contribution Margin
÷ Total Number of Items Sold

Step 7: Label each item as high or low profitability based on whether its item contribution margin is higher or lower than the average weighted menu contribution.

Menu Engineering Categories

Learning Objective 2
Engineer a menu to increase the overall profitability of a foodservice business.

Determining a menu item's relative popularity and profitability is no mere theoretical exercise. The menu planner uses this information to determine what, if any, changes to make to a menu to make it more profitable without reducing revenue or losing customers—no small feat when a menu undergoes a major overhaul. Subtle changes can direct sales to more profitable items or make the less profitable ones more profitable. Dishes that are both low profit and low popularity may need serious reworking, but their role on the menu should not necessarily be abandoned.

A menu planner has various options for improving a menu item's popularity and profitability, but the approaches generally fall into one of three categories—marketing, adjusting food cost, and adjusting sales price. To market a dish, the menu planner must persuade the population of customers as a whole to purchase that menu item more often. The menu planner can attract guests' attention to a dish by enclosing the menu item in a box, highlighting it with a symbol or graphic, or relocating it to a hot zone on the menu. Servers can assist with marketing a dish by recommending it to customers before taking their orders. Menu planners should also review the descriptive copy to see whether a menu item's description requires rewriting to make it sound more appealing. Unless a business's brand requires ingredient-only descriptive copy, a few well-placed modifiers, like "house-made," "crispy," or "locally sourced," can increase sales of the more vividly described menu items. No matter which approach the menu planner takes, marketing a specific menu item almost always increases that item's popularity.

Adjusting a dish's cost or sales price (or both), a menu planner impacts that dish's profitability and, sometimes, its popularity as well. A menu planner can reduce a dish's cost per portion by shrinking the portion size or switching to lower-cost ingredients. However, customers may notice the change in portion size or ingredient quality. They will almost certainly notice a major shift in price should the menu planner increase or decrease the sales price. For some menu items, small changes will not impact the dish's popularity, but for others, even small price increases can cause a significant drop in sales volume. Because price sensitive items stimulate major shifts in sales from minor changes, a menu planner may consider reducing a menu item's sales price slightly or increasing its portion size in order to significantly increase its popularity. The menu planner must always take into account a potential impact on sales volume whenever considering a change to a dish's cost per portion or sales price.

Before deciding what to do about each individual menu item, the menu planner should first divide the menu items into categories based on their menu-analysis scores. With only two variables (popularity and profitability) and two possible results (high and low) for each, menu analysis classifies all menu items as one of four types. Rather than constantly referencing a dish's popularity and profitability, the industry uses more colorful terms to denote each of the four menu-analysis categories:

Star   A star is a dish that possesses both high popularity and high profitability. From the menu planner's perspective, this dish is doing everything right. It sells well and generates a lot of profit for the business. In general, these dishes should be left alone (though adjustments to other menu items will inevitably impact the sale of stars). In Table 11.1e, the beef, salmon, and crab entrées are all stars.

Plowhorse   A plowhorse is a dish with high popularity but low profitability. This creates for the menu planner a conundrum that requires further research. The goal is to make the plowhorses more profitable without reducing the number sold, but low profitability may be the exact reason that a plowhorse is popular. If a plowhorse attracts lots of customers to the business because they recognize the plowhorse as a value, it may be best to modify the dish only slightly or to leave it alone entirely. These customers may end up purchasing highly profitable beverages or other courses while dining. However, if the plowhorse is popular because of suggestive selling by servers or because of its location on the menu, it may allow for greater flexibility in price and portion size adjustment. To make a plowhorse more profitable and convert it to a star, the menu planner should increase its sales price or reduce its portion size slightly. Too great a change may turn off customers, but small changes should be accepted readily.

Alternatively, if a plowhorse is located in the menu's hot zone or highlighted with a box or icon, the menu planner should consider a change. By highlighting or relocating to the hot zone more profitable items that are not selling as well, a menu planner can squeeze higher profits out of the same menu offerings. Still, the menu planner must be careful not to reduce overall business in the process. If a restaurant is known for one of its plowhorses—i.e., a signature dish—emphasizing that dish may be a necessity to attract and retain a growing customer base. In Table 11.1e, the chicken and the pork are plowhorses.

Puzzle   A puzzle has low popularity but high profitability. The challenge for the menu planner in this situation is to increase sales of the puzzles without decreasing their profitability. Because these dishes are already less popular, there is less risk of losing large numbers of customers by changing a puzzle. Increasing the portion size or decreasing the selling price of a puzzle eats away at its profitability, so this approach should be used only if the food cost or sales price of the puzzle is way out of line compared to the other dishes on the menu. A better approach is to sell and market puzzles heavily. Menu planners should consider relocating a puzzle to the menu's hot zone or rewriting the menu description to make the dish sound more appealing. The menu planner might put a box or other highlight around the puzzle to attract the attention of customers. Suggestive sales pitches by the servers also help to drive sales of puzzles.

Depending on the style of service, a change in presentation or sample portions may help to drive sales of puzzles. For example, a dish with a lackluster presentation could draw the interest of other guests in the dining room just from a rearrangement of the dish's components. The same is true for items presented on a cafeteria line. If a chef believes that customers would order the puzzle repeatedly if they tried it just once, he might consider providing free samples to regular customers, especially those ordering less profitable dishes. Similarly, the company could try to build a loyal fan base for a puzzle by offering it at a reduced price as a special or through a coupon promotion. If customers love the dish, they may return to buy it another day at full price. In Table 11.1e, the lamb is a puzzle.

Dog   A dog is low in both popularity and profitability. It is the biggest drag on a menu's ability to increase total profits. Its ingredients take up space in inventory, and cooks spend time preparing a dish that does not sell particularly well. Worse, the dog takes up menu space that could be devoted to a more profitable dish. The first step in dealing with a dog is to determine the role that the dog plays on the menu. Is it a random dish that does not belong on the menu, or is it there to appeal to a specific segment of the market, like customers with special dietary needs who might not otherwise patronize the establishment? For example, a chicken dish at a seafood restaurant allows larges parties to dine there when a single guest with a seafood allergy might otherwise require the entire group to eat elsewhere. A vegan dish on a menu that includes animal products in all of its other dishes serves a similar purpose.

Whether the dog serves a specific purpose or is simply inappropriate on the menu, the menu planner should first figure out how to increase the dish's contribution margin, so the dog becomes a puzzle. The dog might be modified to reduce its food cost or increase its sales price, or both. Alternatively, the dog could be replaced entirely by another dish as long as the market segment the dog serves continues to have viable options on the menu. Once the dog has been converted into a puzzle, the selling and marketing approaches appropriate for puzzles may be implemented. What a menu planner should not do is attempt to increase sales of a dog without first addressing its low profitability. To do so might pull sales from more profitable stars and puzzles, which in turn reduces the menu's overall profitability. In Table 11.1e, the vegetarian entrée is a dog.

Further Considerations

Within each category, there are further subtle differences to consider. For example, two plowhorses may be ranked as low profitability, but one is likely to be more profitable than the other. If a menu planner cannot make either plowhorse more profitable, he might consider directing sales from the less profitable to the more profitable plowhorse. Such a change will improve the menu's profitability overall. Similar adjustments can be made within each menu-analysis category through the relocation of items on the menu, the reassignment of icons, boxes, and other highlights, and the redirection of suggestive selling programs. For example, dogs are typically thought of as more problematic than plowhorses; however, a dog could have a higher contribution margin than a plowhorse, even though both possess a below-average contribution margin. Were the menu planner to direct sales from the plowhorse to the dog, the menu would increase its profit generation.

Such menu changes are subtle. When a foodservice operation chooses to overhaul its entire menu, it should consider retaining at least a few stars from the original menu to ensure a stable market of customers willing to buy highly profitable dishes. Even menus

Rose's Luxury
717 8th St. SE, Capitol Hill

··

Ok, so here's how this works

- Order yourself a nice cocktail or glass of wine
- Choose a couple of Small/Family Style dishes to share
- Eat, go home, come back tomorrow

··

SMALL DISHES:

cold:
CAVIAR SERVICE ... JUST ASK
BEEF RIBEYE TARTARE, PICKLED RAMPS & CRISPY POTATOES 13
FALL VEGETABLE PANZANELLA 12

warm & grill:
CHARRED CARROTS W/ HARISSA, HOUSEMADE YOGURT & PEARL ONIONS 12
PORK SAUSAGE, HABANERO, PEANUTS & LYCHEE SALAD 13
GRILLED QUAIL W/ BRUSSELS SPROUTS, CAESAR & APPLES 16

other goods:
CRISPY PIG'S EAR SALAD W/ MANGO & CABBAGE (SPICY) 13
VADOUVAN CURRY W/ SWEET POTATO & CARAMELIZED BANANA 13
CONFIT GOAT W/ BBQ SEA ISLAND RED PEAS, RICE & GARLIC BREADCRUMBS 14

pasta:
HAND-CUT CHITARRA W/ CARAMELIZED CAULIFLOWER & WHITE WINE SOFFRITTO 13
PENNE "ALLA VODKA" W/ SQUID & BASIL 14

FAMILY STYLE:

SMOKED BRISKET, WHITE BREAD, HORSERADISH & SLAW 29
PERUVIAN-STYLE CHICKEN W/ FRIED YUCA, SWEET POTATO CEVICHE & PLANTAINS 30

items marked in GRASSY GREEN are vegetarian or can be served vegetarian
please notify your server if you have any dietary restrictions or allergies
all unattended or misbehaving children will be given a shot of espresso and a free puppy

FIGURE 11.1
This restaurant changes its menu periodically. Figure 11.2 shows how the menu changes several weeks later.
Reprinted with permission of Rose's Luxury.

Rose's Luxury
717 8th St. SE, Capitol Hill

•••

<u>Ok, so here's how this works</u>

- Order yourself a nice cocktail or glass of wine
- Choose a couple of Small/Family Style dishes to share
- Eat, go home, come back tomorrow

•••

SMALL DISHES:

cold:
CAVIAR SERVICE . . . JUST ASK
BEEF RIBEYE TARTARE, BLACK GARLIC, FARRO & CRISPY POTATOES 13
WINTER VEGETABLE PANZANELLA 12

warm & grill:
CHARRED CARROTS W/ HARISSA, HOUSEMADE YOGURT & PEARL ONIONS 12
PORK SAUSAGE, HABANERO, PEANUTS & LYCHEE SALAD 13
GRILLED QUAIL W/ BRUSSELS SPROUTS, CAESAR & APPLES 16

other goods:
CRISPY PIG'S EAR SALAD W/ MANGO & CABBAGE (SPICY) 13
CONFIT GOAT W/ BBQ SEA ISLAND RED PEAS, RICE & GARLIC BREADCRUMBS 14

pasta:
SHAVED BLACK TRUFFLES W/ SHELLS & PARMESAN CREAM 24
HAND-CUT CHITARRA W/ CARAMELIZED CAULIFLOWER & WHITE WINE SOFFRITTO 13
PENNE "ALLA VODKA" W/ SQUID & BASIL 14

FAMILY STYLE:

SMOKED BRISKET, WHITE BREAD, HORSERADISH & SLAW 29
PERUVIAN-STYLE CHICKEN W/ FRIED YUCA, SWEET POTATO CEVICHE & PLANTAINS 30

items marked in GRASSY GREEN are vegetarian or can be served vegetarian
please notify your server if you have any dietary restrictions or allergies
all unattended or misbehaving children will be given a shot of espresso and a free puppy

FIGURE 11.2
This is a version, several weeks later, of the menu referenced in Figure 11.1. Notice that most of the dishes have been retained as is. A few have been modified. One completely new dish has been added and an old one removed. While the menu has changed a little, it remains easily recognizable and appealing to the operation's loyal and sizable customer base.

Reprinted with permission of Rose's Luxury.

that adjust with the seasons often maintain elements of their most popular dishes to keep the food recognizable and appealing for their most loyal customers.

Finally, it should be stressed that increasing profits is a process that goes beyond strict menu-analysis computations. On paper, it might seem that the way to maximize a menu's profitability is to reduce the menu to one choice in each menu category—the items with the highest contribution margins. While such an approach would maximize the amount of profit made per customer, it would sacrifice long-term profits for a shortsighted view. Too limited a menu will drive away customers who might otherwise patronize the establishment. While those guests might not order the most profitable dishes, every dish on the menu generates some contribution margin. Unless a dish is priced below its variable cost or a restaurant has more customers than it can accommodate, it is always better to have more customers ordering anything from the menu than it is to lose customers in an attempt to drive them toward more profitable dishes.

Incidentally, a menu should never offer a dish with a sales price that does not cover its food cost plus the additional direct customer expenses, such as server wages, linens, and water, associated with every customer. Such a dish causes the business to lose money every time a customer orders it.

A foodservice company that cannot accommodate all of its customers because of an overabundance of business can usually afford to make more drastic changes to its menu. As long as it still retains enough customers to fill to capacity, such a business could easily increase the prices of its plowhorses and dogs to make them more profitable. Losing a dog from the menu and its small following of customers might merely allow other customers to dine and spend money on more profitable items.

Point-of-Sales Systems and Ongoing Changes

Learning Objective 3
Describe the value of a point-of-sales system in menu engineering.

Any foodservice operation ought to maintain sufficient sales records and recipe costing data to make the process of menu analysis and engineering simple to execute. With the use of a computerized spreadsheet program such as Excel, a menu planner could simply enter the sales and pricing information into a worksheet with a few formulas and rather quickly have the menu items categorized by profitability and popularity. However, the process is time-consuming enough that a menu analysis is not typically performed in such a way every day of the week. When menu planners make adjustments to a menu, they typically wait days or weeks to see whether their recommendations have made a difference in the menu's profitability.

Point-of-sales, or POS, systems streamline the process to make menu-analysis computation an almost effortless activity for any given period of time. A POS system is the computerized system most foodservice operations employ today to place customer orders, generate customer checks, and process customer payments. POS systems come in a range of price points, so not every system has the same functionality. However, some have the ability to perform a menu analysis for a manager upon request. The ease of such a system allows a manager or menu planner to see day by day whether certain process changes and menu adjustments are succeeding.

A POS system can present sales numbers for each menu item at the end of each meal period or day. The menu planner can review this information to see how the menu mix has changed. (Recall that the *menu mix* is the number of each item sold in relation to the other items; it typically describes the sale of each item as a percentage of the total number of items sold.) If a menu planner had hoped to increase the sales of certain dishes relative to others, he can find out instantly whether those shifts in buying patterns have occurred. Similarly, the menu planner can see whether overall sales have dropped as a result of certain changes.

While a menu planner would not normally engineer a menu daily or even weekly to tweak menu mix results, he can recommend other interventions based on daily data. For example, the printed menu might stay the same, but the menu planner might encourage servers to suggestive sell certain dishes. Alternatively, he could recommend an advertising or promotional program to direct sales in other ways. The POS system's sales summary report allows for immediate feedback on the success of a menu change in shifting sales patterns. If the POS system supports recipe costing and contribution margin calculations, it can also generate reports on shifts in overall profitability (though the menu planner obviously knows in advance if he has changed a dish's cost per portion or sales price to make it more profitable and should not adjust sales prices or portion sizes on a daily basis). Menu planners must keep in mind that a single day's data is not sufficient to make major menu decisions, but small changes addressed quickly can help to direct the potential impact of a menu adjustment until a broader trend—positive or negative—takes hold. Operations without POS systems can do the same, but their reaction time is often slower due to the time required to compile daily sales data.

Whether a menu planner tracks the results of menu changes by hand or by computer, the more important point is that menu evaluation and modification never end. A new menu may replace an old ineffective one, but from the moment the new one takes effect, managers begin monitoring the results. Sales and profit data collected over days, weeks, and months can tell a menu planner whether a menu is generating sufficient profit as is, whether it needs minor changes, or whether an immediate overhaul is required. Menu analysis and adjustment is a cyclical process rather than a destination. From a broader perspective, the process of menu creation described over the many chapters of this text is circular rather than linear. From market analysis to sales price calculations, from menu content development to layout considerations, the creation of a menu begins anew from the moment a business's prior menu is implemented.

Summary

The amount of money that an item's sales price contributes to the coverage of fixed costs and profit is called the contribution margin. Items with higher contribution margins are considered more profitable than those with lower contribution margins. To engineer a menu to make it as profitable as possible, a menu planner should first conduct a menu analysis, which considers each menu item's profitability and its popularity. The popularity benchmark is set at 70% of the average number of each item sold. An item's popularity level is determined by comparing the number of units sold to the popularity benchmark. An item's profitability is determined by comparing its contribution margin to the average weighted contribution margin. Using the variables of profitability and popularity,

all menu items are labeled as stars, plowhorses, puzzles, or dogs. Each requires a different intervention to increase the menu's profitability, but all adjustments to the menu must be done in ways that shift buying patterns without driving away customers. The menu modifications are evaluated by conducting a menu analysis after the changes to the menu have been implemented. A POS system can provide instantaneous feedback on how the sales and menu mix have changed, if at all. A completed menu is monitored and evaluated soon after it has been put into operation. Should modifications be required, the menu planner begins the cycle of menu creation all over again but this time with even more information and knowledge about the market and its buying habits.

TECHNOLOGY ASSISTANCE: SETTING UP A MENU-ANALYSIS TEMPLATE IN EXCEL

Creating a template in Excel to perform the menu-analysis calculations is relatively simple. Following are the instructions for doing so in just a few steps.

1. In the first row, write out the menu-analysis heading information. In cell A1 write "Menu Item" and plan on listing all menu items for the category in the cells below. In cell B1 write "Number Sold" and plan on writing the number of portions sold for each menu item in this column. In cell C1 write "Item Sales Price" and plan on writing the sales price for each menu item in this column. In cell D1 write "Item Food Cost" and plan on writing the food cost for each menu item in this column. In cell E1 write "Item Contribution Margin." In cell F1 write "Menu Contribution Margin." In cell G1 write "Popularity" and in cell H1

	A	B	C	D	E	F	G	H
	Menu Item	Number Sold	Item Sales Price	Item Food Cost	Item Contribution Margin	Menu Contribution Margin	Popularity	Profitability
1								
2	From menu	From sales data (POS)	From menu	From recipe costing sheets	=C2−D2	=B2*E2	Compare B2 to B9. Write H or L.	Compare E2 to B10. Write H or L.
3					=C3−D3	=B3*E3		
4					=C4−D4	=B4*E4		
5					=C5−D5	=B5*E5		
6					=C6−D6	=B6*E6		
7	Total	=sum(B2:B6)				=sum(F2:F6)		
8	Avg. No. of Each Item Sold	=B7/5						
9	Pop. Benchmark	=B8*0.7						
10	Avg. Weighted CM	=F7/B7						

TABLE 11.2

Menu-Analysis Worksheet Template

write "Profitability." (See Table 11.2 to see how everything looks when entered properly.)

2. Starting with Row 2, write each menu item's name (in A2), number of portions sold (in B2), its sales price (in C2), and its food cost (in D2). Continue with this information in each of the following rows until you have entered all of the menu items in the category you wish to analyze.

3. In column A in the cell just below the last menu item name, write the heading "Total." In the cell below that, write "Average Number of Each Item Sold." In the cell below that, write "Popularity Benchmark." In the cell below that, write "Average Weighted CM."

4. In the B column, next to the heading "Total" use the sum function to total the number of dishes sold. The sum formula for a column is written as =sum (starting cell: ending cell). (For Table 11.2 this is "=sum (B2:B6)".)

5. In the F column, next to the row headed "Total" use the sum function to total the menu contribution margins. The sum formula is written as =sum (starting cell: ending cell). (For Table 11.2 this is "=sum (F2:F6)".)

6. In the B column, next to the heading "Average Number of Each Item Sold" set up a formula to divide the total number of items sold by the number of menu offerings being analyzed. For example, if there are 5 menu items listed in column A, then divide by 5. The formula is written as =cell directly above this one/number of cells with menu item names. (For Table 11.2, this is "=B7/5".)

7. In the B column, next to the heading "Popularity Benchmark" set up a formula to multiply the average number of each item sold by 0.7. The formula is written as =cell directly above this one*0.7. (For Table 11.2, this is "= B8*0.7".)

8. In the B column, next to the heading "Average Weighted Contribution Margin" write a formula that divides the total contribution margin by the total

number of items sold. The formula is written as =cell in column F in the row labeled "Total"/cell in column B in the row labeled "Total." (For Table 11.2, this is "=F7/B7".)

9. In cell E2, write the formula "=C2−D2" to calculate that item's contribution margin. Copy that formula all the way down the column but stopping just above the row labeled "Total."

10. In cell F2, write the formula "=B2*E2" to calculate that item's menu contribution margin. Copy that formula all the way down the column but stopping just above the row labeled "Total."

The template is now complete. Once the information in columns A–D is entered, the worksheet will perform the remaining calculations. The determination of H or L popularity and profitability should be done and entered manual by comparing the data in column B to B9 (for popularity) and in column E to B10 (for profitability).

Comprehension Questions

1. Using the following chart of a menu's appetizer selection and its sales and cost data, conduct a menu analysis to determine the level—high or low—for the popularity and profitability of each item.

Menu Item	Number Sold	Item Sales Price	Item Food Cost	Item Contribution Margin	Menu Contribution Margin	Popularity (H/L)	Profitability (H/L)
Beef skewers	151	$6.25	$2.88				
Potato skins	209	$5.45	$1.44				
Calamari	439	$6.95	$1.89				
Soup	303	$3.00	$0.48				
Salad	518	$3.75	$1.44				
Total		X	X	X		X	X
Average number of each item sold							
Popularity benchmark							
Average weighted CM							

2. Label each appetizer in question 1 as a star, plowhorse, puzzle, or dog.

3. For each of the appetizers described in question 1, state one thing you would do to that appetizer to increase the menu's overall profitability.

4. Over how long a period of time should the data used in a menu analysis be collected—a day, a week, or a month?

5. What is the value of a POS system as it relates to menu analysis and engineering?

Discussion Questions

1. Imagine that you are a restaurant manager in the process of engineering a menu. You have conducted a menu analysis already. What additional information would you want to know about the menu (beyond what you have learned from the menu analysis) before proposing any menu changes? Where might you get this information?

2. This chapter focused on menus for restaurants, but a menu analysis operates the same way for any menu from which people select items with varying sales prices and food costs. Having conducted a menu analysis for a cafeteria, what changes might a menu planner make to the cafeteria to make the operation more profitable? Remember that a cafeteria sells items of varying sales prices and food costs but does not provide a written menu.

3. Consider an all-you-can-eat buffet. Would a menu analysis be applicable here? Why or why not?

4. Consider a dessert menu for which all of the desserts have the same selling price even though they all have different food costs. Is a menu analysis applicable here? Why or why not?

5. After going two years without changing his restaurant's menu, a restaurant manager has finally overhauled the menu. The manager uses his POS system to carefully track each item and the new menu's overall profitability. Less than a week into the new menu, the manager notices that the new menu is not as profitable as the old one, so he releases another new menu just a few days later. This pattern repeats for four straight weeks with four new menus; though each menu differs in overall profitability, none is as profitable as the original. What could the manager have done before releasing the first menu to improve the potential profitability of that menu? Given the situation he is currently in four menus later, what should the manager do at this point to stabilize the situation and return to the desired level of profitability?

Case Study

A menu planner for a fairly successful suburban family restaurant conducts a menu analysis and discovers the following: The vegan tofu stir-fry is the least popular dish (worse than the menu's dogs) even though its profitability makes it a puzzle. Several other puzzles, including a mac and cheese dish (with the largest contribution margin among the entrées) and a pork chop entrée fall short of the mark to qualify as highly popular. The fried chicken is the most popular dish, but its profitability is the lowest among the entrées, making it a plowhorse. The burger is a star, and the grilled mango shrimp skewer is a dog. The menu planner figures that the vegan stir-fry is there to serve the vegan market, so he leaves it alone. He removes the mac and cheese and the pork chop from the menu since they are not selling as well as he'd like. He decides to drop the portion size on the fried chicken from a half chicken to a quarter chicken; by keeping the sales price the same he hopes to make the chicken far more profitable. Because the burger is a star (and thus, highly profitable), he wants to encourage its sales. To accomplish this, he creates a "build your own burger" section with a large list of possible toppings across the menu's entire hot zone. As the shrimp is a dog, he simply takes it off the menu and uses the extra space for the expanded burger section. The menu planner revises the entire menu and sends it to print.

After several weeks under the new menu, the menu planner notices that his changes accomplished what he had hoped. The tofu stir-fry hasn't changed its percentage in the menu mix. The fried chicken is generating a larger contribution margin per sale. The burger is selling even better than before. While there are other items on the menu, the ones that he removed no longer tie up space in inventory. The menu planner is pleased until he notices that overall restaurant profit has gone down due to a 30% decline in total sales dollars compared to the prior month. Looking around the dining room, the menu planner observes that the room has far fewer customers than usual.

What did the menu planner do wrong? What did he do right? If you were the menu planner, what would you have done differently?

Capstone Project

Step 11: Submit your completed project to your instructor for preliminary review and approval to present it to the class. The instructor will determine the exact date for your project presentation, whether during this class session or at an alternate time. If any components of the project are incomplete, be sure to finish them before your final project presentation. Use the presentation to showcase not only the menu but also all of the advance work that went into the menu's creation. Point out the menu's hot zones, which items you hope to sell the most, and how you have marketed those items on the menu. Plan on describing during the presentation how and how often you will evaluate the menu to improve its profitability.

CHAPTER 12

How the Menu Directs Business

INTRODUCTION

This text has approached menu planning from the perspective that many parameters exist that inherently delimit a menu. The target market has certain desires and needs, including nutritional ones. The staff and equipment are only capable of executing dishes of a certain caliber and style. The price point potential customers are willing to pay impacts the food that can be prepared and sold at a profit. The importance of a menu's fealty to a brand and business concept has been stressed repeatedly as well. In other words, all these factors and more direct the ultimate content and form of the menu.

But can the opposite also be true? Can the menu direct and define the other variables? Yes, sometimes it can. An entrepreneur, foodservice business owner, or manager can create the menu first and then make all other decisions to support the menu. The menu epitomizes the vision and defines the brand. Such an approach is risky for a business and not always appropriate, but it can work under certain circumstances. This chapter addresses this approach to menu planning and the potential benefits and pitfalls associated with putting the menu first.

CHAPTER 12 LEARNING OBJECTIVES

As a result of successfully completing this chapter, readers will be able to:

1. Describe how a menu can create a market and drive revenue.

2. Describe how a menu can guide certain business decisions.

3. State the pros and cons of creating a menu first in the menu-planning process and allowing all other business decisions to follow from there.

CHAPTER 12 OUTLINE

The Menu's Marketing Function

Learning Objective 1
Describe how a menu can create a market and drive revenue.

One of the key functions of a menu is to market the food and drink that the business sells. Sometimes, the menu serves only as an internal marketing tool relegated to the first few minutes after the guest enters the foodservice establishment. Normally, it is the brand, not the menu, that brings customers in the door in the first place. Perhaps they have heard about the business from someone else, or perhaps they have seen an ad describing the place in generic terms. They may like the setting or the reputation for service. They may know the cuisine or type of food, but not necessarily the specific dishes on the menu. However, if the menu is the driving force behind a restaurant, the menu should be placed front and center for all marketing strategies, internal and external. In this case, customers come because they know the menu, even if they know little else about the place.

231

RAW BAR

Bison: *Carpaccio, Pickled Peppers, Hominy*
Bass: *Marinated, Dill, Lemon, Pink Pepper*
Beef: *Tartare, Celery Root, Truffle, Parsley*
Oysters: *Cucumber, Meyer Lemon, Verjus*
Petite Seafood Plateau
Grande Seafood Plateau

APPETIZERS

Shrimp: *Cocktail/Sautéed*
Escargot: *Parsnip Agnolotti, Parsley Nage*
Beef: *Tataki of Prime Beef, Ponzu, Chili*
Foie: *Quail & Foie, Almond Pudding, Saffron*
Crab: *Maison, Capers, Lemon, Parsley, Brioche*
Egg: *Mushrooms, Linguini, Peas, Bacon, Parmesan*

SALADS

Caesar: *A Tableside Classic*
Wedge: *Maytag Bleu, Bacon, Buttermilk*
Kale: *Apples, Peanuts, Ice Wine, Quinoa*

SOUPS

Mussels: *Lemongrass-Coconut Broth, Grilled Bread*
Onion: *Baked-Vidalia Soup, Croûton, Swiss*
Peas: *Chilled Pea Soup, Shrimp, Dill, Lemon*

SEA

Salmon: *Maple-Mustard Glaze, Sweet Potato Hash*
Loup de Mer: *Fingerlings, Crab, Sauce "Bouillabaisse"*
Lobster: *Butter Poached 2# Lobster, Lemon*

RANGE

12oz Bone In Filet
6oz Filet Mignon
16oz Bone In NY Strip: *Au Poivre, Tableside*
16oz Cowboy Rib Eye
14oz Tomahawk Pork Chop
36oz Porterhouse: *(For 2: includes 2 sides, sauce)*
16oz Milk Fed Veal Chop

COUP & GARDEN

Hen: *Artichokes, Yellow-foots, Barley Risotto*
Tofu: *Korean BBQ, Bok Choy, Turnips, Black Beans*

SUPPLEMENTS:

Surf & Turf: *1/2 of a 2# Maine Lobster*   **Oscar:** *Colossal Blue Crab, Hollandaise, Asparagus*   **Foie Gras:** *Seared La Belle Farms Foie*

TEMPERATURES TO CHEF'S SPECIFICATIONS:

Pittsburgh: *Charred, Cold Red Center*   **Rare:** *Cold Red Center*   **Medium Rare:** *Warm Red Center*
Medium: *Hot Red Center*   **Medium Well:** *Hot Pink Center*   **Well Done:** *Hot Brown Center (not recommended)*

TABLE ACCENTS

Potato: *Yukon Potato Butter*
Corn: *Creamed Sweet Corn*
Spinach: *Creamed/Sautéed*
Barley: *"Risotto," Soffrito, Parmesan*
Asparagus: *Lemon Oil, Sea Salt*
Onion: *Signature Onion Rings, White BBQ*
Fries: *Truffled Hand Cut Fries, Ketchup*

SAUCES

Steak: *Signature Steak Sauce*
Horseradish: *Crème Fraîche, Horseradish*
Cabernet: *Cabernet, Shallot, Demi-glace*
Hollandaise: *Vinegar, Egg, Butter*
Béarnaise: *Vinegar, Egg, Tarragon, Butter*
Peppercorn: *Green Peppercorn-Veal, Crème Fraîche*
Chimichurri: *Garlic, Parsley, Coriander, Vinegar*

Executive Chef: Daniel Zeal

Our Sea Island Team take allergies very seriously. Before placing your order or consuming any food or beverage, please alert a service team member about any allergy you or your party may have. Our product may contain wheat, egg, dairy, soy, fish, or other allergens even if not listed on the menu. As required by the State of Georgia, we provide this information: "Consuming raw or undercooked meats, Poultry, Seafood, Shellfish, or Eggs may increase your risk of food borne illness, especially if you have certain medical conditions."

Please let your server know if you would like to see our Wellness Menu.

A service charge of 20% and 6% sales tax will be added to food and beverage service.

FIGURE 12.1

A well-done menu reflects the brand of the business it represents, whether the menu or the business is conceived first. This figure, as well as the others in this chapter, shows a menu from a restaurant alongside a photograph of that restaurant. Notice how the menu always reflects the concept depicted in the photo. Figures 12.1, 12.2, 12.3 are all outlets of the Sea Island Company.

Source: Sea Island Company. Reprinted with permission.

FIGURE 12.1   *(Continued)*

Source: Sea Island Company

A foodservice marketer can post menus in the window of a restaurant that receives a lot of foot traffic. She can provide copies of the menu to local offices, hotels, gyms, and other places where people might use a menu to make a decision about where to dine. Print ads sometimes have sufficient space to include a menu or a portion of one. A business's web page can and should include its menu, too. Any foodservice business, no matter its approach to menu planning, can utilize these marketing techniques to drive revenue. However, when a foodservice operation begins with a menu to direct its business decisions, the menu's role in marketing is slightly different and absolutely critical. Rather than photos of the dining room or the people, advertising in a menu-forward operation focuses almost entirely on the menu itself to promote the company's vision. Such a menu must communicate the feel of the establishment—its atmosphere, style of service, and quality of food and drink. The menu descriptions must be evocative, the layout and images suggestive of the ambiance. Because the menu precedes the business in this situation, the owners and managers design everything about the company to support the menu's vision, not the other way around. If the menu is vague in what it communicates about the operation, both managers and customers will be unsure of what to expect from the business.

While most company leaders choose to create a concept and vision first and then a core menu to support it, it is not uncommon for business owners to sprout ancillary services and products from nothing more than a menu. For example, a restaurant may advertise its catering services through its restaurant menu. In reality, no plan for catering may exist yet, but customers may trust the restaurant and assume that the catering operation would be similar in style and quality. The chef or owner may only begin the logistical planning for the business's catering side once a customer expresses interest. The chef can then develop a special catering menu, and in time, the catering division of the restaurant takes off on its own.

Restaurants can market temporary or periodic events on their menus as well. For example, a restaurant might promote a special food and wine dinner, a beer tasting, a weekly pasta night, or a special holiday menu. Often in these situations, the menu is created first to promote the event, and the logistics are planned afterward. In reality, the menu planners already know the restaurant's staff and equipment, but they might make small changes for a special event.

FOOD MENU · ERIC FULLEM - CHEF DE CUISINE

SOUPE

FRENCH ONION
caramelized onion, baguette crouton, Gruyère cheese

WHITE BEAN
white beans, andouille sausage, collard greens

MELON GAZPACHO
cantaloupe soup, watermelon gelee, basil

HORS D'OEUVRES

EGGPLANT AND SUNFLOWER SEED HUMMUS
marinated feta, espelette, grilled pita

QUICHE LORRAINE
frissée, lardon, gruyere

MUSSELS BI BILLI
PEI mussels, aromatic cream sauce

DEVILED EGGS
black truffle, chives

SALMON CRU
raw shaved scottish salmon, lemon shallot vinaigrette, boiled egg, olive, caper, croutons

CHARCUTERIE ET FROMAGE
chef's selection of artisan cheeses and meats

ACCOMPAGNEMENTS

SAFFRON RICE PILAF

ROASTED SPRING VEGETABLES

SWEET CORN POLENTA

SALADE

MELON AND CRAB SALAD
bibb lettuce, cantaloupe, honeydew, basil citrus vinaigrette

CAESAR SALAD
hearts of romaine lettuce, croutons, parmesan cheese, house made caesar dressing

GARDEN SALAD
mixed greens, toasted nuts, carrots, cucumbers, bleu cheese, balsamic vinaigrette

10 VEGETABLE SALAD
spring vegetables, herbs, sunflower seed vinaigrette · 1

LE POULET | **LE CREVETTE** | **LE POISSON DU JOUR**
CHICKEN 8 | SHRIMP 11 | FRESH CAUGHT FISH MP

FOR ADDITIONAL LIGHTER FARE OPTIONS
ASK TO SEE OUR WELLNESS MENU

PLATS PRINCIPAUX

ROASTED LAMB LOIN
ratatouille, cous cous, spiced lamb jus

CRISPY DUCK BREAST
tagliatelle, foie gras cream, chantarelle, prosciutto, black cherry

DAURADE
sea bream, provencal tomatoes, florence fennel, fresh tomato sauce

CHICKEN BASQUEZE
braised organic chicken, roasted sweet peppers, charred onion, sweet garlic polata

ROASTED HALIBUT
lobster bisque, mussels, clams, tomato, shrimp

STEAK FRITES

BAVETTE OF BEEF
hanger steak
STRIPLOIN OF BEEF
12 oz. New York striploin

LA SAUCE

BLACK TRUFFLE BUTTER

BÉARNAISE

BORDELAISE

TURN THE PAGE TO VIEW OUR MEMBER'S CLASSIC MENU

A service charge of 20% and 6% sales tax will be added to Food and Beverage service. As required by the State of Georgia, we provide this information: "The consumption of raw or under cooked foods such as meat, fish and eggs which may contain harmful bacteria, may cause serious illness or death."

FIGURE 12.2

A menu and a photo of the operation it represents.

Source: Sea Island Company. Reprinted with permission.

FIGURE 12.2 *(Continued)*

Source: Sea Island Company.

Hotels commonly promote one of their foodservice operations through another of their foodservice outlets. For example, the room service menu might invite guests down to the lounge for a drink. The lounge menu might suggest breakfast in the hotel restaurant. Because all of the money ultimately flows to the hotel, the food and drink outlets all benefit when they direct customers to each other. Hotel guests can tire of eating in the same place every day, but encouraging them to rotate locations within the hotel allows the hotel to keep more of the customers' business. When a parent restaurant company owns multiple concepts, similar cross-promotion usually occurs. Like a hotel, the parent restaurant group would prefer to keep its customers within the family of businesses, so the restaurants promote each other on their menus and in their advertising. While the menu providing the promotion in this situation is not the menu of the business being promoted, the customer base typically assumes the same level of quality will be present in all of the outlets.

Normally, a menu planner surveys the market to ensure that a customer base for the intended product exists. However, an entrepreneur, passionate about her product, might prefer to create the menu and the concept and then build a market for the product. If such an approach is to succeed, there cannot be too wide a disconnect between the concept and the market. For instance, a low-income community will not be able to afford a five-course, high-end gastronomic tasting menu no matter how much they might want to enjoy it. However, if a survey of a small town shows that the residents enjoy Chinese food, a restaurateur might successfully gamble that they will patronize a Thai restaurant, even if there is no suggestion in the psychographic survey that they crave such a restaurant. A persuasive menu could convince locals to sample and ultimately return regularly to the Thai place. The risk comes in that the entrepreneur may guess wrong, and the market may never materialize. Creating the menu out of known market needs is a much safer approach.

Antipasti

BRUSCHETTA— Balsamic Marinated Tomatoes, House Made Ricotta, Olive Almond Tapenade, Country Bread
CARPACCIO— Sliced Wagyu Beef, Mushrooms, Carrots, Mustard Aioli
CAESAR— Romaine Lettuces, Toasted Brioche, Parmigiano Reggiano
DI CAMPO— Broadfield Lettuces, Cucumber, Heirloom Tomatoes, Red Onion, Herb Vinaigrette
CAPRESE— Heirloom Tomatoes, House Made Burrata, Arugula, Balsamic Glaze
COZZE— Mussels "Fra Diavolo," Calabrian Peppers, San Marzano Tomato Broth
AFFETTATI— Assorted Cured Italian Meats, Artisanal Cheeses, Apple Mustardo
*ARANCINI— Saffron Rice Balls, Mozzarella Crema, Pomodoro
POLPI AL FERRO— Flat Iron Grilled Octopus, Tonnato Sauce, Chicory Salad

Pizza

MARGHERITA— Hand Pulled Mozzarella, Stewed San Marzano Tomatoes, Basil
*TAVOLA— House Made Sausage, Rapini, Aged Gouda
FUNGHI PAZZO— Porcini Garlic Sauce, Pioppini Mushrooms, Mozzarella, Mushroom "Croccante," Ricotta Salata, Truffle Oil
FICHE— Marinated Dried Figs, Speck, Goat Cheese, Fried Sage Oil, Arugula
N'DUJA— Cured Sausage, Red Pepper, Provolone, Calabrian Peppers, Red Onions
PIZZA DEL GIORNO— Pizza Chef's Daily Creation

Pasta

LINGUINI— Thin Cut Saffron Pasta, Georgia Shrimp, Sea Scallops, Jumbo Crab Meat, Calamari, Calabrian Pepper
TAGLIATELLE ALLA BOLOGNESE— Fresh Ribbon Pasta, House Recipe Meat Sauce
TORDELLI FROMAGGI— Spinach Ricotta Filling, Spring Vegetables, Golden Tomato, Balsamic Glaze
STRACCI— Pasta Ribbons, Roasted Mushroom Ragù, Pancetta, Heirloom Tomatoes
MEAT LASAGNA— Bolognese, Bechemella, Parmigiano Reggiano, Ricotta Cheese
STROZZAPRETI— Hand-Shaped Pasta, Georgia Shrimp, Spicy Sausage, Peas, Cream, Bread Crumbs
RISOTTO— Jumbo Crab Meat, Yellow Corn, Goat Cheese, Lemon, Mint

Carne & Pesce

ZUPPA DI PESCE— "Fish Soup," Calamari, Mussels, Fish, Scallops, Shrimp, Octopus, Potato, Tomato
SCALLOPS OREGANATA— Sea Scallops, Lardo, Oregano Bread Crumbs, Fennel, Heirloom Tomato
FILETTO— Beef Tenderloin, Yukon Potatoes "Vesuvio," Roasted Garlic, Oregano, Peas, Cipollini
PULCINO— Roasted Chicken, Rosemary, Black Pepper, Lemon, Zucchini, Squash, Peppers
VEAL SCALOPPINI— Roasted Artichokes, Pine Nuts, Pickled Carrots, Black Olives, Lemon
*POLLO PARMIGIANA— Breaded Chicken Breast, Spaghetti, Pomodoro, Basil
PESCE DEL GIORNO— Chef's Daily Fish Selection

Contorni

Zucchi, Zucchini, Yellow Squash, Roasted Red Peppers
Fettuccine, Alfredo, Parmigiano Reggiano
Broccolini, Lemon Zest

Spaghetti, Pomodoro, Parmigiano Reggiano
Asparagi, Roasted Asparagus, Marcona Almonds
*Cavolfiori Fritti, Fried Cauliflower, Sultanas, Capers, Colatura di Alici

Please see server for healthy menu options.
* Item cannot be prepared gluten-free.
"The consumption of raw or undercooked foods such as meat, fish and eggs which may contain harmful bacteria, may cause serious illnes or death"

FIGURE 12.3

A menu and a photo of the operation it represents.

Source: Sea Island Company. Reprinted with permission.

FIGURE 12.3   *(Continued)*

Source: Sea Island Company.

The Menu as a Control Tool

Learning Objective 2
Describe how a menu can guide certain business decisions.

In addition to driving revenue, the menu has the ability to direct certain management decisions. Again, most operations take stock of their facility and employee constraints before writing the menu, but a brand-new business or one undergoing a complete overhaul has the opportunity to build the business concept around the menu. The food and beverage offered on the menu determine the specific equipment needed to execute those menu items. The operation purchases the equipment needed to prepare those dishes and drinks and passes over all other potential equipment purchases. For a complete renovation or new construction, the layout of the kitchen and dining room may be designed to facilitate the menu efficiently. The menu may guide the planning for everything from ventilation, holding equipment, and hotline layout to the purchase of specialty china, utensils, and dining room equipment. The potential pitfall, of course, is that future menus are tied to the new equipment, too, so the initial construction must be flexible enough to accommodate future menu changes.

The menu can guide staffing levels and required employee skill sets as well. While an existing foodservice operation may write a new menu that falls within the abilities of its current staff, a new business may write job descriptions to attract and hire only those employees capable of executing the menu. By not hiring overqualified workers, management helps to control labor cost to some degree. Alternatively, a menu that makes everything from scratch, incorporates advanced knife cuts, and cross-utilizes product to reduce waste may have a lower food cost but require a well-paid, highly trained kitchen staff to execute it. The menu dictates the language used in advertisements for employees, job specification standards, and interview questions. The work hours needed to properly prepare and serve the menu's offerings guide the staffing levels. The business ends up employing the exact number of workers it needs.

Every country has a story that can be told through its cooking. To experience that story, all you have to do is taste the lost dishes that sustained those who came before us. Our country has an incredible culinary diversity across its states; but it also has an incredible depth through the centuries. America Eats Tavern is a place where you can travel through time to find the moment when our American identity was forged in a pot, skillet and bowl.

SEAFOOD BAR

A delectable assortment of chilled fresh seafood from local shores.

LITTLENECK CLAMS*   **DEVILED KING CRAB COCKTAIL**   **SHRIMP AND KING CRAB COCKTAIL**
9 half-dozen   19   19
                        ROCK SHRIMP COCKTAIL   **OYSTER COCKTAIL***
                                 19   19

OYSTERS

DAILY SELECTION OF FRESH OYSTERS ON THE HALF-SHELL*
Lemon, fruit vinegar, cocktail sauce
Market price
ask your server for daily selection

GRILLED   **PICKLED***   **SLIDERS**
Thomas Downing, New York City, 1825   New York City, 18th Century   Nashville hot chicken-style fried oysters,
Fresh butter, mace   House-made saltines, pickled vegetables   warm Parker House rolls
16   17   15

AMERICAN ARTISANAL CHEESE

Served with spiced pecans, house-made jam, walnut-cranberry bread
14 assortment of three
19 assortment of five

COUNTRY HAMS

JOHNSTON COUNTY CUREMASTER'S RESERVE, NC 12   BENTON'S HICKORY SMOKED COUNTRY HAM, TN 9

OLLI BECKER LANE HAM, AGED 14 MONTHS, VA 11   LA QUERCIA ROSSA BERKSHIRE HAM, IA 11

JOHNSTON COUNTY HAM, NC 9

SELECTION OF ALL FIVE HAMS 24
Rolled biscuit, whole grain mustard, redeye mayonnaise,
pickles, Amish-style pickled eggs

Head Chef Nate Waugaman
General Manager Peter Johnson

* This item may be served with under-cooked ingredients. Consuming raw or under-cooked meats, poultry, seafood, shellfish, or eggs may increase your risk of foodborne illness, especially if you have certain medical conditions.

FIGURE 12.4

A menu and a photo of the operation it represents.

Source: José Andrés ThinkFoodGroup. Reprinted with permission.

SOUPS

CREAM OF MUSHROOM SOUP
Goat cheese mousse, cranberry-walnut tulle
11

BUTTERNUT SQUASH SOUP
Spiced pumpkin seeds, pumpkin oil
11

MANHATTAN CLAM CHOWDER
Littleneck clams, ham hock, potato, tomato broth
15

SALADS

WEDGE SALAD
Iceberg lettuce, jalapeño pickled egg,
1000 island dressing, cherry tomato,
watercress
10
with poached chicken 13
with poached shrimp 16

CAESAR SALAD
Fourth of July, 1924
Baby romaine lettuce, Caesar dressing,
anchovies, croutons, parmesan
10

SALMAGUNDI
Mary Randolph, Virginia Housewife, 1831
Ham, chicken, anchovy, roasted winter
vegetables, egg, field greens, capers,
raisins, walnuts
16

WALDORF SALAD
Oscar Tschirky, New York City, 1893
Apples, celery, walnuts, mayonnaise, walnut catsup,
mixed baby greens
9

ROASTED BEET SALAD
Fannie Farmer, The Boston Cooking School Cookbook, 1906
Red and gold baby beets, raspberries, walnuts,
mixed baby greens, yogurt
12

SMALL PLATES

**HUSH PUPPIES WITH
SOUTH MOUNTAIN CREAMERY HONEY BUTTER**
A Southern fisherman's favorite, fried over an open fire with the leftovers to keep the dogs quiet.
At some point, humans figured the corn cake was a perfect match with freshly caught fish...or trout roe.
8
with trout roe 15

1964 BUFFALO CHICKEN WINGS
Frank and Theresa's, Anchor Bar, Buffalo, NY 1964
House-made Buffalo sauce,
smoked blue cheese, celery
12

CRAB FLAKE AND HAM
Restaurant Haussner, Baltimore, MD 1955
Broiled blue crab, Virginia ham,
lemon butter air
19

TWICE BAKED POTATO
Potato espuma, Vella Dry Jack Cheese,
chives, potato chips, bowfin caviar
19

DEVILED EGGS
Jalapeño, beet and mustard pickled eggs
9

SHRIMP AND GRAPEFRUIT COCKTAIL
Irma Rombauer, Joy of Cooking, 1931
Shrimp, grapefruit, mustard dressing
16

STEAK TARTARE AMERICAN*
Raw chopped beefsteak first appeared on French menus at the turn of the
20th century and was originally called "beefsteak à la Américaine."
It really became popular after WWII in the 1950s.
Raw Roseda Farms beef, warm Parker House rolls
19

VERMICELLI "MAC" 'N' CHEESE PREPARED LIKE PUDDING
The first recipe was first written down by Lewis Fresnaye, a refugee from the
French Revolution. One of America's first commercial pasta-makers, Fresnaye
handed out this recipe with the coiled pasta he sold. Philadelphia, 1802
Vella Dry Jack Cheese 11
with ham and chives 15
with King crab 19

VEGETABLES
7 each

CRISPY BRUSSELS SPROUTS
'Chups cranberry glaze, dried
cranberries, spiced pecans

HARVARD BEETS
Roasted beets, sugar vinegar glaze,
biscuit topping, goat cheese cream

ROASTED CAULIFLOWER CASSEROLE
Cauliflower purée, dry jack cheese,
crispy capers

WHERE THE WILD THINGS ARE
Foraged seasonal vegetables, hen of the woods mushrooms,
mushroom catsup

CREAMED SPINACH
Sautéed spinach, spinach purée,
crème fraiche, bread crumbs, garlic chips

* This item may be served with under-cooked ingredients. Consuming raw or under-cooked meats, poultry, seafood, shellfish, or eggs may increase your risk of foodborne illness, especially if you have certain medical conditions.

FIGURE 12.4 *(Continued)*

SANDWICHES
All sandwiches served with house-made Saratoga chips

MAINE LOBSTER ROLL
John D. Rockefeller, Mount Desert Island, ME, 1910
Classic chilled lobster salad, toasted New England roll
25

JOSÉ'S LOBSTER ROLL
Warm butter-poached fresh Maine lobster,
mayo espuma, celery, toasted butter roll
25

OYSTER PO' BOY
New Orleans, 1929
Crispy fried oysters, lettuce,
tomato, remoulade
19

A BURGER STORY
There are as many possible origins of the humble hamburger as there are possible toppings. Hannah Glasse's Art of Cookery described a "Hamburgh Sausage" of chopped beef on toasted bread. But the first menu to list a hamburger was Delmonico's two decades later. The invention of the refrigerated railroad car allowed fresh beef to travel to local butchers who could use a newly invented mechanical meat chopper to grind it down. When the burger arrived at the St. Louis World's Fair of 1904, it quickly grew into a national sensation.

BLUE CHEESE BURGER*
Buttermilk blue cheese, mayonnaise,
mustard, caramelized onions
and mushrooms
17

STEAK, HAMBURG*
Delmonico's, NY, 1826
Lettuce, tomato, onion,
mayonnaise, mustard
14

FOIE GRAS BURGER*
Hudson Valley foie gras, caramelized
onions, huckleberries, grain mustard
25

LARGE PLATES

EISENHOWER STEW
Beef short rib, charred baby carrot,
pearl onion, cherry tomato
28

MUSHROOM HOPPIN' JOHN
Carolina Gold rice cakes, cow peas,
roasted maitake mushrooms
21

GRILLED SPANISH MACKERAL
Twice-cooked fingerling potatoes,
parsley, mustard seed vinaigrette,
tomato-mustard sauce
25

NASHVILLE HOT CHICKEN
Thornton Prince, 1930s
Fried chicken, spicy glaze, dill pickles,
Parker House rolls
23

NEW ENGLAND BAKED SCALLOPS
Garlic-chive cream, lemon,
garlic chips, anise bread crumb
24

SHRIMP 'N' GRITS
Jamestown, 1607
Byrd Mill grits, Meadow Reserve
cheddar, pearl onion petals, ham hock
17

PHEASANT WITH CELERY SAUCE
Early American Cookery
"The Good Housekeeper," 1841
Pan-roasted pheasant, celery sauce,
roasted turnip, wild mushroom
28

STEAKHOUSE SIRLOIN WITH CATSUPS*
Walnut, modern tomato,
mushroom, oyster
29

MUTTON WITH OYSTERS
Esther Allen Howland,
The New England Economic Housekeeper, 1843
Braised Shenandoah lamb neck,
fried oysters, crispy potatoes, oyster
catsup, tiny vegetables
26

CAROLINA RICE KITCHEN
Please allow a 30 minute cook time
Large to share between at least two / Individual

SUCKLING PIG JAMBALAYA
Braised suckling pig, Andouille sausage, okra, sofrito,
Carolina Gold Plantation Rice
37 / 21

SHRIMP JAMBALAYA
Sarah Josepha Hale, New Household Receipt-Book, 1853
Andouille sausage, chicken, okra,
Carolina Gold Plantation Rice
42 / 25

* This item may be served with under-cooked ingredients. Consuming raw or under-cooked meats, poultry, seafood, shellfish, or eggs may increase your risk of foodborne illness, especially if you have certain medical conditions.

FIGURE 12.4   *(Continued)*

CHEF'S EXPERIENCE

Allow José Andrés to take you on a journey featuring his ode to the dishes and recipes
that tell the culinary story of America while celebrating the native ingredients of Virginia

HUSH PUPPY WITH TROUT ROE

OYSTER SLIDER

BUTTERNUT SQUASH SOUP

ROASTED BEET SALAD

SHRIMP & GRAPEFRUIT COCKTAIL

BUFFALO WINGS

CRISPY BRUSSELS SPROUTS

BLACKENED SCALLOPS

MUTTON WITH OYSTERS

KEY LIME PIE

55 per person
We request the entire table participate.

CATSUPS

Today we only think of tomato, but historically there were dozens of catsups, used with meat and fish. An English import, probably of Chinese origin, the first American catsups were thinner and spicier than today's ketchup.

Produced by hand in Washington, DC, 'Chups Fruit Ketchups offer the same tangy, sweet, savory, and spicy ketchup taste, but are made with different fruits instead of tomatoes.

| MODERN TOMATO | 'CHUPS PLUM | 'CHUPS MANGO | 'CHUPS SPICY PINEAPPLE | 'CHUPS CHERRY |

AMERICA EATS TAVERN
BY JOSÉ ANDRÉS

Located at The Ritz-Carlton, Tysons Corner
1700 Tysons Boulevard
McLean, VA 22102
(703) 744-3999

www.americaeatstavern.com
 americaeatstvrn americaeatstavern americaeatstvrn

FIGURE 12.4 *(Continued)*

FIGURE 12.4   *(Continued)*

Source: José Andrés/ThinkFoodGroup

No matter when in a business's evolution the menu planner creates the menu, the menu items dictate the ingredient requirements. There is no point in purchasing ingredients that the operation does not need. However, the size, layout, and equipment needs of the storeroom may change when the menu drives managerial decisions. A menu with few frozen desserts or ingredients may need only a reach-in freezer while another menu based on large quantities of prefabricated products may require a walk-in freezer. An operation with a streamlined menu that utilizes the same ingredients across multiple dishes may get by with less shelf space than can one with an extensive menu that does not repeat ingredients.

Typically, a menu planner would not include an ingredient on a menu if she were not certain that she could source that product from her purveyors. A menu-first approach might require the chef to partner with farmers to produce those ingredients specifically for the establishment. Similarly, if a chef wants to create a restaurant based on a menu that highlights exotic ingredients, she can reach out to specialty purveyors and ask them to source and carry those ingredients in their product line. If they cannot, she might consider contacting producers overseas and asking them to ship directly to her operation.

When the menu precedes the business, creating a budget may become a simpler process. Managers can more accurately calculate food cost percentages and contribution margins for each dish with menu prices and recipes already in place. While forecasting customer counts still requires educated guessing, the menu helps with estimating an average check and thus, overall revenue from the forecast number of guests. This information, in turn, aids in the creation of all remaining budget lines. Adhering too closely to a budget, particularly in a company's first year, can be an exercise in futility at best and a recipe for disaster at worst, but the menu itself provides some concrete basis on which to ground the budget until the business opens and collects further data.

Stuck in the traffic on Reforma?

To bear the wait : guacamole made right before your eyes, with green tomatillo, serrano chile, crumbled queso fresco and a basket of fresh tortilla chips $13.50

Add our salt air margarita for $12.00
Milagro Silver, Combier L'Original, fresh lime, topped with a salt air

Or our flaco margarita for $7.50
orange infused tequila, fresh lime, grapefruit bitters and a splash of soda water

ANTOJITOS the little dishes from the streets
Ceviches / Marinated seafood salads

Camarones en escabeche
Wild caught Gulf Coast white shrimp poached with vinegar and served with onions, jalapeños, jicama and cucumbers $12.50

Ceviche de atún Pacífico
Ahi Tuna with Maggi-lime marinade, scallions, avocado, toasted pecans, fresno chiles and crispy amaranth $13.00

Ceviche con cítricos
Striped bass in a pineapple-habanero marinade with citrus, jicama and fresno chiles $13.50

Ceviche de hamachi y coco
Sliced Japanese hamachi with fresh coconut sauce, serrano water, fresh Hamakua Farms hearts of palm and slivered almonds $13.00

Cayo en aguachile
Bay scallops tossed with apples, pickled red onions and fresh Hamakua Farms hearts of palm, served with a sauce of lime, cilantro, serrano pepper and apple $12.00

Ceviche Veracruz
Lightly poached squid and striped bass ceviche with a tangy tomato sauce, fried capers, green olives, tomatoes, and pearl onions $13.00

Ceviche de chamoy
Sliced Hawaiian Ono dusted with chile pequín and tossed in a mango and chile mulato chamoy, cacahuetes Japonés, cucumber, onion, lime, and cilantro $12.00

Ensaladas / Salads

Ensalada de palmitos
Fresh Hamakua Farms hearts of palm, grapefruit, orange, radish and avocado, with a tamarind dressing $10.00

Ensalada de aguacate y remolacha
Mexican avocados, roasted beets, tomatillo, pickled red onion, jicama and orange dressing $8.50

"Gaspacho" estilo Morelia
From the historic city of Morelia, a salad of seasonal fruit, jicama root, cucumbers, queso fresco and housemade hot sauce $8.00

Ensalada de Alex-César Cardini
The classic Caesar salad of Romaine lettuce, anchovies, a soft boiled egg, Parmesan cheese and house-made croutons $9.00

Nopalitos in pasilla de Oaxaca
Fresh cactus paddles tossed in a pasilla de Oaxaca chili oil with pickled onion, serrano chile, queso fresco, and green beans $10.00

Ensalada de atún estilo Mazatlan
A confit of Ahi Tuna with creamy avocado dressing topped with a smoked local tomato, spinach and herb salad $11.00

Ensalada de chayote
Mexican squash salad with crumbled queso fresco and crushed peanuts, in a hibiscus dressing $8.00

Verduras / Vegetables

Papas al mole
José Andrés' favorite potato fries in a mole poblano sauce of almonds, chiles and a touch of chocolate, topped with Mexican cream and queso fresco $6.50

Arroz de huitlacoche con queso fresco
Rice sautéed with black Roy Burns Farm Mexican corn truffles, queso fresco and epazote herb oil $10.50

Queso fundido con tequila
Melted Chihuahua cheese flambéed with tequila and served with fresh hand-made tortillas $8.00
Add spicy chorizo $10.00

Machuco y calabaza relleno de frijol con salsa negra
Plantain and butternut squash fritters stuffed with black beans and served with a chipotle chile and piloncillo sugar sauce $8.00

Quesadilla huitlacoche
Traditional folded corn tortilla with Chihuahua cheese and Roy Burns Farm Mexican corn truffle $9.50

Frijoles refritos con queso
Slow-cooked refried beans stuffed with melted Chihuahua cheese, served with Mexican cream and fresh tortillas $8.00

Frijoles Rebosero
Heirloom Rebosero beans, fresno chiles and seasonal vegetables in a mulato chile dressing $10.00

Tortillas
Five hand-made tortillas made fresh in house — the perfect way to mop up your little dishes $4.00

Col de bruselas estilo San Quintín
Crispy brussels sprouts with a chile de árbol sauce, pumpkin seeds, peanuts and lime $8.00

Nopal asado con salsa molcajete
Grilled fresh cactus paddles served with a salsa molcajete of grilled tomatoes, tomatillos, green onions, cilantro and green chiles $8.00

Acelgas con nuez de Castilla
Sautée of swiss chard, cabbage, shallots, toasted hazelnuts, dried cranberries and raisins with a spiced apricot purée, topped with pickled swiss chard $8.00

Chilaquiles con salsa de tomatillo, queso y cilantro
Fresh hand-made tortilla chips with melted Chihuahua cheese, green tomatillo salsa, cilantro and onion $8.50

Huatape de hongos
Locally foraged mushrooms sautéed and served over an herbaceous masa sauce of cilantro, epazote and jalapeño $10.00

Head Chef	General Manager
Colin King	Jason Wiles

FIGURE 12.5
A menu and a photo of the operation it represents.

Source: José Andrés ThinkFoodGroup. Reprinted with permission.

Pescadilla sinaloa
Smoked fish cooked in a traditional broth served in crispy housemade corn tortillas, pickled slaw and a chile pequin salsa $10.00

✳ Cayo con salsa negra
Seared scallops with wild mushrooms, cauliflower and vegetable escabeche with a black bean chipotle chile and piloncillo sugar sauce $15.00

Mariscos / Seafood

✳ Pescado con mostaza
Recado negro blackened seasonal fish roasted tomato and pasilla de Oaxaca chile salsa, pickled mustard seed purée and pickled mustard seeds $14.00

✳ Camarones al mojo de ajo negro
Wild caught Gulf Coast white shrimp sautéed with shallots, árbol chile, poblano pepper, lime and sweet aged black garlic $12.00

Pulpo en recado blanco con pipian rojo
Sour orange braised Spanish octopus served with an onion purée and a savory sesame seed and red fresno chile sauce $14.50

COCINA MEXICANA

Pollo con mole poblano
Half of a grilled young chicken with epazote herb rice and a mole poblano sauce of almonds, chiles and a touch of chocolate $13.00

Albóndigas enchipotladas con queso doble crema
Meatballs in chipotle sauce with crumbled 'double cream' cheese and cilantro $8.00

✳ Huevos enfrijolados
Fried organic egg with black bean sauce, house-made chorizo, salsa verde and tortilla $8.50

Puerco en chile morita
Local pork spare ribs braised and lacquered in salsa of chile chipotle morita, served with jalapeño escabeche, pickled tomatillo and red onion $12.00

Tamal verde
Shredded chicken tamal with green sauce of tomatillo, chile, garlic and cilantro $8.00

Carnes / Meats

✳ Pato en mole pasilla
Braised Hudson Valley duck leg with a mole of pasilla de Oaxaca and ancho chiles, served with roasted kabocha squash $14.00

Gorditas de pato
House-made masa cakes topped with Hudson Valley duck confit and salsa chile árbol and served with a relish of local apples, habanero and piloncillo $12.00

Quesadilla de chicharrones
Pasture-raised Rock Hollow Farms pork belly fried until crisp and served in a house-made tortilla with Chihuahua cheese and a sauce of five chiles $9.00

Chile en nogada
Poblano pepper stuffed with ground pork, pinenuts and apples, served in a creamy Westfield Farm goat cheese and walnut sauce, topped with fresh pomegranate seeds $10.00

Enchilada de pollo con salsa verde
Chicken enchilada served with a salsa verde made of serrano and cilantro, topped with melted Chihuahua cheese, rajas and green onions $9.00

Panuchos de pavo con chiltomate
Turkey leg braised in a tomato and habanero salsa, over a black bean stuffed tortilla topped sour orange, habanero, and tomato salsa with pickled onions and avocado $11.00

✳ Costilla de cordero a la barbacoa
Pennsylvania roasted lamb chop with a traditional barbacoa broth with cumin and avocado leaves, zucchini and green beans $18.50

✳ Bistec en chilmole
Local grilled hanger steak with a pumpkin seed, ancho chile and epazote chilmole sauce $15.00

Authentic Mexican TACOS in hand-made corn tortillas

Tinga poblana con puerco
Stew of shredded Rocky Hollow Farms pork with chorizo, chipotle, lettuce and avocado $4.00

Taco de hongos con crema
Sautéed wild mushrooms with shallots and Mexican cream, topped with salsa serrano and pickled red onions $4.00

Carnitas estilo Michoacán con salsa de tomatillo
Confit of baby pig with green tomatillo sauce, pork rinds, onions and cilantro $4.00

Taco de suadero
Braised, roasted and grilled local brisket in a housemade tortilla with salsa verde, onions and cilantro $4.50

Chapulines
The legendary Oaxacan specialty of sautéed grasshoppers, shallots, tequila and guacamole $5.00

Cochinita pibil con cebolla en escabeche
Yucatan-style pit barbecued Rocky Hollow Farms pork with Mexican sour orange and pickled red onion $4.00

Chilorio de res
Shredded beef braised in a rich and tangy sauce of pasilla and guajillo chiles, topped with white onions $4.00

✳ Taco pescado Baja California
Seared mahi mahi with fresh cabbage, house-made mayo, pickled ancho chiles and onions $4.00

Pollo a la parrilla con aguacate
Grilled marinated chicken thigh with guacamole and grilled green onion $4.00

Lengua guisada
Braised beef tongue with radishes and a sauce of roasted pasilla chile, tomatoes, onion and garlic $4.00

Pancita de puerco al pastor
Seared house-cured pork belly in a sauce of tomatoes and guajillo chiles, served with pineapple, onions and cilantro $4.00

Sopas / Mexico's classic soups

Pozole Rojo
Mexico's famous hominy soup, rich with fresh pork and guajillo chiles, served with garnishes of onion, lettuce and sliced radishes $9.00

Sopa tarasca estilo Pátzcuaro
Black bean soup with avocado leaves, light Mexican cream and aged cotija cheese, served with a side of crispy ancho chile, avocado and fried tortilla $9.00

Caldo Tlalpeño
Traditional chicken soup with seasonal vegetables, carrots, avocado, rice, a spoonful of smoky chipotle sauce and a chipotle chile $8.00

Oyamel Experience Menu

Let our Chef Colin King take your party on a culinary tour through Mexico! $55 per person

Add our Artisan Bar Pairing $35 per person
Creative hand-crafted cocktails and wines from around the world
Ask your server for details!

✳ Consuming raw or uncooked meats, poultry, shellfish, seafood or eggs may increase your risk of food-borne illness.

FIGURE 12.5 *(Continued)*

FIGURE 12.5   *(Continued)*

Source: José Andrés/ThinkFoodGroup

The Chicken and the Egg Paradox

Learning Objective 3
State the pros and cons of creating a menu first in the menu-planning process and allowing all other business decisions to follow from there.

All of this discussion about the menu driving the business or being a reflection and supporter of the business is a chicken and the egg conundrum. Can a menu be created without first considering at least some of the other variables for a potential business? Is any business ever truly built and staffed before the menu is developed? Most of the time, both menu and business evolve together. Just as a menu should be revised after it loses its effectiveness, a menu-driven operation may make adjustments to the menu during the construction and hiring phase of the business. Only a fool would hold firm to a menu concept in the face of insurmountable obstacles that threaten the proper execution of the menu. Adjusting to the current circumstances is much wiser. Conversely, a menu planner looking to make minor updates to a current menu can still add one dish that stretches the market's comfort level in order to try to expand the market. The revision might require the hiring of a new employee or the purchase of a single piece of equipment, but such a change is less risky than basing an entire menu on a nonexistent market.

There are some benefits to working with a menu-first approach. Creating menu content and layout is much easier than designing a comprehensive business plan. For operations in which the brand is essentially the chef (think eponymous restaurant), the business will work better to let the chef illustrate her strengths on the menu and then have everything else fall in line behind that menu. It is also much easier to make business decisions to support a concrete menu—even one that has not been laid out yet—than it is to determine staffing, equipment, and purveyor needs for an abstract menu that has yet to be written.

Of course, there are potential pitfalls to the menu-first approach, too. Without conducting market research first, it is easy to misread what the market wants and to end up with no customers for the business. It may be more difficult or more expensive than expected to find staff, equipment, and ingredients when the menu defines the required caliber and quantity of these resources. Finally, some businesses are simply not designed for a menu-first approach. For example, a room service menu planner must know something about the hotel's brand, its guests, and its other dining options before writing a menu. A banquet planner would turn off many potential clients by writing a set-in-stone menu before interviewing the clients to find out what they want in a banquet.

The two approaches to menu planning—working from existing parameters to create a menu and using a menu to define the parameters—come with benefits and pitfalls. Some challenges are easily overcome; some require costly interventions to address or correct. Fortunately, the dance between the menu and the business it represents (or directs) is always in motion. Menus get created, implemented, revised, and rolled out anew regularly. No menu is ever permanent, just as foodservice businesses—their staff, budgets, customers, and products—are perpetually in flux. The goal of the menu planner is not to strive for the perfect menu, but rather to create the best menu possible for the business at that time and then to evaluate and improve it for the continued success of the company it represents and supports.

Summary

Menu planners can create menus to accommodate a range of existing parameters or design the menu first and manipulate the variables to support the menu. Menus help to market the business and drive revenue. In a menu-first approach, the menu must be the main focus of initial marketing strategies. Menus can also define the caliber, quantity, and type of staffing, equipment, and ingredients needed. A menu-first approach works well when the chef is the brand for the business; it also helps to make management decisions somewhat easier to have a concrete menu as a guide. The risk to this approach is that the customers and required resources to execute the menu may never materialize.

Comprehension Questions

1. List three ways that a menu can be used to market a restaurant.

2. Other than the food available for sale at the current meal, what other products or services can a menu promote? (List three.)

3. What three variables can a menu define when the menu is written before anything else in the business creation process?

4. List two benefits that come from a menu-first approach to menu planning.

5. List two potential pitfalls that come from a menu-first approach to menu planning.

Discussion Questions

1. If you were to create a restaurant from scratch, would you begin by writing the menu or by defining the brand in other ways first? Why?

2. The menu does not have to be created first or last when starting a foodservice business. The menu and the rest of the business are often developed simultaneously. What benefits might come from that approach?

3. Beside those mentioned in the chapter, what other management decisions might be directed by the menu in a menu-first approach?

4. Can a foodservice business use a menu-first approach each and every time it revises its menu? Why or why not?

5. Can a menu-first approach be conducted without the menu laid out, finalized, and printed before any other management decisions are made? What parts of the menu-planning process must be performed early in the business development process and which can be left until closer to opening day?

6. In your opinion, what restaurant management functions should always be directed by the menu (rather than having management decisions delimit or define the menu)? Why?

Case Study

Review the figures in this chapter. Look at each menu and its corresponding photo to see how the menu and the restaurant reflect and support each other. What elements of the menu design—font, layout, color, etc.—do you see suggested in the photo? How else does each menu complement its corresponding restaurant?

As an additional activity, select any of the menus presented in the previous chapters. Discuss with classmates how you would imagine this operation's interior looks. To see whether you are correct, visit the company's website and try to locate a photo of the operation online.

INDEX